P9-DNQ-281

Dungeons & Dragons®

Exemplars of Evil

Deadly Foes to Vex Your Heroes™

Robert J. Schwalb

CREDITS

DESIGN
Robert J. Schwalb

ADDITIONAL DESIGN
Eytan Bernstein, Creighton Broadhurst, Steve Kenson, Kolja Raven Liquette, Allen Rausch

EDITOR
Ray Vallese

EDITORIAL ASSISTANCE
Dan Nagler

FREELANCE MANAGER
Gwendolyn F.M. Kestrel

EDITING MANAGER
Kim Mohan

DESIGN MANAGER
Christopher Perkins

DEVELOPMENT MANAGER
Jesse Decker

DIRECTOR OF RPG R&D
Bill Slavicsek

PRODUCTION MANAGERS
Randall Crews, Kris Walker

SENIOR ART DIRECTOR D&D
Stacy Longstreet

ART DIRECTOR
Karin Powell

COVER ARTIST
Ron Spears

INTERIOR ARTISTS
Jason Chan, Eric Deschamps, Randy Gallegos, Tomás Giorello, Jon Hodgson, Ralph Horsley, Warren Mahy, Michael Phillippi, Eva Widermann, Kieran Yanner, James Zhang

CARTOGRAPHER
Mike Schley

GRAPHIC DESIGNERS
Michael Martin, Karin Powell

GRAPHIC PRODUCTION SPECIALIST
Erin Dorries

IMAGE TECHNICIAN
Robert Jordan

Based on the original Dungeons & Dragons® rules created by E. Gary Gygax and Dave Arneson and the new Dungeons & Dragons game designed by Jonathan Tweet, Monte Cook, Skip Williams, Richard Baker, and Peter Adkison.

This product uses updated material from the v.3.5 revision.

U.S., CANADA, ASIA, PACIFIC, & LATIN AMERICA
Wizards of the Coast, Inc.
P.O. Box 707
Renton WA 98057-0707
+1-800-324-6496

EUROPEAN HEADQUARTERS
Hasbro UK Ltd
Caswell Way
Newport, Gwent NP9 0YH
GREAT BRITAIN
Please keep this address for your records

WIZARDS OF THE COAST, BELGIUM
't Hofveld 6D
1702 Groot-Bijgaarden
Belgium
+32 2 467 3360

620-10928720-001-EN
ISBN: 978-0-7869-4361-6
9 8 7 6 5 4 3 2 1
First Printing: September 2007

Visit our website at **www.wizards.com/dnd**

Contents

Introduction

Acererak. Eclavdra. Iggwilv. Rary. Strahd. Warduke. Vecna. Manshoon. Artemis. Bargle. Dragotha. Kitiara. These names and others like them have great meaning to fans of the DUNGEONS & DRAGONS game. They are the iconic villains who have helped to shape the worlds in which we play. In many ways, they are just as integral to the D&D experience as the player characters themselves. Can you imagine what Caramon would have been without Raistlin? Would Drizzt have been nearly as compelling without Artemis Entreri as his foil? Could there have been a Strongheart without a Warduke?

All of these villains have one thing in common—one trait that sets them apart from the anonymous hordes of goblins, creepy crawlers, and walking dead: They have stories of their own to tell. These villains loom large in our imagination because they seem to be living, breathing people: They have complex goals, fleshed-out personalities, and far-reaching purposes. They are more than just numbers. They are characters, as dear to us as the PCs we play whenever we sit down at the table—and when well implemented, they can turn a good game into an exceptional one.

GREAT VILLAINS

Any DM can make a villain. Simply roll up an NPC, drape her with window dressings (a motivation, a few minions, and a dungeon to call home), and give her the desire to rule the world, kill all the halflings, or accomplish some other diabolical goal. Most PCs have faced an adversary of this sort, probably in a dungeon full of monsters to kill, traps to evade, and prisoners to free. And when the adventurers reach her sanctuary, she is waiting for them, cackling madly as lightning dances from her fingertips. With a word, her servants surge out of the shadows. Combat is fierce, but in the end, the PCs win the day. The experience is thrilling, to be sure: It generates the same excitement that PCs always feel when they wipe the floor with the bad guy and take all his stuff. Whether you plug in a blackguard, a half-fiend, a goblin witch doctor, or a surly red dragon, the experience is usually the same. Right?

Well, sometimes. But it could be much more. The foes mentioned above are villains, certainly, but they are not great villains. Rather than sit in a dusty castle, dungeon, or fortress waiting for the good guys to show up and kill them, great villains take action. They have motives. They have reasonable objectives and clear, realistic agendas. Sure, killing a big, evil adversary at the bottom of a dungeon is entertaining, but such villains rarely stand out in the minds of players. They are not the sort of foe that the PCs will think back on years later, cursing the wretch that dogged their every step until the satisfying moment when they finally put an end to his wicked schemes. Distinctive, unforgettable villains spark the imagination and bring players back to the table again and again.

USING THIS BOOK

Exemplars of Evil is a toolbox for creating memorable villains. Chapter 1 presents an overview of the many factors to consider when constructing an opponent for your PCs, including goals, motives, personality, occupation, and organizations. The chapter also offers new feats, spells, and alternative class features to help give your bad guy a fighting chance.

To show you how to put all that advice into action, the rest of the book presents eight new groups of villains. Each chapter is built around one primary villain (or pair of villains) and delves into his or her background, allies, minions, and base of operations. You learn how to use the villain in your campaign, including those set in Eberron and Faerûn. Each chapter gives full game statistics for the major characters, plus three detailed encounters of varying difficulty. In each case, you can drop the whole package into your campaign for a ready-made master opponent, or you can modify details as desired to fit your particular setting, style, or PC group.

SWIFT AND IMMEDIATE ACTIONS

Some of the special abilities, feats, spells, and items in *Exemplars of Evil* use swift actions and immediate actions. These concepts were introduced in previous DUNGEONS & DRAGONS products, but you should find everything you need in the summary below.

Swift Action: A swift action consumes a very small amount of time, but it represents a larger expenditure of effort and energy than a free action. You can perform one swift action per turn without affecting your ability to perform other actions.

Casting a quickened spell is a swift action. Casting a spell that has a casting time of 1 swift action does not provoke attacks of opportunity.

Immediate Action: Much like a swift action, an immediate action consumes a very small amount of time, but it represents a larger expenditure of effort and energy than a free action. Unlike a swift action, an immediate action can be performed at any time, even if it's not your turn.

Using an immediate action on your turn is the same as using a swift action, and it counts as your swift action for that turn.

WHAT YOU NEED TO PLAY

To use the information in *Exemplars of Evil*, you need the three core rulebooks for the DUNGEONS & DRAGONS game—the *Player's Handbook* (PH), *Dungeon Master's Guide* (DMG), and *Monster Manual* (MM).

Throughout this book, superscript abbreviations are often used to denote game elements and other materials that appear in certain supplements. Those supplements and their abbreviations are as follows: *Book of Vile Darkness* (BoVD), *Complete Adventurer* (CAd), *Complete Arcane* (CAr), *Complete Divine* (CD), *Complete Mage* (CM), *Complete Warrior* (CW), *Draconomicon* (Dra), *Dragon Magic* (DrM), *Dungeon Master's Guide II* (DMG2). *Expanded Psionics Handbook* (EPH), *Fiend Folio* (FF), *Libris Mortis* (LM), *Lords of Madness* (LoM), *Manual of the Planes* (MoP), *Monster Manual II* (MM2), *Monster Manual III* (MM3), *Monster Manual IV* (MM4), *Planar Handbook* (PlH), *Player's Handbook II* (PH2), *Races of Stone* (RS), *Spell Compendium* (SC), *Stormwrack* (Sw), and *Unearthed Arcana* (UA). Having any or all of these supplements will enhance your enjoyment of this book, but they are not required.

Illus. by J. Zhang

GREAT VILLAINS

CHAPTER ONE

As a Dungeon Master, you have created a few nonplayer characters, constructed challenging encounters for the player characters, and perhaps written an adventure or two of your own. Therefore, you have the expertise to create compelling and memorable opponents, and this chapter contains resources to help you do just that. Read it straight through, or skip around and focus on the specific advice and mechanics that best suit your campaign. Either way, you should find everything that you need to cook up foes that will keep your players talking for years to come.

BROAD CONCEPTS

Before you start building a great villain, set a few simple design goals. How do you plan to use the villain? Will he be a recurring foe or a one-shot opponent? Should he be a low-level or high-level villain? What about his race? Consider these factors carefully, because they form your villain's foundation. Keep paper handy so that you can jot down notes as you go.

ROLE

A villain's role defines how you will use him in your game. Every villain is either a minor villain or a major villain.

Minor Villains

Minor villains are supporting characters. They have a place and purpose in the plot, but they are not central to it; thus, the PCs can defeat them without derailing the rest of the campaign. Many minor villains are minions of major villains. They might be interesting characters, but they lack the depth of detail and investment of time that you would put into creating a major foe.

Major Villains

Major villains are the principal antagonists in a campaign or adventure. They propel the story, driving the plot and the PCs' actions toward the grand finale. Major villains are powerful and influential, and they pose a significant threat to the player characters.

FREQUENCY

After choosing your villain's role, establish his presence in the campaign by deciding how frequently he will appear. Villains can be either one-shot or recurring foes.

One-Shot Villains

Most opponents of the player characters are one-shot villains: They appear in a single encounter that typically ends with them pushing up flowers in a shallow grave. A one-shot villain gives the PCs a short-term adversary to confront and overcome, after which they can move on to the rest of the adventure. One-shot villains can be interesting, but you need rarely invest enough time to make them compelling.

Recurring Villains

Recurring villains dog the PCs' heels throughout the game. They grow and develop, gaining levels at a rate consistent with the advancement of the player characters. Recurring villains require more maintenance than one-shot villains, but the extra work pays off because you can tailor their abilities to those of the PCs.

TYPE

There are two types of villains (not to be confused with creature types): racial villains and monstrous villains. Racial villains advance by character class only, while monstrous villains can advance by either Hit Dice or class level.

Racial Villains

As with any character, a villain's race offers clues to his traits, motivations, and goals. Avoid making generalizations based on race, but feel free to use a villain's race as a starting point for fleshing out his personality. You can draw on details from his culture and look to the alignment tendencies of his people. Some races, such as orcs, are inclined toward evil, while others, such as elves, lean toward good. An orc makes for an obvious villain; bad behavior is part of his nature. But for an elf, villainy is a deviation from the norm, so you will need a catalyst to explain an elf villain's fall from grace. Ultimately, you decide how and why your villain became what he is, but race is a good place to start mining for ideas.

Monstrous Villains

Monstrous villains include all those that are not fundamentally defined by race. Usually, monstrous villains advance by Hit Dice, but they can also advance by class levels if you wish to make them more distinct from others of their kind. When selecting a monster to be your villain, keep the creature's Intelligence in mind. To be a great villain, a monster must have the ability to formulate plans and see them through. A tyrannosaurus is not a good choice, though one that gained sentience by means of the *awaken* spell might work.

When in doubt, follow these guidelines: To be a major villain, a monster should have an Intelligence score of 10 or higher. To be a minor villain, a monster should have an Intelligence score of 8 or higher. Monsters with an Intelligence score of 7 or lower make good lackeys and fodder for combat encounters, but they do not have the brains to be great villains.

POWER

Gauging a villain's strength can be tricky. He must be powerful enough to achieve his objectives, but not so powerful that the player characters have no chance of defeating him. Finding the right balance is an art, not an exact science, and it starts with the villain's Challenge Rating and level.

Challenge Rating

A villain's Challenge Rating depends on his role and frequency. A one-shot villain might be an intriguing foe, but he is not meant to survive a single encounter (or at most a single adventure). Accordingly, a great one-shot villain should be immediately formidable and impressive, so his Challenge Rating should be a bit higher than normal.

Since a recurring villain appears persistently over a number of encounters, he does not need the initial punch of a one-shot villain. However, he should evolve at about the same rate as the player characters. A minor villain should be near the PCs in terms of power, while a major villain should be at the upper end of what the party can face.

The table below offers benchmark Challenge Ratings based on role and frequency. However, these ratings are guidelines, not constraints—a villain's Challenge Rating should ultimately depend on the character and makeup of the PCs' adventuring party. For example, you might consider altering a villain's Challenge Rating based on the size of the party, reducing his CR by 1 for each PC fewer than four or increasing his CR by 1 for every two PCs beyond four.

VILLAIN CHALLENGE RATINGS

	Frequency	
Role	One-Shot	Recurring
Minor	Average party level +1	Average party level
Major	Average party level +3	Average party level +2

Low-Level Villains

If you are selecting a race for your villain, avoid races that have racial Hit Dice. These races often have base Challenge Ratings, limiting the number of class levels you can apply and therefore restricting your options for customization.

Monsters seldom make great low-level villains, since they are difficult to tailor to individual parties thanks to Challenge Rating constraints. In addition, monsters that have low Challenge Ratings usually are not the kinds of creatures that work well as great villains.

Medium-Level Villains

If you are creating a racial villain, avoid choosing a race with a large number of racial Hit Dice. Alternatively, if you do choose one of these races, make sure that the villain's racial Hit Dice exceed its base Challenge Rating.

If you are creating a monstrous villain, you can make it distinctive by giving it class levels or templates, or by advancing its Hit Dice.

High-Level Villains

High-level villains cast the most formidable spells, wield the most potent magic items, and might lead organizations that span continents or worlds. Usually, you can add a template to a high-level villain without overly compromising his powers.

EVOLVING VILLAINS

Villains do not simply sit around waiting to be slain. They have goals and interests, they undertake adventures, and they change over time. A one-shot villain can become a recurring villain unexpectedly if the PCs cannot overcome him immediately. Likewise, a few bad rolls of the dice (from the villain's perspective) can put a would-be recurring villain in the ground before you know it.

Villains can also shift between minor and major roles. Consider the minion who replaces his master after the PCs defeat the campaign's major villain. The minion might have been nothing more than a supporting character, but suddenly he is thrust into the center of the plot as he continues the work started by his dread lord.

The same can happen in reverse. Perhaps an ambitious wizard seeks a potent artifact that has the power to shatter worlds, but the PCs find it first and manage to destroy it. With the villain's objective removed, he no longer poses a threat. In fact, if he does not set a new goal, he becomes irrelevant to the plot, being reduced to a minor villain or vanishing from the campaign altogether.

Villains can change type, too. A villainous humanoid can gain a template and become undead, while reincarnation spells can wreak havoc with another evildoer's plans. Magical ceremonies and sites can transform a villain of one race into something completely different.

VILLAINOUS ARCHETYPES

The villainous archetypes described in this section are intended to spark ideas and excite your imagination. Great villains rarely fit into just one mold. If you do not find an archetype that matches your concept, feel free to borrow elements from several archetypes and create your own.

DISTURBING VILLAIN

"You cannot know pleasure without first knowing pain."

A disturbing villain is so thoroughly wicked that his presence is an affront to all that is good and wholesome. These characters have few or no redeeming qualities; even when they are at their "best," their behavior is atrocious.

A disturbing villain sees the world from a twisted perspective, confounding pleasure and pain, reveling in perversity, and seeking malfeasance for its own sake. He is selfish at heart, and his personality is founded on his willingness to fulfill his every desire, no matter how vile.

Advantages: Disturbing villains stand out in the players' minds. These adversaries come equipped with so many repulsive traits and objectives that PCs will need little prompting to confront them.

Disadvantages: Disturbing villains might be convenient, but you should resist the temptation to use them gratuitously. If the players put their characters up against unsettling horrors week after week, the experience will become old hat, forcing you to escalate the depravity each time so that the villain carries the same emotional weight. Sooner or later, you will go too far and offend someone.

Tactics: A disturbing villain might carry out the same actions as other villains, but he does so in an especially appalling way. Instead of merely killing his victims, he mutilates them. When he steals, he takes everything. When he indulges in degenerate habits, he does so at the expense of others. A disturbing villain is irredeemable, and his actions show it.

Example: After a long and successful adventuring career, Urian Redblade (CE half-elf fighter 9) settled in a small village to live out his days in peace. The locals welcomed him, resting easy in the knowledge that a skilled adventurer was watching over them. What they did not realize was that Urian owed a fair amount of his success to a vicious drug known as luhix (*Book of Vile Darkness* 42). In fact, he chose the village because it was just a day's travel from the Free City, where the addicted half-elf goes to get his fix.

As it happened, Urian underestimated how far his coffers would go, and after a few months, he was broke. He purchased a few doses of luhix on credit while trying to figure out a way to come up with the funds. But soon his credit ran out, and he fell deep into debt. It was only a matter of time before the dealers came to collect—and the dealers were not known for their mercy.

During his career, Urian had made many contacts, and he knew of a particularly despicable man who dealt in slaves. The half-elf arranged a meeting with the slaver and worked out a deal in which Urian would sell him villagers in exchange for enough gold to pay off his debts. Now, one by one, villagers are disappearing, and fear is spreading throughout the community. The hapless people turn to Urian for help, and they are relieved when he vows to solve the mystery and save as many innocents as he can.

FACELESS VILLAIN

"I can be anywhere or anyone. I could even be you!"

A faceless villain is a looming threat, a hidden enemy who never reveals her identity. She is frustratingly elusive, always one step ahead of the PCs or so well protected that the adventurers have little hope of uncovering her schemes.

There are two kinds of faceless villains. The first kind is the distant but formidable foe who commands incredible power. She interacts with the PCs through her foot soldiers and lackeys, and reaching her lair—if such a task is even possible—is the goal of an entire campaign.

The second kind of faceless villain is the hidden threat who uses her talents to operate outside the party's notice. She works behind the scenes, pulling strings to set her evil plans in motion. She might carry out these actions personally, blending into the scenery or even into the ranks of the party, or she might cloak herself in layers of defense and misdirection that thwart any attempts by the PCs to find her.

Advantages: Since a faceless villain rarely presents herself to the PCs, she can remain anonymous. You need not define every aspect of such a villain from the outset. In fact, you might wait until the campaign is under way and decide the identity of the villain based on how the game develops.

Disadvantages: For this archetype to work, the villain has to remain beyond the PCs' reach. With low-level parties, this restriction is rarely a problem, but as the characters gain levels, they also gain access—or can afford to buy access—to divination spells. Only the most paranoid villains invest in the necessary wards to protect themselves from every divination, and even so, few safeguards are comprehensive enough to block everything. As a result, in games with higher-level characters, the villain's identity is harder to protect, requiring you to divert the PCs' attention with red herrings and multilayered plots.

Tactics: A faceless villain never reveals her true self. She monitors the characters' actions from afar and orchestrates events accordingly. She also deals in information, and might be skilled at gathering facts about her foes or managing a widespread spy network.

Example: After her father passed her over for the throne, installing her younger brother as the new monarch, Princess Elena (NE female human aristocrat 2/rogue 9) was incensed, blaming her brother for what she perceived as a betrayal. Believing that she deserved the crown but realizing that she was powerless to do anything about it, Elena assumed an alter ego and infiltrated the Honest Men, a guild of criminals known for their skill at assassination. By day, she is the beautiful and obedient princess; by night, she is the White Lady, commanding a legion of killers to wreak havoc in her brother's lands. Her agents extort nobles, ambush shipments, smear officials by spreading false rumors, and eliminate anyone who comes close to discovering her identity. Each time her minions act in her name, they leave behind her calling card: a white rose.

NON-EVIL VILLAIN

"Execution is murder. If we permit it, the blood of the accused stains our hands, making murderers of us all."

Villains need not be evil or neutral. Good-aligned characters can stand in direct opposition to the PCs. Such conflicts can arise over differences of opinion, unwitting alliances with evil manipulators, or moral compromises that are struck to achieve a noble end.

Non-evil villains genuinely believe that their actions reflect their own upright principles. Their point of view might be shaped by philosophical differences with the PCs, or by confusion about another character's motives. Some good-aligned villains are unaware that they serve evil masters, unintentionally spreading malevolence as they pursue their lord's cause. Adamant in their beliefs, they do not or cannot see the danger in what they do.

The White Lady strikes again

Illus. by R. Gallegos

Advantages: Non-evil villains make for unusual foes, allowing you to use a new range of characters and creatures. For example, Dungeon Masters seldom throw paladins against the PCs, and most adventurers would find it unthinkable to slay a celestial. However, with the non-evil villain archetype, creatures that ordinarily would be allies of the PCs instead become their enemies. The party must find a way to fight these opponents without killing them, or the PCs risk committing an evil act themselves.

Disadvantages: For a non-evil villain to be effective, he must believe that his actions are correct. At heart, he is a good character, and he does what he thinks is good. No matter how zealously he strives for his goal, no matter how misguided or closed-minded his actions, he will not commit atrocities—at least, not unless he can rationalize them. Odds are that if the PCs can show a non-evil villain the error of his ways, he will stop doing whatever is causing the trouble. That turn of events might be good for the campaign setting, but it can kill the drama and excitement for the players. To avoid this plot development, make sure that the villain can justify his actions. His motives should be sound, even if his objectives are not.

Tactics: A lawful good villain might be a fanatic, forcing his views on others and making enemies of those who do not subscribe to his beliefs. Alternatively, to protect his nation and his people, a lawful good villain might launch a preemptive war against a rival nation in the name of freedom and security.

Whether he knows it or not, a non-evil villain might be the minion of an evil master. Perhaps he commits terrible deeds—burning villages, executing peasants, or sending innocents into exile—because he is following the orders of a superior. He might have misgivings about his duties, but above all he remains loyal to the crown, the high priest, or some other authority figure.

Example: When her brother was wrongly accused of murder and executed, the fiery agitator Merla Thorngage (CG female halfling fighter 2/rogue 6) vowed to oppose the practice of capital punishment. In her mind, whenever the state executes a miscreant, no matter how shocking his crime, it descends to the criminal's level. Merla also believes that the government represents the interests of the public, so allowing the executions to continue makes the people equally guilty. Therefore, she and her followers liberate convicted criminals, breaking into dungeons and smuggling prisoners out of the city so that they can start new lives elsewhere. Although her views are noble, Merla does not realize that the wretches she helps to free simply pick up where they left off: stealing, murdering, or doing whatever sent them to the gallows in the first place.

RIVAL

"You made me what I am. Now it's time to pay the price."

A rival villain is bound to the player characters. Her objectives are tied to the PCs because her primary role is to oppose them and thwart their efforts. A rival can have other plans and goals, but when she crosses paths with the characters, she exhibits a villain's need to compete with, defeat, or destroy the party.

A rival villain can surface for many reasons. Some are driven by professional competition or jealousy; such a villain might share the PCs' objectives or see them as a threat. Either way, she attempts to slow them down whenever she can, pulling out all the stops to reach the goal first.

Other rivals might be the result of the characters' actions. Perhaps the PCs came upon a troubled community, defeated a dragon that lived nearby, and departed. However, they did not realize that the dragon protected the village from hobgoblins that camped in the nearby hills. With the wyrm gone, the hobgoblins raided the village and enslaved nearly all its people. A few managed to escape, including one who becomes the party's rival villain. Rather than kill the PCs, she strives to discredit them and destroy their reputations.

Advantages: You can drop a rival villain into existing adventures as a complication: She can be woven into your game without becoming the primary plot device. A rival also conflicts with the PCs on a personal level. She might compete with a particular character, allowing you to spotlight an often overshadowed member of the party, or she might oppose the whole group. In fact, you could create a band of rival villains that vie against the entire party of PCs.

Disadvantages: Though a rival villain is adaptable, she becomes tiresome if overused. If an age-old enemy sweeps in to complicate every mission, the PCs might grow to hate her so much that they focus on destroying her, losing sight of the adventure at hand.

Tactics: A rival villain is annoying. She works against the PCs every chance she gets, smearing their names and belittling their achievements. She might create additional obstacles for the characters or share their secrets with enemies of the party. In short, a rival spends most of her time competing with the player characters, exulting in her successes and using her failures as further justification for her villainous ways.

Example: After a party of adventurers ransacked a cult of Orcus, a minor cultist named Soryus Jalt (CE female cleric 5) was left among the dead. In the Abyss, she railed against the adventurers that caused her doom. Her passionate hate was so strong that it drew the fearsome attention of Orcus, who in a rare moment of interest listened to the screaming petitioner. Soryus struck a bargain with the demon prince, offering him souls in exchange for a chance to have the revenge she craved. Intrigued by her ferocity and ambition, Orcus restored Soryus to the Material Plane as an angel of decay[LM]. In her new form, Soryus plots to slowly destroy everything the PCs love. She murders their family members, spreads lies about their exploits, and ruins everything they touch, all the while building toward a confrontation in which she reveals herself as the cause of all their grief.

SYMBOLIC VILLAIN

"There are no innocent words."

A great villain does not have to be complicated. Some of the greatest foes are simple characters who represent a particular concept or theme. The symbolic villain archetype encompasses all the evildoers who fit this bill. They do not need motives for what they do; they simply are what they are. Other archetypes encourage you to leave stereotypes behind, but a symbolic villain relies on them. Everything about his personality symbolizes the concept that he embodies.

This concept need not be associated with a moral failing. Villains can represent the dangers inherent in nearly any idea; you can twist any virtue into a villainous characteristic. For example, a villain who exemplifies the virtue of piety could commit horrible deeds in the name of his deity. A villain who represents love might promote his views by forcing unsuitable partners into hopelessly bizarre unions.

Advantages: The DUNGEONS & DRAGONS game is full of symbolic villains—just flip through any *Monster Manual* to find a creature that embodies the concept you have in mind. These monsters, many of which are derived from real-world legends, are steeped in mythic significance. For example, a dragon symbolizes greed and material desire by keeping a hoard of wealth that it cannot use. Likewise, a succubus symbolizes the concept of lust.

Disadvantages: Symbolic villains often are one-dimensional characters. They lack the depth and complexity of other villains, making them less compelling foes. Furthermore, the concepts they represent must figure strongly into the game; otherwise, you will find it difficult to present scenarios in which the villain's theme is the centerpiece.

Tactics: A symbolic villain can be as straightforward or as complicated as needed, but his actions must always reflect his central concept. A villain who symbolizes wrath would be reactive, destructive, and violent, while a villain representing death might keep zombie minions, dwell in graveyards or on the Negative Energy Plane, or be a walking corpse himself.

Example: After his son was killed by inquisitors for conducting research into the forbidden nature of witches, Karl Vederast (CN male human fighter 12) came to blame education for his son's death. If his boy had never studied those damned books, Karl reasoned, he would still be alive. A mercenary captain, Karl set his warriors on a righteous crusade to destroy dangerous knowledge in all its forms. Of course, it is easy to find a reason to condemn any knowledge as dangerous; thus, Karl's soldiers burn books and scrolls, raze universities and libraries, and string up scholars wherever they go.

SYMPATHETIC VILLAIN

"They killed my family. Can you blame me for wanting to kill theirs?"

Player characters have a clear reason to fight the villains they encounter; after all, most evildoers are unnaturally vile, have sinister objectives, or establish themselves as the party's mortal enemies. Some villains, though, have very good reasons for doing what they do. A sympathetic villain is defined by the action or event that caused her to become a villain in the first place. Something horrible, unfair, or just plain nasty happened to her, and her reaction is understandable. Love, grief, and fear for the safety of loved ones are typical motives of sympathetic villains.

Non-evil villains and sympathetic villains are similar in that both claim that their actions are justified, given the circumstances. However, whereas non-evil villains merely think they have a good reason for their actions, sympathetic villains truly do have a good reason. Their motivation does not excuse their villainy, of course, but it might make them seem less nefarious.

Advantages: The player characters can identify with a sympathetic villain; if their roles were reversed, they could see themselves acting in a similar way. The villain plays on their sympathies, and the PCs feel torn about whether to oppose her or help her. As a result, a sympathetic villain often proves to be highly compelling and interesting.

Disadvantages: If the villain's reasons seem strong enough, the PCs might not try to stop her, and might even try to help her. To avoid this situation, try to balance the justification for the villain's goals with the consequences of her actions. Although the PCs might understand what drives the villain, they also must realize that if she succeeds, the region, world, or setting will be far worse for it.

Tactics: A sympathetic villain is a reluctant enemy. She follows her path because she must, not out of a diabolical need to spread malfeasance. However, she is willing and able to set aside her reservations in pursuit of her agenda, and she accepts that people might be hurt or killed along the way. She sees any such events as unfortunate but necessary consequences of her actions, and nothing more.

Example: Although she was two days late, Michella Crent (LN female human ranger 10) could see that tendrils of smoke still snaked through the trees. She raced through the forest until she reached the ruins of her village. Ignoring the charred and skeletal remains of friends and neighbors, she headed for the remnants of her home. There, she found her husband still clutching their daughter in the cold embrace of the dead. From that moment on, Michella vowed that she would not rest until every last soldier had paid in blood for these shattered lives.

She left the frontier and returned to the barony, where the lord's men were bound to be hiding. Stalking the streets at night, she tracked down a handful of the soldiers and butchered them, carving the word "vengeance" into their chests before hoisting them up on signposts for all to see.

This aggrieved woman will not stop until she kills every soldier who destroyed her home and family, and she will not allow anyone to stand in her way. She regrets having been forced to murder a few drunks, prostitutes, and other poor souls who were in the wrong place at the wrong time, but they were witnesses, and sparing them would have compromised her righteous mission.

TWO-HEADED VILLAIN

"No one understands our love, our passion. We're connected, don't you see? We finish each other's sentences, enjoy the same meals, and appreciate life's finer things. When I discovered that he too loved the taste of human flesh, I was sure we were meant to be together . . . forever."

What's worse than one villain? Two villains, of course. The two-headed villain is a pair of linked foes that works exceptionally well together. United by common goals, bonds of love, or mutual distrust, these villains are capable of striking from many directions at once.

The two "halves" of a two-headed villain are identical in terms of role, power, and frequency. However, they can be different kinds of individuals—and if they do diverge in this way, they are often more powerful for it. For example, a dragon and a powerful spellcaster would be a devastating combination, and a brutal warrior alongside his succubus lover would be similarly nasty.

Although this archetype focuses on a pair of villains, that number could expand to include three or more. Evil adventuring parties, for example, often travel in larger groups; these insidious bands are in search of glory, greed, and power—many of the same reasons that drive the PCs.

Advantages: Two-headed villains are more powerful than other villainous archetypes, and not simply because they have two times (or more) the number of attacks. Just as important, they can tailor their abilities to complement each other and to shore up each other's weaknesses.

Disadvantages: Depending on the nature of the villains' relationship, the PCs might be able to pit one against the other. This trick is more likely to work when the villains are bound through alliances of convenience rather than affection. Moreover, as far as game mechanics are concerned, a two-headed villain is more vulnerable than other villainous archetypes: Each element of a two-headed villain has a lower individual Challenge Rating than would a single villain of equivalent Encounter Level. If the PCs manage to separate the villains, they should be able to make short work of the pair by vanquishing them one at a time.

Tactics: A two-headed villain recognizes the dangers of splitting up, so the characters make every effort to act in unison. Often, one member of the duo is dominant and the other is submissive. The submissive villain stays out of battle and focuses instead on pumping up his partner and casting spells to boost her combat abilities.

Example: Trisha Greme (NE female tiefling wizard 11) and Aram Wendelson (NE male human rogue 6/assassin 6) met while adventuring. At first, they could not stand each another, but after months of shared hardship and perilous adventures, they set aside their differences and discovered that they had more in common than they originally thought. Their fellow adventurers did not realize that both Trisha and Aram were secret cultists of Erythnul, and both had joined the party to murder the other characters. Once the evil couple learned the truth about each other, they turned to the dirty work at hand, burning and poisoning their former companions while they slept.

Now, years later, the pair has established a hidden base in a large city, where they lead a sprawling cult of arsonists and killers. But they remain unfulfilled. Trisha and Aram want to celebrate the anniversary of their meeting by consigning the city to flames in a mad act of destruction intended to honor their foul deity. In their secret laboratory, slaves whose tongues have been cut out mix batches of alchemist's fire, and loyal cultists place stashes of the stuff throughout the city, awaiting the order to detonate.

VILLAINOUS PLOTS

Every great villain has a clear agenda, a strategy for achieving it, and a clear reason for carrying it out. This section is designed to help you build your villain's objectives, motives, and plan of action, which can form the foundation of a single adventure or a whole campaign. Remember, even minor, one-shot adversaries want something, and they usually have a decent idea of how to obtain it.

OBJECTIVES

When selecting a villain's objective, think on a grand scale: Whether he seeks vengeance, love, immortality, or something else, the decision you make here will inform all other choices about the character. The sample objectives described below are broad and flexible so that you can adjust them for your needs.

Immortality

"Death, I shall defeat you."

No one wants to die, but most people accept the inevitable and direct their attention to the here and now. A few, though, rail against the unfairness of it all and become obsessed with their own mortality.

A villain whose objective is immortality wants to transcend the limitations of his form and become godlike. This desire might manifest as a frantic effort to halt the aging process, or as a quest to improve the body so that it is no longer affected by age. Many such villains end up making desperate pacts with fiendish powers, dabbling in forbidden knowledge, or setting aside their souls to embrace undeath.

Example: Mageryn Sollestan (LE female human cleric 5/rogue 2/blackguard 8) is a visually striking woman obsessed with beauty. In an attempt to stave off the inevitable effects of aging, she bathes in the blood of innocents.

This villain believes that the blood of her victim will keep her young

Love

"Don't you understand? I did this all for you!"

Love might seem like an odd objective for a villain, but love is a powerful force, especially when it is unrequited. To win affection, villains might go to great lengths—demeaning themselves, compromising their values, and setting aside what's in their best interest.

This objective can be used in many ways. The most common approach is to have a villain do whatever it takes to maintain someone's ardor. For example, a villain in the thrall of a succubus might commit horrific deeds to keep the demon's interest, ultimately sacrificing his soul.

As another option, a villain can desire someone that he cannot have, such as the spouse of another character or an individual whose situation or vows make reciprocation impossible. The villain might be driven to slay the other's lover or destroy the institution that blocks his advances.

Example: When he returned to his woodland village to wed his childhood love, Maiavel (CE male elf scout 7) discovered that his wife-to-be had married another. Enraged, he plans to murder her husband, a diplomat who is mired in tense negotiations with a nearby human village. If Maiavel succeeds, he could plunge his idyllic community into war.

Power

"I have crushed my enemies and driven them before me. My word is law. The fate of all rests in the palm of my hand."

For many villains, the ability to decide life and death, control the fates of others, and do whatever they like is the greatest possible goal. Villains who strive for power usually do not care how they acquire it, only that it becomes theirs eventually. Some such villains seek military might, creating unstoppable armies; others cultivate political influence in order to seize control from within the system. For some evildoers, true power lies only in the mastery of magic—whether arcane, divine, or some other type. Villains who have such power can defy reality, travel the planes, and perhaps confront the deities.

Example: King Herbert (NE male human aristocrat 8/fighter 4) has learned from his spies that a neighboring nation has discovered gold in a mountain range within its territory. Coveting the newfound wealth, the king sends out agitators to spread rumors about an impending attack on his own realm, hoping to rally the populace behind his plan to invade the other nation first.

Illus. by R. Horsley

Recognition

"They'll never ignore me again."

A world of heroes, monsters, and high adventure offers many chances for fame and glory to those with the courage to take them. Recognition also allows a villain to achieve a number of other objectives. For example, widespread notoriety enables a villain to live on in the memories of future generations, granting him a sort of immortality. Recognition also brings power and influence. People look to heroes for guidance and look upon villains with fear and loathing; the ability to inspire such strong emotions is power of a different sort.

Ambitious villains seek accolades for their achievements and push themselves to perform more and more audacious acts. Nefarious leaders might start wars to establish their legacy, and thieves might infiltrate the most heavily guarded palaces just to be able to say they did it. These villains carve their names into history, and for them, that is enough.

Example: Embittered after being passed over for the post of temple patriarch, Father Gordon Bernwell (LN male human cleric 12 of St. Cuthbert) plots to discredit his rival and usurp his status so he can take the seat for himself.

Vengeance

"They'll all pay for crossing me—each and every one."

Most people can sympathize with the need for revenge. Reasonable beings find themselves wanting vengeance at times, burning with the need to punish others who have wronged them, but most overcome this impulse and continue their lives peacefully.

When vengeance is a villain's objective, she cannot move on. Everything she does feeds her desire to get back at people whom she blames (rightly or wrongly) for slighting her. However, the pursuit of revenge rarely ends well. Villains who strive for vengeance are capable of deplorable acts in the name of justice. Their rage and frustration colors everything they do, and their single-minded fixation enables them to justify nearly any deed that brings them closer to satisfaction.

Example: Anna Orbald (LN female human fighter 7) purchased a sword from a shady dwarf shopowner in a nearby city. When she used it to defend her sister from bandits, the cheaply made blade shattered. Anna's sister was dragged away and never seen again. As a result, Anna has sworn that she will not rest until every weapon merchant pays for her loss.

Wealth

"Gold is power."

People attend school, work at jobs, and move from place to place hoping to secure the comfortable life that they believe they deserve. With wealth comes power, influence, security, recognition, material possessions, and other benefits. On its own, the pursuit of wealth is not necessarily an evil objective.

However, it becomes villainous when someone hoards wealth no matter what the cost. He might work his peasants to death, paying them a pittance for the crops they produce. He might steal without a care for the consequences. He might shatter a nation's economy so that he can divert gold to his own coffers. A villain of this stripe will break agreements, betray allies, and sell out friends and family for a few bags of coin.

Example: Vidon Hammerstone (LE male duergar fighter 9) buys slaves from the drow and puts them to work mining mithral in his tunnels. He drives them mercilessly because to him the value of the ore far outweighs the value of the lives he wastes.

MOTIVATION

Now that you have chosen your villain's objective, the next step is to determine why she wants to achieve that goal. Your villain's motive reveals a key component of her personality. On their own, objectives are morally neutral, but they become sinister when wicked motives are attached to them.

The motivations described below are just some of the many reasons why villains want what they want. For each motivation, an example shows how it can put a particular objective into context. If you want further options, consider drawing on *Heroes of Horror*, which offers a variety of motives for truly deplorable villains.

Achievement

Villains motivated by achievement have a need to excel. They hold themselves to a higher standard, striving to be the best they can be at everything they do. The means to that end, no matter how despicable, do not matter.

Example (Wealth): A thief breaks into the local headquarters of the wizards' guild and steals a dangerous artifact to prove his skill to his peers.

Coercion

Some villains are coerced into striving for a particular objective. For example, a villain might follow orders because it is his job to carry out the commands of his superior. Also, possession, curses, evil items, and other forms of magical compulsion can force a character to act against his will.

Fear is a closely related motivation. A villain might commit evil acts to save the life of an imperiled family member.

Example (Power): An aggressive cult of fanatics threatens to kill a wizard's daughter unless he tears open a portal to the Far Realm.

Conviction

A person guided by her convictions does what she thinks is right and condemns anything that deviates from her beliefs. Villains motivated by their convictions believe that they have a moral imperative to achieve their goal. Typically, this motivation masks a deeper impulse, such as envy or hatred, that a villain might wish to deny.

Example (Immortality): A healer researching a cure for a devastating disease forges a pact with a devil to extend her life span so that she will have more time to finish her work.

Discord

Villains who are driven by discord resent institutions that they consider to be oppressive. By attaining their objectives, they can plunge the established order into chaos and revel in the resulting freedom and confusion.

Example (Vengeance): A bard who was outlawed for speaking out against the king vows to shatter the monarchy and break its hold over the land.

Envy

Envious villains pursue their goals because they want what someone else has. They might try to gain similar fortune for themselves, or they might seek to take a prize away from the target of their jealousy. A villain who envies another individual's wealth will not be satisfied by finding his own riches. To him, victory can be achieved only by stealing or ruining the other person's valued treasures.

Example (Recognition): Fed up with the successes of a rival group, a party of evil adventurers plots to smear the characters' good names.

Friendship

Rather than building affiliations through honest means, villains who are motivated by friendship coerce and abuse others, forcing companionship through fear. Although the friendship that results is not authentic, the villains accept the illusion of camaraderie.

Other villains are so desperate to please that they do terrible things to earn the notice of the person they wish to befriend. Of course, these villains seldom realize that their actions just drive that person farther away.

Example (Recognition): Eager to secure an apprenticeship with a famous archmage, a young wizard conspires to steal a potent artifact from a vault beneath Boccob's temple and bestow the gift on the one he wants to be his master.

Guilt

When characters fail, they must deal with the consequences. Feelings of frustration, anguish, and guilt drive many to attempt to correct or atone for their mistakes. Villains motivated by guilt might have made an immoral choice, failed a loved one, or set in motion a series of events that led to disaster. To make up for their part in the outcome, they overcompensate and try to fix whatever went wrong, often making the situation worse.

Example (Vengeance): When a bodyguard failed to stop an assassin because he was drunk in his quarters, he swore off ale and began to brutally attack anyone who he believes played a role in the conspiracy.

Hate

Whether they hate a person, a country, or a whole race of creatures, villains motivated by hatred are implacable and intolerant, capable of dreadful acts in pursuit of destroying the object of their disgust. They aim to do maximum violence to their hated foes, and they might go so far as to commit mass murder or genocide to achieve their ends.

Example (Power): A fanatical and charismatic cleric strives to gain a position of stature within her church so that she can use her institution's resources to stamp out rival faiths.

Illus. by R. Horsley

This beholder's motives are spurred by madness *(see page 15)*

Lust

A villain motivated by lust covets something and is driven to distraction by her desire to acquire it. Lust often implies a physical attraction to another being, but it also includes base greed.

Example (Immortality): Believing that elves hold the secret of eternal life, a power-mad warlord musters his armies to conquer the natives of an ancient sylvan forest so that he can graft their flesh to his own.

Madness

Insanity allows villains to pursue the most unlikely goals and commit the most horrific atrocities. A villain driven by madness might have delusions about the outcome of his objective, or perhaps he works toward the goal for no particular reason at all.

Example (Immortality): A disturbed beholder captures and petrifies halflings so that he can memorialize them forever.

Order

In the face of terrifying monsters, ambitious criminals, and countless other calamities, some believe that the only solution is to impose absolute order. These villains try to force their views on others because they are convinced that they are right.

Example (Recognition): To prove the necessity of order, a cleric of St. Cuthbert secretly provokes a tribe of hobgoblins into attacking his city. When the citizens start to panic, the priest emerges as a leader, arguing that only his draconian policies can protect the people from the invading monsters.

THE VILLAIN'S PLOT

With your villain's objective and motivation in place, it's time to hatch the details of his plan. At this point, you might not have developed any statistics for the villain other than his Challenge Rating and perhaps his race. That's fine—let his class, feats, spells, and magic items serve the story, rather than the other way around.

This section gives you the basic elements for building your villain's plot. It is not a crash course on adventure design or a discussion of the merits and flaws of linear adventures. Instead, these guidelines are intended to help you organize your thoughts when creating scenarios and villains. It is up to you to fill in the blanks.

SPECIFYING THE GOAL

Your villain has an objective and a motivation. Now, use them to determine exactly what he hopes to achieve. Be specific: If the villain wants immortality, choose the precise form—will he become a lich, seek a place in the court of Asmodeus, extend his natural life, become a deity, or pursue some other strategy? Remember to consider his motives, which will guide you through the many options and help you settle on the perfect choice.

CONSEQUENCES

Before delving into the specific steps of the villain's plan, decide what is at stake if the PCs fail to stop her. The potential consequences will compel them to become involved in the first place and will ensure that they continue to fight the villain throughout the adventure or campaign. The possible outcome should be significant enough to pose a real danger to the world; it might even threaten the setting's very existence. Consequences that dramatically alter a setting can serve as the basis for future campaigns, giving you the ability to start over with new heroes striving to right the wrongs of the old.

SCHEME

At last, it is time to map out the villain's scheme and choose the steps he will take to reach his objective. As you flesh out the details, keep in mind the basic components of great villains. The plot of a one-shot villain should have relatively few steps, since the character will not survive long enough to reach his ultimate goal. A recurring villain's scheme can be more complex. As a rule of thumb, a one-shot villain should be able to attain his goal in the space of a single adventure, but a recurring villain might not reach his goal until the end of the campaign.

One way to design the villain's scheme is to work backward. State the goal as if the villain had already achieved it, and then, moving in reverse, write down each step that he took to reach that point. In the process, you might come up with several different ways for the villain to achieve his objective. For now, choose one path and keep the others in reserve. If the PCs thwart the villain in the early stages of his scheme, you can switch to one of the other plans.

RESOURCES

With the scheme mapped out, you are ready to outfit your villain with the appropriate materials. His resources might include minions and lackeys, magical power, political influence, a particular class or prestige class, a feat, ranks in a specific skill, or a magic item. Make a list of everything that the villain should have. These resources become the building blocks for creating the villain's statistics and forming his organization.

When the list is finished, set it aside for now. Later, when you generate the villain's statistics, return to the list and use it to guide your decisions.

ADVANCING THE PLOT

The trickiest part about running a great villain is advancing his plot. Over the course of a campaign, the player characters should have plenty of chances to ruin the villain's plans. Their successes can spell the villain's doom or just set him back temporarily, forcing him to find another path to his goal.

The objectives of one-shot villains are immediate, so you might assume that the villain has been working toward his objective in the background the whole time. When the PCs come onto the scene, they can stop the villain at a crucial moment and put an end to his scheme.

Recurring villains require a bit more finesse. From the moment you introduce one into your game, he is working toward his goal. Even when the PCs are busy elsewhere, the villain keeps advancing his plots; the trick lies in gauging his progress behind the scenes.

The Encounter Level of encounters in the lowest or starting plot element should be 1 or 2 lower than the party level, while the EL of encounters involving the climactic plot element should be commensurate with the highest level you expect the characters to attain while the villain is active in the campaign. As the average party level rises, so too does the villain make progress toward his goal.

Advancing the Villain

A one-shot villain appears and dies in the space of one adventure, but a recurring villain grows with the player characters, attaining higher levels as they do. You can advance the villain at the same rate as the PCs, but that means that he improves regardless of their success or failure. Instead, consider advancing him based on the PCs' accomplishments. At the conclusion of each adventure, look at what the party achieved and its effect on the villain's scheme.

If the PCs failed to complete their mission or stop the villain's plans, the villain attains two levels for every level attained by the PCs during the adventure.

If the PCs thwarted the villain's plans but did not set him back significantly, the villain attains one level for every level attained by the PCs during the adventure.

Finally, If the player characters set back the villain's plans significantly, leaving him in a worse situation than he was in at the start of the adventure, the villain attains one level for every two levels attained by the PCs during the adventure.

PORTRAYING A VILLAIN

Although the decisions you have made so far allow you to draw some conclusions about your villain, they paint an incomplete picture, revealing nothing about how to roleplay the character. To help you understand how the villain behaves and what he is like, this section offers sample occupations, personality traits, and behaviors to make your scoundrel stand out.

The "Typical Classes" sections in the discussions that follow mention many standard classes that are presented in supplements. Those classes and their sources are as follows: archivist (*Heroes of Horror*), ardent (*Complete Psionic*), beguiler (*Player's Handbook II*), binder (*Tome of Magic*), crusader (*Tome of Battle*), divine mind (*Complete Psionic*), dragon shaman (*Player's Handbook II*), dragonfire adept (*Dragon Magic*), dread necromancer (*Heroes of Horror*), duskblade (*Player's Handbook II*), favored soul (*Complete Divine*), healer (*Miniatures Handbook*), hexblade (*Complete Warrior*), incarnate (*Magic of Incarnum*), knight (*Player's Handbook II*), lurk (*Complete Psionic*), marshal (*Miniatures Handbook*), ninja (*Complete Adventurer*), psion (*Expanded Psionics Handbook*), psychic warrior (*Expanded Psionics Handbook*), samurai (*Complete Warrior*), scout (*Complete Adventurer*), shadowcaster (*Tome of Magic*), shugenja (*Complete Divine*), soulborn (*Magic of Incarnum*), soulknife (*Expanded Psionics Handbook*), spellthief (*Complete Adventurer*), spirit shaman (*Complete Divine*), swashbuckler (*Complete Warrior*), swordsage (*Tome of Battle*), totemist (*Magic of Incarnum*), truenamer (*Tome of Magic*), warblade (*Tome of Battle*), warlock (*Complete Arcane*), warmage (*Miniatures Handbook*), and wu jen (*Complete Arcane*).

OCCUPATIONS

A believable villain has a life, a means of income, a network of connections, and a function in your setting. Occupations reflect the villain's place in your world and help you add another layer of complexity to his character.

Academic

An academic villain is a brilliant mind, an erudite scholar, and an expert on a variety of subjects. These villains include wizards, sages, professors, and others who have an extensive education and devote time to the pursuit of scholarship.

Academics thirst for more knowledge, more influence, or the ability to continue learning without interference from others. Some academics become evil through exposure to forbidden lore, while others enter into infernal pacts to gain power in exchange for their immortal souls.

Typical Classes: Archivist, ardent, binder, cleric, shadowcaster, truenamer, wizard, wu jen.

Example: Perceiving the inherent dangers of certain religions and their adverse effect on society, Jasper (LN male human archivist 12) confiscates the holy books of all faiths to assess if their teachings might threaten the structure of his community.

Portraying the Academic: Speak eloquently, formally, and with precision, and go to great lengths to explain yourself. You might correct characters who cast spells, lecturing them on the proper methods of spellcraft.

Agitator/Fanatic

Agitators are revolutionaries and rabble-rousers. They question the status quo, campaign for a variety of causes, and exult in the discord they create. Whether the targets of their diatribes are politicians, nobles, priests, or the inequitable woes of the commoner, agitators are adept at riling up the people and spreading confusion and chaos.

More often than not, an agitator does not care what cause he champions, as long as people listen to him and rally to his side. Villainous agitators travel from community to community, looking for problems and controversial subjects. When they find an issue to push, they stand on the steps of a temple or a government building, hand out pamphlets, and shrilly denounce whatever it is they oppose this time.

Sometimes an agitator believes so strongly in his mission that he can no longer tolerate other points of view, and anyone who disagrees with him becomes the enemy. He stops championing the cause of the day and becomes consumed by his cause, transforming him into a frothing, intolerant bully.

Typical Classes: Bard, beguiler, cleric, crusader, favored soul, marshal, sorcerer.

Example: Ralda Renforth (CN female half-elf beguiler 8) travels from village to village, questioning the right of the privileged to rule and filling the heads of commoners with treasonous talk. She initiates riots and general upheaval by calling for the redistribution of wealth and the destruction of temples and marketplaces. In short, she puts a torch to the tinderbox that is the social structure of a community. During the commotion, Ralda slips from house to house, stealing any valuables she can grab, and then sneaks off to the city for a life of excess. When her money runs out, she travels to another village and starts again.

Portraying the Agitator/Fanatic: Pepper your speech with inflammatory remarks that are designed to set people at each other's throats. For example, gripe about how priests want nothing but the hard-earned coin of the working class, or denounce elves for keeping secrets from humanity. Blame everyone and everything for all the troubles in the world.

Assassin/Bounty Hunter

Assassins kill and bounty hunters capture, but both are in the business of tracking down prey. They develop many of the same skills, including stealth, combat ability, and a streetwise nature. These professionals care little or nothing for their victims—a job is a job.

Characters in the business of killing for money are evil by definition, but bounty hunters need not be. In fact, some bounty hunters believe that they are doing the world a service by taking dangerous criminals off the streets. They become villains when they cannot or will not question the nature of their job, especially when it's clear that their quarry is innocent.

Typical Classes: Beguiler, duskblade, lurk, monk, ninja, psychic warrior, ranger, rogue, sorcerer, soulknife, spellthief.

Example: Hyrum Shent (NE male whisper gnome[RS] ninja 5/assassin 5) takes nearly any job, no matter how unsavory, because he craves the thrill of the hunt. Unsavory governments hire him to bring in political enemies, fugitives, and sometimes random citizens—rulers find that spreading fear makes it easier for them to maintain their iron grip on the populace.

Portraying the Assassin/Bounty Hunter: These villains are professionals. They might enjoy their work, but they are all business all the time.

Criminal/Spy

Most villains are criminals of one sort or another. Whether they are murderers, thieves, extortionists, or counterfeiters, they profit by defrauding others. Many pursue their line of work because they believe that honest jobs are for suckers, and they view other people as marks, dupes, and victims.

Spies can be considered criminals, too. They are thieves of a sort, but instead of pilfering coins or goods, they steal information. Spies might serve foreign powers, evil religions, or anyone with an interest in a particular subject.

Typical Classes: Bard, beguiler, duskblade, hexblade, lurk, psion, rogue, spellthief, swashbuckler, wizard.

Example: Wensly Phelps (CE male maenad[EPH] lurk 6) works the marketplaces of a large city, picking pockets and cutting purses. Unlike some thieves, he does not target only victims who look like they can afford to lose a few coins. He steals from everyone he can.

Portraying the Criminal/Spy: Criminals are accustomed to looking over their shoulders and often are nervous or skittish. To roleplay this trait, talk quickly and assume a tense posture. Look around frequently, and glance back over your shoulder every now and then.

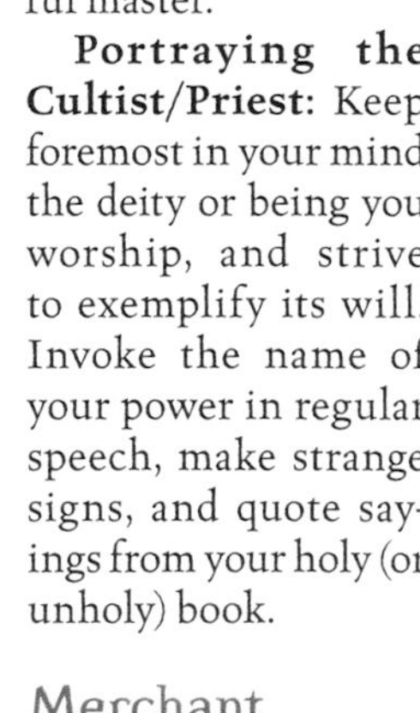

A villainous cultist pays homage to her master

Illus. by J. Zhang

Cultist/Priest

Though cults and religions differ in size, they are similar in many respects. Both groups serve what is believed to be a divine entity. Both groups have authority figures who claim a deeper understanding of that entity. And both groups teach that devotion to the principles of the organization will improve the lives—or the afterlives—of their members. However, in the DUNGEONS & DRAGONS game, cults and religions tend to be separated by a major doctrinal distinction. Religions follow the edicts of deities, while cults serve lesser powers of a suspicious or sinister nature.

A villainous cultist or priest has beliefs that are at odds with those of the player characters. The villain might honor the same god the PCs do, or a different deity that is noted for being good, but her methods of worship or her interpretation of divine will conflicts with that of the party. More commonly, villainous cultists and priests serve evil deities or fiend lords, such as archdevils and demon princes.

Typical Classes: Archivist, ardent, binder, cleric, crusader, divine mind, dragon shaman, incarnate, paladin, shugenja.

Example: Reinia Trent (CE female human aristocrat 2/cleric 3 of Graz'zt) lives a double life. In public, she is the beautiful wife of an influential noble and enjoys wealth, a massive estate, many children, and the envy of every other woman in the city. But behind closed doors, Reinia is the high priestess of a cult that venerates the Six-Fingered Hand. She and five other women regularly gather in the cellar of her sumptuous home to perform dark rituals to their dreadful master.

Portraying the Cultist/Priest: Keep foremost in your mind the deity or being you worship, and strive to exemplify its will. Invoke the name of your power in regular speech, make strange signs, and quote sayings from your holy (or unholy) book.

Merchant

Merchants are masters of commerce and trade. They have connections in most large cities, giving them a long reach and the means to monitor the PCs' activities. A merchant can be anyone from a small, one-man outfit to a powerful prince who controls massive trade consortiums, putting him on par with the mightiest of kings.

A villainous merchant uses his wealth, contacts, and power to acquire more of all three, which he then bends toward his ultimate goal.

Typical Classes: Bard, beguiler, hexblade, psion, rogue, swashbuckler, wizard.

Example: By day, Ferben Nackle (NE male gnome fighter 2/rogue 2/illusionist 2) runs a legitimate business selling curios and alchemical goods. By night, he is an infamous drug lord known as Bishop, pushing all manner of addictive poisons into the poorer sections of the city.

Portraying the Merchant: Everything is for sale—it is just a matter of settling on the price. Show off your wealth by offering to buy the PCs or their equipment, and throw a lot of money around.

Noble/Politician

Courtiers, nobles, knights, monarchs, and other aristocratic villains are born into their positions. Most already have plenty of wealth and power and might pursue villainous objectives out of boredom. Occasionally, aristocratic villains find themselves in danger of losing their status or facing destitution, and they resort to distasteful means to secure their place at the top of society.

Political villains are active in a community's government, whether that means working with or against the local rulers. Bureaucrats, politicians, terrorists, and other such villains derive power from exploiting the public. Some enjoy a special status in the community, and many have a number of supporters who believe their every word.

Typical Classes: Bard, beguiler, cleric, fighter, knight, rogue, samurai, swashbuckler, wizard.

Example: Sir Tybalt of Crois (LE male human knight 13) is known for his brutal methods of handling prisoners. He dismembers his captives and mounts their heads on poles as a warning to those who dare stand against him.

Portraying the Noble/Politician: Depending on the situation, try to come off as arrogant and haughty, quick-witted and slimy, or both at the same time. Insult those who are beneath you, and ingratiate yourself to those who are above you or on the same footing.

Recluse

Not all villains can assimilate into civilized society. Some flee the structure and societal demands of cities to live without condemnation or judgment in the wilderness. The most heinous villains have no choice in the matter and must eke out a rugged existence far from the law.

This occupation can also include villains from other lands or other planes of existence. These foreign characters might live alongside the locals, but they stand apart because of their strange appearance, manner, or customs.

Typical Classes: Binder, divine mind, dragon shaman, dragonfire adept, dread necromancer, druid, monk, psion, ranger, scout, swordsage, wu jen.

Example: Calara the Foul (CE female human rogue 3/druid 3/cancer mage[LM] 4) fled to the sewers when she enraged the head of the local assassins' guild. Her time spent hiding amid the effluvia, rats, and diseases has left her . . . changed.

Portraying the Recluse: This kind of villain has a hard time communicating with others. Speak awkwardly, in terse phrases, in a heavy accent, or in a language that no one understands. If the character is a true hermit, you can remain silent, keeping your head down as if intimidated by contact with other people.

Savage

At home in the wild, savage characters are comfortable far from civilization. They include druids, rangers, trappers, and other characters with wilderness occupations, but they also encompass strange and monstrous creatures that fundamentally oppose all things good and virtuous. A savage character might become a villain to keep civilization from encroaching on his unspoiled lands. Alternatively, he might have been forced into exile due to a hideous or unusual appearance, making him a villain who lashes out because he is misunderstood.

Typical Classes: Barbarian, binder, druid, ranger, scout, sorcerer, spirit shaman, totemist, warlock.

Example: After a band of orcs destroyed his people's hive and scattered the survivors, Ixot (LE male abeil[MM2] ranger 8) has taken it upon himself to seek revenge on all humanoids.

Portraying the Savage: Be aggressive, violent, and destructive. Try to deal with every situation by breaking things. Talk in a loud voice and speak in simple phrases.

Soldier

Born for warfare, a soldier is a trained combatant who makes her living with her sword or her spells. This occupation encompasses foot soldiers, cavalry, officers, and warlords. Most soldiers are martial characters, but this occupation is also appropriate for combat-oriented spellcasters.

Villainous soldiers could be jaded mercenaries, war-weary officers, or embittered generals tired of inept governments. These characters often have military allies, and if they are not in charge of a force, they can rely on the support of their fellow troops.

Typical Classes: Crusader, duskblade, favored soul, fighter, healer, knight, marshal, paladin, psychic warrior, ranger, samurai, scout, soulborn, warblade, warmage.

Example: Kastya Rathra-da (CE female githyanki psychic warrior 10) leads a force of githyanki onto the Material Plane to prepare for an invasion that will capture the world for the Lich Queen.

Portraying the Soldier: Pay careful attention to the battlefield and always keep an eye out for strategic advantages. Keep the odds in your favor by preparing for the PCs' arrival as comprehensively as possible.

PERSONALITY TRAITS

To help you portray a villain, give her some typical villainous personality traits that reveal facets of her nature. These traits determine how she might act in any given situation. Choose at least two traits, and select one to be dominant. For a twist, consider giving a villain a contradictory trait as well—a little depth will prevent her from appearing to be a stereotype.

In the brief discussion that follows, each contradictory trait is defined immediately beneath the typical villainous trait to which it applies.

Arrogant

Proud, vain, and full of self-importance, an arrogant villain shows a blatant disregard for the feelings and wellbeing of others. She spends a lot of time talking about herself and her achievements. These villains are often lawful.

Humble: Shy and unassuming, a humble villain feels herself to simply be doing the best thing. She is motivated by deep-seated beliefs and strives her utmost to contribute to this grander goal. She might be a faithful lieutenant of a higher villain or truly dedicated to a god or a cause.

Avaricious

Covetous and greedy, an avaricious villain plots to acquire items that belong to others. She takes risks to steal, and her mind is usually on what she can gain from any situation. These villains are usually chaotic.

Generous: A generous villain steal, kills, and does horrible things in order to acquire wealth, but then does not hold fast to these gains. The villain's family, friends, and even acquaintances are showered with gifts. Servants are paid well. Charities receive large contributions. Stolen artwork might be donated to museums. A generous villain glosses over murder, torture, theft, and other crimes and thinks only of how an acquired item or money would make a perfect gift.

Cruel

A cruel villain derives pleasure from the suffering of others. Sadistic and merciless, she causes harm and pain merely for the sake of doing so. As might be expected, cruel villains are always evil.

Kind: A kind villain feels that what she's doing is a service for her victims. She might be an assassin who murders people because she believes that "life is pain" and by killing them, she's sending them on to a better place in the afterlife or next life. A kind thief might believe that wealth makes people miserable because they focus only on money. By financially devastating a rich family, the thief gives them the opportunity to reassess their values, rely on each other, and become better people.

Duplicitous

Duplicitous villains are liars, cheats, and traitors. They honor no alliances or bonds of friendship and use other people to serve their needs. Duplicitous villains are always chaotic.

Trustworthy: A trustworthy villain's word is her bond. Such a villain might promise to aid someone in acquiring a powerful weapon. She also might sell the information about the weapon's whereabouts to a rival organization, if she never promised not to tell anyone else about it. Or, if the agreement is simply to help someone get the weapon, once that obligation is fulfilled, she then might try to take it from that individual. Devils are the ultimate example of this personality trait in a villain. Trustworthy villains are always lawful.

Envious

Incensed by the success of others, envious villains belittle the accomplishments of everyone around them, while secretly wishing to achieve the same things for themselves. Envious villains are often evil.

Complimentary: Generally self-confident, a complimentary villain hands out praise when it's deserved. She'll compliment the rogue who bypassed the traps she used to protect her hideaway. She'll exalt the fighting expertise that took out her guardian golems. If she survives to face the PCs again, she'll cheerfully set up harder and harder challenges to protect herself, while admiring the PCs' tenacity.

Gluttonous

Gluttonous villains consume more than their share and hoard treasures to deprive others of the chance to enjoy them. They frequently stockpile food, drink, and wealth, but they can also hoard resources or the attentions of a companion. Gluttons are always evil.

Moderate: A moderate villain blends easily into society. Without grand passions or vices, she lives a fairly ordinary-seeming life. She doesn't hoard wealth, get drunk, or flaunt her talents. Her coworkers or neighbors assume her to be a simple clerk. She is perceived as boring. Searching her home reveals nothing unusual or exciting. She is never the topic of gossip or bards' tales. Only when committing crimes does she step outside this seemingly faultless and mundane life.

Intolerant

Intolerant villains refuse to accept the customs, values, and beliefs of other people and choose to persecute them for their differences. They might react to someone who is dissimilar with malice, laughter, or violence. Intolerant villains are always lawful.

Tolerant: A tolerant villain benefits from diverse groups of lackeys and hirelings. She recruits folk from a variety of races and allegiances. It is in her employ that a half-orc warrior leads a band of gnolls supported by a human cleric and a pixie scout. As long as the folk she uses are loyal to her and her cause, she doesn't care who they are or where they come from.

Lascivious

Fueled by sexual desire, lascivious villains are driven by bodily impulses and ardent for physical gratification. They speak in innuendos and double entendres, and they are aggressive in matters of the flesh. These characters are often chaotic.

Chaste: A villain who focuses on chastity eschews sex and physical pleasure. She avoids lewd speech and provocative clothing. In extreme cases, she seeks to remove all potential temptations from her world, perhaps assassinating anyone who so much as seeks to flirt with her.

Mad

Mad villains might have any number of mental ailments, ranging from paranoia and delusions to psychotic behavior. Their erratic and sometimes hostile actions can repel others quickly. Mad villains are usually chaotic.

Logical: A villain who relies on logic is consistent and sensible. Impassionate and unemotional, she makes decisions based on facts and information.

Manipulative

Manipulative villains exploit and use people. They let others take risks on their behalf, coercing them with false promises and lies. These villains are usually evil.

Direct: "Here's what's going to happen . . ." is the typical approach of a direct villain. She'll tell you exactly what she wants, what she expects of you, and what happens if you succeed or if you fail. Direct villains tend to be lawful.

Nihilistic

Nihilistic villains defy social conventions, having little use for custom or proper behavior. They actively oppose anything they deem to be tradition, and they mock people who seem shackled by convention. Nihilistic characters are usually chaotic.

Traditional: Traditional villains fall into two categories: those who value the status quo and don't want any significant changes in society, and those who want to return society to an often illusory "golden age" of long ago when life was so much better.

Obsessive

Once an obsessive villain latches onto an idea, she will not let go of it easily. The object of her focus might be a pattern of behavior, a phrase, or a goal. Obsessive characters are always lawful.

Capricious: Nothing holds the attention of a capricious villain for long. Ever active, she starts many different schemes and launches a wide variety of endeavors, but sees very few through to completion. She gets bored easily and changes plans by whim to add variety and spice.

Slothful

Slothful villains are rarely motivated to do much of anything. They spend their time lazing about, letting their lackeys and servants attend to them. If they manage to cook up a scheme, they rely on their minions to make it happen. Slothful villains demand that their orders be carried out and thus are usually lawful.

Organized: Meticulous and hard-working, an organized villain prioritizes tasks and gets the job done. A heist involves careful planning, accounting for all possibilities, and setting up contingencies. Such villains prepare for both the likely and the unlikely. An organized villain is rarely surprised.

Vain

Consumed with appearances, vain villains spend much of their time perfecting their looks and those of their servants. They pay close attention to small details and never present themselves unless they are flawless. Vain villains are often lawful.

Modest: A modest villain doesn't draw attention to herself, her body, or her wealth. She wears simple clothing and gear and little or no jewelry. Often, modest villains in charge of an organization favor uniforms. The emphasis is on the group and its accomplishments. Individuality is downplayed. Modest villains generally use "we" instead of "I" when talking about deeds.

Vindictive

A vindictive villain never forgets a slight or lets go of a grudge. Whenever someone crosses her, she visits the same offense on them tenfold. Vindictive villains are usually lawful.

Forgiving: A forgiving villain rarely moves against her rivals or unruly subordinates. Any punishments she metes out are mild. For instance, if one of her underlings attempts to assassinate her, she'll overlook the transgression, perhaps banishing the person or even just letting the offense go if the would-be assassin apologies. Forgiving villains rarely last for long on their own, but a forgiving mastermind with a vindictive or protective second in command can have a very long and prosperous career.

VILLAINOUS BEHAVIOR

Many villains have signature techniques that serve as hallmarks of their wicked nature. By assigning an idiosyncratic behavior to your villain, you evoke her whenever the PCs come across one of her victims. Feel free to choose some of the sample behaviors below or come up with your own.

Habits: Adultery, betrayal, cannibalism, cheating, deviance, drugs, fiend worship, fiendish pacts, idolatry, lechery, lies, neglect.

Minions: Aberrations, animals, constructs, demons, devils, dragons, goblinoids, magical beasts, monstrous humanoids, orcs, plants, undead.

Tactics: Ambushes, arson, assassination, assault, blackmail, bounty hunting, bribery, burglary, deception, disguise, duels, espionage, fraud, gambling, genocide, impalement, kidnapping, looting, murder, paralysis, poaching, rebellion, seduction, slander, slavery, smuggling, sniping, stabbing, stalking, terrorism, tyranny, warfare.

Techniques: Blinding, branding, crucifixion, decapitation, disfigurement, dismemberment, drowning, executions, flaying, garroting, hanging, massacres, mutilation, sacrifice, scalping, stitching, suffocation, torture, whipping.

Tools: Acid, charms, droughts, electricity, evil magic, illusion, monsters, petrification, plagues, poison, psionics, puzzles, storms, traps.

Roleplaying a Villain

When the player characters encounter a villain, they should have the sense that she is more than a collection of numbers. A villain should be special, scary, and thoroughly dangerous. Her capabilities, spells, minions, and environment can help make the point, but in the end, it comes down to roleplaying.

Expressions: Body language, facial expressions, and hand gestures can make your villain stand out. You do not have to be a trained actor—just come up with something distinctive that the villain might do, and then do it. Coughing, drumming your fingers, or darting your eyes around the table are subtle but important expressions that bring a villain to life.

Catchphrase: A classic villain might have a trademark phrase—such as a battle cry, a prayer, or a curse—that is distinctive and memorable. This catchphrase should be keyed to her personality and motivations. A villain driven by greed might declare, "I'd buy that for a gold piece!" whenever she sees something she wants. Similarly, a villain driven by vengeance might scream, "For the blood of my sister!" before charging into battle.

Props: Props can be extremely helpful when roleplaying a villain, especially if you do not use them too often. Props give the players a visual cue that something important is about to happen. When you put on a hat, wear a monocle, or light a candle, you separate the villain from the foes of more mundane encounters.

ALTERNATIVE CLASS FEATURES

Villains need specialized skills to fulfill their wicked plots, and so they might develop slightly atypical abilities as they grow in power. These unusual talents reflect their sinister character and their exposure to fell magic and abominable creatures. This section provides alternative class features for some of the classes in the *Player's Handbook* and other sources.

Alternative class features replace class features found in the original class description. If a villain has already reached or passed the level at which he can take the feature, he can use the retraining option (*Player's Handbook II* page 192) to gain an alternative class feature in place of a normal feature that was gained at that level.

Unless otherwise indicated, the alternative class features detailed below are extraordinary abilities.

Illus. by W. Maby

BLASPHEMOUS INCANTATION

Not all evil deities or fiendish powers are concerned with undead. Some grant their mortal servants the ability to channel their unholy will in the form of a blasphemous incantation.

Class: Cleric.

Level: 1st (cleric).

Special Requirement: To select this class feature, you must be evil. If your alignment changes to something other than evil, you lose access to this class feature until your alignment is restored to evil.

Replaces: If you select this alternative class feature, you lose the ability to rebuke undead.

Benefit: You can call upon your evil master to smite your enemies. All good creatures within 30 feet must succeed on Fortitude saves (DC 10 + 1/2 your caster level + your Cha modifier) or become sickened for a number of rounds equal to your Charisma modifier (minimum 1 round).

You can utter a blasphemous incantation a number of times per day equal to 3 + your Cha modifier. If you have 5 or more ranks in Knowledge (religion), the DC of the Fortitude save increases by 2.

Blasphemous incantation is a supernatural ability.

CELESTIAL SLAYER

Rangers specialize in hunting and defeating certain sorts of foes. Sometimes, a ranger's choice of enemy—as well as his single-minded pursuit of that enemy's destruction—draws the dread attention of evil entities from the Lower Planes. The character becomes better able to resist and combat the forces of good, at the expense of his soul.

Class: Ranger.

Level: 1st.

Special Requirement: To select this alternative class feature, you must be evil. If your alignment changes to something other than evil, you lose access to this class feature until your alignment is restored to evil.

Replaces: If you select this class feature, you do not gain wild empathy, animal companion, or woodland stride.

Benefit: You gain spell resistance equal to 10 + your class level against spells and spell-like effects that have the good descriptor.

In addition, when you roll to confirm a critical hit against a creature of the good subtype, you gain a +4 competence bonus on the roll.

Favored of the Fiends gives a cultist fearsome claws

FAVORED OF THE FIENDS

Cultists of archdevils and demon princes are uncommon and secretive, but they are a potent force for evil in the world. On occasion, when a servant proves his devotion to his vile masters, he undergoes a profound transformation.

Class: Favored soul (*Complete Divine* page 6).

Level: 3rd.

Replaces: If you select this class feature, you do not gain the Weapon Focus feat at 3rd level, nor do you gain the Weapon Specialization feat at 12th level.

Benefit: Your nails lengthen into ragged claws and your teeth extend into sharp fangs, dealing damage as indicated on the following table.

Size	Bite Damage	Claw Damage
Fine	1	—
Diminutive	1d2	1
Tiny	1d3	1d2
Small	1d4	1d3
Medium	1d6	1d4
Large	1d8	1d6
Huge	2d6	1d8
Gargantuan	3d6	2d6
Colossal	4d6	3d6

Your claws are your primary natural weapons. When you are not wielding a weapon, you can use your claws when making an attack action. When making a full attack, you can use both claws and your bite. When wielding a weapon, you can use the weapon as your primary attack and your bite as a natural secondary attack. In addition, if you have a free hand, you can also attack with a claw as an extra natural secondary attack.

Your natural attacks count as if they were evil-aligned for the purpose of overcoming damage reduction.

FEIGN DEATH

A clever villain has many contingencies in place, so that if a plan goes awry, he can beat a hasty retreat. In exchange for some ability to evade damage, he can enter a state that is indistinguishable from death.

Class: Monk, ranger, or rogue.

Level: 2nd (monk or rogue) or 9th (ranger).

Replaces: If you select this class feature, you do not gain the evasion ability. If your class would grant you improved evasion at a higher level, you instead gain evasion.

Benefit: As an immediate action, you can enter a catatonic state in which you appear to be dead. While feigning death, you cannot see or feel anything, but you retain the ability to smell, hear, and otherwise follow what is going on around you.

While under the effect of this ability, you are immune to all mind-affecting spells and abilities, poison, sleep, paralysis, stunning, disease, ability drain, negative levels, and death effects. Attempts to resuscitate you, such as *raise dead* or *reincarnation*, automatically fail, though *resurrection* and *true resurrection* immediately end your feign death ability.

Spells and other effects that assess your current condition, such as *status* and *deathwatch*, indicate that you are dead. However, a character who succeeds on a Heal check (DC 15 + 1/2 your level + your Con modifier) can discern that you are actually alive.

You can remain in the catatonic state indefinitely, though you still require food, water, and air. Emerging from feigned death is a standard action.

INSPIRE HATRED

Motivated by a desire to spread havoc and sow discord, some villainous bards abandon the techniques that inspire heroes to greatness. Instead, they prey upon secret longings and buried frustrations to awaken the hate that resides in mortal hearts.

Class: Bard.

Level: 9th.

Special Requirement: You must have 12 ranks in a Perform skill to use this ability.

Replaces: If you select this class feature, you do not gain the bardic music ability to inspire greatness.

Benefit: You can use music, poetics, or fiery oratory to evoke hatred in a single living creature within 30 feet that has an Intelligence score of 3 or higher. For every three levels you attain beyond 9th, you can target one additional creature with a single use of this ability (two creatures at 12th level, three at 15th, four at 18th, and so on). To inspire hatred, you must sing, speak, or perform, and the target must hear you. The target is entitled to a Will save (DC 10 + 1/2 your bard level + your Cha modifier) to resist this mind-affecting ability. The effect lasts for as long as the target hears you and for 5 additional rounds thereafter.

An affected creature develops an unreasoning hatred of another creature that you indicate. The affected creature attacks the object of its hate as directed, to the exclusion of other opponents. If the affected creature is attacked, it can defend itself as normal, but as soon as possible, it resumes attacking the object of its hate.

Creatures compelled to attack an ally can attempt a new Will save each round to break free from this supernatural effect.

INVISIBLE FIST

Monks who follow the Path of the Invisible Fist learn to harness their *ki* to conceal themselves from detection. With further training, these monks learn to blink between the Material Plane and the Ethereal Plane. To gain this versatility, they sacrifice their ability to escape unscathed from area effects.

Class: Monk.

Level: 2nd.

Replaces: If you select this class feature, you do not gain the evasion ability, nor do you gain improved evasion at 9th level.

Benefit: As an immediate action, you can become invisible for 1 round. You must wait 3 rounds before you can use this ability again.

At 9th level, as an immediate action, you can use *blink*, as the spell, for a number of rounds equal to your Wisdom modifier (minimum 1 round). You must wait 3 rounds before you can use this ability again.

Invisible fist is a supernatural ability.

MIMIC

Many villains specialize in avoiding detection so that they can work behind the scenes to achieve their nefarious goals. To this end, they spend a fair amount of time developing techniques to mask their appearance, at the expense of their normal training in foiling traps.

Class: Rogue.

Level: 1st, 3rd, 6th, 9th, 12th, 15th, and 18th.

Special Requirement: You must have a Charisma of 12 or higher to select this alternative class feature.

Replaces: If you select this feature, you do not gain the trapfinding ability.

Benefit: Once per day, you can use *disguise self* as a caster whose level equals your class level. At 3rd level and every three levels thereafter, you can reduce your bonus on trap sense by 1 to gain an additional use of mimic.

At your discretion, when using *disguise self*, you can spend two uses of the spell-like ability to produce the effect as a swift action rather than a standard action.

SPONTANEOUS AFFLICTION

Druids who give up their rapport with most wild creatures can call upon the assistance of nature's smallest beings. Such characters punish those who would despoil the wilderness by infecting them with a mild illness.

Class: Druid.

Level: 1st.

Replaces: If you select this class feature, you do not gain the ability to spontaneously convert prepared spells into *summon nature's ally* spells.

Benefit: You can transform the stored energy of a spell you have prepared and use it to weaken your enemies.

To use spontaneous affliction, you must spend a standard action and sacrifice a prepared spell. All humanoids within 30 feet of you must succeed on a Fortitude save (DC 10 + 1/2 your class level + your Cha modifier) or become sickened for a number of rounds equal to the level of the spell sacrificed.

UNHOLY FURY

When a barbarian taps into his buried anger, he unleashes his wrath and turns into a brutal killing machine. Although many barbarians learn to control this violence, some exult in it, reveling in the slaughter they create.

Class: Barbarian.

Level: 1st.

Special Requirement: To select this alternative class feature, you must be chaotic evil. If your alignment changes to anything else, this ability reverts to the standard rage ability until your alignment is restored to chaotic evil.

Replaces: If you select this class feature, you do not gain the barbarian's standard fast movement ability.

Benefit: Once during a rage, you can unleash your unholy fury to smite a nonchaotic evil creature. You add your Charisma bonus to your attack roll and deal an extra 1 point of damage per barbarian level. If you accidentally use this ability against a creature that is chaotic evil, the smite has no effect, but the ability is still used up for the duration of your rage.

VILLAINOUS FEATS

Many villains have access to the same types of abilities and features that are available to player characters. This section presents a number of new feats tailored specifically for villains. Some of these feats might be appropriate for PCs as well, though consider carefully before revealing such secrets to the players.

CEREMONY FEATS

A ceremony feat grants you the knowledge and training needed to complete several specific ceremonies. Each feat uses the Knowledge (religion) skill to gauge the depth of your study. As you gain more ranks in that skill, you gain access to more ceremonies.

A creature can benefit from one ceremony at a time. If you attempt a second ceremony on the same creature, the first ceremony's benefits immediately end, and the second ceremony's benefits apply.

Each ceremony has a cost in time and resources. The ceremony consumes its needed materials when it ends, not when the benefit ends. If the ceremony is disrupted—for example, if an opponent attacks you before you finish—the material components are not lost.

VILE FEATS

Some of the feats presented in this book are vile feats, a category of feats first introduced in *Book of Vile Darkness*. Only intelligent creatures of evil alignment can select these feats.

FEAT DESCRIPTIONS

The feats in the following section are presented in the normal format and summarized in Table 1–1: Villainous Feats. (Blessing of the Godless is both a ceremony feat and a vile feat, so it appears twice in the table.)

Illus. by R. Gallegos

A dark ritual conducted with Blessing of the Godless

Table 1–1: Villainous Feats

General Feat	Prerequisites	Benefit
Divine Denial	Knowledge (religion) 9 ranks, Iron Will	+2 to saves against divine spells
Embody Energy	Energy Substitution[CAr], Spell Focus (conjuration)	Wreathe your body with damaging energy
Evasive Maneuvers	Caster level 11th, evasion, Cunning Evasion[PH2], Spell Focus (illusion), ability to cast *invisibility*	When using evasion, you can cast *invisibility* as an immediate action
Generous Sacrifice	Evil, Con 15	Donate negative levels to a willing target
Gruesome Finish	Base attack bonus +6	Give up remaining attacks to make a disabled foe die instead
Maiming Strike	Evil, sneak attack +2d6	Sacrifice 2d6 sneak attack damage to deal 1 Cha damage
Mask of Gentility	Cha 15, Bluff 9 ranks, Disguise 9 ranks	Defeat divination attempts and make it harder to discern your motives
Proteus	Caster level 10th, Spell Focus (illusion)	Exchange a prepared spell for an illusion (glamer) spell
Slippery Skin	Escape Artist 9 ranks, Combat Reflexes	Substitute Escape Artist check result for touch AC
Strength of Conviction	Smite evil or good	Swap smite evil or good for smite
Twist the Knife	Sneak attack +2d6, Improved Critical (melee weapon)	Forego critical damage to impose a penalty on foe's attacks, damage, saves, and checks
Uncanny Forethought	Int 17, Spell Mastery	Reserve slots to cast Spell Mastery spells
Ceremony Feat	**Prerequisites**	**Benefit**
Blessing of the Godless	Evil, Knowledge (religion) 6 ranks	Gain warding rituals
Fell Conspiracy	Wis 13, Knowledge (religion) 4 ranks	Forge a link that enables easy communication
Vile Feat	**Prerequisites**	**Benefit**
Blessing of the Godless	Evil, Knowledge (religion) 6 ranks	Gain warding rituals
Evil Brand	—	Gain +2 bonus on Diplomacy and Intimidate checks made against evil creatures
Beloved of Demons	Evil, caster level 6th, Knowledge (the planes) 6 ranks, Evil Brand, Power Attack	Slay good or lawful creature and gain temporary hit points
Hellsworn	Evil, Knowledge (the planes) 9 ranks, Evil Brand, Weapon Focus	Gain extraplanar subtype and one infernal ability

BELOVED OF DEMONS [VILE]

The tanar'ri reward you with unholy vitality whenever you defeat their enemies.

Prerequisites: Evil, caster level 6th, Knowledge (the planes) 6 ranks, Evil Brand, Power Attack.

Benefit: Whenever you strike a lawful or good creature and reduce it to the dying or dead condition, you gain a number of temporary hit points equal to 1/2 your class level. Temporary hit points gained from this feat disappear after 1 minute.

As an immediate action, you can sacrifice up to 5 temporary hit points to gain damage reduction 5/good for 1 round.

BLESSING OF THE GODLESS [CEREMONY, VILE]

You invoke the dreadful power of darkness and evil to fill your allies with terrible power.

Prerequisites: Evil, Knowledge (religion) 6 ranks.

Benefit: You gain access to ceremonies based on your ranks in Knowledge (religion). Each ceremony allows you to provide up to five allies with malevolent energy. Each rite takes 6 minutes to perform, and requires unholy water and the dung of an evil creature (see below). Each participant stands at one of five points, forming a pentagram with you in the center. The effects of each ceremony last for 24 hours unless otherwise noted.

Dark Pact (6 ranks): You spew the hateful words of true wickedness, investing the malevolence of the Lower Planes in the gathering. You create a pool of reserve hit points equal to your class level × the number of participants. Henceforth, all participants can draw a number of hit points equal to their class level from this pool as an immediate action. These reserve hit points can only be used to recover lost hit points, so any drawn in excess of the character's maximum hit point total are wasted. When the pool is depleted, the effects of the ritual end.

Anoint the Wicked (9 ranks): Your filthy words imbue your allies with an incredible sense of purpose, enough to quench any misgivings. Each participant gains a +4 morale bonus on checks made to oppose Intimidate checks and on saving throws against spells and spell-like effects that have the fear descriptor.

Shield of the Godless (12 ranks): In a sharp voice, you speak the reversed names of thirteen good deities, denying their existence and imbuing your allies with wards of unbelief.

Each participant gains a +4 morale bonus on saving throws against divine spells. The participants also gain damage reduction 5/— against smite attacks made against them. In addition, if any participant is affected by a divine spell, all participants within 60 feet gain a +2 morale bonus on attack rolls and damage rolls for 1 round.

DIVINE DENIAL

You harden your will against the power of the deities.

Prerequisites: Knowledge (religion) 9 ranks, Iron Will.

Benefit: Whenever you are the target of a divine spell, you gain a +2 bonus on saving throws to resist the spell. If the spell does not allow a saving throw, you can make a Will save against the spell's DC as if it allowed a save. If you succeed, you negate the effect of the spell.

EMBODY ENERGY

You can sacrifice prepared spells to shroud your body in a particular type of energy.

Prerequisites: Energy Substitution[CAr], Spell Focus (conjuration).

Benefit: You can sacrifice a spell that has an energy descriptor that matches the energy type you selected for Energy Substitution. By doing so, you wreathe your body with the energy for 1 round per level of the spell sacrificed. You are immune to the energy generated, and your natural attacks and attacks made with weapons deal an extra 1d6 points of damage of the appropriate type. Creatures that attempt to grapple you or that successfully attack you with a natural weapon or an unarmed strike take 1d6 points of damage for each hit or round of sustained contact.

Special: You can select this feat multiple times. Each time, it applies to a new type of energy that you have selected for the Energy Substitution feat.

EVASIVE MANEUVERS

You can vanish into the confusion created by area spells.

Prerequisites: Caster level 11th, evasion, Cunning Evasion[PH2], Spell Focus (illusion), ability to cast *invisibility*.

Benefit: Once per encounter, if you are caught within an area attack whose damage you completely avoid due to evasion or improved evasion, you can cast a prepared or known *invisibility* spell as an immediate action.

EVIL BRAND [VILE]

You are physically marked forever as the servant of an evil power greater than yourself. The symbol is unquestionable in its perversity, depicting a depravity so unthinkable that all who see it know beyond a doubt that you serve an evil patron.

Benefit: Evil creatures automatically recognize the symbol now emblazoned upon you as a sign of your utter depravity and your discipleship to a powerful creature of evil, although the brand does not necessarily reveal your patron's identity. You gain a +2 circumstance bonus on Diplomacy and Intimidate checks made against evil creatures.

FELL CONSPIRACY [CEREMONY]

You forge a connection with a target to ease communications and to keep you apprised of developments in the field.

Prerequisites: Wis 13, Knowledge (religion) 4 ranks.

Benefit: You gain access to ceremonies based on your ranks in Knowledge (religion). These ceremonies forge a link between participants who work toward a common cause. During each ceremony, all participants huddle together and speak in hushed tones, conveying the dark purpose of the conspiracy. Each ceremony takes 20 minutes, and its effects last for 24 hours.

Common Cause (4 ranks): You confide in each ally, whispering your plans into his ear. Once you have finished, you nick each other's ears with a sharp blade (no damage). Henceforth, each participant can cast the *message* spell at will at your caster level.

This ceremony requires a masterwork dagger.

Conspiratorial Bond (8 ranks): You concoct a paste of potent herbs and apply it to the eyes and ears of all participants, including yourself. While doing so, you intone a resonating, rhythmic incantation. All participants gain a +2 bonus on Listen checks and Spot checks for every other participant in range. In addition, all participants within 100 feet can communicate telepathically.

This ceremony requires rare herbs worth 50 gp.

Inviolate Link (12 ranks): Using a concoction of blood and hair from each participant mixed with rare herbs and diamond dust, you paint an eye onto the forehead of each ally. As long as they remain within 100 feet of you, none of you can be caught flat-footed unless all of you are, and none of you can be flanked unless all of you are.

This ceremony requires a bit of blood and hair from each participant, rare herbs worth 50 gp, and diamond dust worth 100 gp.

GENEROUS SACRIFICE

You can relieve your afflictions by donating them to an ally.

Prerequisites: Evil, Con 15.

Benefit: Whenever you gain one or more negative levels, you can transfer some or all of them to a willing creature that you touch.

GRUESOME FINISH

You deliver a terrifying blow to finish off a victim and strike fear into the hearts of your enemies.

Prerequisite: Base attack bonus +6.

Benefit: Whenever you make a full attack and reduce an opponent to 0 or fewer hit points, you can give up any remaining attacks you have in the round to force the target to make a Fortitude save (DC 10 + 1/2 your level + your Cha modifier). If the target fails the save, he dies instead of becoming disabled, and all creatures within 30 feet must succeed on Will saves against the same DC or become sickened for 1 round.

Special: You can use this feat only if you have still have one or more attacks left in a round after reducing your target to 0 or fewer hit points.

HELLSWORN [VILE]

You have made a pact with a foul devil from the Nine Hells. In exchange, you can channel the power of that dreadful plane.

Prerequisites: Evil, Knowledge (the planes) 9 ranks, Evil Brand, Weapon Focus.

Benefit: You gain the extraplanar subtype. Your native plane is now the Nine Hells of Baator, and you can select one of the following infernal gifts.

Hell's Fury: Once per round, as a free action, you can designate a single target that you can see. Your melee attacks and ranged attacks against that target—if made with a weapon for which you have the Weapon Focus feat—deal an extra 1d6 points of unholy damage.

Brimstone Caress: When casting spells or spell-like effects that have the evil descriptor, your caster level increases by 1. Once per encounter, you can increase the save DC of any spell you cast by 1. If the spell deals damage, half the damage dealt is unholy.

Special: If you are slain, your soul is dragged to the Nine Hells of Baator. You cannot be restored to life by any means short of a *miracle* or *wish* spell.

MAIMING STRIKE

You can make dreadful attacks that disfigure your opponents.

Prerequisites: Evil, sneak attack +2d6.

Benefit: Whenever you make a successful sneak attack on a target creature, you can reduce your extra damage and deal Charisma damage instead. For every 2 dice of extra damage that you sacrifice, your attack deals 1 point of Charisma damage.

MASK OF GENTILITY

You cunningly hide your true motives and nature behind a facade of camaraderie and gentility.

Prerequisites: Cha 15, Bluff 9 ranks, Disguise 9 ranks.

Benefit: If you are subjected to a divination spell that normally would reveal your alignment, your alignment registers as neutral. In addition, if someone tries to use

FEATS FROM OTHER SOURCES

Some of the characters detailed in this book have feats that first appeared in various D&D supplements. Those feats are accompanied by a superscript abbreviation in a character's statistics block that identifies the source (see the introduction for more information). When possible, the benefit of a feat is incorporated directly into a character's statistics. If further explanation is needed, the mention of the feat is accompanied by a page reference to this sidebar, and that information is provided below.

Able Learner (Kjarlo): You lose one spell slot from each level of wizard spells that you can cast. You gain an additional prohibited school. In return, you can prepare two additional divination spells per day.

Arcane Strike (Emmara): You can channel arcane energy into your melee weapon, unarmed strike, or natural weapons as a free action. By sacrificing one of your spells, you gain a bonus on your attack rolls for 1 round equal to the level of the spell sacrificed, as well as extra damage equal to 1d4 points × the sacrificed spell's level.

Battlecaster Offense (Oros, Nillaien, and Hloethdrin): If you deal damage to a foe with a spell, you gain a +1 bonus on the first melee attack you make against that foe in the following round.

In addition, if you make a melee attack against a foe, the save DC of the first spell you use against that foe in the following round increases by 1. The higher DC applies only to the foe you attacked, not to any other creature affected by the spell.

Black Lore of Moil (Kastya): You can cast necromancy spells as Moilian spells, dealing an extra 1d6 points of negative energy damage + 1d6 points per two spell levels. If the spell normally allows a save to reduce the damage, the extra damage is similarly reduced on a successful save. A Moilian spell requires a special expensive material component called a runebone. For each die of extra damage, the runebone must be worth 25 gp.

Clinging Breath (Albrathax): Your breath weapon clings to anything caught in the area, an effect that lasts for 1 round. On the round following the use of the breath weapon, the clinging breath weapon deals half the amount of damage it dealt on the previous round. Creatures that avoided the initial damage from the breath weapon do not take the extra damage.

A foe can take a full-round action to remove the clinging breath weapon by making a successful Reflex save against the same DC as the breath weapon. Rolling on the ground grants a +2 bonus on the save. A clinging breath weapon cannot be removed or smothered by immersion in water, but it can be magically dispelled (DC equal to that of the breath weapon).

Using this feat adds 1 to the number of rounds between uses of the breath weapon.

Divine Vigor (Calais and Helthra): You can expend a command undead attempt as a standard action to increase your base speed by 10 feet and gain 2 temporary hit point per character level. These benefits last for 1 minute.

Elemental Adept (Valbryn): You can spontaneously cast a spell of the element you have mastered by sacrificing a prepared spell slot of 3rd level or higher.

Energy Substitution (Valbryn): You can modify any spell with an energy descriptor to instead use a type of energy you choose.

Lifebond (Kastya): Whenever you are within 60 feet of your chosen creature, you gain a +4 bonus to turn resistance and a +2 bonus on saves. If your chosen creature dies, you lose the bonuses and instead take a –2 penalty on saves for 24 hours.

Magic Sensitive (Kjarlo): You can cast *detect magic* at will as long as you have a divination spell prepared. This is a supernatural ability with a range equal to 5 feet per level of the highest divination spell you have available. Activating this ability is a standard action that does not provoke attacks of opportunity.

In addition, the caster level of your divination spells increases by 1.

Maximize Breath (Albrathax): If your breath weapon is used as a full-round action, all variable numeric effects are maximized. Using this feat adds three to the number of rounds between uses of the breath weapon.

Monkey Grip (Thaden): You can wield a light, one-handed, or two-handed weapon that is Large or larger with a penalty of –2, but with the same amount of effort as a Medium weapon of the same type.

Oversized Two-Weapon Fighting (Thaden): You treat one-handed off-hand weapons as light weapons.

Quicken Breath (Albrathax): Using your breath weapon is a free action. Using this feat adds 4 to the number of rounds between uses of the breath weapon.

Rapid Metamagic (Valbryn): You can apply metamagic feats to a spontaneously cast spell in the normal casting time.

Telling Blow (the Urdred): When you make a critical hit against a target, the attack deals sneak attack damage as well.

Verminfriend (Edgar Tolstoff and Katarin Tolstoff): You can attempt a DC 20 Charisma check to prevent vermin from attacking you for 24 hours.

the Sense Motive skill to get a hunch about your purpose or nature, she must succeed on a DC 30 check to obtain an accurate impression.

Normal: Getting a hunch requires a DC 20 Sense Motive check.

PROTEUS

You are a master of masking your features behind a myriad of disguises.

Prerequisites: Caster level 10th, Spell Focus (illusion).

Benefit: You can sacrifice a prepared spell to cast any lower-level illusion (glamer) spell. In addition, you can cast a prepared illusion (glamer) spell as an immediate action by sacrificing another spell of the same level.

SLIPPERY SKIN

You can expertly avoid the grasp of your enemies.

Prerequisites: Escape Artist 9 ranks, Combat Reflexes.

Benefit: If a creature makes a touch attack against you to initiate a grapple, you can sacrifice one of your attacks of opportunity as an immediate action to make an Escape Artist check. You must use the check result in place of your touch Armor Class, even if the result is lower.

STRENGTH OF CONVICTION

You can channel the fury of your deity against a foe.

Prerequisites: Smite good or smite evil.

Benefit: Each day, you can sacrifice one use of smite evil or smite good to smite a single target regardless of his alignment. You gain no additional bonus on the attack roll, but if you hit the target, you deal a number of extra points of damage equal to your class level.

TWIST THE KNIFE

You can make a vicious attack that leaves your victim gasping in pain.

Prerequisites: Sneak attack +2d6, Improved Critical (melee weapon).

Benefit: Whenever you confirm a critical hit while wielding a melee weapon for which you have the Improved Critical feat, you can forego the extra damage and wrack the target with pain instead. For a number of rounds equal to the weapon's critical multiplier, the target takes a –3 penalty on attack rolls, weapon damage rolls, saving throws, ability checks, and skill checks.

UNCANNY FORETHOUGHT

You cunningly prepare your spells for any exigency.

Prerequisites: Int 17, Spell Mastery.

Benefit: When preparing your daily allotment of spells, you can reserve a number of spell slots equal to your Intelligence modifier. As a standard action, you can use one of these slots to cast a spell that you selected for the Spell Mastery feat. The level of the slot used must be equal to or greater than the level of the spell you intend to cast.

Alternatively, as a full-round action, you can use a reserved slot to cast any spell that you know. The spell is resolved as normal, but for the purpose of the spell, your caster level is reduced by two. The level of the slot used must be equal to or greater than the level of the spell you intend to cast.

VILLAINOUS SPELLS

The new spells described in this section are intended for use by villains. With your permission, player characters can acquire and learn these spells, but given their often sinister nature, these spells might not be appropriate for all games.

ASSASSIN SPELL

1st Level

Alibi: Target believes he encountered you recently.

BARD SPELLS

1st Level

Alibi: Target believes he encountered you recently.

Treacherous Weapon: Target's manufactured weapon takes a penalty for 1 round.

3rd Level

Phantasmal Injury: Implant illusion that subject is disabled.

Stiffen: Touch imposes penalties to Dex and speed and reduces maneuverability.

4th Level

Phantasmal Wasting: Touch causes foe to believe he has aged and become weaker.

CLERIC SPELLS

3rd Level

Infallible Servant[M]: Target is utterly destroyed if slain or captured.

Stiffen: Touch imposes penalties to Dex and speed and reduces maneuverability.

Willing Sacrifice: Subject takes 1d10 damage; you gain a profane bonus equal to half the damage.

4th Level

Alliance Undone: Suppress team-oriented effects.

DRUID SPELLS

4th Level

Friendly Fire: Redirect ranged attack against another target within 30 feet.

Infallible Servant[M]: Target is utterly destroyed if slain or captured.

Phantasmal Wasting: Touch causes foe to believe he has aged and become weaker.

9th Level

Ring of Fire[M]: Create a spreading area of lava.

HEXBLADE SPELLS

1st Level

Treacherous Weapon: Target's manufactured weapon takes a penalty for 1 round.

2nd Level

Alliance Undone: Suppress team-oriented effects.

SORCERER/WIZARD SPELLS

1st Level

Alibi: Target believes he encountered you recently.

Treacherous Weapon: Target's manufactured weapon takes a penalty for 1 round.

3rd Level

Infallible Servant[M]: Target is utterly destroyed if slain or captured.

Phantasmal Injury: Implant illusion that subject is disabled.

Willing Sacrifice: Subject takes 1d10 damage; you gain a profane bonus equal to half the damage.

4th Level

Alliance Undone: Suppress team-oriented effects.

Friendly Fire: Redirect ranged attack against another target within 30 feet.

Stiffen: Touch imposes penalties to Dex and speed and reduces maneuverability.

5th Level

Phantasmal Wasting: Touch causes foe to believe he has aged and become weaker.

Touch of Chaos[M]: Touched target transforms into a mass of quivering flesh.

9th Level

Ring of Fire[M]: Create a spreading area of lava.

Infallible servant takes its deadly toll

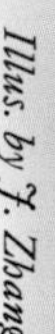

SPELL DESCRIPTIONS

The spells herein are presented in alphabetical order.

ALIBI

Illusion (Phantasm) [Mind-Affecting]
Level: Assassin 1, bard 1, sorcerer/wizard 1
Components: V
Casting Time: 1 swift action
Range: Close (25 ft. + 5 ft./2 levels)
Target: One living creature
Duration: Instantaneous
Saving Throw: Will disbelief
Spell Resistance: Yes

Your target's expression changes as he suddenly recalls seeing you before.

You implant a memory of your presence in a target's mind. The creature recalls speaking with you or interacting with you sometime within the last 24 hours. The phantasm is completely believable and the target's mind adapts to the mental intrusion, filling in any gaps in logic.

ALLIANCE UNDONE

Transmutation
Level: Cleric 4, hexblade[CW] 2, sorcerer/wizard 4
Components: V, S, M/DF
Casting Time: 1 standard action
Range: Close (25 ft. + 5 ft./2 levels)
Area: 10-ft./level radius
Duration: 1 minute
Saving Throw: None
Spell Resistance: No

You chant words of discord and unrest while making a breaking motion with your hands. Those around you fall quiet as suspicion and distrust take root in their hearts.

Alliance undone suppresses the benefits gained from alliances, including, but not limited to, the effects of ceremony feats, teamwork benefits, companion spirits, and affiliations.

Material Component: A severed cord.

FRIENDLY FIRE

Abjuration
Level: Druid 4, sorcerer/wizard 4
Components: V
Casting Time: 1 immediate action or 1 full round; see text
Range: Personal
Target: You
Duration: Instantaneous or 1 round/level; see text

With an arcane word, you create a shimmering field of golden light around your body that pulses and wavers before vanishing.

Whenever you are the target of a ranged attack or a ranged touch attack, you can cast this spell to deflect the attack toward another target within 30 feet. Use the same attack roll. If the redirected attack hits the new target, resolve it as normal. Otherwise, the attack fails.

If you extend the casting time to 1 full round, the duration changes from instantaneous to 1 round per caster level.

INFALLIBLE SERVANT

Necromancy [Evil]
Level: Cleric 3, druid 4, sorcerer/wizard 3
Components: V, S, M
Casting Time: 1 minute
Range: Touch

Target: Creature touched
Duration: 1 hour/level (D)
Saving Throw: Will negates; see text
Spell Resistance: No

You rub dung onto your minion's brow, intoning dark words to bind his life to your cause.

With a touch, you give a target a powerful motivation to avoid failure. If the target is captured by non-evil creatures or is slain, his body dissolves into foul sludge. The target is utterly destroyed and cannot be affected by any spell or effect that restores life (such as *true resurrection*) or a semblance of life (such as *animate dead*) short of *miracle* or *wish*.

When the target dissolves, all creatures within 30 feet must succeed on a Fortitude save against the spell's DC or become nauseated for 1d4 rounds.

Material Component: Dung from an evil creature.

PHANTASMAL INJURY

Illusion (Phantasm) [Fear, Mind-Affecting]
Level: Bard 3, sorcerer/wizard 3
Components: V, S
Casting Time: 1 standard action
Range: Medium (100 ft. + 10 ft./level)
Target: One living creature
Duration: 1 round/level (D)
Saving Throw: Will disbelief
Spell Resistance: Yes

You cast out your senses to fill your foe's mind, causing him to believe that he has suffered a mortal wound.

You create the sensation in the target's mind that he has been disabled (reduced to 0 hit points), restricting him to a single move action or standard action each turn. If the target takes a standard action (or any kind of strenuous action), he takes 1 point of damage from *phantasmal injury*. The target remains conscious unless the damage would actually reduce his hit points below 0. This damage is real and remains after the spell's duration has expired.

PHANTASMAL WASTING

Illusion (Phantasm) [Fear, Mind-Affecting]
Level: Bard 4, druid 4, sorcerer/wizard 5
Components: V, S
Casting Time: 1 standard action
Range: Touch
Target: One living creature touched
Duration: 1 round/level (D)
Saving Throw: Will disbelief
Spell Resistance: Yes

Your touch infects your foe's senses, leading him to believe that he has grown feeble and ancient.

With a touch, you cause a target to believe that he has lost his vitality and vigor. For the duration of the spell, the target takes a –6 penalty to Strength, Dexterity, and Constitution.

RING OF FIRE

Conjuration (Creation) [Fire]
Level: Druid 9, sorcerer/wizard 9
Components: V, S, M
Casting Time: 1 round
Range: Medium (100 ft. + 10 ft./level)
Effect: 10-ft.-radius area of lava; see text
Duration: 1 round/2 levels
Saving Throw: Reflex partial
Spell Resistance: No

You utter deep, rumbling tones as you make arcane gestures over the basalt disc, causing it to glow white hot and evaporate in your hand. When you finish, the ground tears open and hot lava wells up from the depths of the earth.

You create an area of lava. All creatures in the area that make successful Reflex saves take 1d6 points of fire damage plus 1 point per caster level. Creatures that fail their saves take 1d6 points of damage per caster level, to a maximum of 20d6 points. Creatures that take at least 1 point of damage from *ring of fire* take an extra 1d6 points of fire damage each round for 3 rounds.

Each round after the first, the area of lava expands by 10 feet, becoming a 20-foot-radius ring on the second round, a 30-foot-radius ring on the third round, and so on. As the *ring of fire* spreads, all creatures in its area must make new saving throws as described above.

When the spell's duration expires, the lava cools rapidly. All creatures in the area at that time are held fast and cannot move until they make a successful Strength check or Escape Artist check against the spell's DC. Breaking free of the lava is a full-round action.

Material Component: A disc of basalt (5 gp).

STIFFEN

Necromancy
Level: Bard 3, cleric 3, sorcerer/wizard 4
Components: V, S
Casting Time: 1 standard action
Range: Touch
Target: Living creature touched
Duration: 1 round/level (D)
Saving Throw: Fortitude partial; see text
Spell Resistance: Yes

As you touch your foe, blue spiderwebs appear on his skin, slowing him down and gradually paralyzing him.

Upon touching a target, you set in motion a devastating effect that gradually deadens his nerves. On the first round, the target takes a –4 penalty to his Dexterity score, and all his movement rates are reduced by 5 feet. If the target can fly, his maneuverability is reduced by one step.

On the following round, the target can make a new Fortitude save to halt the spell's progress. If the save fails, the penalty to Dexterity worsens to –8, his movement rates are reduced another 5 feet, and his maneuverability is reduced by another 2 steps. This deterioration continues each round until the target succeeds on his save, at which point his condition no longer worsens, or until the target's Dexterity drops to 0. Targets whose movement rates drop to 0 feet cannot move, and targets whose maneuverability drops below clumsy cannot fly. All penalties vanish when the spell's duration expires.

TOUCH OF CHAOS

Transmutation [Chaos, Evil]
Level: Sorcerer/wizard 5
Components: V, S, M
Casting Time: 1 standard action
Range: Touch
Target: Living creature touched
Duration: 1 round/2 levels
Saving Throw: Fortitude negates
Spell Resistance: Yes

With a hand dripping with pale violet slime, you touch your foe, causing him to collapse into a pile of shifting tissue.

Your touch causes a creature to undergo a terrifying transformation. A target that fails its save collapses into a spongy mass of flesh and sinew and takes 1 point of Wisdom drain.

Each round, as a free action, the target can attempt a new Fortitude save to regain its form. If the save fails, the target remains transformed and takes another 1 point of Wisdom drain.

A target afflicted with *touch of chaos* cannot use possessions or cast spells. It takes a –4 penalty to Dexterity, its land speed drops to 10 feet, and it loses all other modes of movement. The target can lash out with tentacles that burst from its flesh, but it attacks the closest creature, whether friend or foe. The attack is made at a –4 penalty and has a 50% miss chance. If a tentacle hits the creature, it deals damage based on the afflicted target's size (Small, 1d3 points; Medium, 1d4 points; and Large, 1d6 points).

Material Component: Slime from a chaos beast.

TREACHEROUS WEAPON

Transmutation
Level: Bard 1, hexblade[CW] 1, sorcerer/wizard 1
Components: V, S
Casting Time: 1 immediate action; see text
Range: Close (25 ft. + 5 ft./2 levels)
Target: One creature
Duration: 1 round
Saving Throw: Will negates
Spell Resistance: Yes

You make a gesture accompanied by a sharp arcane command, and your foe's weapon gives off a momentary shower of sparks.

You can cast this spell on any creature wielding a manufactured weapon. If the target fails its saving throw, the weapon takes a –1 penalty on attack rolls and damage rolls.

For every two caster levels beyond 1st, the penalty worsens by 1. Thus, at 3rd level, the weapon takes a –2 penalty; at 5th level, a –3 penalty; at 7th level, a –4 penalty; and at 9th level or higher, a maximum –5 penalty.

When this spell is cast on a creature wielding a magic weapon, subtract the weapon's enhancement bonus from the penalty. For example, a 1st-level caster would reduce a +1 *longsword* to a +0 *longsword*.

If you extend the spell's casting time to 1 standard action, the enhancement penalties double.

WILLING SACRIFICE

Necromancy [Evil]
Level: Cleric 3, sorcerer/wizard 3
Components: V
Casting Time: 1 swift action
Range: Close (25 ft. + 5 ft./2 levels)
Target: One creature
Duration: 1 round/level
Saving Throw: None
Spell Resistance: No

You utter a blasphemous phrase, and an ally erupts in pale gray flames. When the fire sputters out, you feel the power of corruption coursing through your veins.

You deal 1d10 points of damage to a single evil creature within range that is a willing target. As a result, you gain a profane bonus equal to half the number of points of damage dealt. As a free action, you can use the bonus on attack rolls, damage rolls, saving throws, ability checks, or skill checks. You can use as much or as little of the bonus as you wish, but you must declare the use before the results of the die roll are known. At the end of the spell's duration, any unused bonus points are lost. The effects of multiple *willing sacrifice* spells are not cumulative; you can benefit from only one spell at a time.

VILLAINOUS ORGANIZATIONS

Villains rarely go it alone. They surround themselves with henchmen and lackeys who do the dirty jobs and insulate their employers from virtuous adversaries. To this end, many villains establish organizations—gathering armies of humanoid soldiers, employing guardian beasts, and conjuring up fiends from the darkest pits to serve their whims.

Sometimes, a villain is merely a part of a larger organization. In a way, the organization becomes the villain, and the defeat of the individual adversary has little or no effect on the structural integrity of the group. Examples include the Emerald Claw from the EBERRON™ campaign setting and the Cult of the Dragon in the FORGOTTEN REALMS™ setting.

MINIONS

Great villains need servants to act on their behalf, eliminate their rivals, and help them achieve their goals. A minion, then, is a minor villain linked directly to a major villain.

When creating minions, develop them the same way you would develop any other villains. They have objectives, motives, complex personalities, and so on, making them compelling characters in their own right. However, minions should never overshadow the principal villain they serve.

A major villain should have one to three minions. A minor villain usually has no minions, but if you wish, you can give her one. A minion's Challenge Rating should equal the villain's Challenge Rating minus 2.

The PCs' first brush with a villain is often through a minion, so these lesser characters should bear some similarity to their masters. Minions can employ similar spells, use magic items that fit a particular theme, or employ lackeys that resemble or reflect the nature of their master.

LACKEYS

Beneath minions in the pecking order are lackeys, less significant characters who live only to serve and protect their master. Lackeys are less impressive than minions and have lower Challenge Ratings. They might have levels in NPC classes, and they resemble the usual types of cannon fodder that player characters fight on a regular basis.

A villain's number of lackeys depends on her Charisma modifier and her Challenge Rating. Add the two values together and consult Table 1–2: Typical Lackeys. (For example, a villain whose CR + Cha modifier equals 14 typically has twenty lackeys of CR 1, four lackeys of CR 2, and two lackeys of CR 3.) The table is meant only as a guide, so feel free to modify the numbers to meet your needs.

TABLE 1–2: TYPICAL LACKEYS

Villain's CR	— Number of Lackeys by CR —									
+ Cha Mod	1	2	3	4	5	6	7	8	9	10
9 or lower	—	—	—	—	—	—	—	—	—	—
10	2	—	—	—	—	—	—	—	—	—
11	5	1	—	—	—	—	—	—	—	—
12	10	2	—	—	—	—	—	—	—	—
13	15	3	1	—	—	—	—	—	—	—
14	20	4	2	—	—	—	—	—	—	—
15	25	5	3	1	—	—	—	—	—	—
16	30	6	3	2	—	—	—	—	—	—
17	35	7	4	2	—	—	—	—	—	—
18	40	8	4	2	—	—	—	—	—	—
19	45	9	5	3	1	—	—	—	—	—
20	50	10	5	3	2	—	—	—	—	—
21	75	15	7	4	2	—	—	—	—	—
22	100	20	10	5	3	1	—	—	—	—
23	125	25	13	7	4	2	—	—	—	—
24	150	30	15	8	4	2	—	—	—	—
25	175	35	18	9	5	3	1	—	—	—
26	200	40	20	10	5	3	2	—	—	—
27	250	50	25	13	7	4	2	—	—	—
28	300	60	30	15	8	4	2	1	—	—
29	400	80	40	20	10	5	3	2	1	—
30	500	100	50	25	12	6	3	2	1	1
Each +1	+100	+30	+10	+5	+2	+1	+1/2	+1/3	+1/4	+1/4

Assembling the Lackeys

You have a lot of freedom when choosing the types, classes, and races of the members of a villain's organization. Although any monster or character could be found in the group, keep in mind the villain's theme and alignment, as well as the alignments of the lackeys you select.

As a rule of thumb, lackeys should have a uniform alignment; when selecting monsters, always use the monster's listed alignment. You should reserve unusual monster and alignment combinations for the minions and villains.

No matter how many lackeys constitute the villain's organization, do not define them all at once. Instead, use them the way that a wizard uses a spell slot. When you build an adventure that features the villain's group, select lackeys that are appropriate to the adventure and the PC levels. When lackeys are slain, simply remove them from the villain's pool of servants.

Minions, Lackeys, and the Leadership Feat

The Leadership feat (*PH* 97 and *DMG* 106) is primarily intended to address how player characters accumulate followers as they gain levels and garner a reputation for greatness. As such, the feat is unsuitable for villains, who often spend more time building a network of servants, brokering deals with monstrous entities, and putting terrifying plots into motion. Furthermore, villains—by their very nature—are not the sorts of individuals who accomplish heroic deeds or have impressive qualities, so their leadership scores often suffer due to bad behavior. Still, if you choose to give your villain the Leadership feat, she gains a cohort and followers in addition to any servants she accumulates by dint of her villainy.

ORGANIZATIONAL STRUCTURE

Taken as a whole, a villain's lackeys and minions constitute her organization. They work on behalf of the villain, undertaking missions, gathering information, protecting her lair, and performing countless other duties and tasks. A villain's servants are representatives of her will in the setting, and the PCs must fight them before they confront the major adversary.

Hierarchy

The villain's hierarchy defines how she organizes her lackeys. This arrangement should reflect her goals and alignment: Chaotic villains have loose hierarchies, and lawful characters have rigid ones.

Loose (Chaotic): A loose hierarchy has no formal structure, and members can come and go over time. For these groups to function, they must have a unifying purpose, a common goal, or some other aspect that is shared by all members. Examples include worship of the same deity, hatred of a particular race, or devotion to a common ideal.

Arranging a loose organization requires little preparation. Simply use the lackeys as you need them, assembling them in whatever structure works best for each situation.

Authoritarian (Lawful): In an authoritarian organization—the opposite of a loose hierarchy—everyone knows their place. The leaders issue orders to various lieutenants, who pass them along to their subordinates, who finally give the commands to the grunts. This kind of organization is the most common type for villains who have a militaristic bent.

An authoritarian hierarchy is easy to assemble. Place the villain at the top, with her minions directly beneath. To each minion, attach one of the highest-level lackeys in the organization. To each high-level lackey, attach an equal number of lower-level lackeys, and continue until you reach the 1st-level lackeys, who should be divided evenly among the 2nd-level ones. Lackeys or minions on the same tier communicate with one another.

Segmented (Any): In a segmented hierarchy, a villain divides her servants into smaller isolated cells. Most members of a particular cell are not aware of the members of any other cells. The villain can have multiple cells perform the same task to ensure that her minions achieve the desired outcome, or she can weave a complex web of orders so that cells unknowingly assist each other. In each cell, one member also belongs to a different cell, and one member from that cell belongs to a third cell, and so on, creating a limited line of communication between all cells. This structure ensures that if one cell is lost, the organization will not be compromised.

To build a segmented organization, place the villain at the top, with her minions beneath. From each minion, branch off clusters of lackeys. From each cluster, branch off more clusters until you account for all the lackeys.

Webbed (Any): A webbed organization is similar to a segmented hierarchy in that most members are not aware of agents in other cells. However, the connections between the various cells are more convoluted, with no clear route to the villain.

To build a webbed hierarchy, place the villain at the center. Then place small clusters of lackeys and minions around her. Some of the groups can be connected, while others should remain freestanding, with no clear lines of communication to the villain.

Filling in the Details

Using the villain as your guide, fill in additional details about the organization, such as where it operates, the location of its headquarters, and its membership requirements. The villain's scheme should be the group's central focus, but you can look to her occupation and archetype for further ideas. When fleshing out the organization, consider the following components, summarized from the information on PC organizations in Chapter 6 of *Dungeon Master's Guide II*.

Entry Requirements: Describe what the organization requires from its candidates and the typical kinds of people who join.

Benefits: List some tangible rewards for joining, such as wealth, gear, services, information, access, and status.

Combat: Describe how members of the organization fight. If the members are spellcasters, decide what kinds of spells they use. If the members are warriors, give them unusual or unique tactics or, at the very least, specify the kinds of weapons they wield.

Advancement: Describe how members are recruited, what steps they must take to join, and how they can advance within the organization.

Missions: Describe the kinds of missions the members undertake and the consequences, if any, for failure.

Responsibilities: Describe what the organization requires from its members in exchange for the benefits it offers. These responsibilities might be simple, such as undertaking missions, or they might involve more complicated duties, such as spying on a rival group, overseeing prayers and sacrifices to a deity, and so on.

NPC Reactions: Place the organization in your campaign setting, and consider how the residents of the surrounding area view the group and how various NPCs react.

Minions and lackeys

Illus. by E. Deschamps

Organizations as Affiliations and Guilds

Player's Handbook II and *Dungeon Master's Guide II* offer alternative approaches for handling organizations. The first approach is the affiliation, a separate system that measures a character's exploits and rewards him by giving him greater standing in the group. The other approach is the guild. Both options are tied to particular occupations and grant characters specific benefits in exchange for certain tasks or duties.

Affiliations and guilds are intended for player characters, but you could modify them for use with minions and lackeys. If you have already established a villainous organization, you could adapt it to become an affiliation or guild and allow the PCs to join and fight it from within.

Maintaining the Organization

Invariably, minions and lackeys die. They are, after all, the villain's first line of defense. Although losing servants is annoying, a great villain can always find fresh recruits who are ready to give their lives for their master.

Dead Minions: If a minion's body is available, the villain could have him raised or transformed into an undead creature. Powerful villains might use *resurrection* to retrieve lost servants. If none of these options is possible, a villain can replace a lost minion with a new one after 30 days. The new

minion is one level lower (or one Challenge Rating lower) than the previous minion.

Dead Lackeys: Lackeys are weaker than minions, and villains expect to go through them more quickly. For each week that a villain spends recruiting (or enslaving), she can regain a number of lackeys equal to 1d6 + her Cha modifier.

INTRODUCING A VILLAIN

Armed with a fully fleshed-out villain, you are just about ready to send him after the player characters. However, while you have established all the details and honed the mechanics, you cannot simply drop your bad guy into the game: It is crucial to give him a proper introduction. Sure, having him lurk in the shadows, send minions after the PCs, and make their lives miserable from a distance is fun, but the first meeting with a villain establishes his unique relationship with the PCs and sets the stage for all the encounters down the road. As such, it should be special. Consider using or adapting any of the following methods of introduction.

FORESHADOWING

The easiest way to introduce a villain is to establish his character and nature before he comes onto the scene. The PCs might pick up a few pieces of information while dredging for rumors in a tavern, or they might stumble across a dead lackey while exploring the city's streets. Worse, the adventurers could encounter the villain's handiwork, and particularly in the case of a disturbing villain (see page 7), the unsettling scene could fan the fires of hatred early on.

Example: For days, the player characters move through a veritable forest of corpses impaled on spikes. On each victim's forehead is a strange sigil: a coiled serpent devouring an orb. When the PCs reach the next village, they find it has been all but burned to the ground. By interviewing the few survivors, they discover that the cruel warlord Roderick the Bloody has passed through these lands in search of his missing wife.

HERO-MADE VILLAINS

Player characters step on toes. They fight in the defense of the poor and downtrodden, brave horrid subterranean depths, expose and destroy cultists, thwart plots to kill kings, and try to right many other wrongs. But often, as soon as their job is done, the PCs move on to their next mission, and the people they leave behind are stuck cleaning up the mess. Sometimes the PCs' exploits can set in motion a disastrous series of events that result in the creation of a nemesis.

The player characters can encourage the birth of a villain in a distressing number of ways. They might dishonor or mistreat a villain-to-be without realizing it. They could make a bad decision with a ruinous outcome that leaves many folks craving revenge. The PCs might antagonize a foe on purpose, never suspecting that they are provoking him into becoming a lifelong enemy. Or perhaps the minion of a defeated master villain escapes before the PCs can catch him, and he now sets his sights on the party. No matter what his origin, a hero-made villain is memorable because the PCs played a role in his creation, making him—and his crimes—partly their responsibility.

Example: Between adventures, the player characters overhear gossip about a haunted castle a few days to the north. The locals claim that the place was run by a grim lord who killed himself in shame when his son was hanged for being a servant of Erythnul. Sensing that the site might still hold some treasure, the PCs head off to plunder the castle. After a few days of butchering goblins and other squatters, they fill their bags with loot and ride off. However, they inadvertently awaken the spirit of the dead lord, who is enraged at the looting of his house. He vows revenge and calls up a horde of hellish ghosts to help him torment and punish the thieves.

VILLAINOUS SERVANT

On occasion, you can introduce a villain by having him pose as a merchant or a servant of the player characters. He might be a hired companion, a henchman, or an NPC who sells them magic items or offers healing. This method also works if the PCs employ a monstrous creature, such as one tied to them by a *planar ally* or *planar binding* spell.

Example: The party has made several forays into an old dwarf hold that has been overrun by trolls. The locals claim that the creatures answer to a dreadful witch. Because trolls are so dangerous, the PCs proceed with care, retreating from the tunnels to rest and receive healing from a wise woman at the edge of town. The adventurers do not yet realize that she is the witch, and that she is assessing their capabilities so that she can design the perfect trap.

PARTY AS SERVANT

Another twist is to place the party in the service of the villain. In this approach, the villain hides his motives well, presenting an agreeable front to ensure that the characters serve his interests. The PCs might be unwitting pawns, or they might be the victims of a magical compulsion, such as a *geas*, undoubtedly foisted on them by the same villain.

Example: When his nation is attacked by a horde of barbarians from the ice-capped mountains of the far north, a king calls upon the PCs to help defend the country. In truth, the greedy monarch provoked the attack by sending his minions to steal an heirloom sword, which is said to hold incredible power and give the wielder command over the barbarians.

ALLY IN DISGUISE

Some villains are born from alliances gone sour. Perhaps a trusted friend is corrupted, possessed, or misled into opposing the PCs. On the other hand, the villain might have been a pretender all along, working with the characters for a time to study their strengths or gain valuable information.

Depending on your group, you might consider permitting one of the PCs to be a villain in disguise, or you could tempt a genuine player character into betraying the rest of the group. However, this twist is not recommended for parties of inexperienced players, who need every advantage they can get, or for newly formed gaming groups, whose players might take a double-cross personally.

Example: The PCs belong to the Watch Knights, a group of warriors who guard the border between their own realm and a land infested by orcs and goblins. While on patrol with NPC allies, the group is ambushed by the monsters. During the attack, one of the PCs sees a member of their party run into the woods after firing a crossbow bolt into the patrol leader's neck.

Illus. by T. Giorello

he orc has fallen far from his rightful place as master of the world. Humans, elves, dwarves—they have all stolen his birthright, his racial destiny. It is the purpose of my life to remind the orcs of what they truly are, and to punish the usurpers for their crimes against our people."

—Zargath Human-Bane

Born in slaughter, raised by his enemies, and beloved of no one, the orc known as Zargath Human-Bane burns with a sacred mission. He will raise his people from their primitive state and crush all those who have kept the orcs from claiming what is rightfully theirs.

BACKGROUND

Zargath Human-Bane was never meant to live beyond childhood. Born small and weak, he was left exposed to the elements by his tribe at an early age. Luck (of a sort) was with him that night, though, because his village was burned to the ground by a group of wandering mercenaries. The young Zargath was discovered by a human named Darved Locathen, the head of a local thieves' guild known as the Gray Knives. Darved had followed the mercenaries in the hope of picking up stray loot. What he picked up instead was a slave in the making.

Zargath spent the next twenty years as a cleaner, servant, and whipping boy at The Grinning Fool, a tavern in the poorest section of a large city. The place was also a front for the Gray Knives. Darved was never quite sure why he had saved the young creature—perhaps he thought it might be amusing to have a full-blooded orc laborer—but it was a decision that he and many others would come to regret.

Zargath learned early the ability to dodge and weave to avoid the many mailed fists and outstretched legs at the tavern. He learned to conceal his anger and his exceptional mind so that he would not anger Darved, who beat him mercilessly while drunk. Through the sly observation of his human "father" and the rest of the Gray Knives, he learned the craft of the rogue, and how to strike from the shadows. Mostly, though, he learned how to hate. He despised humans, elves, dwarves, and practically anyone else who entered the tavern. In his heart, Zargath longed to be reunited with his people, and to live in the great civilization that he was sure he had been stolen from.

He saw his opportunity in Gurn Sirensong, a twisted gnome illusionist/rogue who had recently become second in command of the Gray Knives. Zargath befriended Gurn, and offered to poison Darved and the guild's other top lieutenants if the gnome and his trusted men would purge the ranks of anyone loyal to his father. In return, Zargath wanted only to burn down the tavern and to secure a pledge of eternal friendship from the new head of the Gray

Knives. Gurn accepted, and the slaughter that followed was brutal. Gurn took over the guild, and Zargath left to rejoin the glorious orc civilization.

What he found was disappointment. The orcs had no great empire: They were merely fractious, primitive tribes living in hovels on the edges of humanoid nations. Zargath realized that if he wanted an illustrious orc civilization, he would have to build it himself. He selected the largest and most prosperous local tribes and, over the course of a few years, he moved in, murdered his way into a position of influence, and installed a willing war leader to rule as figurehead. Now, with his hold over the local tribes growing, Zargath and his followers—known as the Black Wolves—look outward, determined to bring the orcs to prominence and every other race to its knees.

GOALS

Zargath is an orc consumed by two desires. The first is to create the orc civilization that he dreamed of during his long years of servitude. The second is to exterminate every human, elf, and dwarf in the world. Unlike most orc warlords, Zargath has no desire to conquer other races and seize their territory or take slaves. When the Black Wolves go into battle, they carry out well-planned missions of slaughter from which no adult or child escapes. The orcs leave behind burned cities, scorched earth, and the gruesome corpses of their impaled victims.

Zargath is not blind to the character of the orcs that follow him. He knows that he will not be able to magically sophisticate the race in his lifetime. His hope is to steer its culture toward laws and values that will eventually result in a civilization as powerful as the one the humanoids have created. To this end, he has been a friend and advisor to a fighter named Grikfell, teaching the bright but somewhat small orc a few rogue tricks that helped him take down his rivals and become the tribe's war leader, second only to Zargath in status and influence.

Since then, Zargath has used his alliance with Grikfell to purge his tribe of the larger, dumber individuals by teaching the smaller, smarter orcs a formerly foreign concept—the value of group pride and group effort over the chaotic selfishness that has kept the orcs weak. The orcs that follow Zargath's philosophy have prospered, triumphing in battle against rival tribes, local monsters, and the hated humanoids. As a result, Zargath's reputation as a spiritual leader has grown. Now, orcs from other tribes seek him out to join the ranks of the Black Wolves, and those that resist the new order are being destroyed.

Reforming orc society is not the only task that occupies Zargath. He has had Grikfell lead many raids into the surrounding countryside on missions of extermination. So far, the orcs have limited their targets to small villages and isolated hamlets. They use the raids to develop tactics and strategies, and Zargath's followers are learning the value of group effort through practical experience.

The other major prong of Zargath's plan involves his alliance with Gurn Sirensong, the leader of the Gray Knives. To Gurn, Zargath is a source of wealth and mercenary muscle. In recent months, many valuable goods have been delivered to the thieves' guild by groups of strangely disciplined orcs. In return, Gurn has been selling the orcs weapons, potions, spell scrolls, and captives—engineers, spellcasters, sages, retired military captains, and others who have the expertise Zargath needs to shape his fanatical band into an army and a civilization.

USING THIS VILLAIN

For lower-level player characters, Zargath makes a challenging opponent over a series of adventures. Orcs are common foes for less skilled PCs, but the Black Wolves are more than just experience points waiting to be awarded. The tribe can be used to give orcs depth, resonance, and a long-term presence in the world, making the campaign setting seem more real. Zargath fits the archetype of the disturbing villain (see page 7), with straightforward motives and plans that feature moral clarity rather than ambiguity. The PCs' course of action is simple: Zargath must be stopped.

They can be introduced to his plans in several ways. In an action-oriented campaign, they might hear disquieting rumors of orcs in the wilderness—orcs as disciplined as any human soldiers. They might encounter a group of Zargath's warriors and note the coordination and skill with which they fight. Perhaps the PCs meet a survivor of one of Grikfell's raids and hear a horrifying account of the attack, or maybe they start to run across the symbol of the Black Wolves—a stylized ebony wolf in a white circle on a red field.

In a campaign that relies more on intrigue, the PCs might first encounter Gurn and the Gray Knives. The guild has recently become flush with cash, and the city has seen an increase in the trafficking of mysterious merchandise—some of it damaged, as if in battle—along with a growing local market in weapons. Furthermore, citizens who have specialized knowledge, such as wizards, engineers (especially dwarves), retired soldiers, and sages, have begun to vanish.

When used as a recurring villain, Zargath can grow in menace as the PCs grow in ability. At first, his stronghold will be too well defended to assault it head-on, so the adventurers might need to oppose him indirectly. They could help to defend a town against one of Grikfell's raids, recover a kidnapped specialist, or go after Gurn to cut off the supply of weapons to the Black Wolves.

Eventually, however, Zargath will grow confident enough (and his army will grow large enough) to begin taking on bigger targets—first towns, then small cities, and finally an important city, perhaps the capital of a humanoid empire. This escalation can lead to a final confrontation in which the PCs defend a city and then launch a counterassault against Zar'Fell, Zargath's headquarters.

ZARGATH HUMAN-BANE IN EBERRON

Zargath Human-Bane served twenty years of servitude in the lower reaches of Sharn until his alliance with Gurn. After his escape, he headed for the Shadow Marches, where he discovered his people living pathetic, pastoral lives. His new tribe worships The Dragon Below, and its first crusade is against the Gatekeepers; the tribe hopes to eventually claim the Eldeen Reaches for the orcs. Zargath's ultimate goal is to exterminate Breland and destroy Sharn. However, he worries about how the hags of Droaam will react to his ambitions.

ZARGATH HUMAN-BANE IN FAERÛN

Zargath Human-Bane served twenty years of servitude in the city of Silverymoon until his alliance with Gurn. After his escape, he found his way to King Obould Many-Arrows in the hope of helping him build a new orc civilization. But with five sons already vying for pieces of his kingdom, Obould would brook no rival and tried to have Zargath killed. Zargath escaped again, this time to the wild orcs at the Spine of the World, where he has begun constructing his own empire to challenge Obould. Although his hatred of humanoids and his desire to destroy Silverymoon have not diminished, Zargath's most pressing concern is the inevitable confrontation with Obould.

Illus. by J. Hodgson

Zargath Human-Bane

APPEARANCE AND BEHAVIOR

Zargath does not cut a physically imposing figure. At 5 feet tall and about 120 pounds, he is shorter and lighter than the average orc. Likewise, his face is rounder, flatter, and more intelligent than the norm for the race, and his gray skin carries a pinkish cast that fuels speculation of human blood in his ancestry. Needless to say, the proud orc does not appreciate such comments and has made gruesome examples of those who indulge in loose talk.

Zargath favors simple, unadorned clothing—usually black—with none of the barbaric flair, trophies, or decoration common among his people. He keeps his hair and beard trimmed short and neat. In combat, he wears a suit of masterwork studded leather armor and a voluminous cloak with a deeply inset hood. He has a hand crossbow strapped to his back, and at his waist he carries several small pouches full of thieves' tools (flash powder, caltrops, and the like). He is rarely seen without his masterwork short sword (which he calls "Pride") and masterwork dagger ("Vengeance"). He loves apples for some reason and eats them almost constantly.

Zargath leaves run-of-the-mill tribal administration to Grikfell and focuses his attention on the big picture. He holds frequent meetings with members of the Gray Knives to haggle over information, slaves, and looted merchandise, and he occasionally hosts leaders of other orc tribes to discuss the terms of their surrender. Zargath spares no effort in gathering intelligence before launching a strike, and is often found in the library at Zar'fell (tactical encounter 2–2), which he refers to as the "brain pen." There, he grills kidnapped experts to learn the intricacies of law, government, history, engineering, and military tactics. He jots down notes and thoughts on these matters in a large leatherbound book, which he believes will one day be the founding document for a new orc empire.

Zargath has little patience for religion. He does not forbid his followers from worshiping Gruumsh and other orc deities, but he views the members of the pantheon as shortsighted failures that have proven themselves powerless to help the orcs achieve greatness. Consequently, there are no clerics among his inner circle, a situation that is highly unusual for an orc leader. This generates resentment among orc priests, who do not feel welcome in Zar'Fell. However, Zargath's reverence for knowledge and study has spawned something of a renaissance among orc sorcerers and other arcane magic-users.

Although his plans seem to be coming together, Zargath remains unsatisfied. Intellectually, he understands that he will not live long enough to do more than start his people down the path to civilization and dominance. But lately, his insatiable hatred for humans and other humanoid races has driven him to make some rash decisions. Grikfell believes that Zargath's penchant for torture and atrocity is drawing more notice from humanoid authorities than the Black Wolves can handle at this point. He also worries that Zargath is not paying enough attention to the growing resentment of those stubborn orcs that refuse to march under his banner.

ZARGATH HUMAN-BANE **CR 5**
hp 15 (5 HD)

Male orc rogue 4
LE Medium humanoid
Init +4; **Senses** darkvision 60 ft.; Listen +7, Spot +7
Languages Common, Orc

AC 18, touch 15, flat-footed 14; Dodge, uncanny dodge
(+4 Dex, +3 armor, +1 deflection)
Resist evasion
Fort +3, **Ref** +8, **Will** +0
Weakness light sensitivity

Speed 30 ft. (6 squares)
Melee mwk short sword +6 (1d6+1) and
mwk dagger +1 (1d4+1)
Ranged mwk hand crossbow +11 (1d4)
Base Atk +6; **Grp** +7
Atk Options sneak attack +2d6
Combat Gear 2 *potions of cure light wounds, dust of dryness, ring of protection +1*, tanglefoot bag, caltrops

Abilities Str 12, Dex 18, Con 8, Int 15, Wis 8, Cha 15
SQ trap sense +1, trapfinding
Feats Alertness, Dodge, Two-Weapon Fighting
Skills Diplomacy +6, Disguise +3, Escape Artist +4, Gather Information +6, Hide +11, Intimidate +6, Knowledge (architecture) +3, Knowledge (geography) +3, Knowledge (history), +3, Knowledge (local) +6, Knowledge (nobility) +3, Listen +7, Move Silently +11, Open Lock +5, Search +3, Spot +7
Possessions combat gear plus masterwork studded leather armor, masterwork hand crossbow with 50 bolts, masterwork short sword, masterwork dagger, masterwork thieves' tools

Light Sensitivity Zargath takes a –1 penalty on attack rolls, Search checks, and Spot checks in bright sunlight or within the radius of a *daylight* spell.

Illus. by K. Tanner

WAR LEADER GRIKFELL

"So many thousands of years wasted. Orc spilling the blood of orc, weakening ourselves while our enemies grew strong and prosperous. That time has passed, and a new era must begin. I shall not lead our people, I shall serve them even as I serve Zargath, and together we shall make ourselves great among nations."
—Grikfell

Grikfell was a competent but second-tier tribe member until Zargath taught him some tricks learned from the Gray Knives, inspired him with a bold vision of an orc nation, and installed him as clan war leader. No mere figurehead, Grikfell willingly serves under Zargath, combining his martial prowess with his master's tactical genius. Lately, however, he has begun to have second thoughts. Grikfell still believes in the dream, but fears that Zargath's growing obsession with exterminating their enemies might jeopardize their chance for ultimate success.

War Leader Grikfell

GOALS

Grikfell always knew that he was not like other orcs. He was smarter than average, certainly, but the difference ran deeper than that: Despite his combat skill, he lacked an essential blood lust that could have vaulted him into the upper ranks of orc society.

Thankfully, Zargath gave him something to believe in beyond the usual orc goals of food in the belly and notches on the battleaxe. Grikfell wholeheartedly endorses his master's vision, and views his own position as war leader as a means to that end. He keeps busy running the day-to-day business of the tribe and is often in the field on missions of extermination. Grikfell takes no particular pleasure in slaughter, but he does not shy away from what he considers a necessary task on the road to empire. He is beginning to harbor some doubts, however, about whether Zargath's obsession with killing all other humanoids is leading him to make the wisest decisions.

USING GRIKFELL

Although not as intelligent as Zargath, Grikfell is bright and has a gift for tactical maneuvering and war craft. A technically proficient fighter, he approaches combat with the same cool, disciplined manner with which he approaches everything else in his life. Player characters who meet him in combat might discover that killing Grikfell will require more than simply confronting him on the battlefield. For one thing, he is always accompanied by Elbeth, his pet worg. For another, the orc can recognize the danger posed by a strong party of adventurers, and he is not afraid to retreat if a fight does not go his way.

Appearance and Behavior

Grikfell is a large, heavily muscled orc fighter who prefers to go into battle with his prized suit of masterwork banded mail and his orc double axe. He also carries a few shortspears strapped to his back, with a few more in a quiver carried by Elbeth. Tied around his waist is a battle net that he uses primarily on mounted opponents.

Like his master, Grikfell is not ostentatious. His equipment is simple, well maintained, and free of decoration. His beard is short and neat, and his long hair is tied into an elaborate tail with his one concession to vanity—a bright yellow ribbon.

WAR LEADER GRIKFELL **CR 3**

hp 25 (3 HD)

Male orc fighter 2
LE Medium humanoid
Init +2; **Senses** darkvision 60 ft.; Listen +2, Spot +1
Languages Common, Orc

AC 19, touch 12, flat-footed 17
(+2 Dex, +7 armor)
Fort +7, **Ref** +2, **Will** –1
Weakness light sensitivity

Speed 30 ft. (6 squares)
Melee mwk orc double axe +9 (1d8+6)
Ranged mwk shortspear +6 (1d6 +4) or
Ranged net +5 (entangle)
Base Atk +3; **Grp** +7
Combat Gear 3 *potions of cure light wounds*

Abilities Str 18, Dex 15, Con 13, Int 13, Wis 12, Cha 10
Feats Armor Proficiency (heavy), Exotic Weapon Proficiency (net), Exotic Weapon Proficiency (orc double axe), Weapon Focus (orc double axe)
Skills Bluff +4, Handle Animal +2, Intimidate +6, Jump +2, Listen +2, Spot +1
Possessions combat gear plus masterwork banded mail, masterwork orc double axe, 3 masterwork shortspears, net, *bracers of armor +1*

Light Sensitivity Grikfell takes a –1 penalty on attack rolls, Search checks, and Spot checks in bright sunlight or within the radius of a *daylight* spell.

GURN SIRENSONG

"Why would I be nervous about Zargath? He does what he does, I do what I do, and we both get what we want. 'Don't ask, don't tell'—that's my motto. Besides, I owe him. He's the one who got me to where I am."

—Gurn Sirensong, Master of the Gray Knives

This twisted gnome is a hedonist and a sadist. Originally a promising illusionist who attended a prestigious magician's academy, Gurn Sirensong quit his studies after several years to explore the world and seek adventure. During his wanderings, he discovered his two great loves: indulging in creature comforts and hurting people. His drift into crime was inevitable.

At first, Gurn knew nothing about an orc revolution, nor would he have cared if he did. Currently, however, his fortunes are tied to the success of Zargath's revolution. Gurn deliberately tries to remain ignorant of the details, but he is smart enough to connect the rumors of strange orc attacks with the battle-damaged merchandise that he fences for his ally. Gurn knows that he's riding a tiger, but he is not sure how to dismount.

Gurn Sirensong

Illus. by E. Widermann

GOALS

Gurn's goal is to make life as comfortable as possible for himself and as uncomfortable as possible for everyone else. However, he badly underestimated the beaten and abused orc who helped him become leader of the Gray Knives—he thought he was using Zargath, but he is starting to realize that it might have been the other way around.

He cannot deny that his alliance with Zargath has been good for him personally and for the thieves' guild overall. The raids provide a steady stream of valuable loot, and the orc is his best customer for illicit weapons and captives. But as he hears more rumors about Zargath's ambitions, Gurn wonders why the orc needs so many weapons—and what really lies behind Zargath's mask of friendship.

USING GURN

Gurn Sirensong is a mercenary who believes that the world owes him a living and that everything exists for his amusement. As such, he is always on the lookout for any opportunity to make a profit or eliminate a rival. This self-centeredness often leads him to take risks in the pursuit of material comforts, but the gnome survives because he pays well and because he is completely ruthless. Gurn takes pleasure in making examples out of people who cross him.

In addition to his work with Zargath, Gurn calls the shots for various criminal enterprises that range from burglary to drug smuggling to assassination. He goes to great lengths to conceal his connection to Zargath and is terrified of what might happen if anyone discovered the truth. For the moment, though, Zargath needs him and his network just as much as Gurn needs the orc's money.

Appearance and Behavior

Gurn Sirensong is an ordinary-looking gnome of average height and weight. His face is rather pinched, however, and his eyes are a bit narrower than normal, giving him a constantly scheming expression. In private, he dresses in luxurious silks chosen more for the way they feel than for their aesthetic value. In public, he dresses in sturdy, nondescript black leather garments designed to let him hide in the shadows. He wears a pouch-filled belt that contains a full rogue's kit and his spell components.

GURN SIRENSONG CR 3

hp 14 (4 HD)

Male gnome wizard 2/rogue 1
NE Small humanoid
Init +4; **Senses** low-light vision; Listen +3, Spot +1
Languages Common, Dwarven, Gnome, Goblin, Gnoll, Orc

AC 15, touch 15, flat-footed 11; +4 against giants (+1 size, +4 Dex)
Fort +0, **Ref** +6, **Will** +4; +2 against illusions

Speed 20 ft. (4 squares)
Melee mwk dagger +3 (1d3)
Ranged light crossbow +6 (1d6)
Base Atk +1; **Grp** –3
Atk Options sneak attack +1d6, +1 on attack rolls against kobolds and goblinoids
Combat Gear 3 *potions of cure light wounds*, *wand of magic missile* (CL 2nd, 20 charges), scroll of *summon monster I*, 2 tanglefoot bags, 2 smokesticks, 2 vials alchemist's fire
Wizard Spells Prepared (CL 3rd):
1st—*disguise self* (DC 16), *magic missile*, *silent image* (DC 16)
0—*arcane mark*, *detect poison*, *flare* (DC 14), *ray of frost* (DC 14)
Spell-Like Abilities (CL 3rd):
1/day—*dancing lights*, *ghost sound* (DC 14), *prestidigitation*, *speak with animals* (burrowing mammal only, duration 1 minute)

Abilities Str 10, Dex 18, Con 10, Int 18, Wis 13, Cha 16
SQ familiar (none at present), trapfinding
Feats Scribe Scroll, Spell Focus (illusion), Greater Spell Focus (illusion)
Skills Concentration +6, Craft +10, Decipher Script +10, Diplomacy +4, Disguise +4, Escape Artist +10, Forgery +5, Gather Information +4, Knowledge (local) +6, Listen +3, Move Silently +5, Open Lock +5, Profession (bookkeeper) +5, Sense Motive +2, Sleight of Hand +5, Spellcraft +10, Spot +1, Tumble +5, Use Rope +4
Possessions combat gear plus masterwork dagger, masterwork thieves' tools, 1 antitoxin vial, light crossbow with 30 bolts, topaz/jade necklace (500 gp), 5 gold earrings (20 gp each), 2 diamond rings (50 gp each), spellbook

ZAR'FELL

When Zargath went looking for the center of his orc empire, he and Grikfell found a ruined manor house only a few miles from the tribe's village. They cleared the place of wandering monsters and renamed it Zar'Fell in honor of their alliance and their friendship.

Today, Zar'Fell is a thriving community of over four hundred orcs, including three hundred noncombatant women and children. Most live in small huts on the grounds that surround the keep, while the higher-status orc families live in renovated stone cottages. Zargath, Grikfell, and other leaders reside in the manor house.

KEY FEATURES

Before the Black Wolves arrived, the manor had been abandoned for so long that the second floor, parts of the first floor, all four of the guard towers, and a good chunk of the exterior western wall had collapsed. Now, construction and repair work proceed around the clock.

Much of the interior has been repaired or reinforced, as has most of the western wall and the southeastern guard tower (see area 10). Temporary walls have been built to block access to the southwestern portion of the keep (including area 11), which has almost entirely fallen into rubble. As the second floor had sustained too much damage to be repaired, the orcs knocked it down, took out the stairs, and covered the house in a new flat roof.

Structural Properties

The following general properties apply to all rooms unless otherwise noted in the area descriptions.

Exterior Walls: The dwarf masonry exterior walls are 3 feet thick and descend about 5 feet below the ground. Unrepaired walls have a break DC of 35, hardness 8, and 300 hit points per 10-foot-square section. Because the walls are crumbling, scaling them is a bit easier than normal (Climb DC 15). Repaired walls have a break DC of 40, hardness 8, and 540 hit points per section.

Interior Walls: The inner walls of the house (Climb DC 20) are 2 feet thick and have a break DC of 35, hardness 8, and 180 hit points per 10-foot-square section.

Scaffolding: Most of the house's exterior is covered by wooden scaffolding; this rises to the roof and has enough platforms and equipment for ten orcs to work at a time.

Floors: In repaired areas of the building, the floors are level and in surprisingly good condition. Due to the construction, however, dust, pebbles, and chunks of debris are everywhere. The presence of so many orcs going back and forth in the dirt makes reading tracks very difficult (Survival DC 30).

Ceiling Height: The ceilings throughout the building are 15 feet high.

Brass Bells: Every 40 feet along the walls is a large brass bell with a hammer. Striking one of these bells puts the house on alert.

Doors: All doors are 7 feet high and are brand new. Each door is 2 inches thick and has hardness 5 and 20 hit points. Except where indicated in the area descriptions, all doors in the house are closed but unlocked (unless an orc puts the house on alert).

Illumination: The interior is lit by torches in sconces every 10 feet along on the walls.

Smells: Zargath likes to be clean, so the house lacks the usual odor of an orc nest (no rotting meat or offal). The major exceptions are the kennels and pens (area 5), which smell of unwashed humanoids and worgs, and the collapsed room (area 11), which reeks of mold. In addition, the air throughout the house is full of stone dust and wood shavings, so any PC who makes a check to identify a smell has a 15% chance of sneezing.

Sounds: Depending on the state of alert, the house and the grounds ring either with the clatter of construction or with the tramp of boots and shouted instructions.

Zar'Fell

Illus. by E. Deschamps

DEFENSES

About forty orc soldiers and five orc captains defend the house when Grikfell and his soldiers are out in the field. Six gnoll mercenaries and a pack of four worgs also reside in the manor. However, the orcs are unaware that the house has several other inhabitants. A gray ooze, a wight, two cockatrices, and several monstrous centipedes lurk in the manor, posing just as much danger to the orcs as they do to the PCs.

Orc Soldier — CR 1/2

hp 5 (1 HD)

LE Medium humanoid
Init +0; **Senses** darkvision 60 ft.; Listen +1, Spot +1
Languages Common, Orc

AC 13, touch 10, flat-footed 13
(+3 armor)
Fort +3, **Ref** +0, **Will** –2
Weakness light sensitivity

Speed 30 ft. (6 squares)
Melee falchion +4 (2d4+4/18–20)
Ranged longbow +1 (1d8/×3)
Base Atk +1; **Grp** +4

Abilities Str 17, Dex 11, Con 12, Int 8, Wis 7, Cha 6
Feats Alertness
Skills Listen +1, Spot +1
Possessions studded leather, falchion, 2 javelins

Light Sensitivity An orc soldier takes a –1 penalty on attack rolls, Search checks, and Spot checks in bright sunlight or within the radius of a *daylight* spell.

Orc Captain — CR 2

hp 11 (2 HD)

Male orc warrior 1
LE Medium humanoid
Init +1; **Senses** darkvision 60 ft.; Listen +1, Spot +1
Languages Common, Orc

AC 16, touch 11, flat-footed 15
(+1 Dex, +5 armor)
Fort +3, **Ref** +1, **Will** –1
Weakness light sensitivity

Speed 20 ft. (4 squares) in chainmail, base speed 30 ft.
Melee greataxe +4 (1d12+3)
Ranged heavy crossbow +2 (1d10)
Base Atk +1; **Grp** +4
Combat Gear *potion of cure light wounds*

Abilities Str 17, Dex 13, Con 13, Int 11, Wis 9, Cha 8
Feats Alertness, Combat Reflexes
Skills Balance +1, Climb +5, Hide +1, Intimidate +1, Jump +3, Listen +1, Spot +1, Survival +1
Possessions combat gear plus chainmail, greataxe, heavy crossbow with 12 bolts

Light Sensitivity An orc captain takes a –1 penalty on attack rolls, Search checks, and Spot checks in bright sunlight or within the radius of a *daylight* spell.

Zar'Fell is open only to orcs and authorized humanoid visitors, the latter of whom must have an orc escort and wear a colored feather as identification. The color of the feather

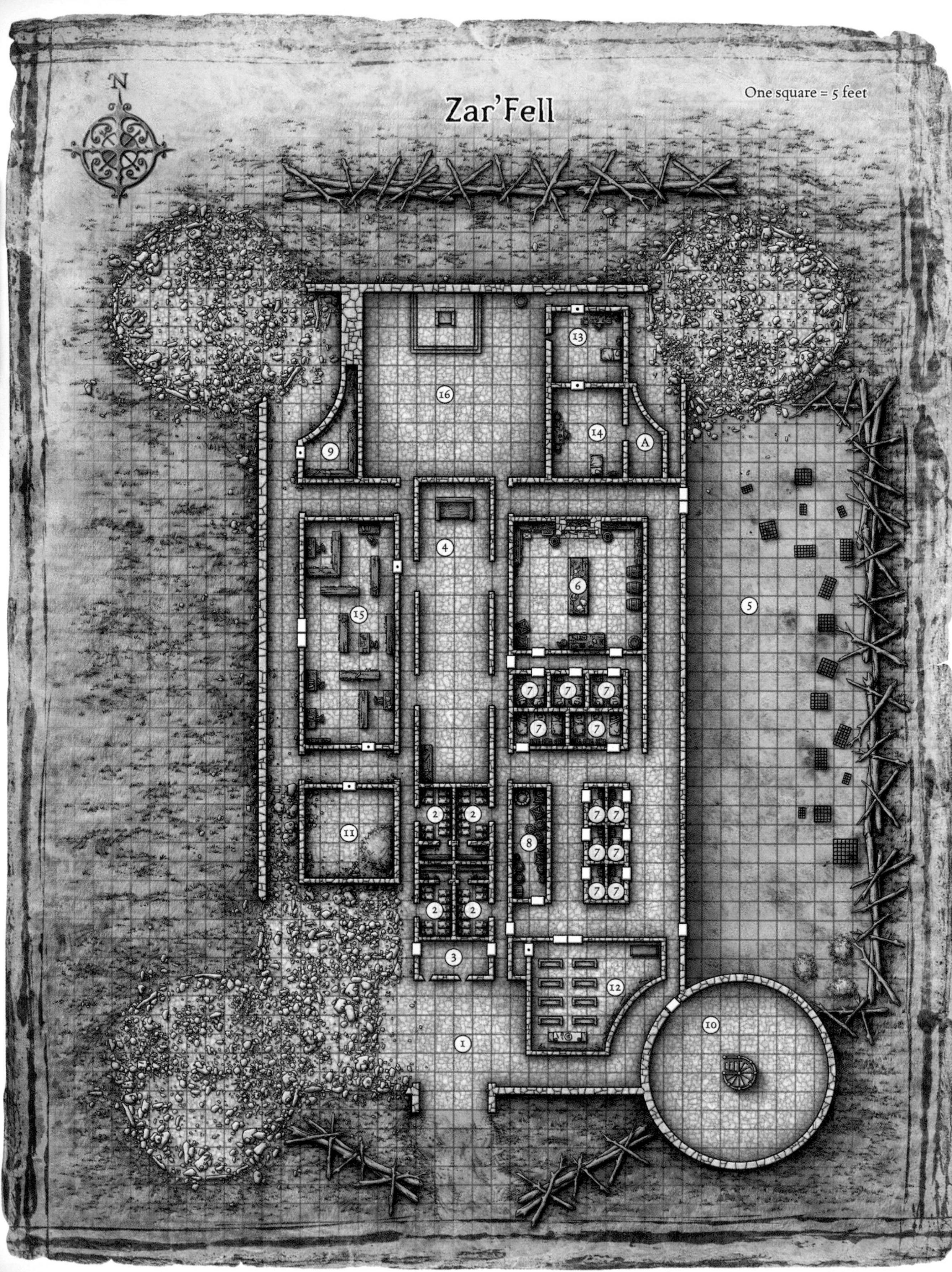
Zar'Fell
One square = 5 feet
N
1
2
2
2
2
3
4
5
6
7
7
7
7
7
7
7
7
7
7
7
7
7
8
9
10
11
12
13
14
15
16
A

changes each week. Unescorted visitors, even those displaying the correct feather, are attacked on sight, no questions asked. Eight orcs armed with longbows patrol the roof to watch the approaches to the house, though the scaffolding obstructs their view of certain areas. The newly rebuilt guard tower (area 10) is occupied at all times by four orcs with longbows.

Zar'Fell has two basic conditions, normal and on alert. Any orc can put the house on alert by ringing one of the brass bells mounted on each wall.

Monstrous centipedes nest in the areas of the map designated as rubble (the two northern towers and the area in the southwest corner of the complex). For every 5 rounds characters spend in an area of rubble, there is a 20% chance that they will be attacked.

Small Monstrous Centipedes (1d10): hp 2 each (1/2 HD); *MM* 286

AREA DESCRIPTIONS

Zar'fell includes not only the ruined house but also a thriving community of four hundred orcs, who live in small huts and stone cottages surrounding the manor. The map does not show these structures or the grounds, but you are free to flesh out the larger orc community as you desire. Additionally, if you want the PCs to run into more orcs while exploring the house, you can restore and populate the second floor.

1. **Entrance:** The entrance to the manor has no door. Until the area can be repaired, it is sealed from the weather with a thick curtain of animal skins. The entrance is guarded at all times by ten orc soldiers, five on each side of the opening behind pointed log barriers.

2. **Guard Barracks:** These rooms can house up to forty sleeping orcs (ten per room). Each barracks has a closet for storing weapons and gear.

3. **Guard Room:** Two orcs with longbows watch the front hall through arrow slits in the south wall.

4. **Arena of Justice:** This former dining hall is now a gladiatorial court. Any orc that has a dispute to settle can bring it to the orc captain known as Magistrate Borak for adjudication or trial by combat. Borak is assisted by supposedly impartial gnoll mercenaries who serve as bailiffs, security, and executioners.

Gnoll Mercenaries (1d6): hp 11 each (2 HD); *MM* 130.

5. **Kennels/Slave Pens:** This courtyard contains a number of large cages; when slaves are not working in the library (area 15), they are held here. Additionally, three worgs lair in the southern half of the courtyard. When not out hunting, the beasts amuse themselves by growling and snapping at the prisoners.

Worgs (3): hp 30 each (4 HD); *MM* 256.

6. **Kitchen:** This room contains a large fireplace, racks of stew pots on hooks, and a long table used to cut meat and prepare food. The ceiling is hung with ducks, geese, and other freshly killed game birds. If anyone other than an orc enters the room, the kitchen staff panics and clangs a brass bell to put the house on alert.

7. **Gnoll Quarters:** These tiny rooms were once used for the manor's servants, but now Borak's gnoll mercenaries live here when they are off duty. The gnolls' personal effects include coins and tiny gems worth a total of 32 gp, and 10 stained silk scarves worth 5 gp each.

8. **Food Stores:** This room is filled with crates and barrels containing a variety of foodstuffs.

9. **Armory:** This chamber is where Zargath stores the weapons and armor that he buys from Gurn, and it is kept under constant guard by a pair of orc soldiers. The door is secured with an expensive lock (Open Lock DC 30) that is trapped with a poison needle; only Zargath and Grikfell have keys.

10. **Guard Tower:** This new tower rises 30 feet into the air and has a commanding view of the area surrounding the manor. Four orc soldiers are stationed here. When the house is on alert, they remain in the tower and support the guards at the entrance (area 1) or shoot anyone attempting to free prisoners from the slave pens (area 5).

11. **Collapsed Room:** The door to this room is locked, and is marked in both Common and Orc with the words, "Do not enter by order of Zargath." Unlocking the door requires a successful DC 15 Open Lock check, but it is jammed shut, and pushing it open requires a successful DC 20 Strength check. Within the room's debris is the nest of a mated pair of cockatrices, which attack any intruders who cross the midpoint of the room. The creatures fight to the death to protect their three eggs, which are worth 50 gp each. Their nest also contains a small gold earring worth 20 gp. During the battle, any explosive or sonic spell has a 25% chance to cause a piece of the roof to collapse and strike a character, dealing 1d8 points of damage.

Cockatrices (2): hp 27 each (5 HD); *MM* 37.

12. **Trophy Room:** The altar, pews, and sarcophagi reveal that this chamber used to be a chapel, but Zargath has turned it into a trophy room. Behind the altar hangs a large banner bearing a stylized black wolf on a white circle in a red field. Piled along the curved walls are broken weapons and armor, souvenirs from past battles.

Five orcs are busy looting a sarcophagus in the room. When the PCs enter, run tactical encounter 2–1 (page 42).

13. **Zargath's Quarters:** Like Zargath himself, these quarters are simple and utilitarian. The room has a human-style bed, a table with three chairs, and a small footlocker that contains a few changes of clothes. The walls are covered with maps, some of local areas and some of sites halfway around the world, all marked with scribbled notes. A bookstand supports a large, leatherbound journal, in which Zargath records his thoughts on the dominant orc civilization that is his dream.

14. **Grikfell's Quarters:** This room is furnished similarly to Zargath's quarters. The door leads to an open interior patio where Elbeth, Grikfell's pet worg, sleeps.

15. **Library:** Six human prisoners from area 5 spend their days here, writing textbooks for Zargath. Each of the captives is an expert on a subject that interests the orc leader. Watching the prisoners are eight orc soldiers, two orc captains, and Dwarreg—a dwarf who was brutally tortured and brainwashed by Zargath and Gurn to believe that he is an orc. When the PCs enter the library, run tactical encounter 2–2 (see page 44).

16. **Audience Hall:** This room has been refitted as a throne room and audience chamber. Zargath is here, discussing a possible alliance with a bugbear ambassador. Also present are Gurn, Grikfell, Elbeth, and eight orc guards. When the PCs enter this chamber, run tactical encounter 2–3 (see page 46).

Trophy Room

Encounter Level 8

SETUP

This encounter begins when the PCs approach the door to the trophy room (area 12). The door is shut, and if the characters do nothing to announce their presence, the distracted orcs inside will not hear them approach. A PC who succeeds on a DC 10 Listen check hears hammering from within the room and several orcs muttering excitedly.

Four orcs are positioned in the squares around the stone sarcophagus in the northeast corner of the room. A fifth orc is inside the sarcophagus, using a prybar to open the hidden coffin buried inside the crypt. By the time the PCs open the door and enter the room, the fifth orc will be dead, and the others will be about to flee toward the exit.

When the PCs open the door, read:

This room has the look of an abandoned chapel. Two rows of stone pews march up the center aisle to a long, low altar. A Black Wolf banner hangs behind it, and other battle standards are hung randomly around the room. Broken, rusty weaponry is piled in ordered rows along the walls and on the benches. Another door is to the right, and two stone sarcophagi lay in an alcove to the left. Four orcs stand around one of the sarcophagi with their backs to you, peering down inside the open tomb.

Give the PCs a chance to declare their actions. Once they do, read:

You hear an inhuman growl coming from the stone coffin, and an orc's shriek—one that ends with a sharp gurgle. The four orcs turn and charge toward you as pale, clawed hands reach over the lip of the sarcophagus and heave a white-skinned, vaguely humanoid monstrosity into view.

When combat begins, the four orcs are not charging the party, but fleeing from the unearthed wight that has just killed their companion. Depending on the PCs' actions, the orcs either run for the door or stop to fight just long enough to push past the adventurers and escape. The orcs' panic imposes a –2 penalty on their attack rolls for the first 2 rounds.

4 Orc Soldiers **CR 1/2**
hp 5 each (1 HD); see page 39

Gray Ooze **CR 4**
hp 31 (3 HD); *MM* 202

Wight **CR 3**
hp 26 (4 HD); *MM* 255

It takes the wight 1 round to climb out of the coffin. When it reaches the floor, it moves to attack the nearest orc (assuming that the PCs blocked them from escaping). The wight correctly judges the orcs to be a lesser threat and thus the easiest prey to convert to spawn. Two rounds after the wight attacks or after the first orc is killed, the remaining orcs split up. Two head toward the altar along the south wall and dig through the nearby debris for something they can use against the wight and the PCs.

Another orc tries to smash through the locked door (hardness 5, 20 hp) on the western wall. If he breaks through, a gray ooze nesting in the small room beyond surges through the opening and attacks the orc. After dispensing with its first victim, the ooze moves into the trophy room and attacks the nearest living target (ignoring the wight and any spawn).

Both the wight and the gray ooze fight to the death. The orcs fight, but they will flee the room if they have the chance.

DEVELOPMENT

Initially, the wight tries to avoid the PCs and concentrates on killing the orcs to create spawn. Four rounds after combat begins, the first orc slain by the wight emerges from the open sarcophagus as a spawn. Any other orcs killed by the wight also return as spawn 4 rounds after their death. (Slain orcs that have not yet risen as spawn dissolve automatically if touched by the gray ooze.) Four to six rounds after its release, the wight turns on the party, sending the spawn against the PC who shows the most martial prowess, and attacking any clerics or spellcasters itself.

If the wight is turned, it retreats to the southern end of the room next to the altar and starts throwing broken weapons and helmets at the PCs, targeting spellcasters if possible. The missiles deal no damage, but if one strikes a spellcaster, it has the normal chance of disrupting a spell.

Features of the Area

The area has the following features.

Illumination: Sconces along the walls hold torches that provide bright illumination throughout this area.

Trophies: The room is littered with the banners of foes defeated by the Black Wolves, signs and miscellaneous goods from sacked towns, and broken weapons and armor from battlefields. The largest banner is a 4-foot-by-6-foot flag of the Black Wolves, which hangs behind the altar and can be pulled down with a DC 5 Strength check. With the exception of the two masterwork daggers, the weapons and armor piled here are useless.

Sarcophagus: The alcove area contains a stone sarcophagus with a lid engraved with an image of a human warrior in armor. The sarcophagus has been opened, and the bottom has been broken out to reveal a second coffin hidden inside the bier—the wight's burial place. On the lid of the coffin is an inscription in an ancient language. A PC who succeeds on a DC 40 Knowledge check can read the inscription, which says simply, "Betrayer."

Pews: Eight stone pews are arranged in two rows. Characters must spend 2 squares of movement to enter a square containing a pew. Those who climb onto a pew gain a +1 circumstance bonus on attack rolls against creatures on lower ground.

Altar: A low altar stands at the front of the room. The altar is empty and bears no sign of whatever deity used to be worshiped here. The altar provides cover for those crouched behind it (granting a +4 bonus to Armor Class and a +2 bonus on saves).

Small Room: This chamber is devoid of features. The floor has collapsed into a sinkhole that is inhabited by the gray ooze.

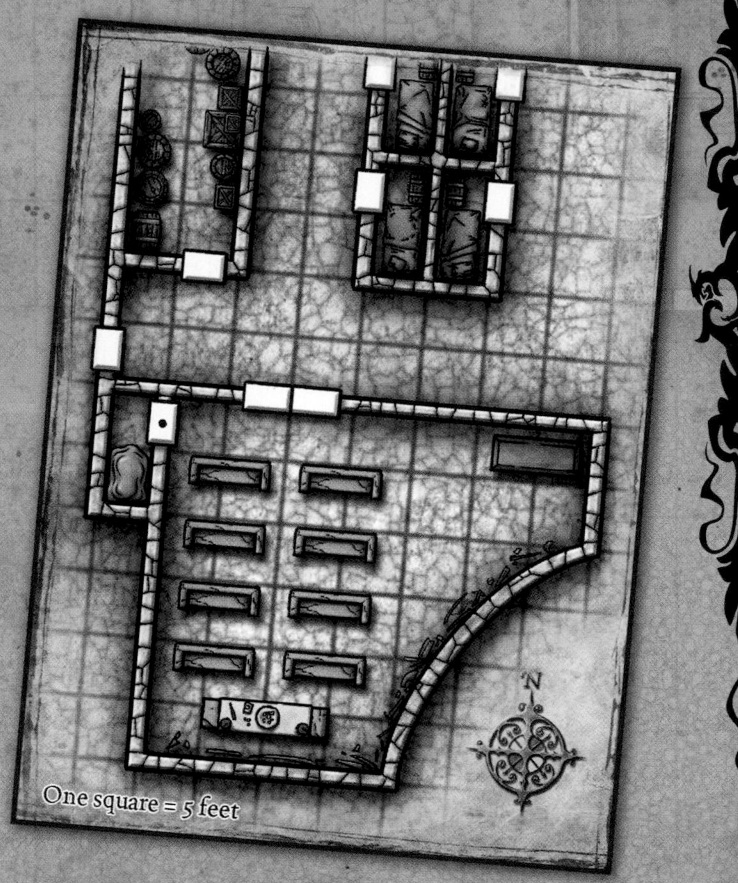

Wight Spawn — CR 3
hp 18 (4 HD); other statistics as for wight (*MM* 255)

2 Gnoll Mercenaries — CR 1
hp 11 each (2 HD); *MM* 130

Orc Captain — CR 2
hp 11 (2 HD); see page 39

9 Orc Soldiers — CR 1/2
hp 5 each (1 HD); see page 39

Once the gray ooze is released, the wight makes every effort to avoid it, but the undead creature will not stop coming after the PCs. If the wight succeeds in grappling with a character, it tries to throw him into the ooze.

If any of the orcs escape, they immediately ring the nearest brass bell, putting the manor on alert. However, the trophy room is not an assigned defensive position, so it takes at least 10 rounds for ten orc guards to arrive.

If none of the orcs makes it out of the trophy room, the commotion of the battle might draw the attention of the gnoll mercenaries resting in their quarters (area 7). After 5 rounds of combat, there is a 20% chance per round that two gnolls arrive to investigate. Upon seeing the wight and ooze, one of the gnolls attempts to shut and hold the door to the trophy room, while the other rings a brass bell and runs for reinforcements. It takes at least 10 rounds for a band of ten orc guards (one captain and nine soldiers) to arrive.

Conclusion

After combat ends, the PCs can sort through the trophy room's piles of junk. Although most of it is useless, diligent examination (Search DC 25) uncovers two masterwork daggers and a small painting of a seascape that is worth 400 gp to the right collector. There is also an amethyst necklace (35 gp) around the wight's neck, and its coffin contains various loose gems and pieces of jewelry worth a total of 1,000 gp.

Library

Encounter Level 7

SETUP

An orc captain stands guard over each entrance to this room. By Zargath's orders, no one is allowed to enter through the southern or eastern door. Player characters who do so are surprised and immediately attacked by the orcs in the room. Those who enter through the western doors are confronted by two orc guards, who first look to see if the intruders have an escort and a feather of the correct color. If the PCs attack as their first action when entering the room through this door, they gain surprise. Otherwise, roll for initiative normally.

If the PCs open the western doors, read:

The door swings open to reveal a tall and mostly empty bookshelf standing directly in front of you, with another to your left. To the right, a miserable and abused human sits at a desk, writing with a quill on a piece of parchment. Two orcs with their swords drawn stand in front of the first bookshelf. "You got business here?" the one on the left snarls.

The library contains tall bookshelves, desks, chairs, and an alchemy station. Six human prisoners (H) sit at desks, filling parchment with information that Zargath has demanded. They are being watched by eight orc soldiers (O), two orc captains (C), and Dwarreg (D), the dwarf who thinks he's an orc.

TACTICS

Once combat begins, four orcs confront the PCs while the rest duck behind bookshelves and try to pepper the intruders with arrows, aiming first at any obvious spellcasters. The four orcs in melee combat try to use the bookshelves to flank the party. Whenever possible, the orcs try to push a bookshelf over onto a party member (for details, see Features of the Area).

The six human captives are noncombatants and try to avoid the orcs and the PCs alike. When combat begins, three hide under their desks, while the rest scramble around the room, trying to escape through any door in the confusion.

As soon as Dwarreg realizes that combat has started, he drinks his *potion of barkskin* and moves to attack the party. Like the orcs, he tries to use the bookshelves as cover, throwing all of the items on his belt at a rate of about 1 per round. He starts by tossing a tanglefoot bag at the first PC he sees, followed by a vial of alchemist's fire. Dwarreg then moves and targets a different PC in the same manner. When he runs out of alchemist's fire, he starts hurling flasks of acid instead. If he sees a PC kill an orc in melee combat, he throws a thunderstone at that character, hoping to deafen her, though he holds one thunderstone in reserve in case he is attacked directly.

The orcs make every effort to stay away from the alchemy station (see Features of the Area) and herd the PCs into its general vicinity. The first time any PC steps within 3 squares of the station, the orcs attempt to detonate the station by firing arrows at it. If they make a successful attack against AC 10, an arrow strikes a volatile object and causes the whole station to explode.

Dwarreg — CR 4

hp 23 (4 HD)

Male dwarf expert (combat engineer) 3
N Medium humanoid
Init +0; **Senses** darkvision 60 ft.; Listen +1, Spot +1
Languages Common, Dwarven, Orc

AC 14, touch 10, flat-footed 14 (+4 armor)
Fort +3 (+5 against poison), **Ref** +1, **Will** +4; +2 against spells and spell-like effects

Speed 20 ft. (4 squares)
Melee mwk morningstar +5 (1d6+2)
Base Atk +2; **Grp** +4
Combat Gear 1 *potion of barkskin*, 3 vials alchemist's fire, 6 tanglefoot bags, 3 thunderstones, 3 flasks acid

Abilities Str 14, Dex 11, Con 16, Int 15, Wis 12, Cha 8
Feats Combat Expertise, Diligent
Skills Appraise +4 (+6 Craft), Balance –1, Craft +9, Decipher Script +5, Diplomacy +7, Disable Device +4, Intimidate +2, Knowledge (architecture) +8, Listen +1, Open Lock +3, Search +2 (+6 secret doors), Spot +1, Survival +7
Possessions combat gear plus masterwork morningstar, masterwork chain shirt

8 Orc Soldiers — CR 1/2

hp 5 each (1 HD); see page 39

2 Orc Captains — CR 2

hp 11 each (2 HD); see page 39

6 Human Captives — CR 1

hp 6 each (1 HD)
Male or female human expert 2
AC 10
Fort +0, **Ref** +0, **Will** +3

DEVELOPMENT

When Dwarreg runs out of vials and flasks, he scurries to the alchemy station (provided it has not been detonated) and attempts to retrieve the four vials of alchemist's fire kept in the steel box. It takes him 2 rounds to unlock the box and pull out the vials. If he cannot retrieve the vials, he uses his last thunderstone on the nearest PC and enters melee combat with his morningstar, fighting to the death.

If Dwarreg is killed or if more than two orcs are slain, two orcs try to flee through the nearest door into the hall to sound the alert and summon help. The remaining orcs have orders to kill the human experts rather than let them escape. Unless directly engaged with the PCs, the orcs pursue the captives wherever they run.

Any time a bookcase is pushed over or a loud noise occurs in combat, there is a 35% chance that two orc captains from the Arena of Justice (area 4) come to investigate. They don't arrive immediately because they must go around the walls to use the approved entrance on the west side.

If the alchemy station explodes, six orc soldiers from area 4 hurry to the library. Additionally, the manor is put on alert.

CONCLUSION

Any captives who survive the encounter latch on to the PCs, begging the adventurers to take them safely out of the manor. The prisoners are leaders in their respective fields, so the PCs would receive a substantial reward for any expert they rescued and returned home.

Treasure: Most of the books on the shelves are common texts on history, government, architecture, and basic engineering. Hidden among the books, however, are ten arcane spell scrolls, as follows:

3rd—*rage, hold person*
2nd—*blur, false life, mirror image*
1st—*ventriloquism, unseen servant, chill touch, shield, grease*

Features of the Area

The room has the following features.

Bookshelves: Each of the eight wooden bookshelves is 2 feet thick, 10 feet long, and 5 feet high, with hardness 5 and 50 hit points. Each unit is about 25% filled with books and can be climbed easily (Climb DC 5). A bookshelf provides cover to anyone behind it (granting a +4 bonus to Armor Class and a +2 bonus on saves).

A bookshelf can be pushed over by someone who succeeds on a DC 15 Strength check, dealing 2d6 points of damage to creatures standing in the squares where it lands (Reflex DC 10 half). It fills those squares with light debris, which increases the DC of Balance and Tumble checks by 2 and imposes a –2 penalty on Move Silently checks. A successful DC 10 Balance check is required to run or charge across light debris. Failure means the character can still act but cannot run or charge this round.

Desks and Chairs: Squares occupied by desks and chairs cost 2 squares to enter. Desks provide cover for those crouching behind them. A creature can also climb on top of a desk, gaining a +1 bonus on melee attack rolls against opponents standing on the floor.

Alchemy Station: Located in the southwest corner of the room, this long table is filled with alembics, beakers, burners, and numerous glass vials of chemicals (each has hardness 1 and 1 hit point). Shattering a vial or applying fire will cause the table to explode in a shower of chemicals and glass, dealing 5d6 points of damage to all creatures in a 20-foot radius. If the blast destroys the steel box containing the vials of alchemist's fire (see below), a second explosion occurs.

Alchemist's Fire Storage: The alchemy station includes a specially designed steel storage box (with hardness 10 and 30 hit points) for vials of alchemist's fire. The box can hold up to 20 vials in two rows, but currently it contains only 4 vials. If the box is destroyed by an explosion or damage from a weapon, the vials inside shatter, throwing flaming liquid out in a 10-foot radius. Creatures struck by the fire take 1d6 points of damage immediately and another 1d6 points of damage from flames in the following round.

Illumination: Sconces placed every 20 feet along the walls hold torches that provide bright illumination. Additionally, a small oil lamp sits on each writing desk.

Acid Bath: The alchemy station has a ceramic basin filled with alchemical byproducts. The acid deals 1d6 points of damage and destroys clothing and armor (Reflex DC 15).

Doors: The three doors to this room are 7 feet high and brand new. Each door is 2 inches thick and has hardness 5 and 20 hit points. The eastern and southern doors are locked.

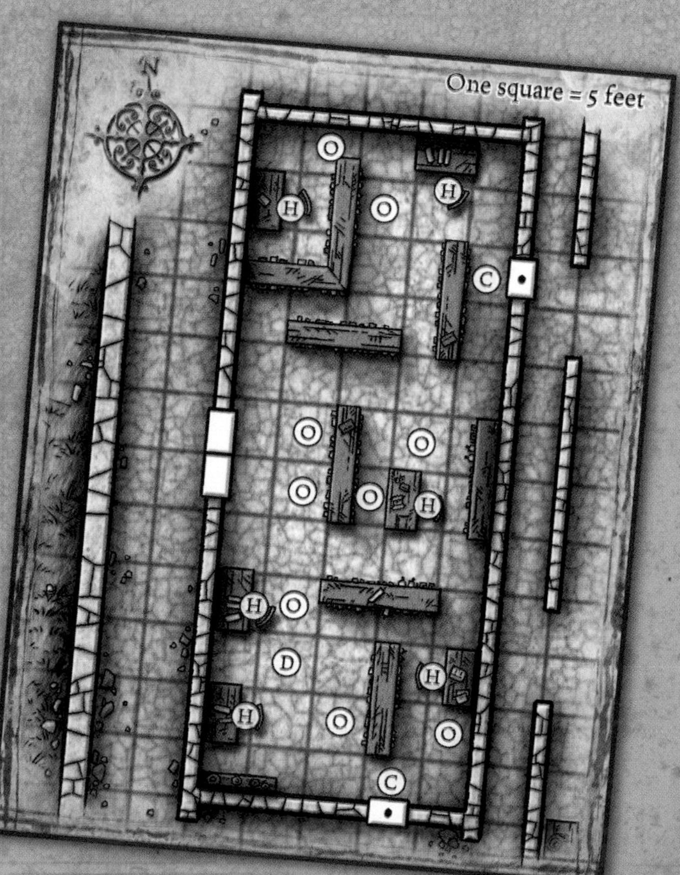

Audience Hall

Encounter Level 10

SETUP

When the manor is not on alert, each of the southern entrances to the throne room and audience chamber has a constant guard of four orc soldiers (O), two on the outside and two on the inside. At any sign of trouble, the guards crouch in defensive positions and call for an alert. All guards will fight to the death, trying to delay the intruders long enough for those in the room to prepare themselves.

Inside the room, Zargath (Z) and Grikfell (Gf) are meeting with a bugbear ambassador (B) to discuss a possible alliance with his people. Gurn (G) is present as well, and so is Grikfell's worg, Elbeth (E).

As soon as the guards raise the alarm, everyone inside the room prepares for an attack.

Gurn drinks his vial of antitoxin, runs to give one tanglefoot bag to Grikfell and the other to a guard, and then heads for the back of the room again. He casts *silent image* to create the illusion of a solid wall hiding the hallway to area 13. Finally, he lights two smokesticks—one in a square in front of him, and the other in a square in front of Zargath—to conceal their presence.

Zargath scatters caltrops in the squares next to the ones covered by the smokesticks. He pours his *dust of dryness* into the 50-gallon barrel of water next to him and retrieves the resulting pellet.

Grikfell stands on the dais in front of the throne, with Elbeth nearby. The worg howls, trying to attract the attention of her packmates in area 5.

The orc guards hold their positions. The bugbear ambassador unlimbers his morningstar and tries to conceal himself in the shadows.

When the PCs enter the room, read:

This dark audience chamber is surprisingly simple and clean for an orc abode. A primitive stone throne sits on a dais in the center of the room, in front of a huge flag with the symbol of the Black Wolves. Decorative weapons and shields are hung on the walls. In front of you, a heavily muscled orc wielding a double axe stands on the dais, next to a huge, snarling black wolf.

ZARGATH HUMAN-BANE **CR 5**
hp 15 (5 HD)

Male orc rogue 4
LE Medium humanoid
Init +4; **Senses** darkvision 60 ft.; Listen +7, Spot +7
Languages *Common, Orc*

AC 18, touch 15, flat-footed 14; Dodge, uncanny dodge (+4 Dex, +3 armor, +1 deflection)
Resist evasion
Fort +3, **Ref** +8, **Will** +0
Weakness light sensitivity

Speed 30 ft. (6 squares)
Melee mwk short sword +6 (1d6+1) and mwk dagger +1 (1d4+1)
Ranged mwk hand crossbow +11 (1d4)
Base Atk +6; **Grp** +7
Atk Options sneak attack +2d6
Combat Gear 2 *potions of cure light wounds*, *dust of dryness*, *ring of protection +1*, tanglefoot bag, caltrops

Abilities Str 12, Dex 18, Con 8, Int 15, Wis 8, Cha 15
SQ trap sense +1, trapfinding
Feats Alertness, Dodge, Two-Weapon Fighting
Skills Diplomacy +6, Disguise +3, Escape Artist +4, Gather Information +6, Hide +11, Intimidate +6, Knowledge (architecture) +3, Knowledge (geography) +3, Knowledge (history), +3, Knowledge (local) +6, Knowledge (nobility) +3, Listen +7, Move Silently +11, Open Lock +5, Search +3, Spot +7
Possessions combat gear plus masterwork studded leather armor, masterwork hand crossbow with 50 bolts, masterwork short sword, masterwork dagger, masterwork thieves' tools

Light Sensitivity Zargath takes a –1 penalty on attack rolls, Search checks, and Spot checks in bright sunlight or within the radius of a *daylight* spell.

TACTICS

When the party enters the room, Zargath throws his *dust of dryness* pellet at the first character through the door. If it hits a PC, the pellet releases 50 gallons of water against the character, possibly knocking her flat (Strength DC 30 to remain standing). The water covers 4 squares of the floor, making them very slippery (–2 penalty on Dexterity checks). After the pellet hits, the orc guards move in, attempting to flank the characters.

Grikfell throws a tanglefoot bag at any PC other than the one hit by the pellet and rushes into melee. Elbeth charges the party and attacks, focusing on any PCs who have been knocked down.

From the back of the room, Gurn tries to target the PCs with his *wand of magic missiles*. The gnome throws a vial of alchemist's fire at any character who comes within 2 squares of him.

Zargath fires crossbow bolts at the intruders as shots become available.

War Leader Grikfell **CR 3**
hp 25 (3 HD); see page 37

Gurn Sirensong **CR 3**
hp 14 (4 HD); see page 38

Bugbear Ambassador **CR 2**
hp 16 (3 HD)

Male bugbear
CE Medium humanoid (goblinoid)
Init +1; **Senses** darkvision 60 ft., scent; Listen +4, Spot +4
Languages Common, Goblin, Orc

AC 17, touch 11, flat-footed 16
(+1 Dex, +2 armor, +1 shield, +3 natural)
Fort +2, **Ref** +4, **Will** +1

Speed 30 ft. (6 squares)
Melee morningstar +5 (1d8+2)
Ranged javelin +3 (1d6+2)
Base Atk +2; **Grp** +4

Abilities Str 15, Dex 12, Con 13, Int 10, Wis 10, Cha 9
Feats Alertness, Weapon Focus (morningstar)
Skills Climb +3, Hide +4, Listen +4, Move Silently +6, Spot +4

Possessions leather armor, light steel shield, morningstar, javelin

Elbeth (Worg) **CR 2**
hp 30 (4 HD); *MM* 256

8 Orc Soldiers **CR 1/2**
hp 5 each (1 HD); see page 39

The bugbear ambassador defends himself if attacked, but otherwise stays in the shadows to watch the battle. He wants to see how his prospective new allies handle themselves in a fight.

Grikfell, Elbeth, and the guards fight to the death.

Development

Depending on how the battle proceeds, you can choose whether Elbeth's three packmates join the fight in 5 rounds, in 10 rounds, or not at all. (The worgs might be occupied chasing escaped prisoners, or they might have been killed by the PCs already.)

If Grikfell falls or if all the guards are slain, Zargath, Gurn, and the ambassador retreat past the illusionary wall. Before leaving, Gurn uses his *summon monster* I scroll to summon a fiendish dire rat to cover their retreat, then casts *flare* at the nearest PC to distract her. Depending on how quickly the villains are pursued, Zargath might stab the ambassador in the back, hoping that the injured or dead bugbear will further distract the PCs. Gurn's last-ditch plan is to use *disguise self* to masquerade as a halfling prisoner and let the PCs find and "rescue" him. Zargath is aware that the gnome plans to betray him, but he leaves Gurn alone, figuring that the diversion will help cover his own escape.

Features of the Area

The room has the following features.

Illumination: This area is dark. Appropriate conditions and concealment penalties apply unless the characters provide their own light source.

Dais: The dais is slightly raised off the ground. A PC who stands on the dais gains a +1 circumstance bonus on attack rolls against an opponent standing on the floor. As noted previously, a secret compartment in the dais holds the orcs' accumulated wealth.

Throne: Zargath's throne is just a massive hunk of gray rock in the approximate shape of a chair. It provides cover for anyone standing behind it (granting a +4 bonus to Armor Class and a +2 bonus on saves).

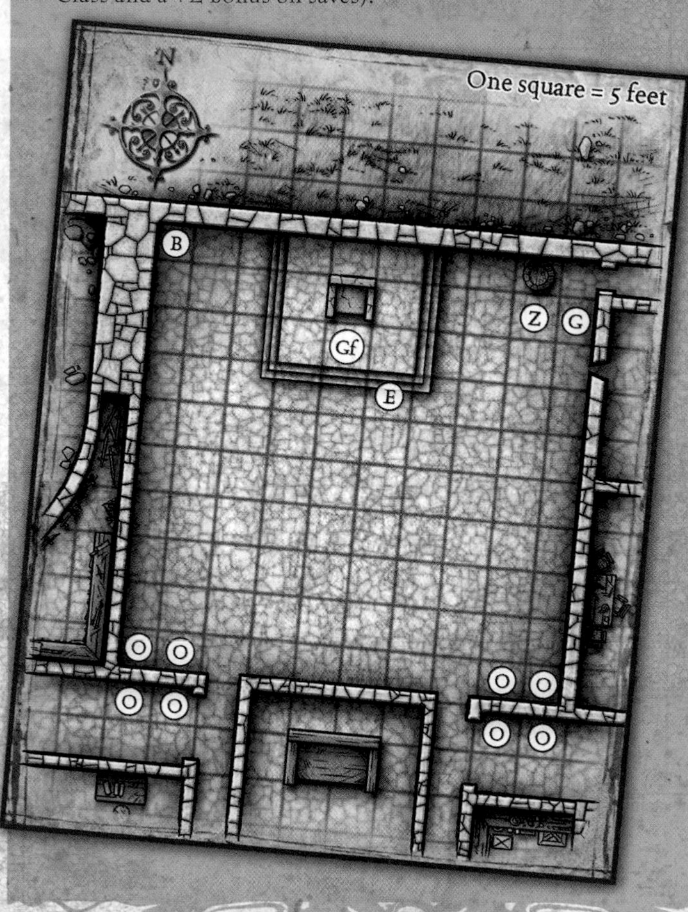

Conclusion

If the PCs are victorious, they can search the throne room for treasure. A successful DC 40 Search check reveals a secret compartment that Dwarreg installed in the dais beneath the throne. (Dwarf racial bonuses do not apply to the check.) In the compartment is a locked box (Open Lock DC 30) that contains the treasury of the Black Wolves—assorted coins and gems worth 7,500 gp.

Illus. by J. Chan

Listen . . ."

"Yes, my love?"

"Do you hear them?"

"Yes. They crawl and writhe, endlessly muttering."

"If you listen, they will drive you mad."

"Ah, but if you serve them . . ."

—Edgar and Katarin Tolstoff

Transformed by the foul whispers heard through the door of a sealed vault, Edgar and Katarin Tolstoff work to liberate an ancient archmage—and to reinvigorate the world-shattering Worm that Walks.

BACKGROUND

It was destiny. They had known since they were children that they would be together forever. They shared an uncommon connection: completing each other's sentences, experiencing the same dreams, and wailing when the other was hurt. Their inexhaustible curiosity kept them together—and their home and the surrounding village gave them plenty of places to explore. They would slip out of the keep and watch the peasants, but sharp whispers and cold stares made them feel uncomfortable, and they ventured forth less and less, turning their attentions to their own crumbling demesne.

They prowled the cavernous corridors below the keep, discovering hidden rooms, secret passages, and many other oddities—but their strangest finding of all lay in the catacombs, a place their mother had strictly forbidden them from entering. Edgar and Katarin knew that the Tolstoff clan had its secrets; knew that not all of their ancestors were kindly or good, despite the self-conscious placidity of their official family history. The catacombs held the evidence of the Tolstoffs' corrupt past, and so had remained untouched for years. The vaults within bore strange glyphs and dire warnings to leave the dead alone. Aside from the occasional creak or susurrus of webs, it was quiet. But one vault was not so silent.

The children heard a guttural whisper coming from within, a demand for them to wait. Intrigued, Edgar and Katarin stopped and listened. The male voice asked for their company—just a small amount of their time—and offered to teach them magic in exchange.

Katarin was thrilled; stories of sorcerers and wizard duels had always captivated the girl. Edgar, on the other hand, was fond of nature, hunting, and exploration, and he had little use for intellectual pursuits—the voice made him frightened and suspicious. He wanted to flee and never return, but he loved his sister and indulged her every whim. With some hesitation, he agreed to stay, and the pair took their first steps on the path to damnation.

Over the next decade, the children descended into the catacombs several times each week. They would relate their experiences to the voice within, and little by little, they learned magic. The master, as they called the voice, seemed pleased and eager to teach them. Edgar never made a great effort to embrace this power, but his sister surprised him with her skill and subtlety.

The baroness, their mother, had hoped to wed Katarin to an important lord, in order to lift the family out of its slow slide into poverty. However, each time she brought a suitor to the keep, Katarin rejected him. Frustrated, her mother tried to force the issue, but any time she set a date for marriage, the young man would go missing, die in a hunting accident, or flee from the hold in fear.

The baroness came to believe that her son, who was equally uninterested in marriage, had something to do with this string of failures. She began to investigate her children, instructing her servants to spy on them and issue regular reports. Yet she learned nothing—all her suspicions seemed groundless. Then, one night, she resolved to follow Edgar and Katarin herself, hoping to confront them directly and expose their wickedness. By doing so, she believed that she would put their unnatural closeness to rest.

In the dead of night, the baroness followed them through a secret door in the feast hall, down the old stairs, and into the dusty tunnels. With each step, her apprehension grew. She dreaded their destination, for she knew what evil lurked below.

Her fears were confirmed. Edgar and Katarin stood before the vault of their grandfather, their very souls at the precipice of annihilation. Terrified, she ran out from her hiding place and pulled at them, screaming, urging them to flee the dreadful thing.

The master spoke, his sadness clear with each word. He told his pupils that their mother would never let them be together, that she would force them to wed others and break up their happy family. His speech had the desired effect. Katarin turned, stared at her mother with hate-filled eyes, and spewed a stream of profanity that shocked the baroness to the core. The woman was filled with revulsion at what her children had become, and she tried to flee to warn others. But Edgar, knowing that she would bring trouble to him and his sister if she escaped, cut his mother down where she stood, spilling her blood onto the dusty tiles of the family tomb.

Since that tragic night, Edgar and Katarin have never been the same. The stain on their souls is too dark, too pronounced for them to resume a normal life. Instead, they live in service to their grandfather, allowing him to extend his influence beyond his prison and corrupt those in and around the keep. He demands that they find a way to loosen the bonds of his vault—promising that, once he is freed, he will usher them into the power of the Worm that Walks.

GOALS

More than anything, Edgar and Katarin want to be left alone, but they are also pragmatic, understanding that their unnatural affection makes them a target for the forces of good. Their grandfather whispers and mutters through the door of his vault, warning the pair that people will come for them, that word will spread of their mother's murder, and that Edgar will be hanged for the crime, forever sundering their love. If only the archmage could be freed from his prison, he would shelter them with his powerful sorcery, destroying anyone who tried to harm them.

Since the murder, Edgar has changed. He rarely leaves the keep by day, and when he does venture out, it is under the cover of a heavy cloak. He refuses to touch Katarin and hesitates even to speak to her, out of fear that he might pass on the disgusting cancer that is eating him alive. Instead, Edgar relies on his remaining guards, who have become physically corrupted (*Book of Vile Darkness* page 186) due to the malevolence in Tolstoff Keep.

Katarin's efforts to open the vault have failed. She drained the meager remains of her family's coffers to acquire the services of potent wizards, conjure up demons, and employ a myriad of magical techniques to breach the wards. Nothing has worked—and her attempts to find a cure for her disease-wracked brother have been equally unsuccessful. Now penniless, she is desperate for coin.

To this end, Katarin left the old keep to install herself in the court of a nearby king. With the help of Draen Raelgal, a gnome wererat who acts as a servant for her and her brother, she looks for unsuspecting nobles to blackmail. She lures them into trysts, gains their confidence, and then threatens to expose their darkest secrets unless they pay her off. Invariably, they give her coins and jewels, which she sends back to her brother, expecting that Edgar will use them to fund their master's liberation.

In the meantime, Edgar has slipped deeper and deeper into madness. The entity that is awakening within him fills his mind with obscene images and dark revelations that drive him into depravity. He orders his corrupted soldiers to round up peasants and bring them to the keep to feed his disturbing lusts. The remains of his victims are thrown to his pets—a psurlon and a gibbering mouther that he keeps hidden in the chapel.

Katarin fears that Edgar's predations will provoke the villagers into rising up against the mad baron. Thus, she returns to the keep frequently to spend time with her brother, hoping to calm and control him, before all their plans fall apart.

THE WORM THAT WALKS

The baroness was well aware of the evil that festered beneath her house. Years ago, her father—then still human—dabbled in forbidden lore, scouring occult texts in search of clues about a deceased god known as the Worm that Walks. He mastered wicked spells, acquired foul magic items, and made pacts with terrifying entities, all in pursuit of the elusive truth about this lost deity. As a reward for his single-minded devotion, the Worm that Walks bestowed its filthy blessing, showering the mortal in a torrent of ravenous worms and maggots. The vermin devoured his physical form, but before he died, his soul transferred to the wriggling host, leaving him immensely powerful but appallingly transformed.

Frightened by his new form, his daughter hired a band of adventurers to destroy him. Over the years, she had spied on her father's terrible doings, and she had overheard enough of his mutterings to know that if he were unchecked, he would unleash great evil on the world. However, even the powerful adventurers could not kill the thing that her father had become. In the end, they settled for sealing him in a vault below the keep. The baroness used her vast wealth to pay for spells strong enough to hold him there, encasing him for eternity (or so she thought) in eldritch bonds.

USING THESE VILLAINS

Edgar and Katarin work best when used together. Although their scheme keeps them in different locations much of the time, they are careful to avoid excessive risks. Katarin is a subtle manipulator, using others to fight her battles for her. Edgar is a paranoid psychopath who hides in the ruins of his family estate, tormented by the voice of his grandfather and the tumor that grows in his gut. He protects himself with corrupted soldiers who share his appalling tastes.

The siblings are not as close as they once were. Katarin believes that Edgar puts the money she sends toward the release of their grandfather, but that is not the case. Meanwhile, Edgar resents the dalliances and trysts that his sister uses to coerce her marks. Thus, tension grows between them; if properly exploited, it could be used to drive a wedge between the two siblings.

Introducing these villains separately is easy, because they move in different circles. The PCs might come across Katarin while spending time in a city and be drawn into her scheme when she tries to ensnare an NPC ally—or perhaps a player character. If the characters try to meddle, she might send Draen and his dire rats after them, while she returns to her family's keep to lie low for a while.

Alternatively, the PCs might face Edgar first. Since the mad baron preys on his subjects, the party could stumble onto a village in mourning or meet refugees fleeing the realm. The tales of woe could lead the PCs back to the keep, where they can confront the siblings in the heart of their lair.

Of course, the pair's superficial schemes mask their true objective, which endangers the entire world. Their entombed grandfather serves the Worm that Walks, a dead god of incalculable power. This terrifying entity means to seize the world for its own despicable purpose and devour everything in it. The nobles' ancestor is a linchpin in the deity's plan: Through him, it can be released from its own sepulcher.

If the PCs manage to thwart or drive off the siblings, Edgar and Katarin return to the keep as soon as possible, more committed than ever before to releasing their grandfather in revenge. They do not realize that the archmage would have no further use for them once freed. Indeed, they will likely be the first victims of the Worm that Walks, as it returns to the world to usher in a new age of despair.

Illus. by K. Tanner

Edgar Tolstoff

THE TOLSTOFFS IN EBERRON

Katarin operates in Korth, the capital of Karrnath; she lives in a small house near Crownhome. She has set her sights on General Thauram (*Five Nations* page 113), a decorated officer who oversees the city's defenses and commands the White Lions brigade—the principal defenders of Korth. Thauram personally interrogates important prisoners, and Katarin believes that by befriending him, she can learn more about wealthy individuals who would be easy to exploit.

THE TOLSTOFFS IN FAERÛN

Situated where the Laughingflow drains into the Evermoors, Tolstoff Keep and the surrounding hamlet have suffered incredibly. Between the trolls, the giants, and the rampaging barbarians, the family has faced extinction on more occasions than anyone can remember. While his sister is away in Silverymoon, Edgar sends his mercenaries to raid the Evermoor Way for supplies. In his growing madness, he has begun to consider raising an army of mercenaries to lay siege to Nesmé, the only town of appreciable size on the Evermoors. Edgar keeps this plot to himself because he knows that Katarin would think it reckless and foolhardy.

APPEARANCE AND BEHAVIOR

Although only in his mid-twenties, Edgar Tolstoff retains neither youth nor vigor. Disease ravages his corpulent body. Festering wounds leak watery pus, while swollen growths burst on his arms and legs. His face, neck, and torso are a forest of fleshy tumors. The most disturbing feature of all is a large distended area that grows in his middle: A thick knot filled with fluid. If anyone could bear to press an ear against it, he would hear horrific utterances emanating from the tumor. Edgar hides his ghastly appearance as well as he can, but the leakage from his various sores and eruptions ruins any clothing he wears.

His sister Katarin is his exact opposite. She shares his sandy hair and startling blue eyes, but her flesh is clean, untouched by corruption. Most of the time, she lets her luxurious locks hang free, but when trying to impress a victim, she takes the time to pile her hair on top of her head, accenting the look with a beautiful dress and some pieces of jewelry that have been stolen by her minion Draen.

Although the siblings differ physically, they are similar in personality. Both are inquisitive, eager to learn and experience new things. They are not unsettled or frightened easily. In fact, Edgar is fond of insects and worms, displaying them in small jars throughout his personal chambers on the second floor of the keep.

Both Tolstoff nobles are extraordinarily loyal. Once they declare their friendship to someone, they are loath to jeopardize it. However, they interpret friendship in unusual ways. They try to anticipate a person's needs and desires, often committing terrible acts because they think the outcome will please their erstwhile ally.

Edgar Tolstoff CR 7

hp 57 (7 HD)

Male human ranger 3/duskblade[PH2] 2/cancer mage[BoVD] 2
NE Medium humanoid
Init +1; **Senses** blindsight 30 ft.; Listen +7, Spot +6
Languages Abyssal, Common; telepathy with cancerous companion

AC 15, touch 11, flat-footed 14
(+1 Dex, +4 armor)
Immune drow poison
Fort +14 (+17 against poison), **Ref** +7, **Will** +3

Speed 30 ft. (6 squares)
Melee *+1 longsword* +10 (1d8+4/19–20) or
Melee *+1 longsword* +8 (1d8+4/19–20) and
+1 short sword +8 (1d6+2/19–20) or
Melee unarmed strike +9 (1d3+3 nonlethal plus disease) or
Melee touch +9 (disease)
Ranged mwk composite longbow +8 (1d8+3/×3 plus poison)
Base Atk +6; **Grp** +9
Atk Options disease, favored enemy humans +2, poison (drow poison, Fort DC 13, unconscious 1 minute/unconscious 2d4 hours), sneak attack +1d6
Special Actions *arcane attunement* 4/day
Combat Gear 3 doses drow poison, *potion of cure moderate wounds*, scroll of *bull's strength*, scroll of *obscuring mist*
Duskblade Spells Known (CL 2nd):
1st (4/day)—*burning hands* (DC 12), *swift expeditious retreat, true strike*
0 (4/day)—*acid splash* (+7 ranged touch), *touch of fatigue* (+9 melee touch, DC 11)
Spell-Like Abilities (CL 7th):
2/day—*contagion* (+9 melee touch, DC 12)

Abilities Str 16, Dex 12, Con 16, Int 13, Wis 8, Cha 15
SQ armored mage, cancerous companion, disease host, wild empathy +5 (+1 magical beasts)
Feats Endurance[B], Combat Casting[B], Deformity (obese)[BoVD], Great Fortitude[B], Poison Immunity[BoVD], Toughness, Track[B], Two-Weapon Fighting[B], Verminfriend[B BoVD] (see page 25), Willing Deformity[B BoVD]
Skills Concentration +9, Gather Information +7, Heal +3, Hide +6, Intimidate +7, Jump +9, Knowledge (nature) +8, Listen +7, Move Silently +7, Search +3, Sense Motive +1, Sleight of Hand +5, Spellcraft +5, Spot +6, Survival +5 (+7 aboveground natural environments), Tumble +5
Possessions combat gear plus *+1 studded leather, +1 longsword, +1 short sword,* masterwork composite longbow (+3 Str bonus) with 20 arrows

Disease (Ex) Shakes—unarmed strike or touch, Fortitude DC 16, incubation period 1 day, damage 1d8 Dex.
Disease (Ex) Slimy doom—unarmed strike or touch, Fortitude DC 16, incubation period 1 day, damage 1d4 Con. When damaged, victim must succeed on a second saving throw or 1 point of damage is drain instead.
Arcane Attunement (Sp) For a combined total of four times per day, Edgar can use *dancing lights, detect magic, flare* (DC 11), *ghost sound*, and *read magic*. Caster level 2nd.
Armored Mage (Ex) Edgar ignores the chance for arcane spell failure imposed by light armor and light shields.
Cancerous Companion (Ex) An intelligent (Int 6) tumor grows inside Edgar. The tumor and Edgar can communicate telepathically. The cancerous companion uses all of Edgar's statistics except Intelligence. The cancerous companion cannot take actions. It bestows Edgar with blindsight out to 30 feet.
Disease Host (Ex) Edgar never takes damage from disease, though he might manifest cosmetic effects. Whenever he encounters a disease, he becomes a carrier and can transmit the disease to others. If Edgar is the target of a *remove disease* spell, he takes 1d6 points of damage per caster level and loses his blindsight for 1d10 days.

Katarin Tolstoff CR 7

hp 30 (8 HD)

Female human aristocrat 1/enchanter 5/mindbender[CAr] 2
NE Medium humanoid
Init +7; **Senses** Listen +5, Spot +5
Languages Abyssal, Common, Draconic, Infernal; telepathy 100 ft.

AC 19, touch 14, flat-footed 16
(+3 Dex, +4 armor, +1 deflection, +1 natural)
Fort +6, **Ref** +5, **Will** +11

Speed 30 ft. (6 squares)
Melee mwk rapier +7 (1d6/18–20)
Ranged light crossbow +6 (1d8/19–20)
Base Atk +3; **Grp** +3
Special Actions *instant daze* 4/day, *push the weak mind* 1/day
Combat Gear *oil of magic weapon, 2 potions of cure light wounds, potion of protection from arrows 10/magic, potion of sanctuary,* scroll of *blink*, scroll of *blur*, scroll of *charm person* (CL 6th), 2 scrolls of *Melf's acid arrow* (CL 6th), scroll of *misdirection*, scroll of *suggestion*, scroll of *summon monster III, wand of invisibility* (25 charges)
Wizard Spells Prepared (CL 6th; prohibited schools evocation and necromancy):
3rd—*dispel magic*, heightened *charm person* (DC 18), *slow* (DC 17), *suggestion* (DC 18)
2nd—*blur, cloud of bewilderment*[SC] (DC 16), *eagle's splendor, touch of idiocy* (+6 melee touch), *whispering wind*
1st—*charm person* (DC 16), *color spray* (DC 15), *disguise self, mage armor*†, *shock and awe*[SC]
0—*acid splash* (+6 ranged touch), *daze* (DC 15), *detect magic, ghost sound* (DC 14), *read magic*
† Already cast

Abilities Str 10, Dex 16, Con 12, Int 18, Wis 12, Cha 16
SQ familiar (none at present)
Feats Eschew Materials, Evil Brand[B] (see page 24), Heighten Spell[B], Improved Initiative, Persuasive, Scribe Scroll[B], Spell Focus (enchantment)[B], Verminfriend[B BoVD] (see page 25)
Skills Bluff +12, Concentration +6, Decipher Script +9, Diplomacy +16*, Disguise +7 (+9 acting), Gather Information +8, Intimidate +14*, Knowledge (arcana) +11, Knowledge (nobility) +9, Knowledge (the planes) +6, Listen +5, Sense Motive +8, Spellcraft +14, Spot +5
* When interacting with evil creatures, Katarin gains a +2 circumstance bonus on Diplomacy and Intimidate checks.
Possessions combat gear plus masterwork rapier, light crossbow with 10 bolts, *ring of protection +1, amulet of natural armor +1, cloak of resistance +1*
Spellbook spells prepared plus all cantrips except evocation and necromancy; 1st—*disguise self, shield*; 2nd—*alter self*; 3rd—*blink*

Illus. by E. Widermann

Katarin Tolstoff

Instant Daze (Sp) Four times per day, when an enemy that has 8 or fewer Hit Dice makes a melee attack against Katarin, she can as an immediate action daze the opponent for 1 round unless it succeeds on a DC 16 Will save.

Push the Weak Mind (Sp) Once per day, Katarin can influence a creature through speech or telepathy as the *suggestion* spell, but with a range of 100 feet and a duration of 7 hours (or until completed); Will DC 17 negates; CL 7th.

DRAEN RALGAEL

"Kill them all. Stab out their eyes. Tear out their tongues! Eat, eat, eat!"

—Draen Ralgael

Edgar and Katarin's most useful and powerful servant is Draen Ralgael, a whisper gnome cursed with lycanthropy. Although he is raving mad, utterly obsessed with eating living flesh, he remains a reliable agent, adept at moving unseen and learning the secrets of their enemies.

Draen was not always evil. He was once a champion of his people—a fearless guardian who helped to patrol the borders of his community, safeguarding it from kobold and goblinoid attacks. The coming of the dark host, a vast army in service to the evil god Nerull, shattered his world, and Draen was one of many who fell to the enemy. Unlike his kin, however, he survived, invigorated by the curse of lycanthropy that he acquired when he was bitten by a wererat during the attack.

GOALS

Draen is filled with self-loathing, haunted by the memories of his old life. He pines for the past, yearning to go home to his people, even though he knows that any survivors are scattered to the winds. Regardless, his curse—and his acquiescence to the dark impulses that accompany it—forever bars him from rejoining his kind. However, he still clings to the hope that if he could somehow escape the beast within, he could resume the life that was stolen from him.

Draen believes that his salvation lies with Edgar. The corrupted Baron has promised to find some way to alleviate the gnome's suffering in exchange for service. Edgar has dangled countless possible cures in front of the gnome, but each one has failed, driving Draen deeper into madness. Despite these disappointments, Draen remains loyal, believing that Edgar's efforts will one day pay off.

USING DRAEN

Draen is the Tolstoffs' problem-solver: their spy, bodyguard, and personal assassin. Currently he is charged with protecting and assisting Katarin as she works to funnel gold back to the estate. Thus, whenever Katarin finds herself in over her head, Draen is always nearby, ready to lift her out of trouble by butchering those around her.

A capable opponent in his own right, Draen sometimes undertakes missions for Katarin. Generally, these jobs entail murder and espionage, but in between such tasks, he is notorious for snatching innocents off the streets and dragging them into the sewers, where he and his dire rat friends eat them alive.

Appearance and Behavior

When in humanoid form, Draen looks like a tall, slender gnome, about 4 feet in height and weighing 40 pounds. His skin is pale green, and he has gray eyes. He favors body art; whorls and patterns cover him from head to toe. He wears two silver rings in his left ear and an iron ring in his nose. He rarely goes without his mithral shirt and always keeps his hand crossbow ready.

When Draen changes shape, his hybrid form and his dire rat form are particularly foul. He looks like a big, bloated rat covered in bristling black fur, with a bright green tail and nose.

Draen has no knowledge of his masters' true goal or the thing that is trapped beneath their keep. In his ignorance, he happily serves. To him, the Tolstoffs are trustworthy, tolerant employers who have accepted him despite his cruel and unpredictable nature. They comfort him when they can, and though they clearly exploit his talents, Draen does not mind since it makes him feel useful.

DRAEN RALGAEL **CR 5**

Male whisper gnome[RS] wererat rogue 3

HUMANOID FORM

hp 25 (4 HD)

CE Small humanoid (gnome, shapechanger)

Init +8; **Senses** darkvision 60 ft., low-light vision, scent; Listen +11, Spot +11

Languages Common, Gnome; rat empathy

AC 21, touch 15, flat-footed 17; Dodge, +4 against giants (+1 size, +4 Dex, +4 armor, +2 natural)

Resist evasion

Fort +5, **Ref** +9, **Will** +6

Speed 30 ft. (6 squares)
Melee +*1 rapier* +7 (1d4+2/18–20)
Ranged mwk hand crossbow +7 (1d3/19–20 plus poison)
Base Atk +2; **Grp** –1
Atk Options +1 on attack rolls against kobolds and goblinoids, poison (black adder venom, Fort DC 11, 1d6 Con/1d6 Con), sneak attack +2d6
Special Actions alternate form
Combat Gear dose of black adder venom, flask of acid, *elixir of hiding, potion of cure light wounds*
Spell-Like Abilities (CL 1st):
1/day—*ghost sound* (DC 10), *mage hand, message, silence* (centered on self)

Abilities Str 12, Dex 18, Con 15, Int 10, Wis 12, Cha 10
SQ trap sense +1, trapfinding
Feats Alertness, Dodge, Improved Initiative, Iron Will[B], Weapon Finesse[B]
Skills Balance +12, Climb +9, Escape Artist +10, Hide +18, Jump +9, Listen +11, Move Silently +14, Spot +11, Swim +9, Tumble +12, Use Rope +4 (+6 bindings)
Possessions combat gear plus mithral shirt, +*1 rapier*, masterwork hand crossbow with 10 bolts

Alternate Form (Su) Draen can assume a bipedal hybrid form or the form of a dire rat.

Hybrid Form

hp 29 (4 HD); **DR** 10/silver

CE Small humanoid (gnome, shapechanger)
Init +11; **Senses** darkvision 60 ft., low-light vision, scent; Listen +11, Spot +11
Languages Common, Gnome; rat empathy

AC 25, touch 18, flat-footed 18; Dodge, +4 against giants (+1 size, +7 Dex, +4 armor, +3 natural)
Resist evasion
Fort +6, **Ref** +12, **Will** +6

Speed 30 ft. (6 squares)
Melee +*1 rapier* +10 (1d4+2/18–20) and bite +4 (1d4 plus curse of lycanthropy) or
Melee 2 claws +9 each (1d4 plus curse of lycanthropy) and bite +4 (1d4 plus curse of lycanthropy)
Ranged mwk hand crossbow +10 (1d3/19–20 plus poison)
Base Atk +2; **Grp** –1
Atk Options +1 on attack rolls against kobolds and goblinoids, poison (black adder venom, Fort DC 11, 1d6 Con/1d6 Con), sneak attack +2d6
Special Actions alternate form
Combat Gear dose of black adder venom, flask of acid, *elixir of hiding, potion of cure light wounds*
Spell-Like Abilities (CL 1st):
1/day—*ghost sound* (DC 10), *mage hand, message, silence* (centered on self)

Abilities Str 12, Dex 24, Con 17, Int 10, Wis 12, Cha 10
SQ trap sense +1, trapfinding
Feats Alertness, Dodge, Improved Initiative, Iron Will[B], Weapon Finesse[B]
Skills Balance +15, Climb +9, Escape Artist +13, Hide +21, Jump +9, Listen +11, Move Silently +17, Spot +11, Swim +9, Tumble +15, Use Rope +7 (+9 bindings)
Possessions combat gear plus mithral shirt, +*1 rapier*, masterwork hand crossbow with 10 bolts

Curse of Lycanthropy (Su) Target must succeed on a DC 15 Fortitude save or contract lycanthropy.
Alternate Form (Su) Draen can assume a humanoid (whisper gnome) form or the form of a dire rat.

Draen Ralgael

Illus. by R. Gallegos

Dire Rat Form

hp 29 (4 HD); **DR** 10/silver

CE Small humanoid (gnome, shapechanger)
Init +11; **Senses** darkvision 60 ft., low-light vision, scent; Listen +11, Spot +11
Languages Common, Gnome; rat empathy

AC 21, touch 18, flat-footed 13; Dodge, +4 AC against giants (+1 size, +7 Dex, +3 natural)
Resist evasion
Fort +6, **Ref** +12, **Will** +6

Speed 40 ft. (8 squares), climb 20 ft.
Melee bite +10 (1d4 plus disease and curse of lycanthropy)
Base Atk +2; **Grp** –1
Atk Options +1 on attack rolls against kobolds and goblinoids, sneak attack +2d6
Special Actions alternate form
Spell-Like Abilities (CL 1st):
1/day—*ghost sound* (DC 10), *mage hand, message, silence* (centered on self)

Abilities Str 12, Dex 24, Con 17, Int 10, Wis 12, Cha 10
SQ trap sense +1, trapfinding
Feats Alertness, Dodge, Improved Initiative, Iron Will[B], Weapon Finesse[B]
Skills Balance +15, Climb +15, Escape Artist +13, Hide +21, Jump +9, Listen +11, Move Silently +17, Spot +11, Swim +15, Tumble +15, Use Rope +7 (+9 bindings)

Curse of Lycanthropy (Su) Target must succeed on a DC 15 Fortitude save or contract lycanthropy.
Disease (Ex) Filth fever—injury (bite), Fort DC 15, incubation period 1d3 days, damage 1d3 Dex and 1d3 Con.
Alternate Form (Su) Draen can assume a humanoid (whisper gnome) form or a bipedal hybrid form.

TOLSTOFF KEEP

At the edge of a large, stinking swamp rises a low hill, on which huddles a mishmash of hovels, houses, and shops. Thrusting up from the center is Tolstoff Keep, an old castle stained dark from centuries of grime, rain, and choking vines. The air is still and silent, except for the occasional screams of swamp-dwelling terrors. A heavy mist swirls about the area, contributing to the hacking cough that afflicts the locals who call this wretched place home.

Few people live in the keep. Aside from Edgar and his sister, the only residents are a handful of guards, all of whom wear disturbing leather masks molded to look like idiotic smiling faces. Villagers whisper that the soldiers are not human—or at least not human any longer. They make no sounds and interact only with one another. No one outside the keep has seen their faces, but some claim that beneath the masks are masses of undulating flesh, not unlike tangles of worms.

KEY FEATURES

The hovels and shacks crowd right up against the castle walls, and the stench of the afflicted and the corrupt hangs like a pall over the area. The castle walls are fashioned from dark stone. Many of the stones have stains that resemble faces twisted with suffering or hands reaching out for help. Indeed, those who brush against the walls find their cloaks snagged by stones, caught in improbable ways.

The keep—the structure within the walls—is two stories tall, though only the main floor is shown on the map. The labyrinthine upper level consists of bedrooms, meeting rooms, and privies, none of which is especially noteworthy—though there are a number of secret passages, isolated rooms, and odd architectural features. Three turrets rise another 20 feet above the second floor, overlooking the outer wall by at least 10 feet.

Structural Properties

The following general properties apply to all rooms unless otherwise noted in the area descriptions.

Outer Wall: The keep is encircled by a wall (Climb DC 20) that is 40 feet tall and that descends 10 feet below the ground to thwart sappers. Near the base, the wall is about 5 feet thick, gradually thinning to 2 feet at the top where crenellations rise to protect the archers who patrol the perimeter. At its base, the wall has a break DC of 50, hardness 8, and 900 hit points per 10-foot-square section. Toward the top, the wall has a break DC of 50, hardness 8, and 360 hit points per section. The crenellations provide cover to creatures standing behind them.

Keep Walls: The exterior walls (Climb DC 20) of the keep are made of superior masonry and are 2 feet thick, with a break DC of 35, hardness 8, and 180 hit points per 10-foot-square section. The internal walls (Climb DC 15)

Illus. by E. Deschamps

Tolstoff Keep

of the structure are masonry and have a break DC of 35, hardness 8, and 90 hit points per section.

Arrow Slits: There are few windows in the keep, though there are numerous arrow slits. These openings grant archers improved cover (+8 bonus to Armor Class and +4 bonus on Reflex saves). Characters attempting to cast spells, such as *fireball,* through the arrow slits must succeed on ranged touch attacks against AC 15. A Small character can squeeze through an arrow slit by making a successful DC 15 Escape Artist check, while a Medium creature can do so by succeeding on a DC 30 Escape Artist check.

Floors: Aside from random splotches of filth and grime, the floors are level and free of debris.

Ceiling Height: The ceilings of the first level are 15 feet high. Dark, writhing shadows roil in the corners as if alive, though they are nothing more than tricks of the light.

Doors: Made from strong wood, all doors are 2 inches thick and have hardness 5 and 20 hit points. They are unlocked.

Illumination: Most rooms are dark, though sconces at 10-foot intervals hold unlit torches.

Smells: The entire place stinks of mildew and spoiled meat. The stench is foul enough to block the use of the scent ability, but it otherwise imposes no penalties.

Sounds: Whenever a character's Listen check result is 25 or higher, she hears a disturbing noise that sounds like something moist writhing around. The first time she hears it, she must succeed on a DC 15 Will save or be shaken for 1 round.

DEFENSES

Most of the keep's defenders have long since died from disease or fled in fear of Edgar's obscene transformation. The guards that remain are utterly corrupted. Ten warriors and two commanders patrol the grounds, and all of them have been physically mutated by the fetid Worm that Walks. If combat breaks out with any of the guards, 1d3 more guards show up every 3 rounds until all have been accounted for (for statistics, see tactical encounter 3–1, page 58). If neither corrupted commander is present at the start of the fight, one of them shows up 4 rounds after combat begins, and the other arrives 4 rounds after that.

Once the PCs arrive, Edgar flees to the catacombs (see tactical encounter 3–3, page 62); if his sister is present, she goes with him. Meanwhile, Draen (for statistics, see page 52) and six corrupted dire rats set out to find and devour the interlopers, attacking the PCs when they are least prepared. The few other denizens of the keep remain in their chambers, confident in their ability to deal with intruders.

CORRUPTED[BoVD] DIRE RAT — CR 1

hp 7 (1 HD)

NE Small aberration (augmented animal)
Init +2; **Senses** darkvision 60 ft., low-light vision, scent; Listen +3, Spot +3

AC 18, touch 13, flat-footed 16
(+1 size, +2 Dex, +5 natural)
Immune acid
Fort +5, **Ref** +4, **Will** +2

Speed 40 ft. (8 squares), climb 20 ft.
Melee bite +3 (1d6+2 plus disease)
Base Atk +0; **Grp** –2
Atk Options disease

Abilities Str 14, Dex 15, Con 16, Int 1, Wis 10, Cha 2
Feats Alertness, Weapon Finesse[B]
Skills Climb +10, Hide +7, Jump +6, Listen +3, Move Silently +3, Spot +3, Swim +10

Disease (Ex) Filth fever—injury (bite), Fort DC 17, incubation period 1d3 days, damage 1d3 Dex and 1d3 Con.

AREA DESCRIPTIONS

Tolstoff Keep consists of several floors above ground and a catacomb below. Nearly all of the action, though, takes place on the main floor. If you wish to expand upon the castle and its contents, feel free to sketch out the upper level to suit your needs. For more on the catacombs, see tactical encounter 3–3 (page 62).

1. Courtyard: Between the outer wall and the keep is the courtyard, an area of churned mud and dead grass. In places, old bones break the surface. Two corrupted human warriors patrol the outer wall. When the PCs enter the courtyard, the guards should be at the extreme northern stretch of wall. Each round, they move 20 feet clockwise. For statistics, see tactical encounter 3–1 (page 58).

2. Entrance: The only entrance to Tolstoff Keep is a single wooden door on the east wall of the structure. Old and stained black from filth, it features a gargoyle's head with a ring through its ears that holds a knocker. The creature's head is real, carefully preserved with foul unguents.

Just inside the keep door, a large room shows its age and neglect. A crimson rug with unsettling patterns covers most of the floor, and two suits of full plate armor flank an archway leading to a hallway. Banners displaying the Tolstoff heraldry—a red-eyed raven on a gray field—hang from the ceiling.

3. Hall of Ancestors: This rectangular hall has two doors, both made of dark wood and bound in rusting iron. A rug runner extends the length of the hall, showing a vine pattern in its weave. Hanging on the walls are a half-dozen portraits of somber people, an equal mix of men and women. At the far end stands a small round table, on which is a skull surrounded by auburn hair. This gruesome decoration is the head of the old baroness. Katarin shattered her jaw to prevent others from contacting her spirit.

4. Feast Hall: This room is a large hall, with multicolored banners rotting on the walls and three rows of tables and benches. Platters of spoiled food, crawling with maggots, cover the tables. Inspection of the fare reveals that someone has recently picked over the old food. Characters who inspect the northwest corner and succeed on a DC 20 Search check discover a secret door. Depressing a concealed stud in the floor opens the door, revealing a narrow hall that ends at a short staircase descending to the catacombs. If the PCs go down the stairs, run tactical encounter 3–3 (see page 62).

Just inside the secret door, a key hangs from a hook. The key opens the door in the antechamber (area 15), which leads to the chapel (tactical encounter 3–2, page 60).

5. Kitchens: The kitchens are far nastier than the feast hall. Against the south wall are six cold ovens. Three tables running down the center of the room hold the rotting remains of three villagers, each bound in place with bloodstained leather straps. They have been opened in the middle and their insides have been scooped out, presumably for a meal.

Beneath one of the tables is a hideous spawn of Kyuss, a fearsome undead horror favored by the Worm that Walks. The creature looks like a thoroughly rotted zombie with green worms writhing in and out of its skull.

Spawn of Kyuss[MM2] **CR 5**
hp 29 (4 HD); fast healing 5

CE Medium undead
Init –1; **Senses** darkvision 60 ft.; Listen +0, Spot +3
Aura fear (40 ft., DC 14)

AC 11, touch 9, flat-footed 11
(–1 Dex, +2 natural)
Immune undead immunities (*MM* 317)
Resist +2 turn resistance
Fort +1, **Ref** +0, **Will** +4
Weakness curative transformation

Speed 30 ft. (6 squares)
Melee slam +6 (1d6+6 plus disease)
Base Atk +2; **Grp** +6
Atk Options create spawn

Abilities Str 18, Dex 9, Con —, Int 6, Wis 11, Cha 15
Feats Stealthy, Toughness
Skills Hide +5, Jump +7, Listen +0, Move Silently +5, Spot +3

Aura of Fear (Su) At the end of each of the spawn's turns, creatures within 40 feet of it must succeed on a DC 14 Will save or become panicked for 7 rounds. A creature that makes its save is immune to this particular spawn's aura of fear for 24 hours.

Curative Transformation (Ex) If a spawn of Kyuss is targeted by a *remove curse* or *remove disease* spell or similar magic, it is instantly transformed into a human zombie (*MM* 266).

Create Spawn (Su) As an immediate action, whenever a spawn of Kyuss strikes an opponent with a slam attack, a melee touch attack, or a ranged touch attack out to 10 feet, it can transfer a worm from its own body into that of its opponent.

Each worm is a Fine vermin with AC 10 and 1 hit point. It can be killed with normal damage or by the touch of silver. On the spawn's next turn, the worm burrows into the host's flesh. (Creatures that have a natural armor bonus of at least +5 are immune to this effect.) The worm makes its way toward the host's brain, dealing 1 point of damage per round for 1d4+1 rounds. At the end of that period, the worm reaches the brain and starts dealing 1d2 points of Intelligence damage per round until it is killed or it slays the host (death occurs at 0 Intelligence). A Small, Medium, or Large creature slain in this way rises as a new spawn of Kyuss in 1d6+4 rounds. Larger creatures gain the zombie template instead. Newly created spawn are not under the control of their creator.

While the worm is inside a host, crawling toward the brain, a *remove curse* or *remove disease* spell will kill it. In addition, a DC 20 Heal check will extract the worm and kill it. Finally, a *dispel evil* or *neutralize poison* spell will delay its progress toward the brain for 10d6 minutes. Once the worm has reached the brain, it can no longer be extracted or slowed. However, it can still be killed with a *remove curse* or *remove disease* spell.

Disease (Su) Kyuss's gift—slam, Fort DC 14, incubation period 1 day, damage 1d6 Con and 1d4 Wis. These effects manifest as rotting flesh and dementia. An afflicted creature derives half the normal benefits from natural and magical healing. A *cure disease* spell removes the affliction.

6. **Sitting Room:** This room holds an oval arrangement of couches and chairs. The upholstery is full of black mold and reeks of mildew. A rotting carpet covers the floor and squelches underfoot. One bookcase is intact against the eastern wall, but bookworms devoured its contents long ago.

7. **Private Rooms:** A short corridor leads to a cluster of passages and doors. Behind the doors are private rooms containing beds, dressers, small rugs, writing desks, chamber pots, and an assortment of miscellaneous items including clothing, old papers, corpses, and dead rats.

8. **Guest Quarters:** A narrow passage widens into a hallway here. Stuffed falcons, eagles, and ravens hang from the ceiling, arranged so that they appear to be flying. Doors on the south wall lead to a mixture of guest chambers, closets, and privies. A staircase on the west end of the hallway leads up to the second floor.

Three corrupted warriors and a corrupted commander patrol the hall. For statistics, see tactical encounter 3–1 (page 58).

9. **Turrets:** The keep has three turrets that rise 50 feet into the air. Arrow slits pierce the exterior walls. Within each turret, a spiral staircase ascends to a large, open room with a conical ceiling.

10. **Archer Platforms:** During its heyday, Tolstoff Keep employed nearly fifty guards. To protect the family, the baron installed archer platforms on the west and south walls, each about 8 feet off the ground, to allow archers a good angle for firing arrows down at attackers. The platforms are enclosed, but careful listeners can hear the scurrying of rats beneath their feet (Listen DC 10).

On the southern archer platform stands a corrupted human warrior, who will shoot at the PCs in tactical encounter 3–1 (see page 58) unless the party finds another way into the keep.

11. **Barracks and Armory:** This cluster of rooms once housed the keep's guards and their armory (the westernmost room in this block). The remaining guards still sleep here, as evidenced by the stink of sour milk and ammonia emanating from their befouled bedrolls. Anyone who makes a successful DC 15 Search check in a room has a 50% chance of turning up 1d12 gp.

12. **Storerooms and Cistern:** These two rooms contain the keep's food and water supply. The northern room holds a dozen kegs of beer and a well that drops to a cistern 30 feet down. The southern room holds sacks of grains, dried vegetables and fruit, and other dry goods.

13. **Male Servants' Quarters:** These rooms once housed the keep's male servants. Since they left soon after the death of Edgar and Katarin's mother, the quarters have been empty for years.

14. **Female Servants' Quarters:** These rooms held the female servants. Like the male servants' quarters, they are long abandoned.

15. **Antechamber:** Thick rugs cover the floor of this chamber. Dozens of religious icons and symbols, representing deities of every alignment, sit on shelves that protrude from the walls at different heights all around the room. Light shines from a pair of floor candelabras laden with fat black candles that are wrapped in incense-soaked oils. The locked door on the northern wall leads to the chapel. The door can be opened with a successful DC 25 Open Lock check, or with the key found behind the secret door in the feast hall (area 4).

Edgar preserves this room in the hope of absolving himself of the sin of matricide. He comes here once each day and lights fresh candles to keep the stench away from the icons.

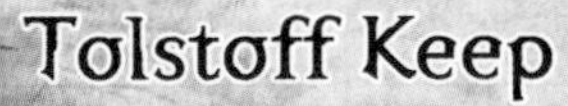

One square = 5 feet

Barbican

Encounter Level 6

SETUP

This encounter occurs when the PCs approach Tolstoff Keep. Two corrupted warriors (G) watch them through arrow slits. A third corrupted warrior cleans his sword in the east barbican tower, and a fourth watches the main gate through an arrow slit in the southern archer platform (area 10). The corrupted commander (C) sits on a stool in the west barbican tower.

Unless the PCs make some attempt to hide, the two guards peering through the arrow slits automatically spot them, and the commander and the east tower guard move to take positions at other arrow slits in their towers.

When the PCs approach the gates, read:

The keep's outer wall looms before you, rising some 40 feet into the air. Two towers flank the main gate, forming a barbican. Arrow slits pierce the walls of the towers.

If the PCs attempt to enter the keep, read:

Four arrows streak toward you from the thin slits in the tower walls. You hear inhuman cackling from within the towers.

TACTICS

When combat begins, the corrupted warriors shoot arrows at the PCs, firing one each round for as long as they have a clear shot. If a PC comes within 10 feet of an arrow slit, the guard at that slit drops his bow and throws a tanglefoot bag (+1 ranged touch) at the character. If the bag hits its target, the PC becomes entangled in alchemical goo, taking a –2 penalty on attack rolls and a –4 penalty to Dexterity. Additionally, the character must succeed on a DC 15 Reflex save or become glued to the ground, unable to move. Even on a successful save, the PC can move only at half speed. A character who fails to save and becomes stuck to the floor can break free with a successful DC 17 Strength check or by dealing 15 points of damage to the hardened goo. In any event, the goo becomes brittle in 2d4 rounds, cracking apart and releasing the character.

The corrupted commander begins the combat by flinging his thunderstone through an arrow slit into the thickest knot of intruders, where it lands with a tremendous bang. Player characters within a 10-foot-radius spread must succeed on a DC 15 Fortitude save or be deafened for 1 hour. Deafened PCs take a –4 penalty on initiative; spellcasters also have a 20% chance of miscasting spells that have verbal components.

4 Corrupted Warriors — CR 1

hp 6 each (1 HD)

Male or female corrupted[BoVD] human warrior 1
NE Medium aberration (augmented humanoid)
Init +4; **Senses** darkvision 60 ft.; Listen +0, Spot +0
Languages Common

AC 21, touch 10, flat-footed 21
(+5 armor, +2 shield, +4 natural)
Immune acid
Fort +4, **Ref** +0, **Will** –1

Speed 20 ft. (4 squares) in chainmail, base speed 30 ft.
Melee longsword +5 (1d8+3/19–20)
Ranged composite longbow +1 (1d8+1/×3)
Base Atk +1; **Grp** +4
Combat Gear *potion of cure light wounds*, 2 tanglefoot bags

Abilities Str 17, Dex 10, Con 15, Int 9, Wis 8, Cha 6
Feats Improved Initiative[B], Weapon Focus (longsword)
Skills Intimidate +2, Listen +0, Spot +0
Possessions combat gear plus masterwork chainmail, heavy steel shield, longsword, composite longbow (+1 Str bonus) with 20 arrows

Corrupted Commander — CR 2

hp 15 (2 HD); fast healing 1

Male corrupted human warrior 2
NE Medium aberration (augmented humanoid)
Init +5; **Senses** darkvision 60 ft.; Listen +1, Spot +1
Languages Common

AC 22, touch 11, flat-footed 21
(+1 Dex, +5 armor, +2 shield, +4 natural)
Immune acid
Fort +6, **Ref** +1, **Will** +0

Speed 20 ft. (4 squares) in chainmail, base speed 30 ft.
Melee mwk battleaxe +8 (1d8+4/×3) or
Melee gauntlet +6 touch (1d3+4 plus 1 vile[BoVD])
Ranged mwk composite longbow +4 (1d8+4/×3)
Base Atk +2; **Grp** +6
Atk Options disruptive attack
Combat Gear *potion of cure moderate wounds*, 2 smokesticks, thunderstone

Abilities Str 19, Dex 12, Con 17, Int 10, Wis 10, Cha 6
Feats Improved Initiative[B], Weapon Focus (battleaxe)
Skills Climb +4, Intimidate +3, Jump –6, Listen +1, Spot +1
Possessions combat gear plus masterwork chainmail, masterwork heavy steel shield, masterwork battleaxe, gauntlet, masterwork composite longbow (+4 Str bonus) with 20 arrows

Vile Damage Unlike normal damage, vile damage can be healed only by magic cast within the area of a *consecrate* or *hallow* spell.
Disruptive Attack (Su) A corrupted commander deals 1 point of vile damage whenever he touches a living, corporeal creature that is not corrupted and is not an outsider.

After throwing the thunderstone, the corrupted commander fires arrows at any enemy spellcasters who escaped its effects or who were outside the radius of the spread.

If the PCs move past the outer wall and enter the keep's courtyard, the guard in the archer platform to the north opens fire with his longbow, targeting lightly armored characters first. The corrupted commander and one of the corrupted warriors emerge from the barbican towers to engage the closest character. The other guards remain in the towers until there are no more PCs outside the walls, at which point the last two warriors also emerge into the courtyard.

The corrupted warriors and the corrupted commander fight intruders to the death.

DEVELOPMENT

When the PCs enter the courtyard, two more corrupted warriors are walking the outer wall at the far northern end. Each round that the combat continues, the warriors move 20 feet clockwise along the outer wall. On the tenth round, if the PCs are still fighting the gate guards, the warriors on the wall attempt DC 22 Listen checks to hear the sounds of battle. If they fail, they walk another 20 feet along the wall, toward the gate. The next round, they attempt another Listen check, this time against DC 20 because they have moved closer to the battle. The warriors keep attempting saves and moving until they finally hear the sounds of combat. At that point, they head toward the gate at a speed of 20 feet.

While the archer in area 10 waits for the PCs to breach the gate, he calls for the other corrupted commander and warriors in the guest quarters (area 8), alerting them to the presence of intruders. It takes 7 rounds for these reinforcements to arrive in the courtyard. If the PCs breach the gate and defeat their initial opponents within 7 rounds, they can slip inside the keep and avoid facing the new arrivals.

CONCLUSION

The towers hold little of interest. They are 50 feet tall and capped with conical roofs. Each tower has four floors, and a spiral staircase leads up past several empty chambers until it ends at the large top floor. The warriors and commander spend their time on the ground floor, which consists of one large room with tables to either side. The table in the west tower holds 1d12 gp and a pair of dice, and the table in the east tower holds a deck of stained cards.

FEATURES OF THE AREA

The area has the following features.

Outer Wall: The keep is encircled by a wall (Climb DC 20) that is 40 feet tall. See page 54 for details.

Main Gate: The main gate is made of 2-inch-thick iron. It has a break DC of 28, hardness 10, and 60 hit points. The gate is secured but can be opened with a successful DC 30 Open Lock check.

Arrow Slits: Due to the slits, the corrupted warriors and commander gain a +8 bonus to Armor Class and a +4 bonus on Reflex saves. Casting spells through the arrow slits requires a ranged touch attack.

Barrels: The barrels in the courtyard are full of old rainwater. If a PC tips one over (Strength DC 25), the spilled water makes an adjacent square extremely slippery, such that the space costs 2 squares of movement to enter.

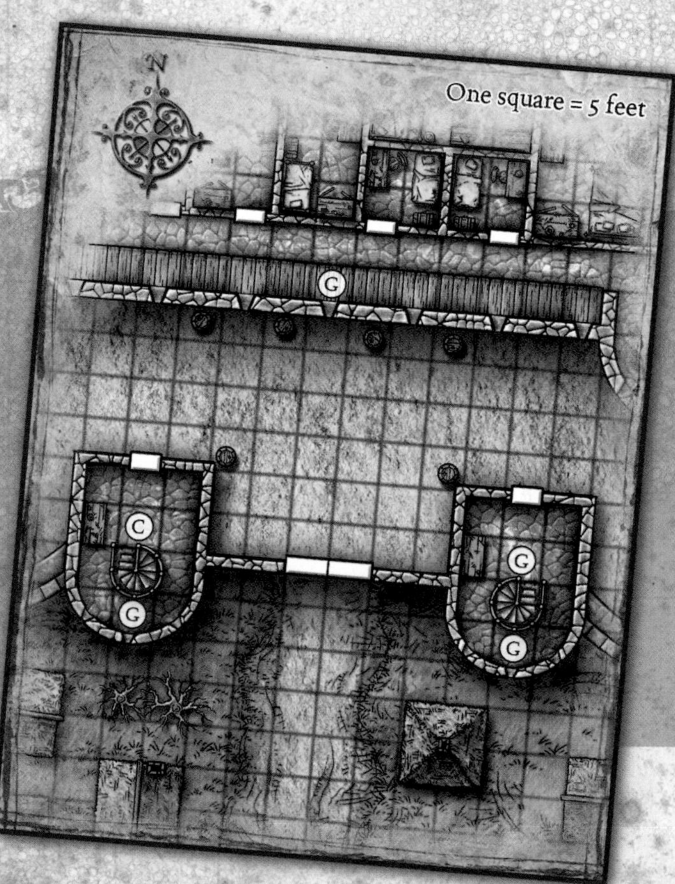

CHAPEL

Encounter Level 7

SETUP

The locked door in the antechamber (area 15) leads to the chapel. If the PCs open the door with the key, they automatically gain surprise. Otherwise, the chapel's residents—a gibbering mouther and a psurlon—are ready for intruders. The gibbering mouther (M) hides in a small alcove in the southwest corner. The psurlon (P) activates its *invisibility* (or *cloud mind*) ability and crouches against the east wall.

When the PCs open the door, read:

As the door swings open, a tremendous stench fills your nostrils. The rows of pews and the altar clearly indicate that the room is a chapel. However, the walls and floor are splashed with gore, and rotting corpses choke the aisles. It's clear from a glance that something has been eating these bodies.

Four angelic statues stand on pillars flanking the dais, each celestial warrior raising a flaming sword into the air. Carved into the front of the altar is a golden face wreathed in fire.

If the PCs enter the room, read:

An awful muttering noise comes from the back corner of the chapel. It fills your head with mad visions and makes your stomach tighten. As you reel from the sound, a streak of lightning shoots toward you from the east wall. The bright bolt dissolves the glamer that concealed the source of the lightning—revealing a horrific creature that looks like a bipedal worm the size of a human, with a head dominated by a wide, fanged maw.

CONFUSED CONDITION

A character who fails his Will save against the gibbering mouther's gibber ability become *confused*. Each round, roll on the following table to determine the character's action.

d%	Action Taken
01–10	Attack the gibbering mouther with melee weapon or ranged weapon; if an attack is not possible, close with the creature.
11–20	Act normally.
21–50	Do nothing but babble incoherently.
51–70	Flee from the gibbering mouther at top speed.
71–100	Attack the nearest creature (a familiar counts as part of the subject's self).

Confused characters who cannot carry out the indicated action do nothing but babble. A *confused* character who is attacked automatically attacks his attackers on the next turn, as long as he is still *confused* at that time. A *confused* character cannot make attacks of opportunity against any creature that he is not already devoted to attacking.

GIBBERING MOUTHER **CR 5**
hp 42 (4 HD); *MM* 126

AVERAGE PSURLON[LoM] **CR 5**
hp 38 (7 HD); **DR** 10/magic

NE Medium aberration
Init +6; **Senses** blindsight 60 ft., darkvision 120 ft.; Listen +11, Spot +1
Languages Undercommon, telepathy 250 ft.

AC 16, touch 16, flat-footed 14 (+2 Dex, +4 armor)
Immune sleep, charm, compulsion
SR 14
Fort +3, **Ref** +4, **Will** +6

Speed 30 ft. (6 squares)
Melee 2 claws +6 each (1d4+1) and bite +4 (1d6)
Base Atk +5; **Grp** +6
Spell-Like Abilities (CL 7th):
At will—*detect thoughts* (DC 15), *mage armor*†, *sound burst* (DC 15)
3/day—*hold monster* (DC 18), *invisibility, lightning bolt* (DC 16), *telekinesis* (DC 18)
1/day—*dimension door*
† Already used

Abilities Str 13, Dex 14, Con 12, Int 18, Wis 13, Cha 17
Feats Combat Casting, Improved Initiative, Multiattack
Skills Bluff +13, Concentration +11, Diplomacy +7, Disguise +3 (+5 acting), Escape Artist +11, Heal +6, Intimidate +5, Knowledge (arcana) +9, Knowledge (dungeoneering) +9, Listen +11, Sense Motive +6, Spellcraft +11, Spot +1, Use Rope +2 (+4 bindings)

If you use *Expanded Psionics Handbook,* make the following adjustments to the statistics block.
NE Medium aberration (psionic)
Psi-Like Abilities (ML 7th):
At will—*concussion blast* (3d6), *inertial armor, read thoughts* (DC 15)
3/day—*brain lock* (all types, DC 15), *cloud mind* (DC 15), *energy bolt* (7d6, DC 17)
1/day—*psionic dimension door, telekinetic maneuver* (+11 check modifier), *telekinetic thrust* (300 lb., DC 16)
Feats Combat Manifestation, Improved Initiative, Multiattack
Skills Bluff +13, Concentration +11, Diplomacy +7, Disguise +3 (+5 acting), Escape Artist +11, Heal +6, Intimidate +5, Knowledge (dungeoneering) +9, Knowledge (psionics) +9, Listen +11, Psicraft +11, Sense Motive +6, Spot +1, Use Rope +2 (+4 bindings)

Features of the Area

The room has the following features.

Illumination: Stained glass windows (each with hardness 1 and 1 hit point) permit some light to shine in from the north end of the room. Additionally, the candles in the antechamber (area 15) produce shadowy illumination in the first 4 squares beyond the door.

Ceiling Height: The ceiling in this room is 20 feet high.

Statues: Four statues flank the altar and dais on the north side of the room. The statues depict bold celestial warriors in the service of Pelor. The statues function as slender pillars. Any PCs who stand in a space occupied by a statue gain a +2 bonus to Armor Class and a +1 bonus on Reflex saves. Each statue has AC 4, hardness 8, and 250 hit points.

Altar and Dais: An altar stands upon a short dais. Characters who stand on the dais gain a +1 circumstance bonus on attack rolls against opponents standing on the floor.

Side Chambers: Two side chambers hold priestly vestments, censers, and other religious accoutrements. The doors are unlocked.

Pews: Twelve pews are arranged in two rows of six. It costs 2 squares of movement to enter a square containing a pew. Those who climb onto a pew gain a +1 circumstance bonus on attack rolls against opponents standing on the floor.

Offal: Characters moving through squares containing offal must succeed on a DC 12 Fortitude save or be sickened for 1 round, taking a –2 penalty on attack rolls, weapon damage rolls, saves, and checks. The gibbering mouther and the psurlon are immune to this effect.

Corpses: The squares containing corpses count as difficult terrain, requiring 2 squares to enter. As with the offal, the mouther and the psurlon are not hindered by the presence of the corpses.

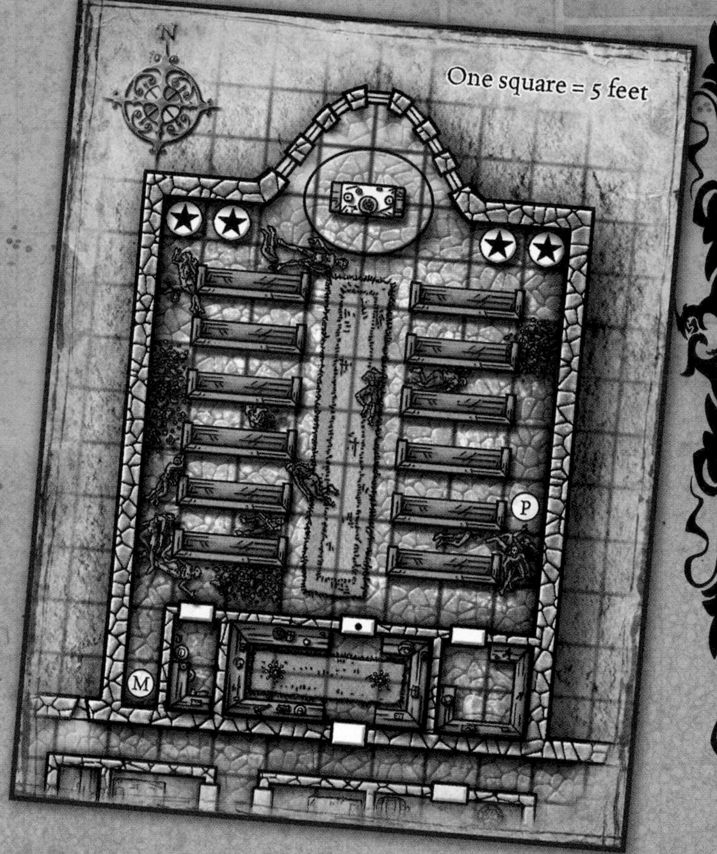

TACTICS

When the PCs enter the room, the mouther starts to gibber in an attempt to confuse them. See the Confused Condition sidebar.

As the gibbering mouther moves forward to engage the PCs, it flings spittle each round as a free action. Anyone who is struck by the spittle and who fails a DC 18 Fortitude save is blinded for 1d4 rounds. While blinded, the victim takes a –2 penalty to Armor Class, loses his Dexterity bonus to Armor Class (if any), moves at half speed, and takes a –4 penalty on Search checks and most Strength- and Dexterity-based skill checks. Checks relying on vision automatically fail.

Each successful bite attack allows the mouther to attempt a grapple as a free action without provoking attacks of opportunity. The creature and its opponent make opposed grapple checks. If the mouther wins, it attempts to swallow its foe by making another opposed grapple check. Characters swallowed by the mouther take 1d4 points of Constitution damage each round that they remain enveloped.

Meanwhile, the psurlon stays back and uses its spell-like (or psi-like) abilities. It uses *hold monster* (or *brain lock*) on the PC closest to the gibbering mouther and follows up with *lightning bolt* (or *energy bolt [electricity]*) and *sound burst* (or *energy bolt [sonic]*) in the next rounds, moving to keep its distance from the PCs. It uses *telekinesis* on any character who comes within 10 feet, using a combat maneuver (*telekinetic maneuver*) or a violent thrust (*telekinetic thrust*) to shove back the pews to slow its attackers down.

The gibbering mouther fights to the death. If the psurlon is reduced to 15 or fewer hit points, it uses *dimension door* (or *psionic dimension door*) to transport 680 feet to the north.

CONCLUSION

The eastern side chamber contains a pile of vestments, icons, and other religious items worth a total of 2,000 gp.

Catacombs

Encounter Level 10

SETUP

When they are at the keep, Edgar (E) and Katarin (K) spend most of their time with their grandfather in the catacombs. They should be positioned in squares adjacent to his vault (A).

If the PCs have not yet defeated Draen, place him (in dire rat form) and six corrupted dire rats wherever you like in the catacombs.

The gloom golem (G) was created by the archmage before he was defeated and sealed away. The golem is under orders to attack anyone who threatens members of the archmage's family, and the PCs clearly meet this criterion.

When the gloom golem begins its howl, the Tolstoff siblings make ready. Edgar reads his *scroll of bull's strength*, which gives him a +2 bonus on melee attack rolls and weapon damage rolls. He then applies a dose of drow poison to his arrows before moving to seek a clear shot at the PCs.

Meanwhile, Katarin casts *eagle's splendor* to make it harder for the PCs to save against her spells. She then reads her scroll of *summon monster* III to summon a fiendish wolverine, which moves to intercept the party. Next, she reads her scrolls of *blink* and *blur* and moves south to circle around the PCs.

When the PCs descend the steps hidden behind the feast hall's secret door, read:

The narrow staircase descends into the earth. The walls are made of old, cracked stone, riddled with hairy orange roots, and thick with glistening worms.

About halfway down, have the PCs attempt DC 5 Listen checks. If they succeed, read:

You hear a faint wailing noise coming from below, a sound of unfathomable suffering. It seems to fill your souls with sorrow.

TACTICS

When the PCs reach the bottom of the steps, they hear the dreadful sound of the gloom golem's wail. The sound does not affect them unless they move within 30 feet of the creature. The golem waits for the PCs to close, readying an action to lash out with its spiked chain at the first adventurer who comes within 20 feet. The gloom golem stays put until it takes at least 20 points of damage, at which point it squeezes out of its room to kill the intruders (use the squeezed statistics). While it is squeezing, each square of movement costs the golem 2 squares of speed.

As the party deals with the golem, Katarin unleashes a barrage of spells. She starts with *shock and awe* to give her brother a chance to deal sneak attack damage. She follows with *slow*, targeting rogues and spellcasters first. She casts *cloud of bewilderment* next. Finally, she casts heightened *charm person* on a PC who seems like a tough fighter. Katarin orders the charmed character to protect her from attackers; this command requires an opposed Charisma check (her modifier is +5 because of *eagle's splendor*).

Meanwhile, the fiendish wolverine charges into the thick of the party. The creature uses smite good on its first attack and then plants itself in one spot. Each round, the raging beast makes a full attack until it is slain or until the spell's duration runs out, sending it back whence it came.

EDGAR TOLSTOFF CR 7
hp 57 (7 HD); see page 51

KATARIN TOLSTOFF CR 7
hp 30 (7 HD); see page 51

GLOOM GOLEM[MM3] CR 7
hp 74 (8 HD); **DR** 10/good

NE Large construct (evil, extraplanar)
Init +2; **Senses** darkvision 60 ft., low-light vision; Listen +0, Spot +0
Aura *crushing despair* (30 ft., DC 16)

AC 22, touch 11, flat-footed 20
(–1 size, +2 Dex, +11 natural)
Immune magic, construct immunities (*MM* 307)
Fort +2, **Ref** +4, **Will** +2

Speed 30 ft. (6 squares)
Melee 2 claws +9 each (1d8+4 plus touch of woe) or
Melee spiked chain +9/+4 (2d6+6 plus touch of woe)
Space 10 ft.; **Reach** 10 ft. (20 ft. with spiked chain)
Base Atk +6; **Grp** +14
Atk Options touch of woe

Abilities Str 18, Dex 15, Con —, Int —, Wis 11, Cha 15
SQ construct traits (*MM* 307)
Feats —
Skills Listen +0, Move Silently –8, Spot +0

Crushing Despair (Su) At the end of each of the golem's turns, any creatures within 30 feet who hear the golem's incessant howl must succeed on a DC 16 Will save or take a –2 penalty on attack rolls, saving throws, skill checks, ability checks, and weapon damage rolls. The penalties remain until the golem is destroyed. A *good hope* spell counters this mind-affecting compulsion.

Touch of Woe (Ex) Any creature damaged by a gloom golem must succeed on a DC 16 Will save or take 1d6 points of Charisma damage. As a victim loses Charisma, it becomes more miserable and withdrawn until, at 0 Charisma, it collapses into a nightmare-filled coma.

When the gloom golem leaves the central room, it is squeezed and uses the following statistics.
AC 18, touch 7, flat-footed 16
Melee 2 claws +5 each (1d8+4 plus touch of woe) or
Melee spiked chain +5/+0 (2d6+6 plus touch of woe)

FIENDISH WOLVERINE CR —
hp 34 (3 HD)

NE Medium magical beast (extraplanar)
Init +2; **Senses** darkvision 60 ft., low-light vision, scent; Listen +6, Spot +6

AC 12, touch 10, flat-footed 10 (+2 Dex, +2 natural, –2 rage)
Resist cold 5, fire 5; **SR** 8
Fort +9, **Ref** +5, **Will** +2

Speed 30 ft. (6 squares), burrow 10 ft., climb 10 ft.
Melee 2 claws +6 each (1d4+4) and bite +1 (1d6+2)
Base Atk +2; **Grp** +6
Atk Options rage
Special Actions smite good 1/day (+3 damage)

Abilities Str 18, Dex 15, Con 23, Int 3, Wis 12, Cha 10
Feats Alertness, Toughness, Track[B]
Skills Climb +12, Listen +6, Spot +6

Smite Good (Su) Once per day, a fiendish wolverine can make a normal melee attack to deal an extra 3 points of damage against a good foe.

When not raging, a fiendish wolverine uses the following statistics:
hp decrease by 6
AC 14, touch 12, flat-footed 12 (+2 Dex, +2 natural)
Fort +7
Melee 2 claws +4 each (1d4+2) and bite –1 (1d6+1)
Grp +4
Abilities Str 14
Skills Climb +10

DRAEN RALGAEL (DIRE RAT FORM) CR 5
hp 29 (4 HD); see page 53

6 CORRUPTED DIRE RATS CR 1
hp 7 each (1 HD); see page 55

Edgar fights viciously. He fires poisoned arrows until the wolverine gets into position; then he drops his bow and charges forward, drawing his melee weapons. Depending on his foe, he might mix in a touch attack with his off hand to infect his opponent with the shakes and slimy doom. When possible, Edgar flanks the PCs, using the wolverine for assistance.

If the battle turns against the siblings—if either one takes at least 20 points of damage, for example, or if the gloom golem is destroyed—Edgar casts *swift expeditious retreat* and falls back to his grandfather's vault. Katarin casts *misdirection* and joins her brother; there, the two make their final stand. Katarin casts *blur* on Edgar and uses attack spells and scrolls to thin the party's ranks. While fighting, Edgar uses his touch as an off-hand attack; if the PCs take his life, he wants to ensure that they will take his contagion, too.

CONCLUSION

Once the PCs deal with the siblings, they are free to explore the vaults. Each vault holds about 300 gp in assorted copper, silver, and gold.

FEATURES OF THE AREA

The room has the following features.

Illumination: Lit torches sit in sconces every 20 feet.

Ceiling Height: The ceiling in this room is 15 feet high.

Vaults: The numerous doors lead to 5-foot-square vaults, each of which contains the remains of a Tolstoff ancestor. Although the doors are not locked, they can be opened only with a successful DC 25 Strength check. Up to two characters can assist an individual on this check.

Vault A: This vault holds Edgar and Katarin's grandfather, the corrupted archmage who was sealed inside by adventurers. The door is sealed shut, locked, and reinforced with potent magic. A permanent *dimensional anchor* spell inside the vault prevents the captive from escaping by magical means.

The release of the archmage is beyond the scope of this encounter, since his power most likely far exceeds that of the PCs. The means of his release—as well as his statistics—are left for you to decide.

Evil characters standing in squares that are adjacent to the vault cast all spells and spell-like abilities at +1 caster level and gain a +1 profane bonus on attack rolls, weapon damage rolls, saving throws, ability checks, and skill checks.

CHAPTER FOUR

CAPTAIN GNASH

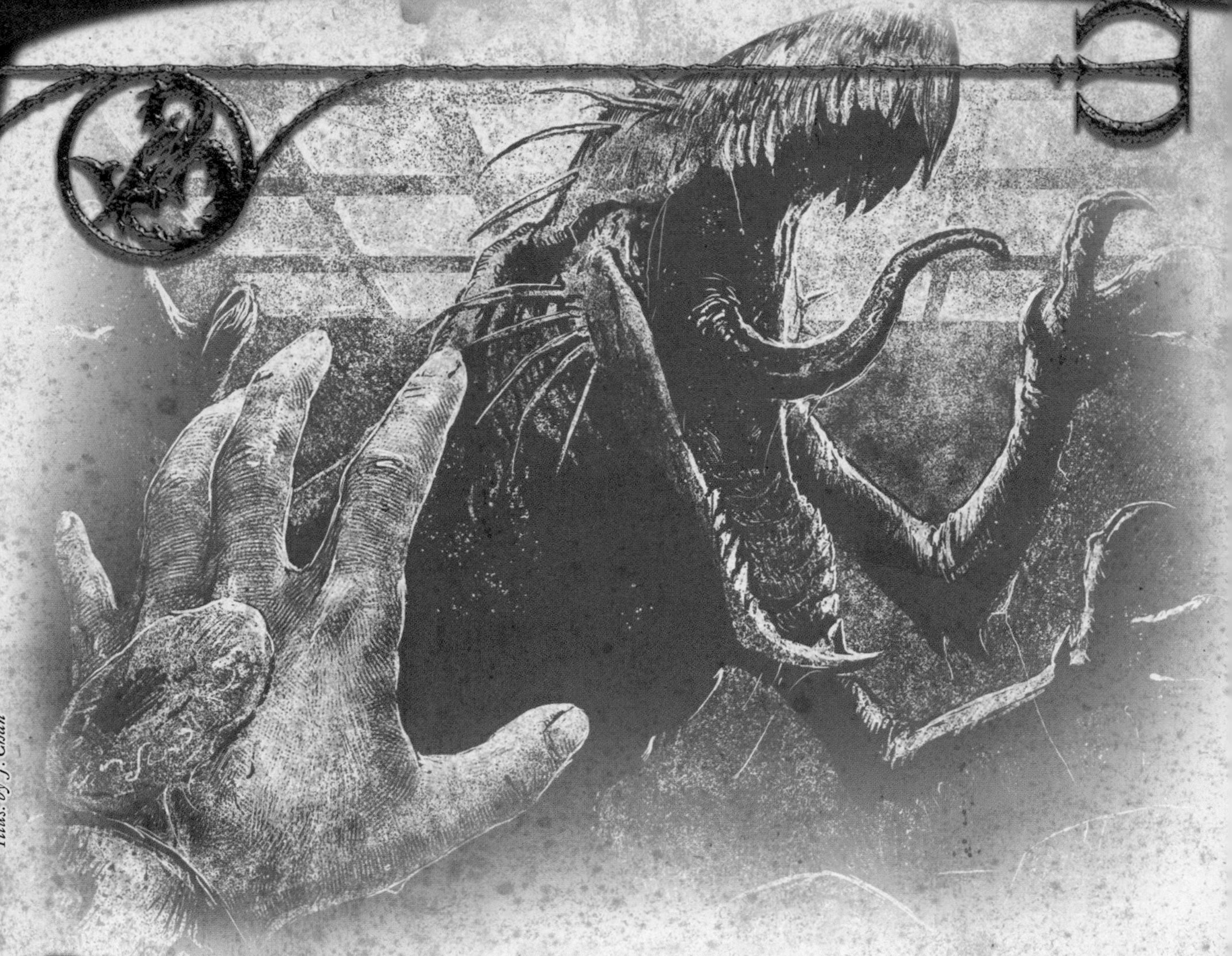

Illus. by J. Chan

Lad, these'n ain't like otha pirates. They do'an care nun 'bout plunder. They jes' essoon walk passa pile o' coin to put a knife in yer gullet and laugh as yeh cry fer yer mamma. These'n cutthroats er the scourge o' da seas, an if nah stop'd, thell be da doom of us all."

—Captain Daniel "The Daft" Simone, dread pirate

In ports and harbors across the sea, the crimson sails of the *Much Kill* inspire terror in all who behold them. The ship is piloted by bloodthirsty, mutated goblinoids. These foul raiders descend on coastal villages to loot, kill, and take slaves, and spill blood in the hold of their vessel to appease the appalling beast they carry. None of their dastardly exploits would be possible, though, without the cruel command of Captain Gnash, one of the nastiest pirates ever to sail the seas.

BACKGROUND

Captain Gnash came to piracy late in life. Before developing his reputation for merciless villainy, the bugbear was a minor thug employed by an ogre warlord known as Scab. His lot was to guard the voracious leader, protect him against attacks by ambitious lieutenants, and ensure that no one disturbed him when he tortured slaves in the privacy of his tent. Gnash would not have been sorry to see Scab dead—indeed, he had his own plans to overthrow the ogre—but he knew that none of Scab's lieutenants would be any better as the leader of the group, so he served, waited, and plotted.

Fate intervened when Scab declared his intent to raze a human city, believing it was a task set before him by his deity. In return for their service, the ogre leader promised his legions "much killing" and plunder, and a chance to butcher soft, spoiled humans. Some of the soldiers had reservations, fearing that such an open attack might provoke a wider war that could result in their annihilation. However, Scab's convictions were powerful, and the chance to visit suffering on the hated humans was too tempting to ignore. Thus, the warlord's armies marched through leagues of dense jungles, impelled by their blood lust. Like spilled ink across a map, the goblinoids streamed out of the undergrowth and fell upon the unsuspecting coastal city.

Goblin sappers burrowed beneath the high stone walls, while disciplined hobgoblin soldiers stormed the gates. Gnash and his fellow bugbears led the charge against the ramparts, scrambling up crude ladders to cut through the unprepared defenders. It was not long before the humans fell back; thus began the slaughter.

After three bloody days of fighting, the city belonged to the goblinoids—but Captain Scab had led his legions to victory at the cost of his own life. Now leaderless, the army

fragmented into smaller knots and factions. The goblins turned against one another, the hobgoblins attacked the bugbears, and creatures strove to tear each other apart as if possessed by madness.

Gnash knew that something was wrong. He knew that Scar had not been strong enough to hold such a fractious brigade together all by himself, which meant that the rank and file must have possessed a sense of community that kept them working together. But now something was affecting their tendency to cooperate . . . something about the city, Gnash supposed.

Now on the alert, the bugbear began to examine the city more closely. Odd statues of squid-headed creatures lined the roads. The construction of the buildings seemed haphazard—some were pyramidal or cylindrical, while others defied the principles of geometry altogether. Strangest of all, the human defenders had not put up much of a fight. Indeed, they seemed resigned to dying.

Gnash came to the conclusion that the city was cursed. He knew that he should flee, but part of him wanted to learn more about the strangely compelling place. The bugbear ventured deeper and deeper into the winding streets. As he explored, he came across an ancient temple that embodied all of the bizarre elements he had witnessed.

Inside, Gnash found an altar to a strange, alien deity. The idol was a stone orb, carved to suggest the surface of the seas. The same aquatic designs covered the columns that lined the altar, as well as the temple's walls, floors, and ceiling. Again, the bugbear felt an urge to run, but again, something held him there. His mind began to fill with impossible images—unsettling landscapes, ancient cities, and endless worlds ripe for the taking, awaiting genocide. Hovering above them all was a ball of roiling water the size of a mountain. An inky tendril extruded from the ball and brushed across the vistas, poisoning everything in its reach.

Gnash knew that he had found his new master. Somehow, he even knew its name—Shothotugg, the Eater of Worlds. And he also knew that he needed to bring this mad abomination to his own world, so that he and all others could know its febrile touch.

Gnash emerged from the temple and addressed the bands of ragged goblinoids, who were still squabbling in the ruins of the city. He spoke of his bizarre master, calling for the warriors to join him; together, he promised, they would pull down the trappings of civilization, destroy and maim, and spread ruin so that all could welcome their new lord from across the stars. They would sail the seas, just as the Eater of Worlds did, and bring its message of death and decay to all they encountered.

On that day, Gnash the guard became Captain Gnash. Supported by a crew of goblins, hobgoblins, and other wretches, he set sail from the dead city to become the scourge of the ocean, a dreadful villain whose name is an epithet and whose deeds have defied imagination.

GOALS

Captain Gnash is insane. Whatever lucidity he possessed as a guard is now behind him, as he campaigns to spread the seeds of destruction and prepare the world for Shothotugg's ascendance. In the depths of the sea, Gnash sees the face of his master, swirling blackly in the foaming waters. His rest is tortured, haunted by nightmares of what will happen when the Eater of Worlds arrives. Though he moans with terror during his sleep, he is reinvigorated each dawn, driven by unreasoning desire to spread suffering to everyone in his path.

Lately, Gnash has dreamed of an island, a windswept outcrop of rock with a single stone pillar thrusting into the sky. He is certain that this place exists—and furthermore, that it can draw Shothotugg's attention, calling the entity from across the stars to scour this world of all life. Obsessed with finding the island, Gnash has bent his crew to his will, taking them to the edges of the oceans in his desperate search for clues.

The bugbear has considered the possibility that the temple in the dead city might reveal the location of the island, and that he somehow overlooked this knowledge when he received his dreadful revelation. His memories of that time are fragmented and disconnected, a montage of sickening sequences that leaves him quailing in fear.

One clear memory from his visit to the temple is the recurring image of a bloated fish-creature bristling with tentacles. The carvings showed the devastating effects of this creature's touch on humans, who were melted into twisted masses. Gnash suspects that one of these aboleths—as he learned they were called—might know of the mysterious island.

Although he is tempted to hunt down an aboleth and tease out its secrets, he remains haunted by the nagging thought that he missed something important in the dead city. Unfortunately for Gnash, he cannot remember where the city is—a fact that fills him with perpetual rage. Accordingly, the captain has begun raiding ports in search of anyone who might have knowledge of the city's location. The smoking ruins of the hapless communities testify to his continued failures, but Gnash has nothing to lose and has vowed to bring this world to its end.

SHOTHOTUGG, EATER OF WORLDS

The Eater of Worlds (*Lords of Madness* page 28) is an Elder Evil, a magnificent and terrible entity whose mere existence is a threat to everything that lives. Most of the Elder Evils dwell in an unknowable, unreachable place, manifesting in the mortal world only when they choose to do so. But Shothotugg exists fully on the Material Plane. It is a mountainous, undulant mass of fluid drifting through space, alighting on the worlds it encounters and poisoning them with its filthy touch. With each destroyed world, the fundamental nature of the Material Plane shifts, creating a palpable effect that ripples throughout the multiverse. Like all Elder Evils, Shothotugg is a being of entropy, and its presence means doom to all.

Illus. by T. Giorello

Captain Gnash

USING THIS VILLAIN

As a disturbing villain, Captain Gnash's plots and goals let you showcase the evil created from a sick mind. The bugbear is fully in the thrall of a strange, otherworldly entity, heedless of the consequences of drawing the Eater of Worlds across the gulf of space. Gnash is a psychopath and his actions and plans are erratic, which makes him a dynamic and adaptable villain.

Gnash does not operate in one stretch of forest, one city, or even one region of the world. Since his base of operations is his ship, the *Much Kill*, he can go anywhere he desires, crossing the oceans with abandon and marauding as he goes. His mobility makes it easy to introduce him to the player characters, because you can place Gnash wherever he is needed in your campaign, rather than orchestrating events to put the PCs in the villain's path.

Perhaps the best way to introduce the dread pirate is to let his reputation do the work for you. Whenever the PCs visit a coastal city or a nearby settlement, they are bound to hear rumors about seas and sailors. Captain Gnash's reputation is particularly fearsome, and his exploits are known throughout the shipping lanes. With each new telling of the tales, the bugbear becomes more of a monster. Some of the speakers exaggerate the extent of his cruelty, but not by much.

If you seed these stories into your game early, the PCs should not hesitate to pursue Gnash when a local lord places an enormous bounty on the pirate's head. Of course, tracking him down is just the start of their trouble: The longer they chase the bugbear, the odder things become. The PCs learn that though the members of Gnash's crew are goblinoids, many of them have been twisted by whatever power they serve and now exhibit strange physical deformities. By talking with survivors in the charred ruins of the villages that Gnash has destroyed, the party discovers that the mad captain is searching for a lost city. Eventually, the PCs learn the truth about his intentions, and at that point, the campaign changes tone. The characters are no longer merely hunting a rogue pirate, but saving the world.

CAPTAIN GNASH IN EBERRON

Captain Gnash spent most of his pirate career sailing the waters south of Darguun, but as his feverish dreams continued to worsen, he found himself venturing deeper and deeper into the Sea of Lost Souls. Members of his crew are becoming concerned; although their captain still raids coastal villages and sacks ships, the band's take from these assaults is small and sporadic. Worse, Gnash has been spending much of his time in his quarters, and rarely appears before the crew. His crew was on the verge of mutiny, until the captain burst out of his chambers and called for a new course—turning the ship toward the mysterious continent of Xen'drik.

CAPTAIN GNASH IN FAERÛN

Gnash was part of a band of goblinoid pirates that prowled the Trackless Sea, raiding the small settlements scattered throughout the Nelanther Isles. Originally the first mate under Captain Scab, a brutal ogre, he served his master loyally—until the *Much Kill* came upon a remote, uncharted island. Exploring the place, the crew discovered an ancient, abandoned city, and Gnash located an old temple. Newly filled with hatred and madness after his visit to that place, he led a mutiny and took command of the *Much Kill*. Today, Captain Gnash still searches for the lost city, but along the way he is content to harass human pirates and plunder their treasures.

APPEARANCE AND BEHAVIOR

Captain Gnash is a hulking brute of a bugbear. He stands just under 7 feet tall and has a bulky frame. His patchy black fur is matted with dried excrement and old blood, but he covers the worst of it with black breeches and studded leather. Though his armor is enchanted, it is no cleaner than the rest of him, stained dark with sweat and with the gore of countless victims.

Despite his great size, Gnash prefers the weapons of a dexterous fighter. From a belt cinched around his waist hangs a fine rapier; the weapon has a sharkskin-wrapped handle and an ornate basket hilt studded with ovoid pieces of jet. When boarding an enemy ship or attacking a settlement, Gnash always straps his steel shield onto his arm. Tied to the spikes that protrude from its surface are cords that hold fingers and toes of his previous victims.

Madness-inducing visions fill the bugbear's mind, but his insanity does not interfere with his cunning in battle. He is a shrewd strategist, and his crew owes much of their success to his brilliant maneuvers. Once invested in a fight, Gnash loathes leaving it; thus, he never attacks unless he can be assured of victory.

His crew has one standing order: Always take thirteen prisoners from any attack or raid. Gnash feeds these living captives to a terrifying creature that he keeps in the ship's hold. He believes that the sacrifices placate the horror and ensure that it will continue to grant him the "dark blessings" he endures when he sleeps. (Gnash does not know it, but the creature is a kython; for details, see tactical encounter 4–3, page 78. In truth, it has nothing to do with his nightmares, but he nonetheless considers it to be Shothotugg's emissary.) Crew members that fail to deliver the required sacrifices are fed to the beast instead; thus, the goblinoids almost always comply with their disturbed captain's wishes.

Captain Gnash **CR 9**
hp 72 (10 HD)

Male bugbear rogue 5/dread pirate[CAd] 2
CE Medium humanoid (goblinoid)
Init +5; **Senses** darkvision 60 ft., scent; Listen +4, Spot +9
Languages Common, Goblin, Orc

AC 26, touch 16, flat-footed 21; uncanny dodge
(+5 Dex, +5 armor, +2 shield, +1 deflection, +3 natural)
Resist evasion
Fort +6, **Ref** +16, **Will** +6

Speed 30 ft. (6 squares)
Melee *+1 rapier* +13/+8 (1d6+5/18–20) or
Melee *+1 rapier* +10/+5 (1d6+5/18–20) and
+1 spiked light steel shield +9 (1d4+2)
Ranged mwk light crossbow +13 (1d8/19–20)
Base Atk +7; **Grp** +11
Atk Options Maiming Strike, Quick Draw, sneak attack +3d6
Combat Gear 2 flasks alchemist's fire, *potion of blur, potion of cure light wounds, potion of cure moderate wounds,* 5 smokesticks, 2 tanglefoot bags

Abilities Str 18, Dex 20, Con 16, Int 13, Wis 12, Cha 13
SQ seamanship, trap sense +1, trapfinding
Feats Evil Brand[B] (see page 24), Iron Will, Maiming Strike (see page 25), Quick Draw, Two-Weapon Fighting[B], Weapon Finesse
Skills Appraise +11, Bluff +6, Climb +11, Diplomacy +3 (+5 evil creatures), Disguise +1 (+3 acting), Hide +8, Intimidate +8 (+10 evil creatures), Jump +7, Knowledge (geography) +3, Listen +4, Move Silently +12, Profession (sailor) +11, Search +6, Spot +9, Survival +1 (+3 following tracks), Swim +10, Tumble +8, Use Rope +9
Possessions combat gear plus *+2 studded leather, +1 spiked light steel shield, +1 rapier,* masterwork light crossbow with 20 bolts, *ring of protection +1, cloak of resistance +1,* 1 gp

Seamanship (Ex) Gnash gains a +2 insight bonus on Profession (sailor) checks. The bonus extends to all allies within his sight or hearing.

Fecar the Unclean

"At first, Gnash seemed mad. I was certain that whatever he found in that city had shattered his mind. Over the last few years, though, I found myself coming to share his vision, and now I look forward to the day when the World Eater arrives."

—Fecar the Unclean

From the beginning, Fecar the Unclean has been one of Captain Gnash's most loyal allies. The two were fast friends for years, setting aside the natural rivalry that exists between bugbears and hobgoblins, and spending long nights swilling ale and playing cards. When Gnash took charge of the remnants of the ogre's marauders, Fecar followed. In return for his loyalty, Gnash named him first mate.

Goals

Although Captain Gnash counts Fecar as one of his most trusted minions, the hobgoblin has plans of his own. Fecar rightly believes that Gnash will eventually expend every member of his crew in his mad quest to find his coveted lost island, discarding carelessly those who die along the way. Fecar agrees that finding the island is paramount, but he has no intention of being sacrificed with the others. Instead, he looks for an opportunity to kill his comrade and take command himself.

Aware of the dangers of leading a mutiny, Fecar has been slow to recruit other crew members in case they reveal his treachery. He watches and waits, listening to the grumbles of the pseudonatural goblins. If one expresses dissatisfaction with the captain, Fecar plucks him from the crew and tortures him until he is convinced that the goblin is on his side. These interrogations are often fatal, and only reinforce Gnash's belief that Fecar is his staunchest supporter—because the captain wrongfully believes that Fecar is discovering and dispatching mutinous soldiers, The goblinoids that survive Fecar's abuse are horribly scarred, but they become unwaveringly loyal to the first mate.

Fecar knows that if he does manage to murder Gnash and take command, he will still have to deal with what the crew calls "the thing in the hold." The monster is loyal to the captain and considers the bugbear to be its mother. To gain the thing's trust and affection, Fecar volunteered for the dangerous task of feeding captives to the monster. Again, Gnash misinterpreted this action as proof of the hobgoblin's allegiance. Now, after weeks of taking its meals from Fecar, the kython has begun to come around, occasionally favoring the first mate with a few splashes of its slippery mucus.

Using Fecar

When the *Much Kill* sails into port, Fecar and a hand-picked team of goblinoids scout the community and search for clues about the lost city or anything else that will help them. As they nose around, they also steal food, weapons, and other equipment before returning to the ship to report their findings. In ports that are particularly hostile to goblins, the *Much Kill* drops anchor in a nearby cove, and the spies infiltrate the city under the cover of darkness. Since Captain Gnash uses this tactic to judge a city's strength before he gives the order to attack, the PCs are likely to encounter

Fecar on one of his forays before they set eyes on the ship or the rest of its crew.

Appearance and Behavior

Fecar has earned the moniker "the Unclean" because a putrid odor follows him wherever he goes. A mixture of brine, sweat, and cheese, the stench comes from his unwillingness to bathe, and his body is covered with leprous sores and colonies of vermin that feast on the sour excreta.

His clothing is similarly soiled, and the once-beautiful artistry of his enchanted mithral shirt is lost beneath years of accumulated filth. His breeches are tattered and torn, stained with pale rings of salt and sweat. Fecar wears old boots stolen from a human captive. When he takes them off; the ghastly stink of his feet is strong enough to repel even the crustiest sailors.

The hobgoblin delights in causing pain, and he giggles with sadistic glee in combat. Whenever he lands a sneak attack, he shrieks with pleasure, laughing for several seconds before he renews his assault.

Fecar the Unclean — CR 7

hp 48 (7 HD)

Male hobgoblin rogue 3/hexblade[CW] 3/scarlet corsair[SW] 1
CE Medium humanoid (goblinoid)
Init +4; **Senses** darkvision 60 ft.; Listen –1, Spot –1
Languages Common, Goblin

AC 21, touch 14, flat-footed 17; Dodge, Mobility (+4 Dex, +5 armor, +2 shield)
Resist evasion, mettle
Fort +4, **Ref** +10, **Will** +3; +3 against spells and spell-like effects

Speed 30 ft. (6 squares); Spring Attack
Melee *+1 longsword* +9/+4 (1d8+3/19–20) or
Melee dagger +8 (1d4+2/19–20)
Ranged mwk composite longbow +11/+6 (1d8+2/×3)
Base Atk +6; **Grp** +8
Atk Options Improved Feint, sneak attack +2d6
Special Actions hexblade's curse 1/day
Combat Gear flask of alchemist's fire, *potion of bear's endurance, 2 potions of cure light wounds, oil of magic weapon,* tanglefoot bag

Abilities Str 15, Dex 18, Con 14, Int 10, Wis 8, Cha 16
SQ trap sense +1, trapfinding
Feats Dodge, Improved Feint[B], Mobility, Spring Attack
Skills Appraise +2, Balance +10, Bluff +12, Climb +6 (+8 ropes), Diplomacy +5, Disguise +3 (+5 acting), Escape Artist +4 (+6 ropes), Hide +8, Intimidate +14, Jump +9, Knowledge (geography) +2, Listen –1, Move Silently +12, Profession (sailor) +4, Spot –1, Swim +7, Tumble +11, Use Rope +9
Possessions combat gear plus *+1 mithral shirt, +1 buckler, +1 longsword,* dagger, masterwork composite longbow (+2 Str bonus) with 20 arrows, *ring of swimming*

Mettle (Ex) If Fecar makes a successful Will or Fortitude save against an attack that normally would have a lesser effect on a successful save (such as any spell with a saving throw entry of Will half or Fortitude partial), he instead negates the effect.

Hexblade's Curse (Su) Once per day as a free action, Fecar can select one visible target within 60 feet and impose a –2 penalty on the target's attack rolls, saves, ability checks, skill checks, and weapon damage rolls for 1 hour unless the target succeeds on a DC 14 Will save.

Illus. by J. Hodgson

Fecar the Unclean

Pog the Navigator

"We owe a great debt to Captain Gnash. We were bound in stone, and he freed us. For ninety-nine turns of the moon, we shall serve him, guiding his ship to the far ends of the world if he requires it."

—Pog the Navigator

When Captain Gnash dropped anchor near a tiny island alone in the middle of a cerulean sea, he thought that he had reached the end of his mission—but alas, it was not the isle that appeared in his nightmares. This one held little more than bent trees, clusters of rock, and a stone statue of a goblin. Intrigued by the statue, Gnash brought it on board, hoping that it was a sign from Shothotugg. He assigned a rotation of crew members to watch the statue day and night, for fear that he might miss some vital clue.

Not surprisingly, the statue remained immobile and unyielding. Eventually it occurred to Gnash that the stone figure might actually be a petrified creature. One day while the ship was in port taking on supplies, the captain brought aboard a wizard he had hired to remove the enchantment. The wizard cast his spell, and—lo and behold!—the statue became a living creature.

Thus was the goblin named Pog released from a long period of petrification. Pog vowed ninety-nine months of service to Captain Gnash as a measure of thanks, and today he serves as the *Much Kill*'s navigator.

GOALS

Pog's time as a statue has left him embittered and full of hatred, though he hides his rage beneath a veneer of serenity. The moment he was released from his stony prison, Pog recalled the circumstances of his fate. He remembered being betrayed by his companions on that small, lonely island, left to be worn away by wind and rain. He has forgotten a few minor aspects of the treachery—such as the identities of those who abandoned him—but sees these details as irrelevant to his quest for revenge.

The goblin sees an opportunity in Gnash and his mad designs. Each time the *Much Kill* descends on a village, Pog snoops around for some sign of the former friends who left him for dead. Though he remembers nothing about them, their deceit still burns in his soul, and he intends to make them pay for his lost years.

So far, Pog has found only one of the traitors, an elf cleric who served the sea god. The goblin thought it was strange that the elf had no recollection of him—or of ever traveling with a goblin—but he still tortured the priest for days before ending the miserable creature's life. Occasionally, when his captive sobbed and pleaded for mercy, Pog felt doubts begin to surface, but he swiftly quashed them.

Pog the Navigator

USING POG

Although Pog is certain that he was the victim of some terrible betrayal, this is not the case. In truth, he lived on the remote island with several other goblins; together, they sought to tear open a hole in the fabric of reality and create a permanent gate to the another plane. The human, elf, and other faces that Pog vaguely recalls are those of adventurers who came to the island to thwart the goblins' sinister plot. These events happened nearly a century ago, so everyone involved is either dead or well beyond Pog's reach.

Thus, his victims are innocent of the crime he claims they have committed. There's no telling when a stranger's name, voice, or facial expression might trigger one of Pog's "memories," but when it does, the goblin sets all else aside. He moves to take his target alive so that he can force the so-called traitor to confess—at which point he cuts the victim's throat.

To Pog, the *Much Kill* is just a convenience. On an emotional level he cares nothing for Gnash, the crew, or their goals, and has pledged his service because it suits his purpose for now. Even though the goblin has pledged his service for a long time, he would not hesitate to turn on Gnash if the captain ever becomes too much of a liability. Pog might leave, throw in with mutineers, or simply kill the bugbear if the circumstances demand it.

Appearance and Behavior

Even for a goblin, Pog is short, just under 3 feet tall. He's thin, malnourished, and more than a bit ragged. While he was petrified, the elements scoured the contours of his body, softening or removing his hair and facial features. When he was restored, he awakened to sheer agony, his sinew and muscle bloody and exposed. Now, months later, his body is covered in patches of scar tissue. His face is almost completely smooth, with only a suggestion of a nose and no lips. Pog's eyes bulge out of his skull, held in place by exposed sinew that he moistens with a special salve, hoping that eventually it will restore his flesh. Fully aware of his unsightly appearance, the goblin wraps his slight body in a voluminous cloak, even though the ship's crew—many of whom are grotesquely misshapen themselves—barely seem to notice his looks.

Pog's physical deformities are matched by a deranged mind. He always refers to himself in the plural, and he suffers from frequent hallucinations and flashbacks that leave him trembling and dazed. When nervous, he picks at his skin, ripping away old scabs and tearing open the scars until he regains his composure.

Pog **CR 7**

Male goblin conjurer 7
CE Small humanoid (goblinoid)
Init +2; **Senses** darkvision 60 ft.; Listen +1, Spot +1
Languages Common, Draconic, Giant, Gnoll, Goblin, Orc

AC 15, touch 14, flat-footed 13; Dodge
(+1 size, +2 Dex, +1 armor, +1 deflection)
hp 24 (7 HD)
Fort +4, **Ref** +5, **Will** +7

Speed 35 ft. (7 squares)
Melee shortspear +3 (1d4–1)
Ranged mwk heavy crossbow +7 (1d8/19–20)
Base Atk +3; **Grp** –2
Atk Options Sudden Still
Special Actions *abrupt jaunt*[PH2] 4/day
Combat Gear *potion of cure moderate wounds*
Wizard Spells Prepared (CL 7th; prohibited schools evocation and necromancy):
4th—*dimensional anchor* (+6 ranged touch), *dimension door, solid fog*
3rd—*dispel magic, fireball* (DC 17), *haste, nauseating breath*[SC] (DC 17)

Illus. by K. Tanner

2nd—*baleful transposition*SC (DC 16), *blur, cloud of bewilderment*SC (DC 16), *Melf's acid arrow* (+6 ranged touch), *see invisibility*
1st—*color spray* (DC 15), *expeditious retreat, feather fall, lesser orb of sound*SC (+6 ranged touch), *obscuring mist, shield*
0 —*acid splash* (2) (+6 ranged touch), *detect magic, read magic*

Abilities Str 8, Dex 14, Con 12, Int 18, Wis 13, Cha 6
SQ tattoo spellbook
Feats Combat Casting, DashCW, Dodge, Scribe ScrollB, Sudden StillB CAr
Skills Climb +4, Concentration +11, Hide +6, Knowledge (arcana) +14, Knowledge (geography) +14, Listen +1, Move Silently +6, Ride +6, Spellcraft +16, Spot +1, Survival +1 (+3 avoid hazards and getting lost), Swim +4
Possessions combat gear plus shortspear, masterwork heavy crossbow with 10 bolts, *ring of protection +1, bracers of armor +1, cloak of resistance +1,* 2 *Quaal's feather tokens (anchor),* small steel mirror, spell component pouch, spyglass
Spellbook spells prepared plus 0—all except for evocation and necromancy; 1st—*animate rope;* 2nd—*whispering wind*

Abrupt Jaunt (Sp) As an immediate action, Pog can teleport up to 10 feet in any direction. He may not bring along other creatures. To gain this alternative class feature, Pog gave up the ability to summon a familiar.
Tattoo Spellbook (Ex) Pog's body is a living spellbook and the spells he knows are tattooed directly onto his flesh. See *Complete Arcane* page 186 for details.

If you use *Expanded Psionics Handbook,* replace Pog's statistics block with the following one.

Pog **CR 7**
hp 34 (7 HD)

Male blue nomadEPH 7
CE Small humanoid (goblinoid, psionic)
Init +2; **Senses** darkvision 60 ft.; Listen +1, Spot +1
Languages Common, Draconic, Giant, Gnoll, Goblin, Orc

AC 15, touch 14, flat-footed 13; Dodge, Psionic Dodge (+1 size, +2 Dex, +1 armor, +1 deflection)
Fort +4, **Ref** +5, **Will** +7

Speed 30 ft. (6 squares); Speed of Thought
Melee shortspear +3 (1d4–1)
Ranged mwk heavy crossbow +6 (1d8/19–20)
Base Atk +3; **Grp** –2
Combat Gear *breath crisis pearl, cognizance crystal 1, potion of cure moderate wounds, power stone of biofeedback, power stone of body adjustment, power stone of psionic levitate*
Power Points/Day: 61; **Powers Known** (ML 7th):
4th—*death urge*A (DC 18), *psionic dimensional anchor* (+5 ranged touch)
3rd—*dispel psionics*A, *energy burst*A (DC 17), *eradicate invisibility*A (DC 17), *time hop*A (DC 17)
2nd—*concealing amorpha, dimension swap*A, *energy stun*A (DC 16), *thought shield*A
1st—*burst, catfall*A, *know direction and location, mind thrust*A (DC 15), *vigor*A
A: Augmentable

Abilities Str 8, Dex 14, Con 12, Int 18, Wis 13, Cha 6
SQ naturally psionic
Feats Combat ManifestationB, Dodge, Psionic Body, Psionic DodgeB, Speed of Thought
Skills Climb +9, Concentration +11, Knowledge (geography) +14, Knowledge (psionics) +14, Listen +1, Move Silently +6, Psicraft +16, Ride +6, Spot +1, Survival +1 (+3 to avoid natural hazards and getting lost), Swim +9
Possessions combat gear plus shortspear, masterwork heavy crossbow with 10 bolts, *ring of protection +1, bracers of armor +1, cloak of resistance +1,* 2 *Quaal's feather tokens (anchor),* spyglass

MUCH KILL

The *Much Kill* is a massive black sailing ship that spreads mayhem and suffering wherever it travels. Twice the size of an ordinary ship of the same structure, it is notorious for shattering smaller vessels, scattering timber and corpses in its wake. The ship's hull and three masts are dark, oozing the cheap resin that was used to seal the wood. The *Much Kill* flies crimson sails from its masts, and the sole black flag snapping from the mainmast bears a red demonic skull atop two red crossed bones.

The caravel has a crew complement of about thirty-five goblins, hobgoblins, and bugbears, many of which are the same creatures that swore service to Captain Gnash in the ruins of the lost city. They scuttle about the ship like roaches, attending to the lines and sails and doing their part to keep the vessel seaworthy. A ship full of goblinoids would be strange enough, but many have become pseudonatural creatures, and their malignant deformities—tentacles, eyestalks, and worse—make the pirates of the *Much Kill* among the most feared in all the seas.

KEY FEATURES

Despite its massive proportions, the *Much Kill* is as quick and agile as its smaller cousin ships. The caravel has a main deck, a lower deck, and a hull, as well as a quarterdeck at the aft and a forecastle at the bow. The bowsprit—the long pole at the front—is solid iron and ends in a harpoon barb. Hanging from the pole are rotting corpses that bob and twist as the ship cuts through the waves. Red sails hang from the yards on three sturdy masts. Severed hands, ears, and feet (taken from prisoners fed to the thing in the hold) decorate the masts, and many of the sailors shake the hands, stroke the feet, or whisper into the ears for good luck.

DEFENSES

The *Much Kill* is a floating fortress. The hull is nearly 2 feet thick and reinforced with iron plates, while steel rings encircle the masts to help protect them from attack. Twin ballistae at each end of the ship fire heavy harpoons, attached to long coils of rope, into enemy ships or large sea creatures, which are then reeled in for food.

Each member of the crew is a capable warrior, as savage and cruel as First Mate Fecar. Some of them have become pseudonatural creatures, their bodies sprouting strange growths and mutations, thanks to the disruptive influence of the Eater of Worlds.

The ship's hold serves as a prison for a kython—a terrible monster conjured from the screams of the mad. Insatiable, the creature needs regular feeding, and when too many days pass without a meal, Gnash is forced to drop one of the crew into the hold. The captain keeps the monster because he believes that it helps to guide him in faithful service to Shothotugg.

AREA DESCRIPTIONS

The *Much Kill* is a large caravel crawling with activity. There are few ways to infiltrate the ship, and adventurers who intend to make a direct assault against Captain Gnash on the deck of his own vessel are in for a tough go.

1. The Sea: Sharks infest the waters around the ship, drawn by the promise of regular feeding. The crew dumps scraps and buckets of offal over the rail to keep them close. At any given time, there are 1d4+1 Medium sharks, 1d3 Medium sharks and 1 Large shark, or 1d3–1 Medium sharks and 1 Huge shark swimming around the hull of the ship.

2. Sterncastle: The crew can reach the sterncastle by two ladders. In the center of the deck is the mariner's wheel, where Pog (see above) spends most of his time peering through a spyglass and making course corrections. A bugbear steers the ship, enduring Pog's shrill insults with incredible patience, and a hobgoblin operates each ballista. Two davits lead to the ship's boats, each of which holds up to twelve Medium passengers (if they squeeze in tightly).

Bugbear Pilot: hp 13 (3 HD); *MM* 29.

Hobgoblins (2): hp 6 each (1 HD); *MM* 153.

3. Forecastle: The forecastle holds the anchor and two ballistae that can fire anywhere in a 90-degree arc. Coils of rope litter the deck, as do scraps of food and old body parts that the pirates kick around when bored. Second Mate Crunglutch spends most of his time here, barking orders through a mass of gelatinous tentacles oozing from his face. Each ballista is operated by a pseudonatural hobgoblin. For their statistics, see tactical encounter 4–1, page 74, but add the following line.

Ranged *+1 ballista* –1 (3d8/19–20)

CRUNGLUTCH, SECOND MATE CR 2

hp 16 (3 HD)

Male pseudonatural[CAr] bugbear
CE Medium outsider (augmented humanoid, goblinoid, native)
Init +1; **Senses** darkvision 60 ft., scent; Listen +4, Spot +4
Languages Common, Goblin

AC 17, touch 11, flat-footed 16
(+1 Dex, +2 armor, +1 shield, +3 natural)
Resist acid 5, electricity 5; **SR** 13
Fort +2, **Ref** +4, **Will** +1

Speed 30 ft. (6 squares)
Melee morningstar +5 (1d8+2)
Ranged heavy crossbow +3 (1d10/19–20)
Base Atk +2; **Grp** +4
Atk Options true strike
Special Actions alternate form

Abilities Str 15, Dex 12, Con 13, Int 10, Wis 10, Cha 9
Feats Alertness, Weapon Focus (morningstar)
Skills Climb +3, Hide +4, Listen +4, Move Silently +6, Spot +4
Possessions leather armor, light wooden shield, morningstar, heavy crossbow with 10 bolts, pouch containing 2d12 gp

True Strike (Su) As the *true strike* spell, 1/day.
Alternate Form (Su) As a standard action, Crunglutch can assume the form of a grotesque, tentacled mass of dripping tissue. While he is in this form, his opponents take a –1 morale penalty on attack rolls.

4. Crew Quarters: Bunks fill this large room. All crew members except for Pog and the officers sleep here in shifts. When every bed is taken, which is often the case, the rest of the crew sleeps on the main deck or on the galley floor.

Since the pirates work in shifts, the crew quarters always has 1d10 goblins, 1d6 hobgoblins, 1 bugbear, 1d6 pseudonatural goblin pirates (see tactical encounter 4–1, page 74), and 1d3 pseudonatural hobgoblin pirates (see tactical encounter 4–1).

Goblins (1d10): hp 5 each (1 HD); *MM* 133.

Hobgoblins (1d6): hp 6 each (1 HD); *MM* 153.

Bugbear: hp 16 (3 HD); *MM* 29.

5. Captain's Quarters: This filthy room serves Captain Gnash as his living quarters. It stinks of sweat, and unspeakable foulness stains the bunk. On a writing desk in the corner

Illus. by R. Horsley

The Much Kill

is a pile of identical drawings, each depicting a huge black disc with smudged edges.

Gnash spends much of his time here, leaving the day-to-day operation of the ship to his first and second mates. He writes nonsense on the walls or hunches over his desk, wildly sketching new pictures of the Eater of Worlds. If the *Much Kill* comes under attack, he bursts out of his quarters to direct the crew's response.

6. **Wardroom:** This room serves as the officer's mess. Captain Gnash, Pog, and the other officers take their meals here, and except for Gnash, they all spend time here when not on duty. The room holds little more than a large table and six chairs. At any given time, the table holds the remains of the last meal or two.

7. **Galley:** The galley is a chamber of horrors. Arms, legs, and torsos hang from hooks set in the ceiling. A butcher block stands in the center; a huge, stained knife is stuck into it. The floor is sticky with gore, and bold dire rats snatch morsels as they slough off the bones. The ship's cooks, a pair of pseudonatural hobgoblins (see page 75), pass time arguing over the finer points of roasting human flesh.

Dire Rats (2d4): hp 5 each (1 HD); *MM* 64.

8. **Pog's Quarters:** When he is not navigating on the sterncastle or taking meals in the wardroom, Pog stays in his quarters. He tolerates the crew well enough, but has no affection for them or their deformities. The room is sparsely furnished with a bunk, a small chest of spare clothes, and a padded chair. Aside from the possessions mentioned in his statistics block, Pog owns nothing of value.

9. **Fecar's Quarters:** This appalling room makes the galley seem pleasant by comparison. It is stripped of everything but a darkly stained mattress on the floor. The walls, floor, and ceiling are splashed with gore, on which maggots dine and flies drop their eggs. Fecar sleeps here when he must, but otherwise spends most of his time elsewhere.

10. **Brig:** This filthy chamber holds prisoners until Gnash is ready to sacrifice them to the thing in the hold. The floor is covered with old straw and excrement, and a sludge-caked bucket sits next to the door. Captives are never fed, since Gnash does not waste food on something he intends to kill anyway.

11. **Crunglutch's Quarters:** A simple cabin equipped with a bunk, desk, lamp, and chair, these quarters hold little of interest. As with the first mate, Crunglutch is frequently busy and rarely in his quarters.

12. **Chain Locker:** This room holds a long coil of heavy chain, which passes up through the ceiling and onto the forecastle, where it is attached to the anchor. Additionally, spare sails, coils of rope, and other supplies clutter the floor.

SHIP STATISTICS

The *Much Kill* is a beefed-up version of the caravel—a relatively advanced type of sailing ship. The statistics block presented here summarizes the most important characteristics of the ship for use in a combat situation. The *Stormwrack* supplement contains much more information on waterborne vessels.

Much Kill

Colossal caravel
Seaworthiness +4

AC section 3, rigging 1
Hull Sections 48 (sink 12)
Section hp 120 (hardness 8); **Rigging hp** 80 (hardness 0)

Speed wind × 30 ft. (average)
Melee ram (6d6)
Ranged 4 +1 *ballistae* (3d8/19–20)
Mounts 4 light
Space 120 ft. by 20 ft.; **Height** 20 ft. (draft 20 ft.)
Complement 60; **Watch** 14
Cargo 240 tons

Seaworthiness: The ship's overall sturdiness. This modifier is applied to any Profession (sailor) checks the captain or master makes in order to avoid foundering, sinking, and hazards that large, well-built vessels avoid more easily than small and frail ones.

AC: The AC of each hull section (see below) and the AC of the rigging (which comes into play when attackers are trying to eliminate or reduce a ship's mobility).

Hull Sections: The number of hull sections the ship possesses.

Sink: The number of destroyed hull sections necessary to sink the ship outright.

Section hp: The number of hit points and the hardness of each hull section.

Rigging hp: The number of hit points and the hardness of each rigging section.

Melee: The damage dealt by the vehicle per 10 feet of speed it currently possesses if it rams another object. For example, a ship with a base ram damage of 6d6 deals 6d6 points of damage if moving at a speed of 10 feet, 12d6 at a speed of 20 feet, and so on.

Ranged: The damage dealt by any projectile weapons the ship possesses. The attack bonus for a ranged attack is based on the creature operating the weapon, modifier for the difference in size between the weapon and the creature. In the case of a ballista (see *DMG* 100), which is a Huge weapon, a Medium creature takes a –4 penalty on its attack roll when operating the weapon.

Mounts: The number of weapons the ship can mount. A light mount is suitable for a ballista. (The *Much Kill* has four ballistae, two on the forecastle and two on the sterncastle.)

Space: The length and width of the area taken up by the ship.

Height: The height of the main deck above the waterline. Most vessels of Huge or larger size have deckhouses, forecastles, or sterncastles that are above this level.

Draft: The amount of the ship's overall height that lies below the waterline.

Complement: The number of crewmembers, passengers, and soldiers who can be carried by the vessel for extended voyaging. For a short voyage (a day or less) a ship might be able to cram two or three times this number of individuals on board.

Watch: The number of crew members necessary to make course changes, adjust for wind changes, and generally handle the ship. Usually the watch consists of a helmsman, a lookout or two, and a small number of deck hands who can go aloft to change the set of the sails as necessary.

Cargo: The capacity of the vehicle's hold, in tons (1 ton = 2,000 pounds). Most ships are slowed to 3/4 normal speed if carrying half this load or more.

The Much Kill

One square = 5 feet

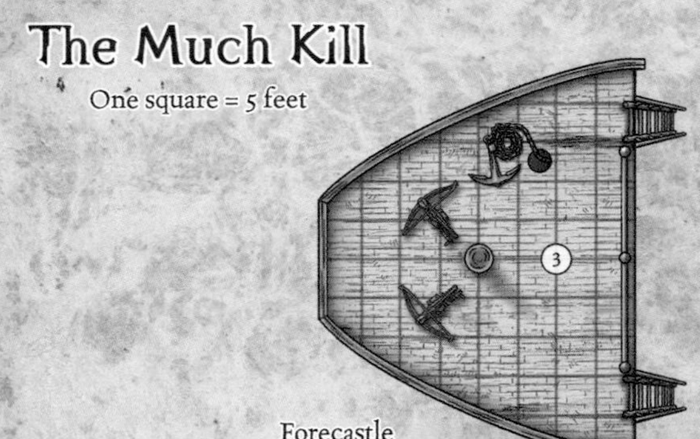

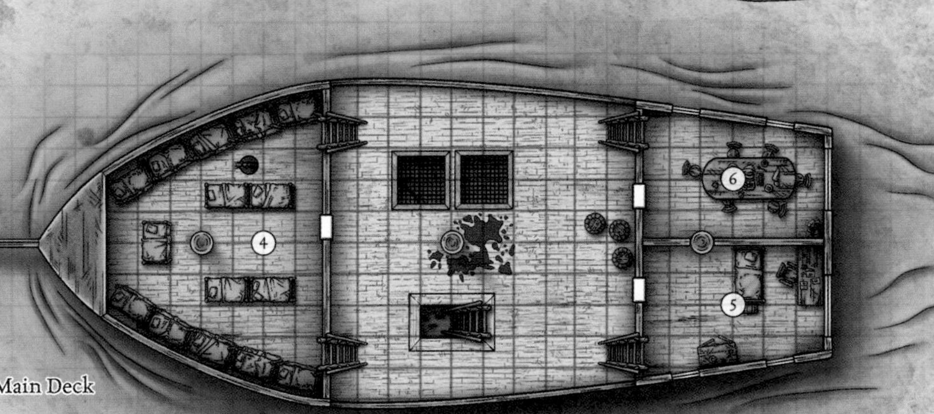

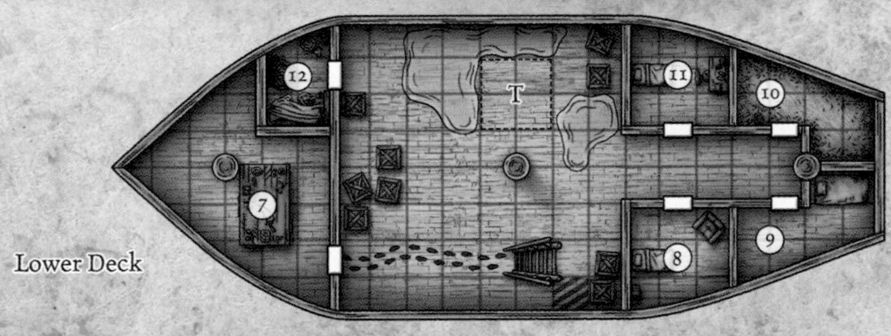

Main Deck

Encounter Level 7

SETUP

The main deck of the *Much Kill* is a busy place. Pseudonatural goblins (G) and pseudonatural hobgoblins (H) go about their business: swabbing the deck, attending to the sails, and avoiding the attention of Crunglutch, who watches their work from the forecastle (area 3). High above the main deck, a goblin lookout hides in the crow's nest (C).

When the PCs first spot the Much Kill, read:

A massive black caravel plows through the waves, propelled by a strong wind that fills its crimson sails. A black flag snaps in the wind, showing a red demonic skull above a pair of crossed bones.

As the characters draw closer, read:

The ship is ghastly. Freshly severed heads hang from the rails, dripping blood onto the ravenous sharks that circle the vessel. Rotting corpses hang from the barbed iron pole at the front of the ship, twisting and breaking apart as the ship cuts through the waves. The deck and rigging crawls with goblins, hobgoblins, and bugbears—but these are no ordinary goblinoids. Purple tentacles emerge from their flesh, eye stalks sprout from their heads, and their features drip and writhe, transforming before your very eyes.

TACTICS

When combat begins, three goblins and two hobgoblins have not yet assumed their alternate forms. On the first round, they do, and then they maneuver to flank any PCs who come aboard.

The other three goblins lob javelins at any player characters who are not yet on the main deck. The other two hobgoblins use their *true strike* ability and then either load their crossbows (if targets are available) or move to engage an opponent in melee.

Once the goblins have exhausted their javelins, they draw morningstars, use true strike, and fling themselves into melee. All of the goblinoids fight to the death.

The goblin lookout begins combat hidden in the crow's nest 30 feet above the deck. He pops up and fires crossbow bolts at the character closest to his location, targeting a spellcaster in preference over someone else if two intruders are the same distance away. Then he drinks his *potion of blur* and continues his barrage.

Goblin Lookout — CR 2

hp 16 (4 HD)

Male goblin rogue 3/fighter 1
CE Small humanoid (goblinoid)
Init +6; **Senses** darkvision 60 ft.; Listen +2, Spot +10
Languages Goblin

AC 16, touch 13, flat-footed 14
(+1 size, +2 Dex, +3 armor)
Resist evasion
Fort +3, **Ref** +7, **Will** +3

Speed 30 ft. (6 squares)
Melee mwk longsword +4 (1d6–1/19–20)
Ranged +1 *light crossbow* +7 (1d6+1/19–20)
Base Atk +3; **Grp** –2
Atk Options sneak attack +2d6
Combat Gear *potion of blur*

Abilities Str 9, Dex 14, Con 10, Int 9, Wis 14, Cha 6
SQ trap sense +1, trapfinding
Feats Improved Initiative, Lightning Reflexes, Rapid Reload (light crossbow)[B]
Skills Balance +10, Climb +5, Hide +12, Jump +7, Listen +2, Move Silently +6, Profession (sailor) +8, Ride +6, Spot +10, Tumble +10
Possessions combat gear plus masterwork studded leather, masterwork longsword, +1 *light crossbow* with 20 bolts

6 Pseudonatural Goblins — CR 1/3

hp 5 each (1 HD)

Male pseudonatural[CAr] goblin warrior 1
CE Small outsider (augmented humanoid, goblin, native)
Init +1; **Senses** darkvision 60 ft.; Listen +2, Spot +2
Languages Goblin

AC 15, touch 12, flat-footed 14
(+1 size, +1 Dex, +2 armor, +1 shield)
Resist acid 5, electricity 5; **SR** 11
Fort +3, **Ref** +1, **Will** –1

Speed 30 ft. (6 squares)
Melee morningstar +2 (1d6)
Ranged javelin +3 (1d4)
Base Atk +1; **Grp** –3
Atk Options true strike
Special Actions alternate form

Abilities Str 11, Dex 13, Con 12, Int 10, Wis 9, Cha 6
Feats Alertness
Skills Hide +5, Listen +2, Move Silently +5, Ride +4, Spot +2
Possessions leather armor, light wooden shield, morningstar, 3 javelins, 1d6 sp

True Strike (Su) As the *true strike* spell, 1/day.
Alternate Form (Su) As a standard action, a pseudonatural goblin can assume the form of a grotesque, tentacled mass of dripping tissue. While a goblin is in this form, its opponents take a –1 morale penalty on attack rolls.

4 PSEUDONATURAL HOBGOBLINS **CR 1**
hp 13 each (2 HD)

Male pseudonatural[CAr] hobgoblin warrior 2
CE Medium outsider (augmented humanoid, goblinoid, native)
Init +1; **Senses** darkvision 60 ft.; Listen +2, Spot +2
Languages Common, Goblin

AC 15, touch 11, flat-footed 14 (+1 Dex, +3 armor, +1 shield)
Resist acid 5, electricity 5; **SR** 12
Fort +5, **Ref** +1, **Will** –1

Speed 30 ft. (6 squares)
Melee longsword +3 (1d8+1/19–20)
Ranged light crossbow +3 (1d8/19–20)
Base Atk +2; **Grp** +3
Atk Options true strike
Special Actions alternate form

Abilities Str 13, Dex 13, Con 14, Int 10, Wis 9, Cha 8
Feats Alertness
Skills Hide +3, Intimidate +0, Listen +2, Move Silently +3, Spot +2
Possessions studded leather, light steel shield, longsword, light crossbow with 10 bolts, pouch containing 1d12 gp

True Strike (Su) As the *true strike* spell, 1/day.
Alternate Form (Su) As a standard action, a pseudonatural hobgoblin can assume the form of a grotesque, tentacled mass of dripping tissue. While a hobgoblin is in this form, its opponents take a –1 morale penalty on attack rolls.

DEVELOPMENT

This encounter escalates each round after combat begins. Crunglutch (see page 71) watches the fight from the forecastle (area 3) in the first round and joins the melee on the second. If any PCs have not yet boarded the *Much Kill* and are in range, the pseudonatural hobgoblins on the forecastle fire the ballistae at them and then spend the next 2 rounds reloading the weapons. If the PCs engage these hobgoblins, they drop what they are doing and fight to the death.

Additionally, Pog, the bugbear pilot, and two ordinary hobgoblins stand on the sterncastle (area 2). The hobgoblins fire their ballistae at the PCs, following the same tactics as their mutated brethren on the forecastle. The bugbear pilot remains at his station unless attacked.

Pog casts *blur* (or manifests *concealing amorpha*) in the first round and then supports his comrades with *fireball (energy burst)* and *Melf's acid arrow (energy stun)*. However, he has no interest in dying. If half the defenders fall or if he is attacked, Pog retreats, cuts the lines that hold one of the rowboats, and then jumps over the rail, using *feather fall (catfall)* to land gently in the boat. If pursued, the goblin tries to use his powers to destroy the party's vessel, but if escape looks impossible, he surrenders.

If the fight lasts for more than 8 rounds, Captain Gnash explodes out of his quarters. The bugbear uses his crew to flank the PCs and tries to make sneak attacks. He uses Maiming Strike frequently, laughing as he disfigures his foes.

FEATURES OF THE AREA

The area has the following features.

Barrels: Three barrels stand between the doors to the captain's quarters (area 5) and the wardroom (area 6). Characters standing in a space that contains a barrel gain cover.

Ladders: The ship has five ladders. Two lead up to the forecastle, two lead up to the sterncastle, and one leads down to the lower deck. Characters on a ladder who fight opponents standing below them gain a bonus for being on higher ground.

Grates: Two wooden grates serve as cargo hatches that lead down to the lower deck. Moving through a space that contains a grate costs 2 squares of movement. Characters can try to move more quickly, but they must succeed on a DC 10 Balance check or their feet slip through a gap and they fall prone.

Spilled Blood: A great deal of blood has been spilled near the main mast. Characters standing in a square that contains spilled blood must succeed on a DC 5 Balance check each round or fall prone.

Main Mast: The main mast (protruding upward from the spot marked C) provides cover to anyone standing behind it. The mast has AC 3, hardness 5, and 200 hit points. Anyone who tries to climb the mast in an attempt to reach the crow's nest, 30 feet above the deck, must succeed on a DC 15 Climb check.

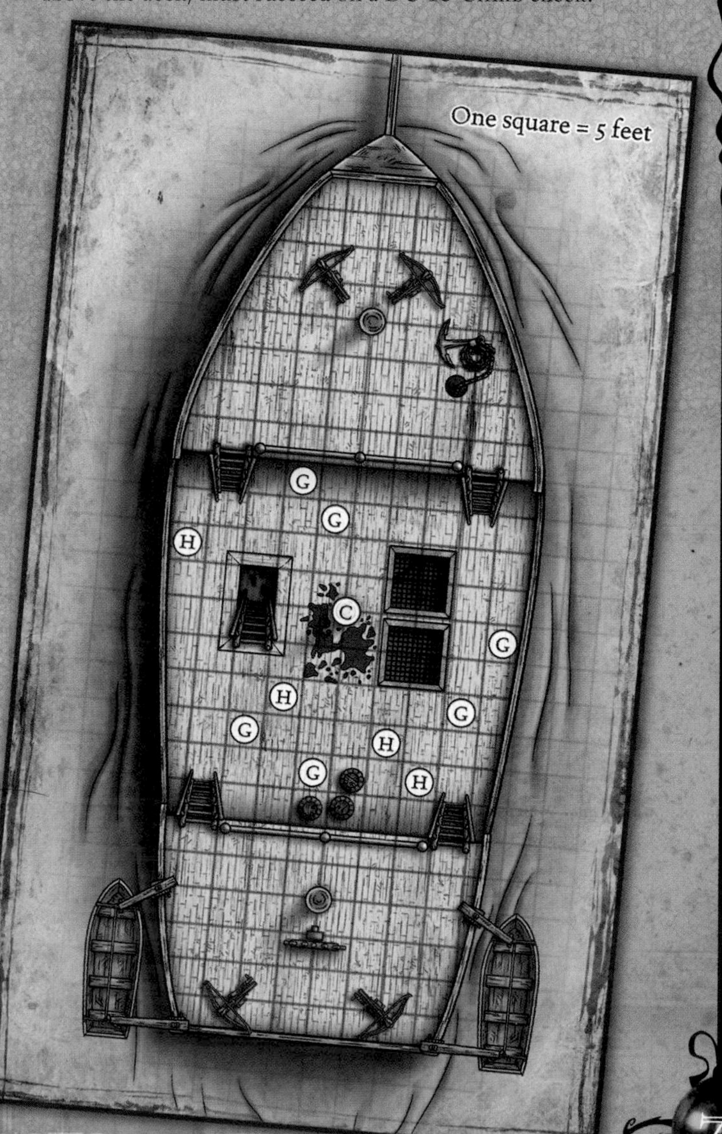

Lower Deck

Encounter Level 9

SETUP

The crew uses the lower deck to store cargo because Gnash insists on keeping the kython in the hold. Crates and boxes are piled in the corners, and water pools on the floor beneath the cargo hatch in the ceiling. The planks are weak in places and sag under pressure.

When the PCs board the *Much Kill*, the sounds of combat from the main deck alert Fecar, who quickly sets up an ambush for the intruders on the lower deck. The map shows the positions of Fecar (F) and a pair of varag barbarians known as Fecar's Boys (V). Just before springing the ambush, the first mate drinks his *potion of bear's endurance* (see his modified statistics below), and each of Fecar's Boys uses his *blur* spell-like ability.

A maximum of three characters can be on the ladder at one time.

When the characters climb down to the lower deck, read:

The stench is particularly foul here, a blend of sweat, blood, and dung. The light from above breaks through the gloom just enough to reveal what looks like a cargo hold. But before you have a chance to assess your surroundings, a filthy hobgoblin springs out of the shadows. The creature screams with rage as it swings its sword.

FECAR THE UNCLEAN **CR 7**
hp 62 (7 HD)

Fort +6
Abilities Con 18
These statistics represent Fecar after he drinks his *potion of bear's endurance*; see page 68 for his full normal statistics.

TACTICS

On their turn, Fecar's Boys each take 5-foot steps to attack the first PCs who come down the ladder. Throughout combat, they use a 5-point Power Attack (+9 attack, +10 damage), regardless of the success or failure of their attacks. They remain at the base of the ladder to restrict entry by other PCs and to make attacks of opportunity against anyone who gets past them. They make full attacks each round for 6 rounds, at which point their *blur* effect ends. For the remaining 3 rounds of their rage, they use Spring Attack to strike and then leap away.

Fecar is more careful. He starts by throwing a tanglefoot bag at the lead character, and while his allies crowd the ladder, he uses Spring Attack to dart in, attack, and leap back, always moving to a space where he can take

2 FECAR'S BOYS **CR 5**
hp 81 each (6 HD); **DR** 5/magic

Male half-farspawn[LoM] varag[MM4] barbarian 3
CE Medium outsider (augmented humanoid, goblinoid, native)
Init +8; **Senses** blindsight 60 ft., darkvision 60 ft., scent; Listen +12, Spot +9
Languages Goblin

AC 18, touch 12, flat-footed 18; uncanny dodge (+4 Dex, +4 armor, +6 natural, –2 rage)
Miss Chance 20% *blur*
Immune poison
Resist acid 10, electricity 10; **SR** 16
Fort +12, **Ref** +8, **Will** +7

Speed 70 ft. (14 squares); Run, Spring Attack
Melee *+1 greatsword* +14 (2d6+13/19–20) and 2 tentacles +8 each (1d4+3)
Space 5 ft.; **Reach** 5 ft.
Base Atk +5; **Grp** +13
Atk Options magic strike, rage 1/day (9 rounds)
Special Actions change shape
Combat Gear *elixir of hiding, potion of cure moderate wounds*
Spell-Like Abilities (CL 6th):
3/day—*blur*†
1/day—*stinking cloud* (DC 14), *touch of idiocy* (+15 melee touch)
† Already used once

Abilities Str 22, Dex 19, Con 22, Int 4, Wis 16, Cha 12
SQ trap sense +1
Feats Improved Initiative, Power Attack, Run[B], Spring Attack[B]
Skills Intimidate +4, Jump +29, Listen +12, Move Silently +18*, Spot +9, Survival +9 (+13 tracking by scent)
*Fecar's Boys can always choose to take 10 on Move Silently checks, even if rushed or threatened.
Possessions combat gear plus *+1 studded leather, +1 greatsword*

Change Shape (Su) Fecar's Boys can transform into horrid, tentacled masses. The ability works as *change shape* (*MM* 306), except as follows: Their movement modes remain unchanged; they retain their tentacle attacks; they become amorphous and immune to flanking and critical hits; and creatures native to the Material Plane take a –1 penalty on attack rolls against Fecar's Boys.

Magic Strike (Su) Fecar's Boys' natural weapons are treated as magic weapons for the purpose of overcoming damage reduction.

When not raging, Fecar's Boys use the following statistics.
hp decrease by 12
AC 24, touch 14, flat-footed 20
Fort +10, **Will** +5
Melee *+1 greatsword* +12 (2d6+10/19–20) and 2 tentacles +6 each (1d4+3)
Grp +11
Special Actions change shape, true strike
Abilities Str 18, Con 18
Skills Jump +27
True Strike (Su) As the *true strike* spell, 1/day.

Features of the Area

The room has the following features.

Illumination: Weak light streams down from the space at the top of the ladder and through the grating of the cargo hatch. The lower deck remains in shadowy illumination, and everyone in the area has concealment.

Ceiling Height: The ceiling in this room rises 7 feet overhead.

Crates: Crates and boxes are scattered around the lower deck. Characters standing in a space containing a crate gain cover.

Footprints: Bloody footprints emerge from the door to the galley (area 7) and stop at the foot of the ladder. The unsettling marks are empowered with fell energy, and evil characters standing in a space that includes a footprint gain a +1 profane bonus on attack rolls and weapon damage rolls.

Ladder: The ladder leads up to the main deck. Characters on the ladder who fight opponents on the lower deck gain a +1 bonus on attack rolls for being on higher ground.

Doors: Several doors lead to other rooms, as shown on the map of the ship (page 73). Each door is unlocked and has hardness 5 and 10 hit points.

Exterior Walls: Each section of the ship's hull has hardness 8 and 120 hit points. If any 5-foot section of the hull is breached, water pours into the lower deck. If twelve sections of the hull are breached, the caravel sinks.

Interior Walls: The lower deck's interior walls have hardness 5 and 60 hit points.

Weak Floor: The floorboards are weak and rotting. Each 5-foot section has hardness 2 and 30 hit points. Medium or larger characters who step on the square that has diagonal shading fall through the floor and land in the hold. They take 1d6 points of damage from the fall and must contend with the kython (see tactical encounter 4–3 on the next page).

Water on Floor: Any creature that enters a square containing water must make a successful DC 10 Balance check to avoid slipping and falling prone.

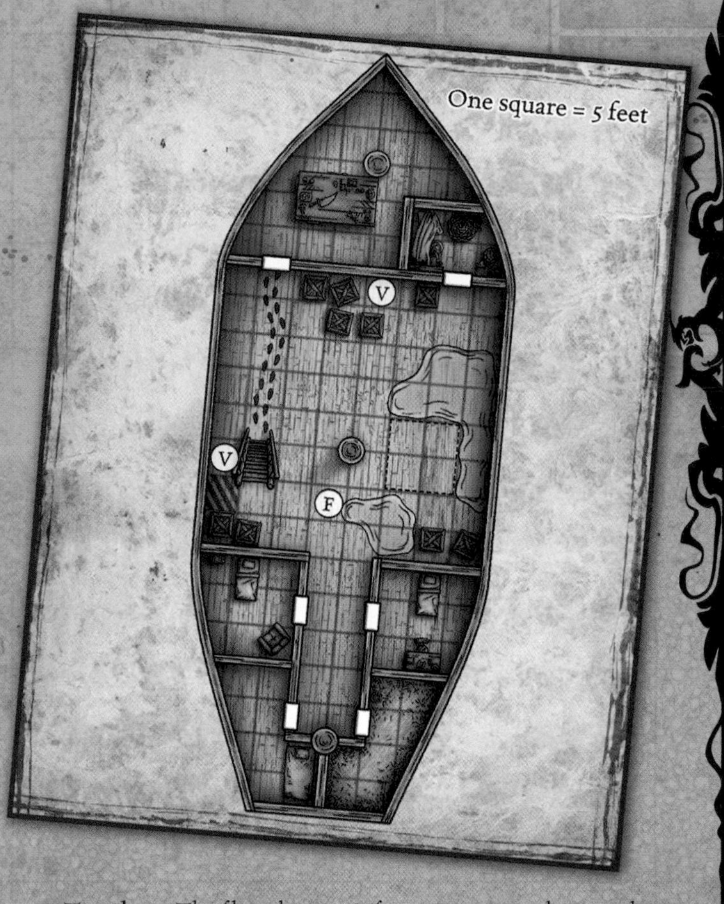

Trapdoor: The floor has a 10-foot-square trapdoor in the space indicated by the dashed line. A successful DC 10 Strength check opens it, revealing the hold below, but there is no ladder to climb down.

Masts: The masts (circular symbols along the center line of the ship) provide cover to anyone standing behind them. Each mast has AC 3, hardness 5, and 200 hit points.

advantage of sneak attack. Fecar uses the Dodge feat against the strongest PC in the group. If the adventurers push past the barbarians, Fecar bestows a hexblade's curse on any character who appears to be some kind of warrior, banking on the possibility that the PC will not be able to resist.

Since escape from the lower deck is unlikely, Fecar and his Boys fight to the death. However, if defeat seems imminent, the first mate breaks his flask of alchemist's fire, hoping to set the ship aflame and take the PCs down with him.

DEVELOPMENT

After 3 rounds of combat, the two hobgoblins in the galley (area 7) join the battle. Heedless of danger, the cooks fight recklessly.

If a section of the hull takes enough damage to spring a leak, water starts pouring in. One or more holes in one section of the hull will not jeopardize the ship, but the water also runs down into the hold below, and the sudden cold shower makes the kython quite unhappy. After 1d6 rounds, it begins roaring and hammering at the floorboards over its head. Each round that the creature pounds the lower deck, all characters standing on the deck must succeed on a DC 10 Balance check or be knocked prone.

THE HOLD OF MADNESS

Encounter Level 10

SETUP

On one of Gnash's many adventures, he discovered a strange, rubbery egg. Believing it was a gift from his insane master, he placed it in the ship's hold. To his surprise, the egg hatched, revealing an otherworldly creature. The thing grew rapidly, and seemed content in the hold as long as it ate regularly. Lately, more and more water has collected in the hold, bringing with it various parasites (including bloodbloaters) that thrive in the stagnant pool. The kython tolerates the cold, fetid water for now, but if the level rises much higher, it is certain to break free.

Disturbances such as combat or flashy spellcasting (*lightning bolts* and the like) send the kython (K) scuttling into the shadows and cause the bloodbloaters (B) to quiver.

If any PCs on the lower deck peer down through the trapdoor, read:

The stench from what looks like a half-flooded cargo hold is overpowering. In the square of light cast by the open trapdoor, you can see the ribs of the ship sticking up out of the dark water. A pale, wrinkled human hand floats on the oily surface.

If the PCs descend, read:

The hold is dark, and the light from above does little to illuminate your surroundings. The thigh-deep water is cold, black, and greasy. Down here, the foul odor is so strong that you find yourself breathing as little as possible.

If the PCs have a light source or use darkvision, read:

Something massive stirs and splashes toward the aft, unfolding itself to reveal a vaguely humanoid creature armored in chitin plates. Its enormous oblong head splits, showing multiple rows of teeth webbed with thick strings of drool. The creature hisses, then surges through the water toward you.

THE THING IN THE HOLD **CR 9**

hp 209 (22 HD)

Male advanced adult kython[BoVD]
NE Large aberration
Init +7; **Senses** blindsight 60 ft.; Listen +12, Spot +2
Languages Abyssal, Infernal

AC 23, touch 11, flat-footed 24; Dodge, Mobility
(–1 size, +2 Dex, +12 natural)
Immune acid, cold
Resist electricity 20, fire 20
Fort +12, **Ref** +9, **Will** +15

Speed 45 ft. (9 squares); Spring Attack
Melee bite +23 (4d6+8/19–20 plus poison) and
3 claws +22 each (2d6+4) and
claw +22 (2d6+4 plus mucus pod)
Space 10 ft.; **Reach** 10 ft.
Base Atk +16; **Grp** +28
Atk Options Cleave, Power Attack, mucus pod, poison (Fort DC 21, 1d6 Str/1d6 Str)

Abilities Str 27, Dex 14, Con 20, Int 10, Wis 14, Cha 11
Feats Cleave, Dash, Dodge, Improved Critical (bite), Improved Initiative[B], Mobility, Multiattack[B], Power Attack, Spring Attack, Weapon Focus (claw)
Skills Escape Artist +13, Hide +14, Jump +12, Listen +12, Move Silently +17, Spot +2, Use Rope +2 (+4 bindings)

Mucus Pod (Ex) A target struck by a kython's fourth claw attack is sprayed by yellow mucus from a pod on the creature's arm. The target must succeed on a DC 26 Reflex save or become entangled for 1d6+4 rounds. Alcohol dissolves the entangling mucus.

7 BLOODBLOATERS[FF] **CR 1**

hp 22 each (2 HD)

N Medium ooze (aquatic, swarm)
Init +1; **Senses** blindsight 60 ft.; Listen –5, Spot –5
Languages none

AC 11, touch 11, flat-footed 10
(+1 Dex)
Immune critical hits, flanking, mind-affecting spells, weapon damage, single-target spells, vision-based effects, poison, *sleep*, paralysis, polymorph, stunning
Fort +6, **Ref** +1, **Will** –5
Weakness vulnerability to area spells and fire

Speed 5 ft. (1 square), swim 30 ft.
Melee swarm (1d6 plus 1 Str)
Space 5 ft.; **Reach** 0 ft.
Base Atk +1; **Grp** +1
Atk Options blood drain
Special Actions distraction

Abilities Str 10, Dex 13, Con 22, Int —, Wis 1, Cha 1
SQ amphibious, ooze traits (*MM* 313), swarm traits (*MM* 315)
Feats —
Skills Listen –5, Spot –5, Swim +8

Blood Drain (Ex) In each round when a bloodbloater swarm deals at least 1 point of damage to a target, it also drains blood and causes 1 point of Strength damage.

Distraction (Ex) Any PC who begins his turn with a swarm in his square must make a successful DC 17 Fortitude save or be nauseated for 1 round. Spellcasting or concentrating on spells requires a successful Concentration check (DC 20 + spell level). Using skills involving patience and concentration requires a DC 20 Concentration check.

TACTICS

Once the PCs are aware of the kython, it wastes no time in attacking. It uses Spring Attack and a 10-point Power Attack on its first full action, then moves toward the thickest cluster of bloodbloaters in the hope of luring the PCs to them. If the characters take the bait, the kython holds its position and makes a full attack each round, modified by a 7-point Power Attack. If it fells any PCs, it leaves them for the bloodbloaters to finish. The kython spreads its attacks among several PCs, but if it entangles a character in a mucus pod, the creature focuses its full attention on that character, using a 13-point Power Attack for each attack until the victim is dead.

The kython continues to use Spring Attack to provoke the PCs into closing with it. After 2 rounds, if they have not done so, the creature gives up and closes on them.

The bloodbloaters move toward the PCs. Since they have to negotiate the beams that stick up out of the water, they travel only 1 square per move action. These mindless combatants gorge themselves on blood and will not pursue a living character if an unconscious or dying victim is closer.

CONCLUSION

If the PCs manage to destroy the kython in its lair without sinking the ship, they gain 1-1/2 times the normal experience points due to the treacherous environment.

Treasure: The dark water hides various items that belonged to the kython's victims. Each round when a PC examines the hold and succeeds on a DC 15 Search check, he finds 1d20 gp (a total of 1,120 gp is scattered across the bottom of the hold). In addition, a searching character has a 20% chance of finding one of the following items:

- a divine *scroll of bear's endurance* in a watertight tube
- *oil of shillelagh* in a sealed ceramic container
- a *potion of protection from chaos* in a tightly stoppered glass vial
- a *wand of magic missile* (CL 1st, 42 charges)
- a dark orange *fire elemental gem*

FEATURES OF THE AREA

The area has the following features.

Illumination: Light streams through the trapdoor and the grating of the cargo hatch, providing shadowy illumination in the area directly below the trapdoor. Any creatures standing in that area gain concealment. The rest of the hold is dark, granting total concealment to its occupants.

Ceiling Height: The ceiling in the hold rises 7 feet overhead.

Trapdoor: The ceiling contains a trapdoor in the space indicated by the dashed lines. From within the hold, a PC can push the trapdoor open by making a successful DC 10 Strength check.

Beams: Parallel beams—the skeleton of the *Much Kill*—crisscross the floor of the hold. Each beam is approximately 1 foot wide. A character can move across the slippery beams at half speed by succeeding on a DC 12 Balance check. Those who move faster than half speed take a –5 penalty on the check. Anyone who fails the check by 5 or more slips into the brackish water. The kython does not have its movement impaired in the hold and can move freely throughout the area.

Water: Water to a depth of 3 feet fills the gaps between the beams. Because the floor is uneven, PCs cannot run or charge while in the hold. If a character is not standing on a beam, entering a water-filled square costs 2 squares of movement.

Exterior Walls: Each section of the ship's hull has hardness 8 and 120 hit points. If any 5-foot section of the hull is breached, water pours into the lower deck. If twelve sections of the hull are breached, the caravel sinks.

Interior Walls: The remains of the hold's interior walls have hardness 5 and 60 hit points. They provide cover to anyone standing behind them.

Debris: Spaces marked with debris are choked with broken timbers, sodden rubbish, and the remains of the kython's meals. Moving into one of these spaces costs 1 extra square of movement.

Masts: The masts (circular symbols along the center line of the ship) provide cover to anyone standing behind them. Each mast has AC 3, hardness 5, and 200 hit points.

Illus. by J. Chan

Sometimes I wake up drenched in sweat. In my dreams, I see myself murdering Pietro while she stands there, laughing. Now, I inhabit her flesh, maintaining her dark alliances and darker schemes. The sins of both our pasts live unwelcome in this body. I must destroy them all to cleanse us of evil."

—Calais Archwinter as Tamesik

Calais Archwinter was an elf priestess of Corellon Larethian, an adventurer, and an opponent of tyranny. Tamesik was a drow priestess, the mastermind behind an illicit trade ring known as the Chelicerata. When they met in battle, Tamesik lost her life, and Calais lost her identity. Cursed to inhabit the drow's body, Calais became what she hated the most. Since her transformation, she has descended toward evil, furthering the drow's plots and intrigues. Fractured and twisted, her mind dwells on only one thing: vengeance.

BACKGROUND

Calais Archwinter was a priestess of Corellon Larethian and part of Freedom's Lance, a band of adventurers. The Lance was famous for its struggle against slavery and corruption. In addition to Calais, its members included Lylok, a human traps expert; Rionan, a barbarian; and Pietro, a half-elf wizard and Calais's lover. Together, the four heroes fought for the downtrodden, the forgotten, the orphaned, and the homeless. They were about to settle down, at least temporarily, when they caught wind of illegal activity in the city where they were based.

Believing that the criminal organization was only a minor threat, the Lance investigated with little fear. Hoping to end their most recent adventuring escapades on a high note, the group followed a lead to a warehouse near the docks. Casing the building, they saw what appeared to be a normal storage facility, filled with crates and staffed by a handful of guards. They did not realize that what they saw was only an illusion—a ruse engineered by Tamesik, a cunning and vicious drow priestess and a powerful servant of Lolth.

Tamesik ran a black-market operation known as the Chelicerata out of the warehouse, which sat above a subterranean complex. Through a tunnel that ran from the building into the Underdark, Tamesik and her drow minions could move illegal goods without being detected.

However, Tamesik was extremely paranoid, and when her spies reported that the adventurers known as Freedom's Lance were in town, she became concerned. Rather than risk allowing the do-gooders to learn the truth, she led them directly into a trap.

Calais and her comrades were ambushed when they entered the warehouse. Trapped in the building by guards and magical defenses, they had no choice but to fight their way out. They took heavy damage, but eventually wiped out the first wave of adveraries. Afterward, though, more powerful drow continued to emerge from the tunnel.

As the battle continued, the drow used potent magic to neutralize Rionan and Lylok, but Calais and Pietro remained. The two adventurers fired back with magic of their own, taking out many dark elves. For a short time, it seemed that Tamesik had underestimated the party, and the drow were nearly defeated.

Then Calais fell victim to a *confusion* scroll. In a frenzy, she turned on Pietro, killing him with her mace, and then attacked the heavily wounded drow priestess. Tamesik attempted to escape, but Calais charged her, stabbing the drow repeatedly with a fallen dagger.

As Tamesik was brutalized, she beseeched the Spider Queen to curse her foe by turning Calais into whatever she hated the most. Lolth answered. In the blink of an eye, the body of the drow priestess changed shape, taking on the form of the elf, and the body of Calais transformed into a perfect likeness of Tamesik. Lolth had not seen fit to heal the former drow body of its wounds, however, and so Tamesik had only a moment of bewilderment before she died.

Coming out of her *confused* state, Calais was shocked by the carnage and the transformation. Not only were her companions dead—Pietro by her own hand—but her own corpse lay at her feet as well. The remaining drow, ignorant of the switch, quickly escorted who they thought was their mistress into the safety of the Underdark. Calais, traumatized and terrified, played along as well as she could, expecting to be identified as an impostor and killed at any moment.

But she was not discovered, perhaps because Lolth felt that a quick end would not have fulfilled the real Tamesik's dying curse. Time passed, and as Calais adapted to her situation, she realized that she had not only the form but also the abilities of the drow priestess. She decided then that the switch had been a blessing in disguise from Corellon Larethian: a chance to bring new powers to bear against the hated drow and to destroy their evil from within.

Calais took steps to learn Tamesik's mannerisms, scrying on other drow to see their impressions of her. She studied her foe's business dealings and came to know her minions and lackeys. Realizing that she would arouse suspicion if she dismantled the Chelicerata, Calais decided that she must continue Tamesik's activities to mask the fact that she was subtly destroying her enemy's legacy.

However, on some level, Calais was only fooling herself. As she descended further into the persona of Tamesik, she lost her faith and morals. Something had snapped in her mind during the transformation. Calais began to justify immoral acts as necessary evils, which appeased her conscience but did not satisfy Corellon Larethian. The deity withdrew his support, judging her unfit for his faith.

At that moment, Lolth stepped in to fill the void. The transition was so smooth that Calais did not notice the change. The domain of Chaos, which Lolth shared with Corellon happened to be the one domain that Calais had access to. Subconsciously, Calais made other changes that allowed her to keep believing that she remained a priestess of Corellon. Somewhere in her mind, Calais knew that she was no longer a force for good in the world. But she ignored the warning signs, justifying the changes however she could and ignoring the reality of her fall from grace.

In her manipulation of Tamesik's affairs, Calais has become just as ruthless as the drow priestess ever was. She uses her new form and abilities as weapons of revenge against anyone connected to the Chelicerata, including human nobles, drow investors, and unwitting merchants. In her troubled mind, anyone involved with the organization deserves to die. Most of her machinations involve finances, but she also hires assassins to terrorize and kill those who displease her. Calais wants to punish Tamesik and her supporters for their wicked ways, and for the evil acts that they have supposedly forced her to commit.

GOALS

Each day, Calais wrestles with her life's contradictions: She hates drow, but she revels in the power of her position and the respect she receives from her minions. On good days, she furthers her scheme to destroy the Chelicerata, weakening the major players and pitting the dark elves against their corrupt human allies. On bad days, she wallows in misery, lashing out at her minions and victims. This erratic and unstable personality is what makes Calais so dangerous. When in control of her mental faculties, she tries not to harm innocents. When consumed by hatred, she sees enemies everywhere.

When her personality changes, so does the nature of her goals. Her primary objective is to weaken and polarize the drow and their human allies. To this end, Calais foments rebellious gossip among the drow houses, disseminates rumors that pit factions against each other, and orders her followers to attend revels in disguise, inciting talk about deceptions and betrayals. She hopes to corrode the power structure of the dark elves and spark an open war. Her minions are eager to follow her orders, duped into believing that their mistress seeks to create a void so that the Chelicerata can fill it.

If Calais focused her energies entirely on the drow, she might never come into conflict with residents of the surface world. Unfortunately for her, however, her manic episodes force confrontations. During her fits, she suspects everyone of collusion with the drow. She directs her minions to attack merchant caravans, searching for evidence of corruption, and orders the assassination of prominent citizens, attempting to weed out potential threats. Usually her targets are evil, but sometimes she sends her squads after the wrong people, and innocents die. During these raids, her minions also terrorize the families of the victims. Calais encourages this behavior at the time, but after her personality shifts back, she is horrified by the results of her hatred.

Even if Calais truly wanted to stop committing evil acts, she would find it nearly impossible: She cannot reverse Tamesik's dying curse, and her mental illness compels her to seek revenge on anyone associated with the trade ring. Moreover, vengeance is really all that Calais has left. Her adventuring companions died in the battle against the drow, and her former friends and allies among Corellon's faithful believe that she met a similar fate. Too proud (and too scared) to consider suicide, Calais is left with nothing but the loyalty of Tamesik's minions and her burning desire for retribution.

USING THIS VILLAIN

Calais is an extremely resourceful villain. She can cast an eclectic variety of offensive and defensive spells, as well as divinations and countermagic, so she is rarely caught unprepared. Furthermore, her extreme paranoia drives her to consider many eventualities and make plans far in advance.

Still, Calais acknowledges her limits. She keeps plenty of minions and lackeys on hand, prizing versatility and rewarding success. Unlike many villains, she is relatively kind to her underlings, though she sometimes punishes them unfairly during her delusional fits. Though she never apologizes for her explosions, she always makes it up to the servants she wrongs.

Calais tries to be a faceless villain, hiding under her *hat of disguise* and subtly spreading gossip and rumors. She might pose as a mysterious benefactor and hire the PCs for missions; alternatively, she could give the party tips about drow activities and evil nobles, acting as a source of information. Her true nature could remain hidden for quite some time, but when Calais is caught up in one of her fits, she is less able to spin a convincing story. If the PCs manage to capture or corner her, she might crumble under interrogation. If truly pressed, she tearfully explains how she was forced into the body of a drow and how she is doing the best she can to poison the dark elves from within. She leaves out the most reprehensible details of her behavior since then, but she sticks to the truth about the rest of her history.

Because of her misfortune, the PCs might find it easy to view Calais as a sympathetic villain. Many characters, especially those of chaotic alignment, might find her actions to be fairly reasonable. Some will not fault her for manipulating and harming drow. Calais tries hard to encourage these perceptions while playing down her role in the raids on nobles and their families. If she succeeds, some of the PCs might be moved to help her escape from the Underdark, while others might go so far as to assist in her scheme to weaken the dark elves.

Regardless of whether Calais wins any of the PCs to her side, it eventually becomes clear that she does not deserve their aid. When the characters learn that she has ordered the murders of innocents, including children, they will turn against her. Calais does everything in her power to keep tabs on the PCs, however, and if she thinks that they are becoming suspicious of her, she tries to distract or eliminate them before they can act.

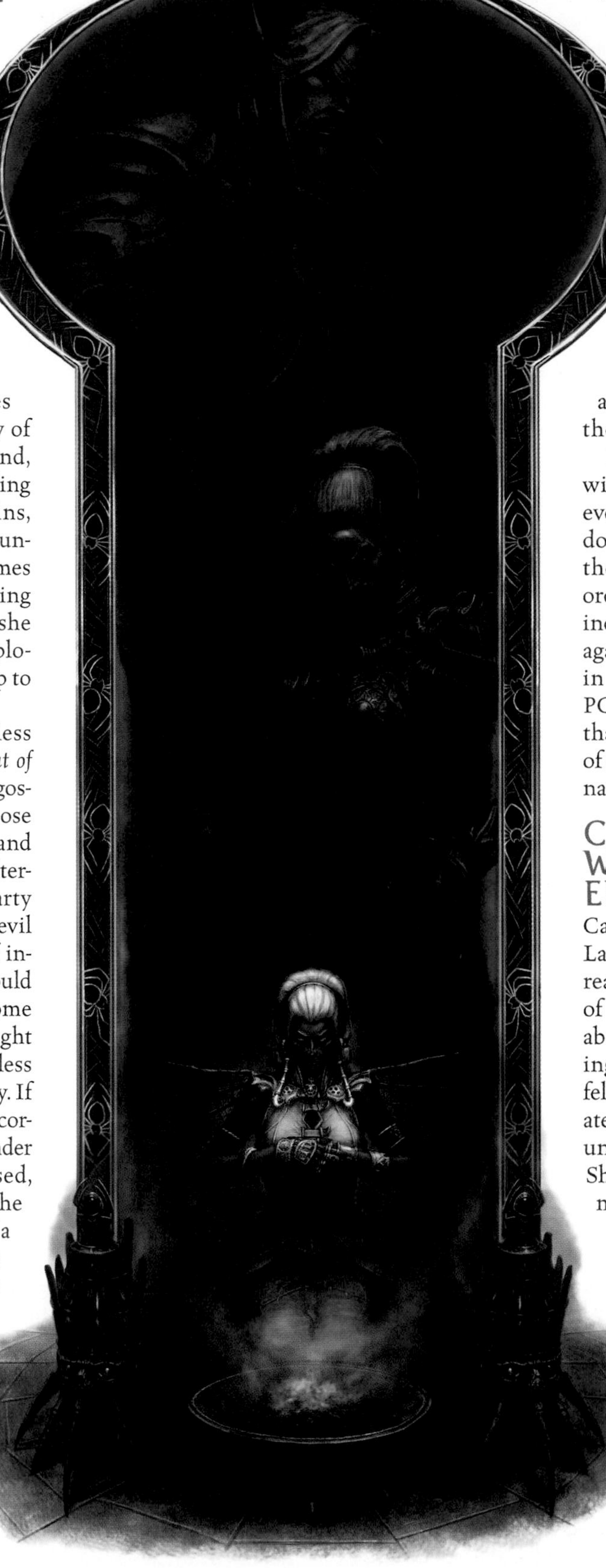
Calais Archwinter

Illus. by M. Phillippi

CALAIS ARCHWINTER IN EBERRON

Calais and the rest of Freedom's Lance were returning to Stormreach when they caught the scent of corruption. Rumors circulated about a high-end slave ring operating off the coast. The adventurers fell into a trap, and Calais now operates Tamesik's organization in and under a warehouse near the docks. She sees the growing drow settlements as a cancer in the heart of Stormreach.

Tamesik had forged alliances with corrupt trade organizations and unsavory mercenaries, including Thrush Xivdrad, a rogue thunder guide. She assassinated officials from many major merchant groups, though they do not suspect her.

Most members of the Chelicerata are drow from splintered Xen'drik, but the organization also includes Sulatar drow and Umragen refugees from besieged Qabalrin. Their resentment against surface dwellers leads them to support Calais.

In Eberron, Tamesik was never a priestess of Lolth, but instead worshiped the Mockery (as an aspect of Vulkoor). Calais still worships Corellon Larethian, but he is a hero honored by the Valenar in their warrior-ancestor religion, not the head deity of the elves.

In opposition to the Valenar, Tamesik had been trying to insinuate her drow into Khorvaire by creeping through the upper levels of Khyber. Considering her people to be the true heirs of elven power, she had hoped to build a base of strength from which to exert greater influence. Her ambition had been divinely inspired—a wave of hubris from Vulkoor. Under the influence of Lolth, a minor demon lord, the scorpion god has grown more prideful, filling his followers with racial zeal. The new powers that Calais wields are partially a manifestation of Vulkoor's divinity and partially derived from Lolth's magic.

CALAIS ARCHWINTER IN FAERÛN

After their latest adventure, Calais and her band of heroes were recuperating in Waterdeep when Rionan received a visit from Myrnd Gundwynd, the leader of the Black Boar Tribe. Myrnd passed along a rumor about a slave ring involving House Gralhund, Anteos, and Rosznar.

Myrnd was unaware of the true depth of the situation. Tamesik was running an illicit trade ring and trafficking with three houses, but few people realized that drow were behind the operation. When Calais and her party stumbled into the warehouse, they were ambushed by dark elves.

Today, posing as Tamesik, Calais controls the trade ring from the warehouse in the docks, using a secret tunnel to Skullport to hide from the Watch. She is on good terms with the slavers, mercenaries, and nobles from Gralhund, Anteos, and Rosznar.

APPEARANCE AND BEHAVIOR

Tamesik was a common-looking drow female. Lacking the bearing of a noble or the clout of a high priestess, she depended on her intelligence, her thoroughness, and the loyalty of her followers. She ran a tight organization but was not as cruel to her subordinates as most drow priestesses are, allowing for small indiscretions and occasional sloppiness.

In her youth, Tamesik's body had a malnourished appearance. When she began to rise above her roots, she made a concerted effort to soften her features, cultivating the appearance of a highborn drow. She tinted her dark, lustrous hair with henna, bringing out the violet in her eyes. She used garnet dust to highlight her eyes and a tincture of jet and ivory to soften her skin and hide blemishes.

Tamesik watched the highborn priestesses, copying the styles and cuts of their clothing. She favored high collars, elaborate outfits, and expensive jewelry, always dressing in fine garments even for simple meetings and procedures in her sanctuary. Such trappings hid her relatively weak frame and small stature.

Since assuming Tamesik's form, Calais has had no trouble keeping up the drow's appearance. As an elf, Calais had always enjoyed using cosmetics and scented oils. She has also taken up Tamesik's luxurious apartment in the complex below the warehouse. When it comes to personality, though, she occasionally falters. At first, Calais had to keep reminding herself to react to situations with the cold cruelty of a drow, not the warm compassion of an elf. She has grown more comfortable in her role, but she still loses her composure under stress now and then, lapsing into her old mannerisms and speech patterns.

When in control, Calais is quiet, using succinct statements and direct commands to get what she wants. When minions address her, she responds tersely, with phrases such as "So noted," or "I will take that into account." She is more talkative with her two most important minions, a handsome drow warlock named Darzemaan and a mysterious human wizard named Kjarlo.

When in the throes of one of her fits, Calais becomes more vocal: taunting her enemies, scolding her underlings, and reveling in chaos. During these periods, she screams puzzling statements about her true past, such as "Now you know what it's like, Tamesik!" or "This is for Pietro!" These outbursts terrify and confuse her minions. They worry that their mistress has gone mad, unable to differentiate past from present or herself from others. Nevertheless, they still support Calais, because they receive better treatment from her than they would from other elite drow.

CALAIS ARCHWINTER (AS TAMESIK) CR 11

hp 59 (10 HD)

Female drow cleric 10
CE Medium humanoid (elf)
Init +0; **Senses** darkvision 120 ft.; Listen +6, Spot +6
Languages Common, Drow Sign Language, Dwarven, Elven, Gnome, Undercommon

AC 23, touch 11, flat-footed 23
(+9 armor, +3 shield, +1 deflection)
Immune magic *sleep* effects
SR 21
Fort +9, **Ref** +4, **Will** +12 (+14 against spells and spell-like effects)
Weakness light blindness

Speed 20 ft. (4 squares) in full plate, base speed 30 ft.
Melee *+1 heavy mace* +8/+3 (1d8+1)
Base Atk +7; **Grp** +7
Atk Options divine counterspell[CM], Magic Disruption
Special Actions Fell Conspiracy, command undead 5/day (+2, 2d6+12, 10th), spontaneous domain casting[PH2]
Combat Gear *potion of cure serious wounds, potion of neutralize poison,* scroll of *fog cloud,* scroll of *lesser restoration,* scroll of *living undeath*[SC], scroll of *mass bear's endurance,* scroll of *prayer,* 2 flasks of anarchic water[PlH]
Cleric Spells Prepared (CL 10th):
5th—*dispel law*[D] (CL 11th, DC 19), *greater vigor, slay living* (+7 melee touch, DC 19)
4th—*chaos hammer*[D] (CL 11th, DC 18), *freedom of movement, lesser globe of invulnerability*[DM] (CL 11th), *poison* (+7 melee touch, DC 18), *restoration*
3rd—*anticipate teleportation*[SC†,DM], *bestow curse* (DC 17), *magic circle against law*[D] (CL 11th), *know vulnerabilities*[SC] (DC 17), *searing light* (+7 ranged touch)
2nd—*close wounds*[SC], *deific vengeance*[SC] (DC 16), *hold person* (DC 16), *lesser restoration, protection from arrows*[DM] (CL 11th), *shatter*[D] (CL 11th, DC 16)
1st—*alarm*[DM], *bless, divine favor, obscuring mist, protection from law*[D] (CL 11th), *resurgence*[SC]

0—*create water, cure minor wounds, detect magic, guidance, purify food and drink, read magic*
DM: Spell learned through the divine magician[CM] alternative class feature (see below)
D: Domain spell. Domain: Chaos
† Already cast

Spell-Like Abilities (CL 10th):
1/day—*dancing lights, darkness, faerie fire*

Abilities Str 10, Dex 10, Con 12, Int 14, Wis 18, Cha 14

SQ notice secret and concealed doors within 5 feet
Feats Combat Casting, Divine Vigor[CW] (see page 25), Fell Conspiracy (see page 24), Magic Disruption[CM]
Skills Concentration +14 (+18 casting defensively), Knowledge (arcana) +7, Knowledge (religion) +15, Listen +6, Spellcraft +12, Search +4, Spot +6
Possessions combat gear plus *+1 full plate, +1 heavy steel shield, +1 heavy mace, hat of disguise, periapt of Wisdom +2, ring of protection +1, darksteel key**, 275 pp and 43 gp (in a chest in her quarters)
* This small key allows its possessor to control a shadesteel golem as if he had created it. The object looks like an ordinary key but is surrounded by shadowy wisps that draw in light. An *identify* spell reveals the command word necessary to activate the key.

The possessions listed above are only the personal items that Calais carries with her; the trade ring's assets far exceed what is detailed here. If Calais were not so focused on revenge, she might make better use of the resources available to her.

Light Blindness (Ex) Abrupt exposure to bright light (such as sunlight or a *daylight* spell) blinds Calais for 1 round. In addition, she takes a –1 circumstance penalty on attack rolls, saves, and checks when in bright light.
Divine Counterspell Four times per day, Calais can counter a spell as a supernatural ability. This ability functions as *dispel magic,* but uses her cleric level rather than her caster level, with a +2 synergy bonus from Knowledge (arcana) (total bonus of +12).
Divine Magician In exchange for giving up access to a second domain, Calais adds a limited breadth of arcane spells to her cleric spell list. Each time she learns to cast spells from a higher spell level, she adds a single abjuration, divination, or necromancy spell from the sorcerer/wizard list to her list of cleric spells.
Magic Disruption As long as Calais has an abjuration spell prepared, she can disrupt the magic of other spellcasters. As an immediate action, she can force another character casting a spell to make a Concentration check (DC 15 + the level of the highest-level abjuration spell she has available, which is usually *dispel law*). If the check fails, the spell is disrupted. Calais casts abjuration spells at +1 caster level.
Spontaneous Domain Casting Calais can lose a prepared spell (other than a domain spell) to cast a spell from the Chaos domain that is of the same level or a lower level. In addition, she can choose to fill any or all of her domain spell slots with *inflict* spells.

Illus. by M. Phillippi

The two faces of Darzemaan

DARZEMAAN

"Power lies in the perceptions of others. My reputation is my strength."

—Darzemaan

Darzemaan was born into a drow house in a distant part of the world—but when his mother was assassinated, he was cast out. Now a warlock servant of the demon lord Graz'zt, he spends most of his time pursuing luxury.

Darzemaan was recruited by Tamesik when he attempted to *charm* the disguised priestess into handing over her jewels. When she promised him a life of extravagance and power, he joined the Chelicerata. The warlock has proven invaluable in spreading rumors and courting new business associates, as well as in intimidation and collection.

GOALS

Darzemaan's main goal is to become the sole consort of Tamesik; he doesn't realize that she has been replaced by Calais. He constantly butts heads with Kjarlo, her only other significant minion—a spellcaster whose abilities sometimes outshine his own. The next most important minions, a set of drow duskblade triplets, have not shown enough ambition to threaten him.

Darzemaan fears the challenges of living as a drow in the surface world, but enjoys the lazy life afforded by his abilities. The Chelicerata provides him with money, fine accommodations, and occasional amorous dalliances with Calais. If he could dispose of Kjarlo, he would become the only minion of any real power serving the drow priestess.

USING DARZEMAAN

Darzemaan serves as the face of the illicit trade ring. Calais prefers to plot from afar, allowing the charismatic warlock to weave his webs over the merchants of the city. He is the most frequent contact encountered by PCs who deal with Calais.

If the adventurers come into conflict with Darzemaan, they have a significant problem. His contacts, *charmed* servants, and demonic powers make him a dangerous foe. In person, he is most formidable at moderate range, where he can use his voice while avoiding the perils of melee combat. The warlock relies on his social skills and his magical talents, not on dealing massive amounts of damage.

Darzemaan believes that the violent strikes that Calais has ordered against noble families are meant to even the playing field among the drow. He suspects that something is amiss with his mistress, but has shown little interest in finding out more.

Appearance and Behavior

When disguised, Darzemaan appears as a handsome human or half-elf with green eyes and shoulder-length auburn hair. He wears expensive, stylish clothes, cultivating a dashing and dangerous look that is just appealing enough to draw romantic attention.

Among his allies, Darzemaan drops his disguise and takes his true form—that of a tall, handsome drow with long silver hair. His fiery orange eyes mark him as a servant of the demon lord Graz'zt.

When he is at ease, Darzemaan is a pleasant, amiable, and courteous gentleman. He genuinely enjoys socializing and negotiation, but he disdains the drudgery and bookkeeping that business often requires. If the warlock becomes angry, he channels the malevolence of Graz'zt, turning cruel and vicious.

DARZEMAAN **CR 9**
hp 39 (8 HD); **DR** 2/cold iron

Male drow warlock[CAr] 8
CE Medium humanoid (elf)
Init +2; **Senses** darkvision 120 ft.; Listen +2, Spot +2
Languages Abyssal, Common, Drow Sign Language, Elven, Gnome, Undercommon

AC 18, touch 13, flat-footed 16
(+2 Dex, +5 armor, +1 deflection)
Immune magic *sleep* effects
SR 19
Fort +4 (+8 against poison), **Ref** +7, **Will** +7 (+9 against spells and spell-like effects); +1 against spells and spell-like effects produced by good creatures
Weakness light blindness

Speed 30 ft. (6 squares)
Melee mwk rapier +6/+1 (1d6–1/18–20)
Ranged mwk hand crossbow +9 (1d4 plus poison/19–20)
Base Atk +6; **Grp** +5
Atk Options poison (drow poison, Fort DC 13, unconscious 1 minute/unconscious 2d4 hours)
Special Actions deceive item, *detect magic* (at will, as the spell, CL 8th), *eldritch blast* 4d6 (+8 ranged touch, CL 8th), eldritch spear, fiendish resilience
Combat Gear 3 doses drow poison, scroll of *fog cloud*, scroll of *web*, *wand of cure light wounds* (CL 1st, 25 charges)
Invocations Known (CL 9th):
Lesser—*charm* (DC 20), *dread seizure*[DrM] (DC 20)
Least—*baleful utterance* (DC 18), *beguiling influence*, *call of the beast*[CM], *eldritch spear*
Spell-Like Abilities (CL 8th):
1/day—*dancing lights, darkness, faerie fire*

Abilities Str 8, Dex 14, Con 12, Int 16, Wis 10, Cha 20
SQ notice secret and concealed doors within 5 feet
Feats Fiendish Heritage[CM], Fiendish Power[CM], Lightning Reflexes
Skills Bluff +22, Concentration +6, Diplomacy +21, Intimidate +20, Knowledge (arcana) +5, Knowledge (the planes) +5, Listen +2, Search +5, Sense Motive +5, Spellcraft +4, Spot +2, Use Magic Device +16
Possessions combat gear plus *+1 chain shirt, cloak of Charisma +2, ring of protection +1, belt of resistance +1* (as *cloak of resistance*), *hat of disguise,* masterwork rapier, masterwork hand crossbow with 20 bolts, 223 gp

Light Blindness (Ex) Abrupt exposure to bright light (such as sunlight or a *daylight* spell) blinds Darzemaan for 1 round. In addition, he takes a –1 circumstance penalty on attack rolls, saves, and checks when in bright light.

KJARLO THE UNSEEN

"He is searching for me, every minute of every day. I have taken all precautions within my ability, but it's never enough. Eventually, my luck will run out and he will find me."

—Kjarlo the Unseen

Kjarlo is a human on the run. When he was still a student in an academy devoted to the arcane arts, he accidentally destroyed a book of tanar'ri magic while conducting research in the library. The act somehow summoned a demon—a balor known as Déoglaubrach. Luckily for Kjarlo, the balor was momentarily stuck in the cramped library. He tried to slip out while the demon extricated itself, but Déoglaubrach spotted the mortal just as he dashed through the door.

Kjarlo fled the city and kept running, spending a few weeks in each new town as a mage for hire and moving on whenever he heard that a balor had been spotted nearby. Eventually, he joined up with Tamesik, who felt that his abilities would be useful to the Chelicerata. Years of evading pursuit (real or imagined) had honed Kjarlo's skills, shaping him into a highly capable information broker with endless tricks up his sleeve.

Soon after Calais supplanted Tamesik, Kjarlo began to suspect that something was wrong. His divinations have revealed the strange fits that occasionally seize her mind, but he has not yet learned her secret. He has not pushed the point, because the Chelicerata complex is a good place to hide from Déoglaubrach. Still, as an information broker, Kjarlo is an expert in blackmail, and if necessary he will use what little he knows as a bargaining chip.

Kjarlo loathes Darzemaan, whom he considers the epitome of vulgarity. He disdains the drow's excessive use of charms as flagrant abuses of magic. He tries to avoid the warlock, but rarely succeeds.

GOALS

More than anything, Kjarlo wants to be free of Déoglaubrach. The threat of the balor is a constant knot in his stomach, a nervous reminder of the consequences of a single mistake. He tries to remain at top form and perpetually improves his skills, hoping to survive long enough for the chaotic demon to lose interest in the chase and indulge in other torments.

Kjarlo worries that his constant competition with Darzemaan is distracting him from this crucial task. Compounding the problem is the warlock's association with Graz'zt, the Dark Prince of the Abyss. Kjarlo fears that the demon lord is somehow aware of his indiscretion and might feed that information to Darzemaan. If the warlock were to learn his secret, Kjarlo's life would be over.

Illus. by J. Hodgson

Kjarlo the Unseen

USING KJARLO

Like Darzemaan, Kjarlo makes an excellent contact for the Chelicerata. Unlike the warlock, he does not openly display his power, preferring to work from the shadows. If the PCs develop a relationship with Calais or her trade ring, Kjarlo is likely to assist them. Although he guards information with extreme care, he helps the adventurers learn enough to carry out whatever mission Calais gives them.

Kjarlo remains concerned about the change that has come over the drow priestess. He has been suspicious ever since she stepped up her attacks on rival drow; in the past, Tamesik's relationship with other dark elves was competitive, but hardly murderous. Kjarlo is not surprised that a drow might choose to assassinate others of her kind, but the killings began so abruptly that he cannot help suspecting that something is amiss. Given the right motivation, Kjarlo would be willing to delve deeper into the mystery.

Appearance and Behavior

Kjarlo's features are common but pleasing. He has close-cropped black hair, dark gray eyes, and a pale, clear complexion. Despite his relative youth, his perpetual nervousness has caused his face to prematurely age. He wears clothing that is well suited to hiding—dark, muted leathers, long coats, and the like. Although not obsessed with cleanliness, he keeps a sharp appearance, ironing his shirts and starching his collars. He wears little ornamentation, favoring only practical accessories. Even his magical headband and ring are nondescript, thin circles of silver.

Kjarlo's mannerisms are like his appearance: simultaneously precise and nervous. Each day, he catalogs his actions in a locked book that is warded by an *alarm* spell. He wastes little motion, striding quickly and lightly, though his pace—always a few steps faster than it needs to be—reveals a bit of fear. Similarly, he uses few words, preferring to conduct short meetings in which he provides his service, receives his compensation, and departs, all in the space of a few moments.

Kjarlo hates flagrant displays of power and disdains flashy combat spells. In fact, when he uses magic, nearby nonspellcasters often fail to notice—especially if he turns invisible.

KJARLO THE UNSEEN **CR 9**
hp 37 (9 HD)

Male human rogue 1/spellthief[CAd] 1/diviner 3/unseen seer[CM] 4
N Medium humanoid
Init +2; **Senses** Listen +10, Spot +14
Languages Common, Drow Sign Language, Elven

AC 18, touch 13, flat-footed 16
(+2 Dex, +5 armor, +1 deflection from tattoo)
Fort +5, **Ref** +8, **Will** +13

Speed 30 ft. (6 squares)
Melee mwk short sword +7 (1d6–1/19–20)

Ranged +*1 hand crossbow* +10 (1d4+1 plus poison/19–20)
Base Atk +4; **Grp** +3
Atk Options poison (drow poison, DC 13, unconscious 1 minute/unconscious 2d4 hours), sneak attack +4d6, steal spell (0, 1st)
Combat Gear 10 doses drow poison, *potion of cure light wounds,* scroll of *fog cloud,* scroll of *hold portal,* scroll of *mount,* scroll of *obscuring mist,* scroll of *silent image*
Wizard Spells Prepared (CL 9th; 1d20+11 to overcome SR for divination spells; prohibited schools enchantment, evocation, necromancy):
4th—*arcane eye* (CL 11th), *greater invisibility, ruin delver's fortune*[SC], *scrying* (CL 11th, DC 21)
3rd—*arcane sight, clairvoyance/clairaudience, enduring scrutiny*[CM], *listening coin*[SC] (CL 11th), *unluck*[SC] (CL 11th, DC 20)
2nd—*chain of eyes*[SC] (CL 11th, DC 19), *create magic tattoo*[SC]* (3), *detect thoughts* (CL 11th, DC 19) (2)
1st—*alarm, critical strike*[SC] (CL 11th), *guided shot*[SC] (CL 11th), *mage armor, sniper's shot*[SC] (CL 11th), *true casting*[CM] (CL 11th), *vigilant slumber*[SC] (CL 11th)
0—*detect poison, ghost sound, mage hand, read magic*
* Tattoo grants +1 deflection bonus to AC, +2 resistance bonus on saves, or +2 competence bonus on attack rolls

---

Abilities Str 8, Dex 14, Con 12, Int 18, Wis 14, Cha 10
SQ enhanced awareness[UA]
Feats Able Learner[CM] (see page 25), Greater Spell Focus (divination), Magic Sensitive[CM] (see page 25), Practiced Spellcaster[CAr], Scribe Scroll[B], Silent Spell[B], Spell Focus (divination)
Skills Craft (painting) +7, Decipher Script +12, Gather Information +10, Hide +14, Knowledge (arcana) +13, Knowledge (local) +9, Listen +10, Move Silently +10, Search +16, Sense Motive +14, Spellcraft +16, Spot +14
Possessions combat gear plus *+1 mithral chain shirt, +1 hand crossbow* with 40 bolts, *headband of intellect +2,* masterwork short sword, 91 gp
Spellbook spells prepared plus 0—all except for spells from prohibited schools; 1st—*identify*; 2nd—*locate object*

Steal Spell (Su) Kjarlo can forego 1d6 points of damage from his sneak attack to steal a 0-level or 1st-level spell from his opponent. If the opponent prepares spells, Kjarlo can steal a specific spell; the opponent loses that spell from memory and cannot cast it for 1 minute, even if she prepared it multiple times. If the opponent is a spontaneous caster, she loses the ability to cast the stolen spell for 1 minute. If the opponent does not cast spells, has no spells prepared, or has no more spell slots, this ability has no effect.

Kjarlo can try to steal a specific spell or allow the DM to choose a spell randomly. If he tries to steal a specific spell that is not available, the stolen spell (or spell slot) is determined randomly.

Enhanced Awareness Kjarlo has Sense Motive on his list of wizard class skills. When he casts *identify*, it takes only 10 minutes, rather than the standard casting time of 1 hour. When Kjarlo casts *arcane eye*, the sensor travels 20 feet per round (rather than 10) while studying surroundings. Kjarlo adds 1 to the saving throw DCs of his divination spells; this improvement stacks with his Greater Spell Focus (divination) feat. To gain this alternative class feature, Kjarlo gave up the ability to summon a familiar.

THE CHELICERATA TRADE COMPLEX

The warehouse that serves as the upper level of the Chelicerata complex was once the storehouse for a brewery, which operated in areas 2 and 3. When Tamesik set her sights on the building, she arranged accidents and disappearances among the brewers. Once the warehouse was hers, she extended the hallway (area 2c), connecting it to small caverns in the Underdark that she and Kjarlo divined. The rest of the caverns were used as guard barracks and bedrooms for Tamesik and her minions.

Since Calais took charge of the criminal organization, little has changed in the layout of the complex. Apart from minor alterations to her own living quarters, Calais has maintained the appearance and everyday operations of the complex.

KEY FEATURES

The complex consists of three sections. The first is the cloaked warehouse on the surface, where the illegal goods are held. A spiral staircase in the warehouse leads down to the second section—the original brewery chambers, which now serve as an office and chapel. Rough tunnels that extend from the original hallway connect those rooms to the third section: small caverns in the Underdark that serve as barracks and quarters.

Structural Properties

The following properties apply to the subterranean rooms of the trade complex. The features and properties of the warehouse are discussed in tactical encounter 5–1 (page 90).

Walls: The walls of the former brewery (areas 1a, 2a, 2b, most of 2c, and 3) are hewn from the rock of existing caverns. They are 3 feet thick and have hardness 10, 600 hit points, and a Climb DC of 25. The walls of the rough tunnels (some of area 2c and areas 4, 5, 6, and 7) are bumpier than those in other parts of the complex. They are 3 feet thick and have hardness 10, 550 hit points, and a Climb DC of 17.

Floors: The floors of the manmade section of the lower complex are smooth stone and have no effect on movement. The floors of the roughly hewn Underdark section are natural, though still relatively smooth. Although movement is not impaired, the DCs of all Balance, Jump, and Tumble checks that begin or end on the floor are increased by 4.

Ceiling Height: The ceilings throughout the lower complex are 15 feet high.

Doors: All doors in the lower complex are 5 feet wide and open inward. Each door is made of 3-inch-thick stone and has hardness 8 and 60 hit points.

Illumination: An *everburning torch* illuminates the spiral stairway from the warehouse (area 1a). The office (area 2a) has a single *everburning torch* in the northeast corner. The long north–south branch of the tunnels (area 2c) is lit by three *everburning torches.* Each of its two smaller branches is lit by one *everburning torch.* The chapel (area 3) and each of the four caverns (areas 4 to 7) contain four *everburning torches,* one in each corner.

Encounter Levels: The encounters in the lower complex range from EL 6 to EL 12. You can increase the EL of an encounter if guards have been mobilized or if Calais or one of her minions moves to the area.

DEFENSES

Tamesik commissioned a powerful wizard to produce an illusion that makes the warehouse appear to be a normal storehouse with a few guards. Intruders have trouble navigating the area and fighting back against rapid assaults.

The chapel (area 3) is protected by a shadesteel golem. This construct is held in a magical rapier that Tamesik found in the Underdark. If the altar is touched by someone who does not possess the appropriate key, the rapier transforms into the golem, which attacks the person who touched the altar and anyone else nearby. Simultaneously, the statues in the sanctuary release hordes of tomb spider broodswarms.

Kjarlo and Darzemaan take turns monitoring activities within the warehouse. In tactical encounter 5–1 (page 90), Darzemaan is overseeing the area, but Kjarlo could easily be lurking nearby. With his powers, the warlock tries to influence the emotions and actions of the PCs. If he fails, he retreats to the lower complex. Kjarlo is always prepared and remains several steps ahead of any intruders—he is nearly impossible to surprise.

If the PCs are detected in the warehouse, word spreads to the lower complex, allowing its inhabitants time to prepare spells, don armor, and take other precautions. Unless the characters overcome the difficulties of entering through the warehouse, they are not likely to surprise the denizens below.

Punishment for touching the altar

Illus. by W. Mahy

AREA DESCRIPTIONS

The Chelicerata complex contains many entrances and exits, allowing villains, minions, and guards a number of possible escape routes. Calais and her minions can be found anywhere in the compound, but are most likely encountered in their respective living areas or as noted in the following area descriptions. These descriptions correspond with the map on page 89.

1. Warehouse: The complex begins in this warehouse. The PCs can enter through locked cargo doors on the southern and eastern walls (Open Lock DC 32), or they can attempt to scale the building (Climb DC 20) and sneak in through the high windows on the northern and western walls. The number of guards varies depending on the time of day, but because drow are mostly nocturnal, the heaviest concentration is present at around midnight. Darzemaan is often found here, ready to *charm* or disable foes. If things go poorly, he flees into the lower complex. Each warehouse guard carries a key to the cargo doors. For more details, see tactical encounter 5–1 (page 90).

1a. Secret Staircase: A spiral staircase hidden under a crate leads down to a landing in the underground complex. From the landing, a set of stairs descends into a series of tunnels (area 2c).

2a. Administrative Office: This small administrative office is always locked (Open Lock DC 32). It contains a writing desk with one drawer and a small bookshelf that holds academic and economic tomes. In the locked desk drawer (Open Lock DC 28) is a fat book of accounts. If anyone reads a page of the book without first uttering the password, a *blast glyph of warding* is triggered. Only Calais and her minions have keys to the office and to the drawer.

Any characters inspecting the desk can attempt a DC 32 Search check; success indicates the discovery of a small secret compartment that houses a silver box. The box is worth 100 gp and contains the treasure listed below.

Glyph of Warding (Blast) Trap: CR 6; spell; spell trigger; no reset; spell effect (*blast glyph of warding*, 16th-level cleric, 8d8 sonic, Reflex DC 14 half); multiple targets (all targets within 5 ft.); Search DC 28; Disable Device DC 28.

Treasure: 400 pp, scroll of *flame strike*, scroll of *heal*, scroll of *restoration*, scroll of *sending*.

2b. Reldeth's Closet: This room used to be a storage closet, but it was abandoned after a drow guard named Reldeth died here during a hazing. Reldeth now haunts the chamber as a spectre. He leaves Calais and her most important minions alone, but he torments any guards who open the closet door, and attacks unfamiliar visitors outright. The closet door is locked (Open Lock DC 25).

Reldeth (Spectre): hp 45 (7 HD); *MM* 232.

2c. Tunnels: Manmade tunnels connect the rooms in the underground portion of the trade complex. The tunnels that lead to the barracks and quarters (areas 4 to 7) are rougher than those in the former brewery.

3. Chapel: Tamesik had consecrated this small chapel to Lolth, and Calais left it intact so as not to raise suspicions

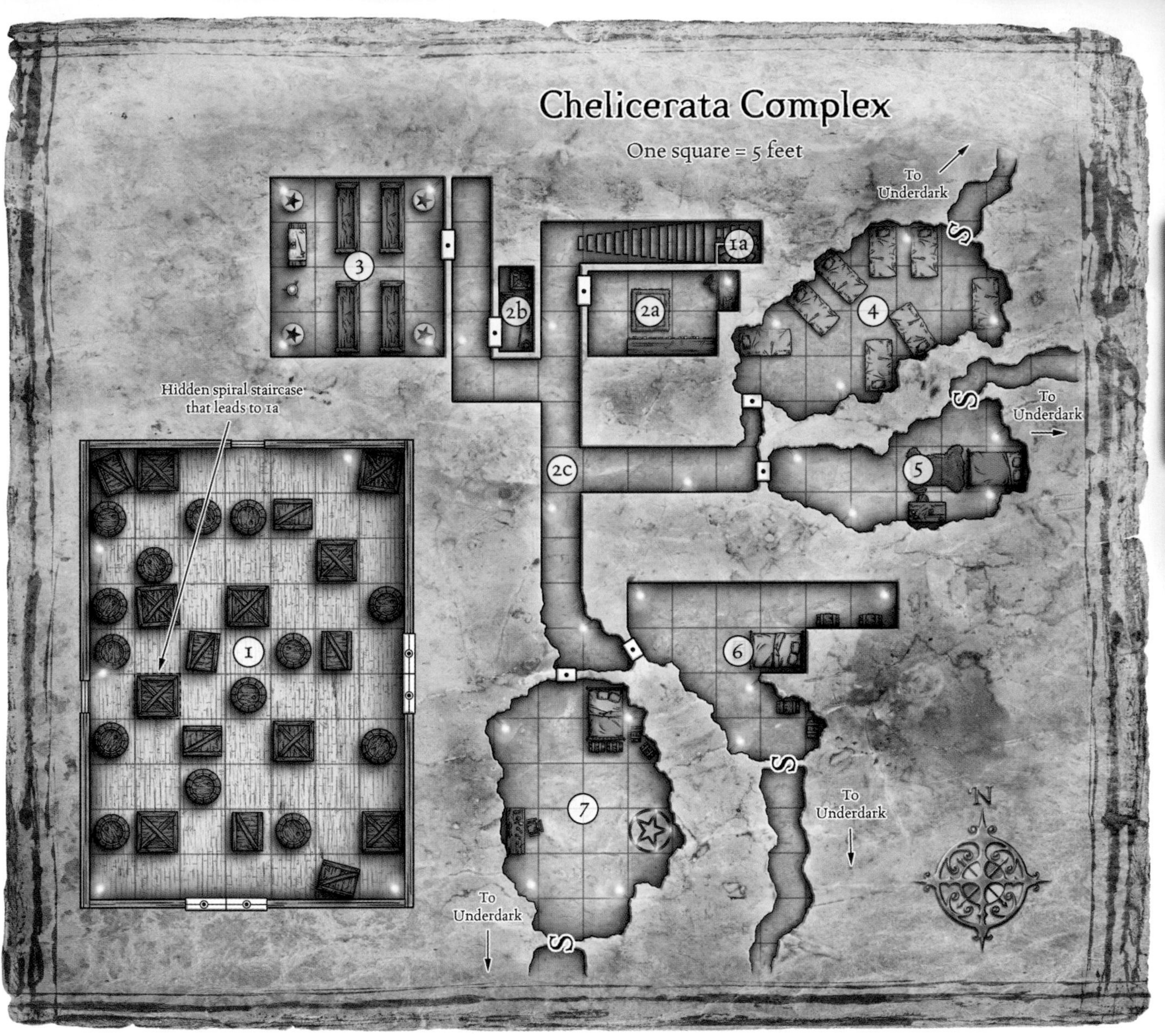

among the drow. She continues to delude herself into believing that Corellon Larethian, not the Spider Queen, is the source of her divine power.

The chapel is locked (Open Lock DC 30). Spider statues loom in the corners of the room, and a nondescript altar sits near the far wall, opposite the chapel's entrance. Above the altar floats an upside-down rapier. Anyone who touches the altar without possessing the proper key causes a shadesteel golem to be released from the rapier. The creature attacks the intruders, fighting until it is slain, they are slain, or they leave the chapel. See tactical encounter 5–2 (page 92).

4. Guard Barracks: Cots and bedrolls fill this room. In the middle of the day, the PCs find many guards here, but at other times they encounter only a few drow.

Chelicerata Guards: hp 12 each (2 HD); see page 90.

5. Kjarlo's Quarters: This room is nicely appointed, though the decor is sensible rather than luxurious. A neatly made bed is pushed against the eastern wall, a soft bearskin rug occupies the floor in front of the bed, and everything is extremely tidy. A secret door in the north wall (Search DC 32) leads into the Underdark.

6. Darzemaan's Quarters: Unlike Kjarlo's room, the warlock's quarters are lavish and completely impractical. Silk sheets cover an overstuffed feather bed, and expensive tapestries and other fabrics fully conceal the walls. Several locked ornamental chests (Open Lock DC 20) contain Darzemaan's personal items, none of which are valuable to the PCs. A secret door on the south side of the chamber (Search DC 32) leads into the Underdark.

7. Calais's Quarters: This room appears to be a natural cave that was shaped and enlarged by stoneworkers. It is lavishly appointed with soft and expensive furnishings. A *teleportation circle* on the east side of the room leads to the city above, and a secret door on the south wall (Search DC 32) leads into the Underdark. For more details, see tactical encounter 5–3 (page 94).

WAREHOUSE

Encounter Level 11

SETUP

Darzemaan and four drow guards patrol within the cloaked warehouse. As soon as the player characters enter the building, the guards make Listen checks. Because the illusion makes the PCs think that the layout of the warehouse is different from the real layout, their movements within the building are clumsy. They take a penalty of –8 on Climb, Hide, Jump, Move Silently, Ride, and Tumble checks. These penalties make it likely that the drow guards, unaffected by the illusion, succeed on their Listen checks.

It takes 1 round of normal movement before the PCs realize that something is wrong. During this round, when moving at full speed, they take 1d4 points of nonlethal damage each time they walk into a square that is occupied by an object hidden by the illusion. If the PCs attempt to climb or move on illusory objects, they take 1d4 points of nonlethal damage from sudden falls and sprains. Once a character has taken damage from such bumps and bruises, he is entitled to attempt a DC 22 Will save to disbelieve the illusion.

Running and charging are impossible, but a character can take a double move. If a character moves at half speed, he can successfully navigate the warehouse without bumping into objects, but his slowness puts him at a severe tactical disadvantage.

Until a PC successfully disbelieves the illusion, Darzemaan and the drow guards are effectively invisible, as from a *greater invisibility* spell with an effective caster level of 8th for the purpose of dispelling.

When the PCs begin to move through the room, read:

As you move around the warehouse, you realize that something is wrong. You bump into objects that you can't see, bruising your body against hidden obstacles. Your legs buckle as you stumble across a floor that feels uneven but looks flat and smooth. You begin to hear strange words of magical power, but their source is hidden.

TACTICS

When the PCs begin to stumble around the illusory warehouse, the drow snipe at them, staying out of melee range unless they have a perfect opportunity for a close attack. The four guards are spaced out around the room, making them hard to affect with area spells and adding to the confusion of the environment. They apply drow sleep poison to their crossbow bolts to incapacitate their targets; this way, Darzemaan (and perhaps Kjarlo or Calais) can question the intruders before killing them. Individually, the guards are not that powerful, but with their many battleground advantages they are a dangerous group.

Meanwhile, Darzemaan attempts to *charm* one of the PCs, trying to confuse the adventurers or turn them against each other. If this tactic fails, the warlock tries to weaken the interlopers with his offensive items and

4 CHELICERATA GUARDS **CR 3**
hp 12 each (2 HD)

Male or female drow rogue 1/fighter 1
CE Medium humanoid (elf)
Init +3; Senses darkvision 120 ft.; Listen +5, Spot +5
Languages Common, Drow Sign Language, Elven, Undercommon

AC 17, touch 13, flat-footed 14
(+3 Dex, +4 armor)
Immune magic *sleep* effects
SR 13
Fort +3, **Ref** +5, **Will** +1 (+3 against spells and spell-like effects)
Weakness light blindness

Speed 30 ft. (6 squares)
Melee mwk short sword +4 (1d6+2/19–20/)
Ranged mwk hand crossbow +6 (1d4 plus poison/19–20)
Base Atk +1; **Grp** +3
Atk Options Point Blank Shot, poison (drow sleep poison, DC 13, unconscious 1 minute/unconscious 2d4 hours), sneak attack +1d6
Combat Gear 4 doses drow sleep poison, 3 *potions of cure light wounds,* 2 *oils of magic weapon*
Spell-Like Abilities (CL 3rd):
1/day—*dancing lights, darkness, faerie fire*

Abilities Str 14, Dex 17, Con 11, Int 12, Wis 12, Cha 10
SQ notice secret and concealed doors within 5 feet, trapfinding
Feats Point Blank Shot, Weapon Focus (hand crossbow)
Skills Climb +9, Hide +7, Jump +7, Listen +5, Move Silently +7, Search +5, Sleight of Hand +7, Spot +5, Swim +3, Tumble +7
Possessions combat gear plus mithral chain shirt, masterwork hand crossbow with 20 bolts, masterwork short sword, masterwork climber's kit, 3 pp, 39 gp, 10 sp

Light Blindness (Ex) Abrupt exposure to bright light (such as sunlight or a *daylight* spell) blinds drow for 1 round. In addition, they take a –1 circumstance penalty on attack rolls, saves, and checks when in bright light.

DARZEMAAN **CR 9**
hp 39 (8 HD); see page 85

Features of the Area

The warehouse has the following features.

Illumination: The warehouse is lit by five *everburning torches.* Four are ensconced in the corners of the room, and another is on the wall directly opposite the eastern cargo doors.

Walls: The walls in the warehouse have AC 3, hardness 9, and 100 hit points. At 14 inches thick, they are sturdier than the walls of a typical storehouse. They are composed of thick wood with overlaid mortar, making them difficult to scale (Climb DC 27).

Ceiling: The ceiling in the warehouse is 30 feet high. There are remnants of catwalks at window height in the upper reaches of the room. Tamesik demolished the walkways to impede any trespassers who broke in through the windows.

Doors: The only doors in the warehouse are 10-foot-wide cargo doors in the southern and eastern walls. The doors are made of reinforced wood and have hardness 7 and 30 hit points. They open both inward and outward.

Staircase: A spiral staircase is hidden under a crate to the left of the center of the warehouse. The crate is empty and offers no resistance when moved.

Upper Windows: The only windows in the warehouse are near the tops of the northern and western walls, about 25 feet above the floor. If the PCs enter through a window, they must find their own way down.

Cargo: The warehouse is cluttered with boxes, crates, and barrels of contraband, including drugs, weapons, poisons, and stolen art and antiquities. The goods in the warehouse have a total value of more than 50,000 gp, though most of the items are very difficult to liquidate.

powers, especially *eldritch blast.* Darzemaan coordinates his attacks with those of the guards to cause as much confusion and disorientation as possible. His *baleful utterance* and *dread seizure* invocations are particularly useful for hindering the PCs and increasing the general chaos. If necessary, Darzemaan uses his scrolls of *fog cloud* and *web* to further impede the party and cover his retreat into the lower complex.

Conclusion

If Darzemaan or the guards are in danger of being defeated, they retreat, using the methods described above to slow the PCs and cover their escape. The drow descend to the lower level, making sure the other members of the Chelicerata are alert and ready.

ALTAR EGO

Encounter Level 11

SETUP

Each corner of the chapel contains one *everburning torch* and a statue of a spider. Near the wall opposite the entrance is a plain altar, above which floats an upside-down rapier. The chapel is usually empty unless Calais comes to pray or conduct a service. Tamesik was more prone to dogma and enjoyed preaching to her minions, but Calais dislikes holding ceremonies. Still, a secret compartment in the altar holds a small store of magic items, so Calais might come here to equip herself for a fight—especially if she has been alerted to intruders in the warehouse.

For the most part, the chapel is safe. However, if anyone touches the altar without possessing a special key, the shadesteel golem in the rapier is awakened. (See Features of the Area, below.) When this occurs, four tomb spider broodswarms emerge from the spider statues in the corners.

If one of the PCs touches the altar without the key, read:

As you touch the cool stone of the altar, the hovering rapier begins to spin in circles. The spinning rapidly becomes faster, creating a whirling ring of shadow and steel. From this dark ring emerges a metallic, skeletal monstrosity. At the same time, hundreds of spiders pour out of the statues in the corners of the room.

TACTICS

The broodswarms heal whenever the shadesteel golem releases its negative pulse wave. Reldeth also heals, which allows him to become a threat again even if he was previously damaged.

These tactics can backfire, however. If a PC succumbs to the poison of a broodswarm, he can be healed by the negative energy of the golem's pulse wave, but only for 1 minute.

CONCLUSION

The golem and the broodswarms attack until the PCs are slain, they are slain, or the intruders retreat. If the shadesteel golem is slain, it returns to the rapier and cannot be released again for 24 hours. If the PCs retreat, the golem returns to the rapier and waits to fulfill its duty. The same is true for the broodswarms, except that they return to the statues.

SHADESTEEL GOLEM[MM3] **CR 11**

hp 119 (18 HD); **DR** 10/adamantine and magic

N Medium construct (extraplanar)

Init +3; **Senses** darkvision 60 ft., low-light vision; Listen +0, Spot +0

Languages —

AC* 34, touch 14, flat-footed 31
(+3 Dex, +20 natural, +1 dodge from *haste*)

Immune magic, construct immunities

Fort +6, **Ref** +10*, **Will** +6

Weakness construct vulnerabilities

Speed* 60 ft. (12 squares), fly 60 ft. (perfect)

Melee* 3 slams +21 each (2d6+7)

Base Atk +13; **Grp** 20

Special Actions negative pulse wave

Abilities Str 24, Dex 16, Con —, Int —, Wis 11, Cha 7

SQ construct traits, *haste*, shadow blend

Feats —

Skills Hide +15, Listen +0, Move Silently +19, Spot +0

Immunity to Magic (Ex) A shadesteel golem is immune to any spell or spell-like ability that allows spell resistance. In addition, certain spells and effects function differently against the creature, as noted below.

A magical effect that has the light descriptor (such as *continual flame*) causes the golem to speed up for 2d4 rounds as if affected by a *haste* spell. The golem is also *hasted* if it is subject to a positive energy effect, such as the turning attempt of a cleric, which might happen if a cleric mistakenly identifies it as a nightwalker or other undead.

If a shadesteel golem is targeted by or within the area of a spell that has the darkness or shadow descriptors, the golem heals 1 point of damage per level of the spell.

Negative Pulse Wave (Su) A shadesteel golem can radiate a burst of inky black negative energy as a free action every 1d4+1 rounds. The pulse wave drains life from all living creatures within 40 feet of the golem, dealing 12d6 points of negative energy damage. A successful DC 19 Fortitude save halves the damage. Undead creatures within the area are healed of 12d6 points of damage instead, and any turning effect they are under is broken. A *death ward* or similar effect protects a creature from a shadesteel golem's negative pulse wave.

Shadow Blend (Su) A shadesteel golem has concealment in any illumination other than full daylight.

* Affected by a continuous *haste* spell that is in effect because of the *continual flame* spells cast on the *everburning torches*. The *haste* effect (granting one extra attack when making a full attack, +1 bonus on attack rolls, +1 dodge bonus to Armor Class, and +1 dodge bonus on Reflex saves) is negated if all the *continual flame* spells are dispelled or if the area is brought into darkness.

4 Tomb Spider Broodswarms[MM3] CR —

hp 22 each (3 HD)

NE Tiny magical beast (swarm)
Init +5; **Senses** darkvision 60 ft., low-light vision, tremorsense 60 ft.; Listen +9, Spot +9
Languages —

AC 17, touch 17, flat-footed 12 (+2 size, +5 Dex)
Immune swarm immunities
Resist half damage from piercing and slashing weapons
Fort +5, **Ref** +8, **Will** +6
Weakness swarm vulnerabilities

Speed 20 ft. (4 squares), climb 20 ft.
Melee swarm (1d6 plus poison)
Base Atk +3; **Grp** —
Atk Options distraction, poison (DC 13, 1d4 hp/1d4 hp)

Abilities Str 7, Dex 20, Con 15, Int 1, Wis 16, Cha 2
SQ swarm traits, tomb-tainted soul, web walk (not used)
Feats Alertness, Iron Will
Skills Climb +13, Hide +11, Jump +2, Listen +9, Move Silently +7, Spot +9

Distraction (Ex) Any creature that begins its turn with a swarm in its square must make a successful DC 13 Fortitude save or be nauseated for 1 round. Spellcasting or concentrating on spells requires a successful Concentration check (DC 20 + spell level). Using skills involving patience and concentration requires a DC 20 Concentration check.
Poison (Ex) Creatures affected by a tomb spider broodswarm's poison are healed by negative energy and harmed by positive energy as if they were undead. This effect lasts for 1 minute after a failed save.
Tomb-Tainted Soul (Ex) A tomb spider broodswarm is healed by negative energy and harmed by positive energy as if it were undead.
Skills A tomb spider broodswarm can always take 10 on Climb checks, even if rushed or threatened.

Treasure: A secret compartment in the altar can be found on a successful DC 32 Search check. The compartment holds 1,000 pp, two diamonds worth 4,000 gp each, a *+1 shocking dagger*, a scroll of *banishment*, a scroll of *blade barrier*, a scroll of *greater restoration*, a *wand of slashing darkness*[SC] (CL 7th, 22 charges), and an extra *darksteel key* that can control the golem.

The compartment also contains a set of eight small parchments that are sacred to the devotees of Lolth. The parchments have no inherent magical or material value, but they are antiquities to the church, making them effectively priceless. The golem was placed in the chapel to guard the parchments, not the other treasure.

Features of the Area

The chapel has the following features.

Illumination: *Everburning torches* light the four corners of the room. They cause the shadesteel golem to act as if under the effect of a continuous *haste* spell.

Darksteel Rapier: The *darksteel rapier* is considered magic and evil for the purpose of overcoming damage reduction, though it does not have an enhancement bonus. The owner of a special *darksteel key* tied to the weapon can touch the altar without releasing the shadesteel golem. The key also enables its owner to control the golem once released. The owner can insert the key into the pommel of the rapier, allowing the item to be carried as a normal weapon.

To set the rapier, the owner of the key places the weapon, blade down, in midair above or near the object to be guarded. Then he removes the key from the pommel while concentrating on the object (in this case, the altar), and the rapier becomes attuned to that object. In all other ways, the weapon acts like an *immovable rod*, except that it releases the golem when the altar is touched.

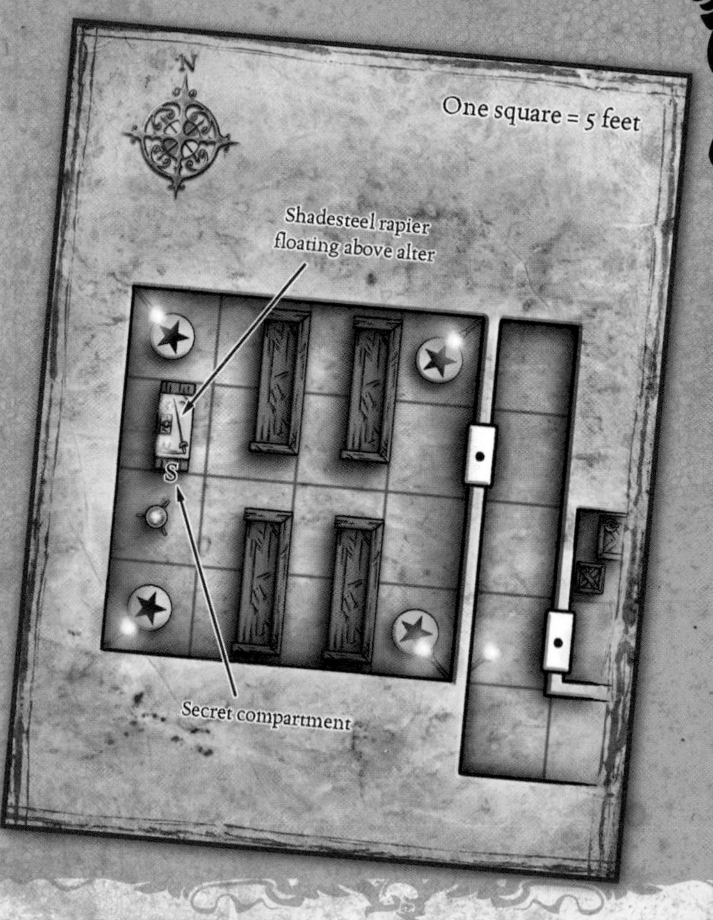

Calais's Chamber

Encounter Level 12

SETUP

Assuming that the PCs were detected in the warehouse, Calais (C) has had time to prepare for an assault. Even if the adventurers successfully navigate the defenses of the complex, Calais uses her *prying eyes* spell to look for intruders. When she gets word that the complex is under attack, she summons her most powerful guards (D)—duskblade triplets named Oros, Nillaien, and Hloethdrin—to her quarters (area 7). Although her bedchamber is small, it is fairly defensible because it has two escape routes: the *teleportation circle* and the secret door to the Underdark.

Oros, Nillaien, and Hloethdrin are unshakably devoted to Calais, whom they believe to be Tamesik the drow. Tamesik rescued them from slavery when they were on the verge of being sold to a gladiatorial arena; since that day, the triplets have loyally served the priestess. Although they realize that something is amiss with their benefactor, they do not suspect that she is an impostor. If they were to learn the truth about how Calais killed and replaced Tamesik, their reaction would be extreme.

When the PCs enter this room, read:

The door opens to a surprising scene. Three drow males in breastplates stand in a defensive line, protecting their mistress with their glowing longswords. Behind this wall of living steel stands an elegantly robed drow female, preparing to unleash the divine force of her dark goddess.

TACTICS

As soon as Calais has gathered her guards, she casts a series of defensive spells. First, she casts spells that protect herself and the triplets. In the first round, she uses her scroll of *mass bear's endurance*. In the next round, she casts *bless*, followed by *magic circle against law*.

CALAIS ARCHWINTER **CR 11**
hp 59 (10 HD); see page 83

OROS, NILLAIEN, AND HLOETHDRIN **CR 6**
hp 31 each (5 HD)

Male drow duskblade[PH2] 5
LE Medium humanoid (elf)
Init +2; **Senses** darkvision 120 ft.; Listen +2, Spot +2
Languages Common, Drow Sign Language, Draconic, Elven, Gnome, Undercommon

AC 18, touch 12, flat-footed 16 (+2 Dex, +6 armor)
Immune magic *sleep* effects
SR 16
Fort +5, **Ref** +1, **Will** +4 (+6 against spells and spell-like effects)
Weakness light blindness

Speed 20 ft. (4 squares) in breastplate, base speed 30 ft.
Melee *+1 longsword* +9 (1d8+3/19–20)
Ranged mwk hand crossbow +8 (1d4 plus poison/19–20)
Base Atk +5; **Grp** +7
Atk Options poison (drow sleep poison, Fort DC 13, unconscious 1 minute/unconscious 2d4 hours)
Special Actions *arcane attunement*, arcane channeling, quick cast 1/day
Combat Gear 2 doses drow sleep poison, scroll of *see invisibility*
Duskblade Spells Known (CL 5th):
2nd (3/day)—*ghoul touch* (+7 melee touch, DC 15)
1st (6/day)—*ray of enfeeblement* (+7 ranged touch), *resist energy, shocking grasp* (+7 melee touch, DC 14), *swift expeditious retreat, true strike*
0 (6/day)—*acid splash* (+7 ranged touch), *disrupt undead* (+7 ranged touch), *ray of frost* (+7 ranged touch), *touch of fatigue* (+7 melee touch, DC 13)
Spell-Like Abilities (CL 5th):
1/day—*dancing lights, darkness, faerie fire*

Abilities Str 14, Dex 14, Con 12, Int 17, Wis 10, Cha 10
SQ notice secret and concealed doors within 5 feet, armored mage (medium), spell power
Feats Battlecaster Offense[CM] (see page 25), Combat Casting[B], Weapon Focus (longsword)
Skills Concentration +9 (+13 casting defensively), Knowledge (arcana) +11, Knowledge (religion) +11, Listen +2, Search +5, Sense Motive +8, Spellcraft +13, Spot +2
Possessions combat gear plus *+1 breastplate, +1 light steel shield, +1 longsword*, masterwork hand crossbow with 10 bolts, 7 pp, 5 gp

Light Blindness (Ex) Abrupt exposure to bright light (such as sunlight or a *daylight* spell) blinds drow for 1 round. In addition, they take a –1 circumstance penalty on attack rolls, saves, and checks when in bright light.
Arcane Attunement (Sp) For a combined total of six times per day, each of the triplets can use *dancing lights, detect magic, flare* (DC 14), *ghost sound*, and *read magic*. Caster level 5th.
Arcane Channeling (Su) Each triplet can cast any touch spell he knows (*ghoul touch, shocking grasp*, or *touch of fatigue*) and deliver it through his longsword with a melee attack. This channeling requires a standard action and does not provoke attacks of opportunity. If the attack is successful, the attack deals damage normally, and then the effect of the spell is resolved.
Quick Cast Each triplet can cast one spell per day as a swift action, as long as the spell's normal casting time is 1 standard action or less.
Armored Mage (Medium) (Ex) Each triplet can cast arcane spells with no chance of arcane spell failure while wearing medium armor and using a light shield.

On subsequent rounds, Calais employs individual defensive spells, including *neutralize poison, freedom of movement*, her scroll of *living undeath, dispel law, lesser globe of invulnerability, protection from arrows*, and *guidance*.

The duskblades have few defensive spells. If the *prying eyes* that Calais used to spy on the PCs observed a pattern in the elements cast by one or more party members, the triplets use their *resist energy* spells to ward themselves and Calais against this element. If time allows, they also use their scrolls of *see invisibility*, especially if the *prying eyes* reported attacks coming from unseen foes.

In combat, each triplet focuses his blade and his spells on a single opponent, making the most of his Battlecaster Offense feat. Calais prefers to stand to the side, casting ranged spells and occasionally stepping in to use a deadly touch spell such as *slay living*.

DEVELOPMENT

Calais can move to the chapel and control the actions of the shadesteel golem (see tactical encounter 5–2, page 92), but she does so only if her organization has the advantage over the intruders. If any of the triplets are driven from her quarters, they either join her in the chapel or retreat through the secret tunnels.

FEATURES OF THE AREA

The bedchamber has the following features.

Illumination: The room is lit by four *everburning torches*, one in each corner.

Teleportation Circle: Calais and her minions have keys to the *teleportation circle*. To open the portal, a creature must stand within the circle and utter a complex activation phrase ("Rynoch Toelira Krekhtvbern Lylrocharian") three times, which takes 1 full round. Once the portal has been opened, any number of travelers who have keys can go through it, space permitting. The *teleportation circle* can function three times per day, and the portal stays open for 1 round each time.

CONCLUSION

If Calais and her bodyguards believe that they might lose the battle, they retreat. If they are in a hurry or on the brink of death, the drow flee through the passage; if they have a little more time, they use the *teleportation circle*, which takes 1 round to activate (see Features of the Area, below).

After retreating, they heal themselves with their remaining potions and spells, and then return to the complex if it is feasible to do so.

Treasure: If the PCs poke through the luxurious furnishings of the chamber, they easily find several plain wooden chests (Search DC 10) that contain clothing, jewelry, and personal items worth about 2,000 gp. In one chest, identical to the others, an additional 275 pp and 43 gp are hidden among the garments (Search DC 18). All the chests are unlocked.

Illus. by T. Giorello

"It's you or me, I'm afraid, and I don't want to die."
—Emmara Ishandrenn

Emmara Ishandrenn was once a potent force for good in the world until she was captured, tortured, and cursed by a lich known as Restarann. His curse stripped away her goodness, cloaking her soul in deep, festering shadow. Now driven half mad by terrifying dreams, Emmara believes that she must perpetrate acts of unspeakable evil to survive. From her lair in the Soth Tarnel, a faded tomb in a lonely, crumbling sea stack, she plots her revenge against all who abandoned her.

BACKGROUND

Emmara Ishandrenn—once an acclaimed adventurer, follower of Pelor, and hero of the Free City—is now one of its most implacable and dangerous enemies. A native of the city, she spent her formative adventuring years exploring the hills and woodlands of the surrounding area with her compatriots, known as the Band of the Eternal Sun. They grew in power and fame until, one day, an influential local lord sought them out.

The lord told Emmara and her companions a harrowing tale of ancient evil reawakened. A lich called Restarann had stirred from his deathless slumber and, for some unknowable reason, was sending agents deep into the city. Victims slain by the agents were terribly mutilated, arranged in strange poses, and surrounded by arcane shapes drawn in their own blood or formed from their entrails. This depravity could not be permitted to continue.

Thus, the Band of the Eternal Sun set out to find and slay Restarann. After weeks of searching, they discovered his lair and began their assault. The adventurers easily bested the lich's lesser guardians, but Restarann was far too powerful for the intruders. Emmara's companions were cut down by mighty death magic, and she alone survived—barely.

It pleased the sadistic Restarann to spare Emmara a quick demise. Instead, he tortured her for weeks before placing a powerful curse upon her. The curse destroyed her honor and morality, replacing it with a hatred for all things good and fair. The lich was surprised by the depth of her conversion and her newfound capacity for evil, and so he allowed Emmara to live on as his servant. That night, however, terrifying dreams began to haunt the former adventurer.

Emmara's transformation brought more than nightmares. With it came boundless ambition and an insatiable lust for revenge. She hated her new master with a passion, for though she truly embraced the darkness, she could not forget the pain and suffering that Restarann had visited upon her.

Therefore, she slowly worked to subvert her master. Subtly placed clues and garbled accounts from survivors eventually led another band of heroes to Restarann's lair. The adventurers bested him in an epic battle, not suspecting that Emmara had already taken steps to weaken the lich. Having laid her plans carefully, Emmara survived her master's fall and escaped with a significant portion of his treasure and magic. She used this wealth to establish herself in the isolated Soth Tarnel, a tomb dedicated to a long-fallen hero. From her new lair, she contacted the most skilled of Restarann's former spies and assassins and bound them to her service with promises of bountiful loot.

GOALS

Emmara's descent into evil has not been without great personal cost. The frightening dreams that started on the night of her conversion have grown in intensity ever since.

In these nightmares, she hurtles through the pitch black toward a bright light. All around her loom images of herself committing acts of depravity and violence. She recognizes some of these crimes as actions she took while in Restarann's service, but others are unknown to her. The comforting darkness begins to fade, replaced by a painful burning sensation. As she draws closer to the light, it intensifies and expands, engulfing her. Agony wracks her body as her very soul is peeled away. At that point she awakens, terrified.

Emmara has developed a deranged belief that the nightmares show the passage of her remaining life and that the bright light represents death. Because the dreams presumably show actions that she has yet to take, Emmara has come to believe that the more wanton cruelty she commits, the longer she will live.

Emmara has several goals. First and foremost, she wants to survive: The prospect of death and the loss of her soul terrifies her, and she will commit any atrocity in the hope of extending her life. To this end, she has waylaid many small groups of travelers and attacked isolated farmsteads. Emmara kills most of her victims immediately, but a few are mutilated and tortured first. She is careful to cover her tracks, having seen how overconfidence led to Restarann's destruction.

She has also come to regret forging relationships with the lich's spies and assassins. At the time, her vanity compelled her to prove that she was the equal of her former master, if not his better. Now, however, she realizes that the agents know too much about her, and that they are not particularly loyal—if they were captured by the forces of good, they might barter for their lives with information about her activities. Thus, Emmara wants them all killed before they can talk.

Finally, her hatred has grown into an all-consuming lust for vengeance against the Free City and the lord who sent her after Restarann long ago. In her twisted view, both are complicit in the pain and suffering she endured at the hands of the lich. Emmara's long-term goal is to shatter the security of the city's residents and give them a taste of the misery that she has known.

Emmara Ishandrenn

USING THIS VILLAIN

Using Emmara in your campaign is simple. The details of her home (the "Free City") and her former employer are left vague; you can choose any large community on or near a coast and name any local noble as her employer. The lord who sent her after Restarann might be someone the PCs have also worked for.

Depending on the amount of campaign time you want to devote to Emmara's schemes, the PCs can encounter her in a variety of ways. Consider how far her plans have developed and how deeply you want the party to become involved in her story.

The simplest approach is to introduce Emmara as little more than a random encounter. The PCs could be among a group of travelers that she attacks; if she escapes, the PCs can track her back to her lair and try to finish her off. Alternatively, the player characters could come upon the aftermath of one of Emmara's assaults, or discover a lone survivor who provides a chilling account of the massacre.

Rather than begin with Emmara herself, you can hook the party by using Restarann's old network of spies. While in the Free City, the PCs foil the attempted murder of a former agent of the lich. Afterward, the grateful spy confesses his sordid past and begs for help. He recognized his assailant as one of Emmara's new agents, and he tells his rescuers what he knows about the ex-adventurer. From there, the adventurers follow a trail of clues that lead to the Soth Tarnel.

Finally, you can have the PCs run into Emmara's minions first. A prominent nobleman lies dead, and murderous gangs of cutthroats stalk the streets of the Free City. A group of local citizens begs the PCs to end the violence. The adventurers intercept and defeat a gang of Emmara's lackeys led by Farror, her most talented spy. Farror flees to warn his mistress of the unexpected resistance, and Emmara begins plotting the PCs' downfall before they can derail her plans.

EMMARA IN EBERRON

Emmara is a native of Sharn. Her employer was Sava Kharisa, the City Council representative for Lower Central. Sava is an outspoken individual whose support for the city's common folk has made her many enemies on the council.

Restarann laired beneath the Graywall Mountains, several hundred miles north of Sharn. Hidden deep within the mountain range, his lair extended hundreds of feet below the ground. In these dark tunnels, the lich's mindless servants discovered adamantine—and a rare vein of byeshk. Before Restarann's death, substantial amounts of both metals were mined and hidden away. Emmara knows the location of the

Illus. by J. Zhang

secret storage facility, and, if endangered, she offers to trade that knowledge for her life.

EMMARA IN FAERÛN

Emmara is a native of Waterdeep, and her employer was a fat, hard-drinking fellow known as Mirt the Moneylender. Although not a true nobleman, Mirt is widely believed to be one of the mysterious Lords of Waterdeep, and he aims to leave Faerûn better than he found it. Thus, he had great interest in the destruction of Restarann.

Emmara and her companions tracked the lich to a half-submerged castle hidden deep within the Mere of Dead Men. There, her comrades were slain and she was turned to evil. Although Restarann now lies dead, whole sections of tunnels under his lair have never been cleared. If necessary, Emmara offers her knowledge of these passages—and the treasures they contain—in exchange for her life.

APPEARANCE AND BEHAVIOR

Emmara is a middle-aged female human of indeterminate heritage. Almost skeletally thin, she stands 5 feet 7 inches tall and seems to weigh almost nothing. Her skin is pale, nearly white, and entirely free of blemishes. Her raggedly cut, dirty blonde hair hangs down to her shoulders and obscures much of her face. Dark rings, the result of many sleepless nights, surround her hate-filled eyes, giving her an even more haggard appearance. Although she is only forty years of age, she appears to be at least a decade older.

Strangely, Emmara is fastidious about her appearance; her clothes and equipment are extremely clean. She usually wears full plate armor and is never without her sword, which she has named Ebon Death. The blade of this large falchion is jet black, and mystical symbols representing undeath, suffering, and magic decorate the pommel.

Emmara is cruelty personified. She is also somewhat deranged, a consequence of the torture she endured from Restarann and her involuntary conversion to the path of darkness. Her mental condition is worsened by her chronic sleep deprivation, which makes her erratic and irritable. She often slurs her words and occasionally has hallucinations—waking dreams in which she believes that she is going to die. While in this state, she lashes out at anyone nearby, attempting to prolong her life by committing more vile acts.

Emmara is unforgiving and can hold a grudge for years. If the PCs thwart her plans, they earn her wrath, and she makes special efforts to track them down.

EMMARA ISHANDRENN **CR 15**
hp 91 (15 HD)

Female human fighter 4/transmuter 7/blackguard 4
NE Medium humanoid
Init +0; **Senses** Listen +7, Spot +8
Aura despair (10 ft., –2 on saves), evil (moderate)
Languages Common, Draconic, Infernal

AC 24, touch 12, flat-footed 24
(+9 armor, +2 shield, +2 deflection, +1 natural)
Fort +15, **Ref** +9, **Will** +11

Speed 20 ft. (4 squares) in full plate, base speed 30 ft.
Melee *+1 thundering falchion* +17/+12/+7 (2d4+10 plus 1d8 sonic/18–20)
Base Atk +11; **Grp** +16
Atk Options Arcane Strike, Cleave, Gruesome Finish, Improved Sunder, Power Attack, poison (deathblade, Fort DC 20, 1d6 Con/2d6 Con), smite good 1/day (+4 damage), sneak attack +1d6
Special Actions rebuke undead 3/day (+0, 2d6+2, 4th)
Combat Gear 2 *potions of cure serious wounds, potion of fly,* scroll of *stoneskin,* 2 vials deathblade poison
Wizard Spells Prepared (CL 7th; arcane spell failure 40%; prohibited schools enchantment and evocation):
4th—*dimension door,* stilled *haste*
3rd—stilled *wraithstrike*[SC] (3)
2nd—*blur, false life, resist energy* (2), *see invisibility*
1st—*enlarge person, feather fall, hold portal, obscuring mist, true strike, ventriloquism*
0—*dancing lights, detect magic, light, mage hand, prestidigitation*
Blackguard Spells Prepared (CL 4th):
2nd—*summon monster II*
1st—*corrupt weapon, cure light wounds*
Spell-Like Abilities (CL 4th):
At will—*detect good*

Abilities Str 20, Dex 10, Con 14, Int 14, Wis 12, Cha 11
SQ dark blessing, familiar (howler; see tactical encounter 6–3, page 108), poison use, share spells
Feats Alertness[B] (if familiar within 5 ft.), Arcane Strike[CW] (see page 25), Cleave[B], Gruesome Finish (see page 24), Improved Familiar, Improved Sunder, Lightning Reflexes, Power Attack, Scribe Spell[B], Still Spell, Weapon Focus (falchion), Weapon Specialization (falchion)
Skills Concentration +16, Jump +8, Knowledge (arcana) +12, Knowledge (religion) +6, Knowledge +12, Listen +7, Ride +16, Spellcraft +14, Spot +8
Possessions combat gear plus *+1 full plate, +1 buckler, +1 thundering falchion, belt of giant strength +4, cloak of resistance +3, amulet of natural armor +1, ring of protection +2, gloves of Dexterity +2,* 650 gp
Spellbook spells prepared plus 0—all except for prohibited schools; 1st—*disguise self, expeditious retreat, mage armor, shield*; 2nd—*protection from arrows, web, whispering wind*; 3rd—*fly, vampiric touch, water breathing*; 4th—*Evard's black tentacles, scrying*

FARROR

"Hello, my dear. What a pretty young thing you are. Would you do me the honor of allowing me to buy you a drink?"
—Farror, in disguise

Handsome, charismatic, and devilishly charming, the erinyes called Farror is a cad and a bounder. Farror once served as the eyes and ears of the lich Restarann, spying on people and events in the Free City. Now he works with Emmara because their alliance gives him opportunities to indulge his two greatest passions—gratuitous violence and pleasures of the flesh.

GOALS

Farror is not particularly loyal to Emmara and would never consider dying for her. He sees her as dangerously unstable, but he enjoys participating in the mayhem and slaughter that she makes possible.

The erinyes revels in the here and now, and wastes little time making plans or worrying about the future. He fancies himself a connoisseur of females, and when not carrying out Emmara's directives, he spends most of his time pursuing the latest object of his lust.

USING FARROR

As Emmara's spy, Farror scouts out her targets and keeps watch over the Soth Tarnel, warning her of approaching vessels and adventurers. The PCs could encounter him almost anywhere.

In combat, Farror relies on his aerial mobility and his ranged attacks. If he faces serious opposition or is badly wounded, he teleports out of danger to warn Emmara. If she has already been killed, the erinyes instead teleports far away, never to return.

Farror knows that he is hated by Jebrix, Emmara's minotaur battle champion, but he does not care. He views Jebrix as a blood-crazed beast and pays no attention to his reports and opinions.

Appearance and Behavior

Farror resembles a handsome and muscular human male, though his large, white, feathery wings and his glowing red eyes betray his extraplanar nature. He wields a red bow that glows with an unnatural light.

The erinyes flaunts his good looks and his apparent angelic heritage to awe commoners and nobles alike, trusting in his *ring of mind shielding* to defeat any attempts to determine his true lineage. Exceptionally vain and superficial, Farror wears only the finest garments, which are tailored and cut to show off his impressive physique.

Unlike many devils, Farror does not hold grudges; apart from the pleasures of the flesh, he really does not care about anything enough to bother. He is loquacious among strangers but says little of worth, using his natural talents to gain as much information as possible.

Farror maintains rooms at several of the city's best inns, teleporting between them as needed. When he appears in public, it is often in the taprooms of these hostelries, surrounded by a gaggle of impressionable (or *charmed*), young, beautiful women.

FARROR **CR 13**
hp 176 (18 HD); **DR** 5/good

Male erinyes scout[CAd] 8/fighter 1
LE Medium outsider (baatezu, evil, extraplanar, lawful)
Init +7; **Senses** darkvision 60 ft., see in darkness, permanent *true seeing* (CL 14th); Listen +24, Spot +24
Languages Celestial, Common, Draconic, Infernal; telepathy 100 ft.

AC 29, touch 16, flat-footed 29; Dodge, Mobility, uncanny dodge; +2 when skirmishing
(+6 Dex, +5 armor, +8 natural)
Immune fire, poison, outsider immunities
Resist acid 10, cold 10, evasion; **SR** 20
Fort +19, **Ref** +21, **Will** +15
Weakness outsider vulnerabilities

Speed 40 ft. (8 squares), fly 50 ft. (good); Shot on the Run
Melee mwk longsword +22/+17/+12/+7 (1d8+5/19–20)
Ranged *+1 flaming burst composite longbow* +23/+18/+13/+8 (1d8+6 plus 1d6 fire/×3) or
Ranged *+1 flaming burst composite longbow* +23/+23/+18/+13/+8 (1d8+6 plus 1d6 fire/×3) with Rapid Shot or
Ranged *+1 flaming burst composite longbow* +15 (1d8+6 plus 1d6 fire/×3) with Manyshot
Base Atk +16; **Grp** +21
Atk Options skirmish +2d6, Point Blank Shot, Precise Shot
Special Actions entangle, *summon baatezu*
Combat Gear *elemental gem (air)*, 2 *potions of cure serious wounds*
Spell-Like Abilities (CL 12th):
At will—*greater teleport* (self plus 50 pounds of objects only), *charm monster* (DC 19), *minor image* (DC 17), *unholy blight* (DC 19)

Abilities Str 21, Dex 23, Con 21, Int 14, Wis 18, Cha 20
SQ battle fortitude, camouflage (use Hide in terrain that does not grant cover or concealment), fast movement, flawless stride, outsider traits, trapfinding, trackless step
Feats Dodge[B], Evil Brand (see page 24), Hellsworn (see page 24), Improved Rapid Shot, Manyshot, Mobility[B], Point Blank Shot, Precise Shot, Rapid Shot, Shot on the Run, Weapon Focus (longbow)
Skills Balance +16, Concentration +17, Diplomacy +7, Escape Artist +26, Hide +25, Intimidate +9, Jump +12, Knowledge (religion) +14, Knowledge (the planes) +14, Listen +24, Move Silently +26, Search +21, Sense Motive +22, Spot +24, Survival +4 (+6 on other planes or following tracks), Tumble +19, Use Rope +9
Possessions combat gear plus *+1 mithral shirt*, *+1 flaming burst composite longbow* (+5 Str bonus) with 60 arrows, masterwork longsword, *cloak of resistance +3*, *ring of mind shielding*, *quiver of Ehlonna*, 50 gp

Entangle (Ex) Farror carries 50 feet of stout rope that entangles opponents of any size, as an *animate rope* spell (CL 16th). He can hurl the rope 30 feet with no range penalty.
Hellsworn (Hell's Fury) Once per round as a free action, Farror can designate a single target that he can see. All his ranged attacks with his longbow against that target deal an extra 1d6 points of unholy damage.
Summon Baatezu (Sp) Once per day, Farror can attempt to summon 2d10 lemures or 1d4 bearded devils with a 50% chance of success. This ability is the equivalent of a 3rd-level spell.

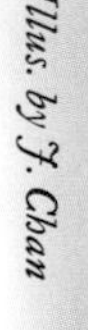

Illus. by J. Chan

Farror

JEBRIX

"The Lord of Slaughter is strong within this human, though she does not know it. I must honor her as I would my lord."
—Jebrix, explaining his allegiance to Emmara

A powerful minotaur cleric dedicated to Erythnul, the deity of slaughter, Jebrix is a creature without morals or conscience. As Emmara's battle champion, he revels in the death and suffering he wreaks in her name. Jebrix leads a small band of berserkers who serve as her personal guard and shock troops.

Illus. by K. Tanner

Jebrix

GOALS

Emmara is not a worshiper of Erythnul, but Jebrix is loyal to her because she seems to abide by the deity's tenets zealously. As long as she continues to serve the God of Slaughter, whether intentionally or unwittingly, Jebrix will follow her.

The minotaur dislikes Farror, knowing instinctively that the erinyes is not truly sworn to Emmara. In fact, he views the arrogant devil as a threat to his mistress and to himself. Although Jebrix does not have the intelligence to actively plot against Farror, he does not help the erinyes in battle unless explicitly ordered to do so by Emmara.

USING JEBRIX

As Emmara's bodyguard, Jebrix normally stays close by her. If the PCs invade the Soth Tarnel, they almost certainly run afoul of him and the two minotaur guards under his command (see tactical encounter 6–2, page 106).

On occasion, however, Jebrix leaves the tower to lead attacks against particularly reviled foes of his mistress. The PCs could encounter him as they guard one such individual. Alternatively, Jebrix and his raging minions could attack the PCs as they camp in the wilderness.

Appearance and Behavior

Tall and massively muscled, Jebrix looks like a human covered in thick fur, and he has the head of an enormous bull. One of his ears has been chewed off, and his black, almost lifeless eyes gleam with hate. He dyes his fur deep red in homage to his deity, and his jet black *+2 full plate* is splattered with the dried blood of his victims.

Jebrix is a simple, unimaginative creature, overwhelmingly committed to the tenets of Erythnul. He lives to spread the suffering and evil demanded by his lord. The screams of the dying and the hot splash of a foe's blood on his fur excite him beyond all reason.

Jebrix uses his cleric powers to heal his companions as needed or raise them from the dead. These actions are not signs of compassion on his part; rather, he views his fellow minotaurs as vital tools in his mission to spread the dogma of Erythnul throughout the world.

He has little need for gold, treasure, or other material goods. The only items he covets are those that help him slaughter the innocent and the helpless. Jebrix exhibits little initiative, preferring to leave strategy to Emmara. Once given orders, however, he follows them with a single-minded purpose that borders on the fanatical.

JEBRIX **CR 13**

hp 156 (18 HD)

Male minotaur cleric 13
CE Large monstrous humanoid
Init +3; **Senses** darkvision 60 ft., scent; Listen +8, Spot +8
Languages Common, Giant

AC 26, touch 11
(–1 size, –1 Dex, +10 armor, +3 deflection, +5 natural)
Immune *maze* spells
Fort +16, **Ref** +10, **Will** +18

Speed 20 ft. (4 squares) in full plate, base speed 30 ft.

Melee mwk greataxe +22/+17/+12 (3d6+9/×3) or
Melee gore +22 (1d8+3) or
Melee mwk greataxe +22/+17/+12 (3d6+9/×3) and gore +17 (1d8+3)
Space 10 ft.; **Reach** 10 ft.
Base Atk +15; **Grp** +25
Atk Options Improved Bull Rush (+10), Power Attack
Special Actions blasphemous incantation, powerful charge, spontaneous casting (*inflict* spells)
Combat Gear *pearl of power* (1st level), scroll of *cure critical wounds*, scroll of *stoneskin*
Cleric Spells Prepared (CL 13th):
7th—*blasphemy*[D] (CL 14th, DC 22), *destruction* (DC 22)
6th—*animate objects*[D], *blade barrier* (DC 21), *mass cure moderate wounds*
5th—*dispel good*[D] (CL 14th), *flame strike* (DC 20), *righteous might*, *spell resistance*, *wall of stone* (DC 20)
4th—*chaos hammer*[D] (CL 14th, DC 19), *cure critical wounds*, *divine power*, *restoration*, *sending*, *spell immunity*
3rd—*dispel magic* (2), *magic circle against good*[D] (CL 14th), *invisibility purge*, *prayer*, *protection from energy*
2nd—*calm emotions* (DC 17), *cure moderate wounds*, *hold person* (2), *shatter*[D], *resist energy* (2)
1st—*bless*, *deathwatch* (CL 14th), *entropic shield*, *magic weapon* (2), *obscuring mist*, *protection from law*[D] (CL 14th)
0—*create water*, *cure minor wounds* (2), *detect magic*, *detect poison*, *read magic*
D: Domain spell. Deity: Erythnul. Domains: Chaos, Evil

Abilities Str 22, Dex 8, Con 19, Int 6, Wis 21, Cha 10
SQ natural cunning
Feats Great Fortitude, Improved Initiative, Improved Bull Rush, Lightning Reflexes, Power Attack, Track, Weapon Focus (greataxe)
Skills Concentration +16, Listen +8, Spot +8
Possessions combat gear plus *+2 full plate*, masterwork greataxe, *periapt of Wisdom +2*, *ring of protection +3*, *amulet of health +2*, 100 gp

Blasphemous Incantation (Su) Three times per day, Jebrix can call upon the power of Erythnul as a standard action. All good creatures within 30 feet must succeed on a DC 16 Fortitude save or become sickened for 1 round. (Jebrix gave up the ability to rebuke undead when taking this alternative class feature.)
Powerful Charge (Ex) When charging, Jebrix can make a single gore attack with an attack bonus of +22 that deals 4d6+9 points of damage.
Natural Cunning (Ex) Jebrix is immune to *maze* spells, never gets lost, and is never caught flat-footed.

THE SOTH TARNEL

Emmara Ishandrenn lairs in the Soth Tarnel, an ancient tomb dedicated to a long-forgotten hero. The sepulcher is cut into Elliast's Spire, a spray-drenched, gull-haunted pinnacle separated from the mainland by half a mile of turbulent water. Carved into the rock is the shape of a massive greatsword, fully 200 feet from its tip to its pommel, which soars the full height of the spire. At its base, a sea cave known as Durrin's Rest penetrates the sword's tip, giving the illusion that the weapon is broken.

Little vegetation grows on the stark cliffs of Elliast's Spire, and few creatures live here except for sea birds, which nest in the stack's many crevasses and ledges. Vicious riptides and barely submerged rocks make swimming and boating near the spire dangerous. At high tide, the dark, turbulent waters of the sea completely cover the opening to Durrin's Rest. At low tide, however, it is possible to enter the cave.

Within the tomb itself, the Stair Martial spirals up from Durrin's Rest to the top of the spire, where a small network of chambers houses Emmara and her minions.

KEY FEATURES

Skilled stonemasons built the Soth Tarnel hundreds of years ago, but the sea's constant pounding has taken its toll. All that remains of the beautifully carved, intricately detailed greatsword is a vague silhouette from a forgotten time.

Unless the PCs can fly, they must cross turbulent waters to reach the tomb. At 200 or more feet from the spire, the water is rough and can be crossed only with successful DC 15 Swim checks or DC 15 Profession (sailor) checks. Within 200 feet of Durrin's Rest, the numerous riptides and the complex topography of the sea bed make the waters stormy, increasing the DCs of the Swim and Profession (sailor) checks by 5.

The cliffs of Elliast's Spire are steep and slick, but they can be scaled with successful DC 20 Climb checks. Scaling the carved greatsword is more challenging, adding 5 to the DC of Climb checks.

Structural Properties

Inside Soth Tarnel, many intricate details still survive.

Illumination: The chambers of the Soth Tarnel are lit by *continual flame* spells cast on iron balls that hang 3 feet down from the ceiling on thin iron chains. Corridors and stairways are unlit.

Ceiling: Hallways are normally 10 feet high, and most rooms extend up to at least 15 feet. The ceilings are vaulted throughout and are buttressed by stone ribs.

Slender Pillars: In each room, the stone ribs of the ceiling connect to slender pillars (*DMG* 64). Each pillar has AC 4, hardness 8, and 900 hit points.

Doors: The doors are made of stone and have nested hinges (*DMG* 62) that allow them to open in either direction. The outer face of each door is carved with scenes depicting humans slaying orcs. Each door is 4 inches thick and has hardness 8, 60 hit points, and a break DC of 28. All doors are unlocked.

Walls: The walls are hewn from 3-foot-thick stone and have hardness 8, 540 hit points, and a break DC of 50. They can be scaled with successful DC 22 Climb checks.

Floor: The floors throughout the Soth Tarnel are made of polished granite. In Durrin's Rest, they are slick with seaweed and other detritus.

DEFENSES

Emmara prefers solitude. Thus, only a few of her trusted minions dwell with her in the Soth Tarnel. Fanatically loyal to Emmara, these elite minotaur guards use the lower ceremonial landing (area 3) as a base. Although they are some distance from Durrin's Rest (area 1), they likely hear any combat that occurs in the sea cave. As soon as they do, Jebrix casts *sending* to alert Emmara, then joins the battle to delay the intruders as long as possible.

Two of the tomb's original guardians—a pair of stone golems—survived the Soth Tarnel's decline. When Emmara

Illus. by R. Gallegos

Elliast's Spire

moved in, she found their controlling amulet and moved the golems to the Chapel of Reverence (area 5). Their standing orders are to kill anything that enters the chamber. They do not attack creatures in the Grand Processional (area 4) unless the intruders attack them first.

If the PCs reach this point before Emmara's minions are able to warn her, she almost certainly hears the sounds of battle with the golems and prepares for combat, as detailed in tactical encounter 6–2 (page 106). When ready, Emmara moves from the Chambers of the Keepers (area 6) to the Chapel of Reverence and casts *hold portal* on the doors to slow down the intruders.

AREA DESCRIPTIONS

The PCs might find it difficult to surprise Emmara. They must likely approach her lair from the sea, enter at the bottom, and make their way to the top—defeating berserker minotaurs along the way—before they can confront her. The following areas correspond with those on the map on page 103.

1. Durrin's Rest: Set at the base of the Soth Tarnel, Durrin's Rest is a large sea cave that floods almost completely at high tide. Low tide, however, reveals a long, low rock shelf covered in seaweed. The water has eroded the shelf, making its surface uneven. Two worn, seaweed-wrapped statues of humans wearing plate armor and carrying greatswords flank a broad staircase (area 2).

A scyllan lurks below the black waters of Durrin's Rest, attracted by the rich pickings of the vessels that sail to and from the Free City. Whenever the creature detects movement in the cavern above, it surfaces to attack. If intruders flee up the stairs, the scyllan does not pursue them. (See tactical encounter 6–1, page 104.)

2. The Stair Martial: These steep stairs wind up from Durrin's Rest into the heart of the Soth Tarnel. The broad, wide steps are heavily shrouded with dust, but otherwise unaffected by the passage of time. A successful DC 10 Search check reveals tracks going up and down the stairs, made by one or more Medium humanoid creatures.

3. Ceremonial Landing: The Stair Martial is interrupted in three places by flat landings; these feature intricate carvings of human warriors battling a host of orcs. Small alcoves with seats carved into the wall were meant to give mourners a place to rest before continuing their ascent.

Emmara's elite guards—two barbarian minotaurs led by Jebrix—use the lowest ceremonial landing as a barracks and guard chamber. From here, they watch and listen for signs of trouble from below. Their landing is roughly 70 feet from Durrin's Rest, so the guards take a penalty of –7 on Listen checks to hear fighting in the sea cave. (See tactical encounter 6–2, page 106.)

4. Grand Processional: The Stair Martial opens into this domed chamber, which is pn the same level as the carved greatsword's crossguard on the cliffs outside. Cunningly fashioned windows in the crossguard allow some natural light to filter in while keeping the weather at bay, but much of the chamber remains darkened. Sound echoes eerily here.

The chamber is 60 feet long and 35 feet wide. Four rows of slender pillars support the domed roof, which is 40 feet high at its center. Opposite the Stair Martial, a door opens to the Chapel of Reverence.

5. Chapel of Reverence: This balconied chamber has only one light source: a narrow shaft cut into the ceiling, directly above an enormous shattered sarcophagus in the center of the room. Thus, the coffin is brightly lit, while shadowy illumination surrounds it to a radius of 20 feet. The sarcophagus has long since been battered open and looted. Treat its squares as dense rubble and the squares adjacent to it as light rubble.

From here, a narrow spiral staircase wends upward to the Chambers of the Keepers.

If Jebrix has alerted Emmara, the PCs encounter her here, along with her howler familiar and two golem guards. (See tactical encounter 6–3, page 108.)

6. Chambers of the Keepers: The former keepers of the tomb—followers of the fallen hero—used these chambers as living quarters. From here, they guarded the Soth Tarnel and escorted mourners coming to pray at the tomb.

These chambers have little original furniture left; mounds of brittle and shattered wood are stacked in the corners. One area served as a kitchen. A chimney that pierces one wall can be used to reach the top of Elliast's Spire, but it is a tight squeeze (Climb DC 10).

Emmara has claimed these chambers as her living quarters. If the PCs get this far, they find many of her mundane possessions, including two large chests containing the funds she uses to finance her plans—a total of 28,000 gp. They might also discover her spellbook (Search DC 20), hidden beneath a false panel in the floor of the kitchen area.

7. Atop the Spire: A cleverly hidden secret door (Search DC 30) stands at the head of the spiral stairs. The walls here are very rough, made to look as if the builders simply stopped tunneling.

Beyond the secret door lies a small natural cave. Its floor is slick with rainwater; treat the cave as a shallow pool (*DMG* 64). A wet, narrow ledge (Balance DC 17) ascends one of the cavern's walls—at its highest point, there is an opening that leads to the zenith of Elliast's Spire.

Durrin's Rest

Encounter Level 13

SETUP

This encounter begins when the player characters enter the sea cave. If they swim into the cave or enter by boat, the lurking scyllan immediately becomes aware of them and attacks. If the PCs fly in, the scyllan must make a successful Spot check to notice the interlopers.

At low tide, the roof of the cave mouth is 15 feet above sea level. At high tide, the entrance is completely submerged. Inside, the cave ceiling quickly rises to a height of 40 feet above the wall pierced by the Stair Martial. A narrow, seaweed-encrusted stairway leads up from the water to the rock ledge.

When the PCs enter the cave, read:

Ahead of you, a large natural cave extends away into darkness. The water here is choppy, but not as tumultuous as the sea outside. Still, the sounds of crashing waves echo throughout the cave.

Barnacles and hanging clumps of seaweed cover the lower portions of the cavern walls. A narrow staircase, barely visible in the shadowy light, leads up from the water to a rock ledge. Beyond, a set of broad stairs, flanked by two seaweed-draped statues of warriors, leads upward.

If the scyllan notices the PCs, read:

Suddenly, a monstrous creature bursts out of the rough water. Its upper body is a heap of lashing tentacles surrounding two viciously curved claws. Its massive, fishlike head has a toothy maw that opens wide as the creature begins to wail.

TACTICS

As soon as the scyllan becomes aware of the player characters, it bursts forth to do battle. The creature produces its frightful noise and then uses *control water* to raise the water level in the cavern by 32 feet. This action fills the

SCYLLAN[SW] **CR 13**

hp 184 (16 HD); **DR** 10/magic and silver

LE Huge outsider
Init +7; **Senses** darkvision 60 ft.; Listen +24, Spot +24
Languages Aquan, Infernal

AC 29, touch 11, flat-footed 26
(–2 size, +3 Dex, +18 natural)
Immune outsider immunities
SR 27
Fort +17, **Ref** +13, **Will** +15
Immune outsider vulnerabilities

Speed swim 50 ft. (10 squares)
Melee tentacle +25 (1d8+11) or
Melee 4 tentacles +25 each (1d8+11) and 2 claws +23 each (2d6+5)
Space 15 ft.; **Reach** 15 ft. (30 ft. with tentacles)
Base Atk +16; **Grp** +35
Atk Options constrict 1d8+11, improved grab, swallow whole
Special Actions *control water*, frightful noise

Abilities Str 33, Dex 17, Con 25, Int 8, Wis 20, Cha 6
SQ outsider traits
Feats Ability Focus (frightful noise), Improved Initiative, Improved Natural Attack (claw), Multiattack, Swim-By Attack[SW], Weapon Focus (tentacle)
Skills Hide +14, Intimidate +17, Jump +38, Knowledge (nature) +20, Listen +24, Spot +24, Survival +26, Swim +19

Constrict (Ex) A scyllan deals 1d8+11 points of damage with a successful grapple check made with a claw.
Improved Grab (Ex) If a scyllan hits with a tentacle, it can start a grapple as a free action without provoking attacks of opportunity. If it wins the grapple, it establishes a hold and can transfer the grabbed creature to a claw as a free action or attempt to swallow it whole. If it transfers the creature to its claw, the scyllan can constrict the creature.
Swallow Whole (Ex) A scyllan can try to swallow a grabbed creature whole by making a successful grapple check. A swallowed creature takes 2d8+16 points of bludgeoning damage plus 2d6 points of acid damage per round. A swallowed creature can cut its way out by using a light slashing or piercing weapon to deal at least 25 points of damage to the maw (AC 17). Once the creature exits, muscular contraction closes the hole; other swallowed creatures must cut their own way out. A scyllan's maw can hold two Large creatures, eight Medium creatures, 32 Small creatures, 128 Tiny creatures, or 512 Diminutive or smaller creatures.
Control Water (Sp) 1/hour; CL 16th (*PH* 214).
Frightful Noise (Su) A scyllan produces a wailing sound that unsettles creatures within 100 feet that have 16 or fewer Hit Dice. It starts its wailing as a move action and can end it as a free action. Creatures that make a successful DC 18 Will save against the wail are immune for 24 hours. On a failed save, creatures that have 4 or fewer Hit Dice are panicked for 2d6 rounds, and creatures that have between 5 and 16 Hit Dice become shaken for 2d6 rounds. This is a mind-affecting compulsion.
Swim-By Attack A scyllan can take a move action and take another standard action (such as an attack) at any point during the move. It cannot take a second move action during a round when it makes a swim-by attack.
Skills A scyllan has a racial bonus of +8 on Swim checks to perform a special action or avoid a hazard. It can take 10 on a Swim check even if distracted or endangered. It can use the run action while swimming, as long as it swims in a straight line.

Features of the Area

The sea cave has the following features.

Illumination: If the PCs come here during the day, some light filters into the cave. The first 20 feet beyond the cave entrance is in bright illumination, the next 20 feet is in shadowy illumination, and the remainder of the cave is in darkness.

Water: The water in the cave is rough (Swim DC 15), but the relative shelter keeps it from being as turbulent as the water outside. At low tide, the water in the cavern is 30 feet deep.

Slick Rock Floor: The surfaces of the rock ledge and the partially submerged rock shelf are extremely slippery and uneven. A successful DC 15 Balance check is required to run or charge across either surface. A failed check indicates that the character cannot move farther in that round (but can take other actions).

Steep Stair: The Stair Martial is a steep stair and affects the movement of creatures climbing up or down the steps (*DMG* 63). In addition, while on the stairs and attacking opponents below them, creatures gain a +1 melee attack bonus for fighting from higher ground.

Narrow Staircase: As the steep stair, detailed above, but only 5 feet wide and heavily eroded. Treat the narrow stairs as light rubble (*DMG* 60). At low tide, the stairs end just above sea level.

Seaweed-Covered Statues: These worn, seaweed-draped statues depict human warriors clad in archaic plate armor holding greatswords in front of them, point down.

Walls: Up to a height of 10 feet above the entrance to the Stair Martial, the walls are slippery (Climb DC 20). Beyond that level, however, the walls are drier and easier to negotiate (Climb DC 15).

entire cavern, floods 20 feet of the Stair Martial, and creates a hump of water 50 feet long that extends out into the open sea. Once the waters recede, the flooded portion of the Stair Martial remains slick, increasing the DC of Balance checks on the steps by 5.

In subsequent rounds, the scyllan attacks submerged characters, trying to swallow them whole. It swims up the narrow staircase in search of prey but remains in the water, gaining improved cover against opponents on land. While completely submerged, the scyllan has total cover against opponents on land unless they are under a *freedom of movement* effect.

The scyllan does not pursue foes up the Stair Martial, but otherwise it fights to the death. After all, the PCs have invaded its home.

CONCLUSION

If a battle occurs in Durrin's Rest, Jebrix and the minotaur guards might hear it from their position on the lowest ceremonial landing (area 3). Each minotaur can attempt a DC –10 Listen check, which includes a –7 penalty because of the distance. If the minotaurs hear the battle, they prepare for combat. (See tactical encounter 6–2, page 106.)

The scyllan lairs underwater below the rock ledge. If the PCs kill the beast, they can search the waters for treasure (see Features of the Area, below).

Treasure: Scattered on the cavern floor are the remains of the scyllan's previous victims and various items they carried. If the PCs dive underwater and search the floor, they find a corked *bottle of air*, a type II *necklace of fireballs*, 1,000 gp worth of coral, and 500 gp in mixed coins.

CEREMONIAL LANDING

Encounter Level 15

SETUP

This encounter takes place on the lowest ceremonial landing (area 3), where Jebrix and two minotaur guards reside, and on the stairs leading up to the landing. If they hear the sounds of battle filtering up from Durrin's Rest, the minotaur guards move to the top of the Stair Martial and prepare to heave rocks down upon anyone they hear climbing the steps. Meanwhile, Jebrix casts *sending* to warn Emmara of intruders before moving farther back on the landing, using one of the alcoves for cover.

As soon as the guards hear movement on the Stair Martial (DC 0 Listen checks, modified by the relevant distance), they hurl chunks of masonry down at the intruders. Each minotaur can throw one chunk of masonry per round. Each piece of masonry has an attack bonus of +10 and deals 1d6+1 points of damage. Treat each chunk as a line effect that makes an attack roll against every target in the squares it passes through.

While the PCs are still on the stairway, Jebrix casts *animate object* on three chunks of masonry, which he directs down the stairs before casting *divine power* and *righteous might* on himself.

When the minotaurs first hurl masonry down the stairway, read:

With a thunderous crash, two chunks of stone bounce down the stairs toward you.

When the PCs reach the entrance to the landing, read:

Two brawny minotaurs stand at the top of the stairs. Each wields a greataxe and wears a thin chain shirt. At your appearance, they roar in defiance. The minotaurs block the entrance to a landing, but you can make out a few details behind them. Alcoves open to the left and the right of the long, narrow chamber, and on the far wall, an archway leads to more rising stairs.

2 MINOTAUR GUARDS (RAGING) — CR 11

hp 156 each (13 HD); **DR** 1/—

Male minotaur barbarian 7
CE Large monstrous humanoid
Init +1; **Senses** darkvision 60 ft., scent; Listen +10, Spot +6
Languages Common, Giant

AC 18, touch 8, flat-footed 18; improved uncanny dodge, uncanny dodge
(–1 size, +1 Dex, +5 armor, +5 natural, –2 rage)
Immune *maze* spells
Fort +16, **Ref** +11, **Will** +12

Speed 40 ft. (8 squares)
Melee *+1 greataxe* +21/+16/+11 (3d6+13/×3) or
Melee gore +20 (1d8+4) or
Melee *+1 greataxe* +21/+16/+11 (3d6+13/×3) and gore +15 (1d8+3)
Ranged javelin +16 (1d6+8)
Space 10 ft.; **Reach** 10 ft.
Base Atk +13; **Grp** +25
Atk Options Power Attack
Special Actions powerful charge, rage 2/day
Combat Gear *potion of cure serious wounds, potion of displacement, potion of haste*

Abilities Str 27, Dex 13, Con 22, Int 8, Wis 10, Cha 6
SQ fast movement, illiteracy, natural cunning, trap sense +2
Feats Great Fortitude, Iron Will, Lightning Reflexes, Power Attack, Track
Skills Climb +13, Jump +16, Listen +10, Spot +6
Possessions combat gear plus *+1 chain shirt, +1 greataxe, cloak of resistance +1*, 390 gp

Powerful Charge (Ex) When charging, a minotaur can make a single gore attack with an attack bonus of +20 that deals 4d6+9 points of damage.
Natural Cunning (Ex) A minotaur is immune to *maze* spells, never gets lost, and is never caught flat-footed.

When not raging, a minotaur guard has the following changed statistics:
hp decrease by 26
AC 20, touch 10, flat-footed 20
(–1 size, +1 Dex, +5 armor, +5 natural)
Fort +14, **Will** +10
Melee *+1 greataxe* +19/+14/+9 (3d6+10/×3) or
Melee gore +18 (1d8+3) or
Melee *+1 greataxe* +19/+14/+9 (3d6+10/×3) and gore +13 (1d8+3)
Ranged javelin +14 (1d6+6)
Grp +23
Abilities Str 23, Con 18
Skills Climb +11, Jump +14

JEBRIX — CR 13

hp 156 (18 HD); see page 100

Features of the Area

The lowest ceremonial landing has the following features.

Steep Stair: The Stair Martial is a steep stair and affects the movement of creatures climbing up or down the steps (*DMG* 63). In addition, while on the stairs and attacking opponents below them, creatures gain a +1 melee attack bonus for fighting from higher ground.

Shrine of Erythnul: Jebrix has set up a small shrine to Erythnul in one of the alcoves. The centerpiece of the shrine is a bloodstained chest banded in iron. Atop the chest sit a number of grisly offerings to the deity of slaughter, as well as a few broken and shattered weapons taken as trophies from the slain.

Living Area: The minotaurs use the other alcove as their living space. Much of the floor is covered in a thick layer of rugs, discarded cloth, and the half-eaten remains of unidentifiable food. Treat the area as if it were light rubble (*DMG* 60).

Crevasse: A crevasse 10 feet wide and 30 feet deep cuts through the center of the landing. It can be crossed on a successful DC 10 Jump check; anyone who fails the check falls in and takes 3d6 points of damage. The walls of the crevasse are rough, so anyone who falls in can climb back out with a successful DC 15 Climb check. The minotaurs use the crevasse as a dumping ground for garbage, and it holds all manner of foul, unwholesome, and useless objects.

Empty Plinth: In front of each side alcove stands a plinth that is 10 feet square and 5 feet high. Each plinth grants cover to anyone behind it. Originally, a stone golem stood on each plinth, but Emmara has moved the golems to the Chapel of Reverence (tactical encounter 6–3, on the next page).

3 Animated Chunks of Masonry — CR 3

hp 42 (4 HD); hardness 10

N Medium construct
Init +0; **Senses** darkvision 60 ft., low-light vision; Listen +0, Spot +0
Languages understand Common

AC 14, touch 9, flat-footed 14 (+4 natural)
Immune construct immunities
Fort +1, **Ref** +1, **Will** –4
Weakness construct vulnerabilities

Speed 30 ft. (6 squares)
Melee slam +2 (1d6+1)
Space 5 ft.; **Reach** 5 ft.
Base Atk +1; **Grp** +2

Abilities Str 12, Dex 10, Con —, Int —, Wis 1, Cha 1
SQ construct traits
Skills Listen +0, Spot +0

TACTICS

Jebrix prepares for combat by using his scroll of *stoneskin*, then casting *invisibility purge*, *prayer*, *spell immunity* (*dispel magic*, *fireball*, and *lightning bolt*) and *spell resistance*. He casts his other protective spells as time allows.

As soon as they see the PCs, the guards rage. The minotaurs stay at the top of the stairs as long as possible to gain the benefit of higher ground. Jebrix hangs back from melee combat, supporting the guards with *blasphemy*, *destruction*, and *flame strike*.

If the guards are forced back into the room, Jebrix blocks the stairs with a *blade barrier* after a few PCs enter the landing. On subsequent rounds, all three minotaurs attempt to bull rush opponents into the blades.

Jebrix and the guards are fanatical followers of Erythnul and fight to the death.

CONCLUSION

If the PCs dispatch the minotaurs, they can proceed upward through the stairs on the far side of the landing.

Chapel of Reverence

Encounter Level 15

SETUP

In the Chapel of Reverence (area 5), Emmara, her howler familiar, and her two stone golems prepare to battle the intruders (provided that Emmara has been alerted of their arrival). Before the PCs arrive, Emmara casts *hold portal* on the chamber door.

When she first claimed the Soth Tarnel, Emmara discovered an amulet that gave her command over the tomb's stone golem guardians. They originally stood on the lowest ceremonial landing, but she moved them to the chapel for better protection. As soon as Emmara becomes aware of trespassers, she commands the golems to flank the door and attack anything that steps through. During combat, she rants and raves at the PCs.

When the player characters enter the chapel (through the west door), read:

Ahead of you, in the center of this domed chamber, lies a large stone sarcophagus surrounded by rubble. The sarcophagus seems to have been shattered. A line of slender pillars runs down each side of the chamber, and caltrops have been scattered directly in front of the door. Standing slightly back from the entrance are two hulking stone statues, easily 10 feet tall.

If Emmara has managed to cast *obscuring mist*, modify the text to mention the vapor.

TACTICS

As soon as her minions warn her of intruders, Emmara prepares for combat. She uses a scroll of *stoneskin* and casts *see invisibility*, *false life*, *resist energy (fire)*, and *resist energy (cold)*—sharing all spells with her familiar—before donning her *+1 full plate*. Next, she casts *corrupt weapon* on her falchion and moves in front of the entrance, where she attempts to cast *obscuring mist* to limit the intruders' line of sight into the room. She then scatters bags of caltrops near the door to break up the PCs' movement. Finally, Emmara ducks behind the ruined sarcophagus and coats her falchion with deathblade poison.

If possible, Emmara fights while mounted on her howler. When the PCs break through the door, she casts a stilled *haste* (shared with her familiar). If a PC clears the caltrops and any *obscuring mist* present, the howler charges. Emmara uses a swift action to cast a stilled *wraithstrike* (shared with her familiar; treat all their attacks in that round as touch attacks) and uses her Power Attack feat for 5 points. As a free action, she sacrifices a 1st-level spell to fuel her arcane strike, gaining a bonus of +1 on attack rolls and dealing an extra 1d4 points of damage per attack. If Emmara reduces an opponent to 0 or fewer hit points, she uses her Gruesome Finish feat to kill him.

The howler charges into combat, preferring to make full attacks whenever possible. The beast is keenly loyal to Emmara and fights to the death. If the howler is slain, Emmara retreats, jumping atop the shattered sarcophagus or running to the balcony.

EMMARA ISHANDRENN **CR 15**
hp 91 (15 HD); see page 98

HOWLER (IMPROVED FAMILIAR) **CR —**
hp 45 (6 HD)

CE Large outsider (chaotic, evil, extraplanar)
Init +7; **Senses** darkvision 60 ft.; Listen +13, Spot +13
Languages understands Abyssal, empathic link, can speak with Emmara and other howlers

AC 21, touch 12, flat-footed 18
(–1 size, +3 Dex, +9 natural)
Immune outsider immunities
Resist improved evasion
Fort +12, **Ref** +8, **Will** +9
Weakness outsider vulnerabilities

Speed 60 ft. (12 squares)
Melee bite +16 (2d8+5) or
Melee bite +16 (2d8+5) and 1d4 quills +11 each (1d6+2)
Space 10 ft.; **Reach** 5 ft.
Base Atk +11; **Grp** +20
Atk Options Combat Reflexes, deliver touch spells
Special Actions howl, quills

Abilities Str 21, Dex 17, Con 15, Int 9, Wis 14, Cha 8
SQ grant Alertness, outsider traits, share spells
Feats Alertness, Combat Reflexes, Improved Initiative
Skills Climb +14, Hide +8, Jump +25, Listen +13, Move Silently +12, Search +7, Spellcraft +9, Spot +13, Survival +2 (+4 following tracks)

Howl (Ex) Each hour that a nonoutsider is within hearing range of the howler, that creature must succeed on a DC 12 Will save or take 1 point of Wisdom damage. This is a sonic mind-affecting ability.
Quills (Ex) A howler's neck bristles with long quills. While biting, the creature thrashes about, striking its foe with 1d4 quills. An opponent hit by a howler's quill attack must succeed on a DC 16 Reflex save, or the quill breaks off in his flesh. Each lodged quill imposes a cumulative penalty of –1 on attack rolls, saves, and checks. A quill can be removed safely with a successful DC 20 Heal check; otherwise, removing a quill deals an extra 1d6 points of damage.

2 Stone Golems CR 11

hp 107 each (14 HD); **DR** 10/adamantine

N Large construct
Init –1; **Senses** darkvision 60 ft., low-light vision; Listen +0, Spot +0
Languages understand Common

AC 26, touch 8, flat-footed 26
(–1 size, –1 Dex, +18 natural)
Immune magic, construct immunities
Fort +4, **Ref** +3, **Will** +4
Weakness construct vulnerabilities

Speed 20 ft. (4 squares)
Melee 2 slams +18 each (2d10+9)
Space 10 ft.; **Reach** 5 ft.
Base Atk +10; **Grp** +23
Special Actions *slow*

Abilities Str 29, Dex 9, Con —, Int —, Wis 11, Cha 1
SQ construct traits
Skills Listen +0, Spot +0

Immunity to Magic A stone golem is immune to any spell or spell-like ability that allows spell resistance. In addition, certain spells and effects function differently against the golem. A *transmute rock to mud* spell *slows* a stone golem (as the *slow* spell) for 2d6 rounds with no saving throw, while *transmute mud to rock* heals a wounded golem of all its lost hit points. A *stone to flesh* spell does not change the golem's structure, but the spell negates the creature's damage reduction and immunity to magic for 1 round.

Slow (Su) Range 10 feet; duration 7 rounds; Will DC 17 negates. A stone golem can use a *slow* effect (as the spell) as a free action once every 2 rounds.

Conclusion

Emmara does not want to die and tries to leave if combat goes badly. Ordering any surviving golems to cover her retreat, she uses *dimension door* to transport herself (and her howler, if it is still alive) to the Chambers of the Keepers (area 6). She quickly grabs her spellbook from its hiding place and uses the secret door to reach the top of Elliast's Spire. Once there, she drinks one or more *potions of cure serious wounds* and waits to see if the PCs discover her bolthole. If they find her, she drinks her *potion of fly* and flees to the mainland.

Features of the Area

The Chapel of Reverence has the following features.

Shattered Sarcophagus: Treat these squares as dense rubble (*DMG* 60). Nothing remains within the shattered sarcophagus except the jumbled bones of a powerfully built male human. Characters who stand atop the sarcophagus can gain a +1 melee attack bonus for fighting from higher ground.

Light Rubble: Squares adjacent to the shattered sarcophagus contain light rubble (*DMG* 60).

Slender Pillar: Each pillar has AC 4, hardness 8, and 900 hit points. Slender pillars grant a +2 cover bonus to Armor Class and a +1 cover bonus on Reflex saves to characters in the same square.

Balcony: A flight of 5-foot-wide stairs leads up to this 10-foot-high balcony. Characters on this terrace using weapons with reach can strike targets in floor squares that are adjacent to the balcony. The stairs are considered steep stairs and affect the movement of creatures climbing up or down the steps (*DMG* 63). In addition, while on the stairs and attacking opponents below them, creatures gain a +1 melee attack bonus for fighting from higher ground. Finally, a low stone balustrade around the balcony grants cover to anyone behind it.

Illus. by R. Horsley

The king was a waste of fire giant spark. Gilgirn is well rid of him. My countrymen needed a leader to ignite their souls. I never imagined that it would fall on me to coax those flames, but so be it. For now, the hard work is done. Our enemies fear us again, but that is not enough. Those who made sport of my kind in the past will learn what it means to have fire licking at their skin."

—Excerpt from the private journal of Valbryn Morlydd

Tired of ruling in the shadow of Balthur, an incompetent king, Valbryn murdered her spouse and became queen of Gilgirn, the seat of power in a dwindling fire giant kingdom. Valbryn restored pride to the fire giants with the help of the Urdred, her vicious agents, and she now plies arcane magic to uncover forgotten secrets deep within the belly of a dormant volcano.

BACKGROUND

Since the beginning of fire giant history, there was Gilgirn, a fiery mountainhold that became the birthplace of the fire giant civilization. Gilgirn is situated inside a dormant volcano that sits atop a magma reservoir; the volcano has simmered without erupting for untold millennia. Mythology speaks of the first fire giants climbing out of the magma at the dawn of their age and carving a home for themselves out of the ash and lava.

Easily the greatest asset of the fire giants, the magma beneath Gilgirn contains a higher concentration of iron than normal. A talented smith can extract and work the magma into virtually any iron object—including armor and weapons. Because of this bountiful and naturally occurring resource, Gilgirn has remained the seat of fire giant power, and is now a fortress for the race's ruling caste. It has been a sacred and highly defended locality for countless generations. That is, until recently.

Balthur was the latest fire giant king to rule over Gilgirn, but he was born into the position and turned out to be ill suited for leadership. He preferred to hunt the many creatures native to the region rather than handle affairs of state. By necessity, much of the decision-making fell to his young queen, Valbryn, who had not yet reached adulthood.

Valbryn was a strong and highly intelligent giant, but the king's frequent absence attracted invasions from adjoining kingdoms, whose forces coveted Gilgirn's resources. Valbryn saw only one solution. She arranged for the assassination of Balthur during one of his hunts and sent her loyal agents—known as the Urdred, or "death maidens"—to make it look like an accident. The mantle of leadership passed cleanly to Valbryn, and she changed her surname to "Morlydd," which means "bold vindicator." Nobody has uttered the name "Balthur" since then.

The young queen set about restrengthening her kingdom's reputation, knowing that the surrounding nations would underestimate her resolve. To this end, Valbryn divided the Urdred into groups and dispatched them down out of the mountains with complements of ettins and trolls. The death maidens stormed every realm that had attacked the fire giants during the reign of the late king, razing villages and cities alike. Before long, the greatest heroes of each nation arrived at the gates of Gilgirn in the custody of the Urdred, bearing generous gifts and pleas to end the war.

Once again secure, the fire giant kingdom began to thrive. Valbryn, now an adult, took up an interest in arcane magic, gleaning insight from some of the tomes that the envoys had brought as gifts. The queen studied forgotten lore, determined to unlock mysteries that were said to be hidden in the magma beneath Gilgirn. Her studies also revealed spell secrets that, among many other magical effects, could alter her size and shape for long periods of time.

GOALS

Of course, Valbryn's principal goal is maintaining her reign over the fire giants and extending her realm as far as possible. She believes that the most important means to this end is locating and controlling the gateway to the Elemental Plane of Fire that lies beneath her fortress.

Through her studies of lore and magic, Valbryn eventually discovered why the magma reservoir under Gilgirn had been dormant for so long. Following a clue in one of her arcane tomes, Valbryn descended into the molten rock and found a secret portal to the Elemental Plane of Fire, through which lava once flowed. Ancestral fire giants had magically sealed the portal so that nothing could pass through in either direction.

According to legend, the fire giant race was born in the magma of Gilgirn. Based on this story, the queen surmises that the first fire giants were natives of elemental fire who came through the portal. Valbryn believes that if she can unseal the portal, she will find masses of fire giants on the other side—legions she can use to bolster Gilgirn's army. The kingdom's forces were nearly depleted in the war against the neighboring realms, and Valbryn has no intention of honoring the peace treaties she established; thus, she is eager to rebuild her military. As soon as she can muster an army large enough to launch a multipronged invasion, she means to crush the smaller races and pick their bones clean. Valbryn has therefore made opening the portal her primary objective.

Accordingly, she has dispatched Helthra, Thaden, and members of the Urdred to acquire information about portals to other worlds. So far, the group has learned of a minor artifact known as a *planar trestle* that can force open portals between planes. Once the scattered, constituent pieces of the *planar trestle* are identified, deciphered, and assembled, Valbryn hopes to use it to unseal the portal to the Elemental Plane of Fire. If the queen finds allies on the other side, the results could be disastrous for the surrounding kingdoms.

USING THIS VILLAIN

Valbryn is a formidable female giant who has the resources of a wealthy kingdom at her disposal. However, she wishes to conceal her nation's true strength, and so avoids extravagant displays of power. When her legions are again ready to march, she wants the smaller races to be complacent and unwary. To keep up the pretense of peace, Valbryn operates by proxy through her Urdred. Fortunately for the queen, fire giants are so independent in nature that whenever her

HOW THADEN MET VALBRYN

The queen of the fire giants and a mighty human ranger: Seldom has a more mismatched pair of individuals turned out to be companions.

The saga of Valbryn and Thaden began several decades ago. The ranger battled stalwartly but unsuccessfully against the raiders that the queen had sent forth to subjugate the humanoid realms that adjoined the territory around her fortress.

Valbryn had ordered her assault squads to subdue the most valiant survivors among the nations the Urdred defeated and bring those captors before her. Then she selected one member of each vanquished force to carry back her terms of surrender and had the others killed. Thaden turned out to be an exception to that rule; the raiders that captured him, unconscious and near death, related tales of his pride and fighting spirit. They spoke highly of his skill at combating the giant invaders, which led the queen to conclude that it might be wiser to keep him alive and persuade him (through torture, if necessary) to reveal those special techniques. Accordingly, she ordered him to be imprisoned in a cell beneath her quarters and nursed back to health.

After the ranger's wounds healed, he proved to be an uncooperative yet gregarious prisoner. He would not speak of his special skill at fighting giants—not even under threat of pain—but he deflected the queen's anger by flattering her and encouraging her to converse with him on a personal level. As time went on, Valbryn grew to prefer Thaden's company over that of her subjects—most of whom were sorely lacking in intelligence (compared to her) and did not share her interest in spellcasting.

Originally, Thaden's use of flattery and conversation was a stalling tactic—he was trying to stay alive long enough to figure out a way to escape. But the longer he acted the part of the friend and confidant, the more he genuinely enjoyed the role. He captured Valbryn's trust to such an extent that the queen allowed him to serve as a surrogate father to her daughter Helthra.

Today, Thaden spends much time with Valbryn in her personal quarters, even though he is still "officially" confined to his cell. Their emotional bond is a mutual one, and equally strong on both sides. The ranger will fight on behalf of the queen if her fortress or her reign is threatened, and Valbryn will not hesitate to bring her spells and her weapons to bear against anyone—even another fire giant—who opposes her companion.

agents are spotted in neighboring lands, she can attribute the foray to a rogue element that is being hunted down and punished.

In truth, the death maidens do Valbryn's secret bidding. These warriors are female giant ninjas whom she has trained to fulfill their current roles without fail. The Urdred have full discretion to exercise their will as they see fit; they command the hell hounds of Gilgirn and are accountable to no one but Valbryn. She keeps their numbers limited and promotes new candidates as needed.

Illus. by T. Giorello

Valbryn Morlydd, Queen of the Fire Giants

Because the Urdred frequently lead expeditionary forces, the PCs will likely encounter them before meeting any other members of the fire giant kingdom. Thus, the death maidens are a good way for characters to experience Valbryn's machinations firsthand in an encounter outside Gilgirn. In such encounters, the Urdred are almost always found plundering repositories of knowledge.

As the PCs attain higher levels and grow more capable of handling the Urdred in combat, the nature of the encounters shifts. Valbryn has finally identified the items needed to build the *planar trestle*, and the death maidens begin searching other lands in earnest for obscure historical objects. The diplomatic gloves come off, and the Urdred go to increasingly greater lengths to secure the component parts of the minor artifact.

VALBRYN MORLYDD IN EBERRON

Valbryn struggles for dominance among the indigenous dark elves of Xen'drik. However, as a fire giant wu jen, she craves the convenience and resources of Khorvaire. There are plenty of runes to explore on each continent, any of which can lead to the discovery of another component of the *planar trestle*.

VALBRYN MORLYDD IN FAERÛN

Valbryn is eager to raise the profile of her kingdom by taking back the fire giants' ancestral home, which is currently occupied by gold dwarves. The dwarves do not know about the portal to the Elemental Plane of Fire, so Valbryn is the only individual capable of acquiring the knowledge to unlock the gate. What she discovers on the other side might help or hinder her cause.

APPEARANCE AND BEHAVIOR

Early in her adulthood Valbryn had no ambitions to rule the fire giant kingdom, but leadership becomes her. Once the young bride of a crude and self-indulgent king, she now thrives as the queen of Gilgirn, basking in the inferno of limitless power and unforeseen possibilities. To her court, she appears more confident and vital nowadays than ever before.

Valbryn makes no effort to hide her curves (such as they are with a fire giant's physique), and she accentuates her shape

MINOR ARTIFACT: PLANAR TRESTLE

A planar trestle is an amalgamation of esoteric objects that are unique to the plane on which the artifact was created. Once the components are interlocked in one specific way, the amalgamated object cannot be physically sundered or harmed by any type of energy. When a planar trestle is brought into contact with a portal to another plane, whether sealed or inactive, that portal is forced open permanently, destroying the artifact.

Strong conjuration (calling); CL 20th; Weight 5 lb.

without provocatively revealing any flesh. She usually wears her long, blood-red hair down, letting it frame her face and securing it with a modest circlet rather than a formal tiara. Her garments range in hue from black and gray to black and twilight blue. However, she always decorates herself with a red sash and never wears anything white; these color restrictions are dictated by one of the taboos that she observes as a wu jen.

When addressing her military leaders or the fire giant population as a whole, Valbryn wears an ornate tailored masterwork breastplate so that she appeals to the warriors. Beyond the use of these trappings, she finds the pomp and circumstance of royal appearances bothersome.

This informal spirit carries over into most aspects of her rule. Valbryn is a strong and unyielding monarch, but she has a sultry charm and eloquence that puts others at ease. She uses these talents to disarm and relax her enemies, the better to catch them off guard.

The queen's greatest weakness is vanity, stemming from a deep-rooted desire to be considered beautiful—a quality that few fire giants value. When Thaden Felstrom was first captured and imprisoned, he exploited this vanity in a successful attempt to save his life.

VALBRYN MORLYDD — CR 17

hp 248 (29 HD)

Female fire giant wu jen[CAr] 9/geometer[CAr] 5
NE Large giant (fire)
Init +5; **Senses** darkvision 60 ft., low-light vision; Listen +2, Spot +13
Languages Common, Draconic, Giant

AC 30, touch 15, flat-footed 27
(–1 size, +3 Dex, +4 armor, +3 deflection, +1 insight, +10 natural)
Immune fire, giant immunities
Fort +18, **Ref** +10, **Will** +18; +2 against fire spells
Weakness vulnerability to cold, giant vulnerabilities

Speed 40 ft. (8 squares)
Melee *+2 adamantine flaming longsword* +27/+22/+17/+12 (2d6+15/19–20 plus 1d6 fire) and slam +20 (1d4+4) or
Melee 2 slams +25 each (1d4+9)
Ranged *+1 composite longbow* +18 (2d6+10)
Base Atk +17; **Grp** +30
Atk Options Awesome Blow, Energy Substitution (cold), Improved Bull Rush, Improved Sunder, Power Attack
Special Actions rock catching, rock throwing
Combat Gear *2 potions of cure serious wounds*, scroll of *telekinesis*, scroll of *tongues*, *wand of rope trick* (25 charges)
Wu Jen Spells Prepared (CL 18th):
7th—*decapitating scarf*[CAr] (DC 23), *sword of darkness*[S CAr] (CL 19th)
6th—*fire seeds* (CL 20th, DC 22), *globe of invulnerability*[S]† (CL 19th), *greater dispel magic*[S] (CL 19th), *transfix*[S CAr] (CL 19th, DC 22)
5th—*arc of lightning*[S CAr] (CL 19th, DC 21), *fire breath*[S CAr] (CL 21st, +18 ranged touch), *teleport*[S] (CL 19th), *vitriolic sphere*[S CAr] (CL 19th, DC 21)
4th—*dimension door*[S] (CL 19th), extended *greater invisibility*[*S] † (CL 19th), extended *polymorph*[*S]† (CL 19th), *stoneskin*[S] (CL 19th), *wall of fire*[S] (CL 21st)
3rd—*displacement*[S] (CL 19th), *haste*[S] (CL 19th), *fire wings*[S CAr] (CL 21st), *protection from energy*[S]† (CL 21st), *remove curse*[S] (CL 19th)
2nd—*cat's grace*[S] (CL 21st), *detect thoughts*[S] (CL 19th, DC 18), extended *alter self*[*S] (CL 19th), *hold person*[S] (CL 19th, DC 18), *see invisibility*[S] (CL 19th), *gaseous form*[S] (CL 19th)
1st—*endure elements*[S] (CL 21st), *fiery eyes*[S CAr] (CL 21st), *hail of stone*[S CAr] (CL 19th), *jet of steam*[S CM] (CL 19th, DC 17), *magic missile*[S] (CL 19th), *shield*[S] (CL 19th)
0—*detect magic*[S] (CL 19th), *prestidigitation*[S] (CL 19th), *ray of frost*[S] (CL 19th, +18 ranged touch), *read magic*[S] (CL 19th)
* Spell secret
S: Spellglyph replaces verbal and material components
† Already cast

Abilities Str 28, Dex 12, Con 20, Int 22, Wis 16, Cha 13
SQ book of geometry, elemental mastery (fire), giant traits, pass sigil, powerful spellglyph, sigilsight, spell secrets, taboos, watchful spirit
Feats Awesome Blow, Combat Casting, Elemental Adept[CM] (*fireball*) (see page 25), Energy Substitution[CAr] (cold) (see page 25), Improved Bull Rush, Improved Initiative, Improved Sunder, Maximize Spell[B], Power Attack, Practiced Spellcaster[CAr], Rapid Metamagic[CM]
Skills Bluff +6, Climb +14, Concentration +18 (+22 when casting defensively), Decipher Script +19, Diplomacy +12, Disable Device +11, Disguise +1 (+3 when acting), Intimidate +8, Jump +18, Knowledge (arcana) +19, Knowledge (nobility and royalty) +11, Listen +2, Search +13, Sense Motive +8, Spellcraft +21, Spot +13, Survival +3 (+5 when following tracks)
Possessions combat gear plus *+2 adamantine flaming longsword*, *+1 composite longbow* (+9 Str bonus) with 40 arrows, *amulet of natural armor +2*, *bracers of armor +4*, *ring of protection +3*, *headband of intellect +4*, *ioun stone (dusty rose)*, *bag of holding (type I)*, highly polished silver mirror for *scrying* spell, spellglyph inks, royal wu jen outfit, 160 pp, 10 gp
Spellbook spells prepared plus 0—all; 1st—*accuracy*[CAr], *charm person, comprehend languages, disguise self, melt*[CAr], *protection from good, true strike, unseen servant;* 2nd—*bull's strength, mirror image, rope trick, whispering wind;* 3rd—*dispel magic, fireball, gaseous form, tongues;* 4th—*fire shield, locate creature, scrying;* 5th—*dominate person, passwall, telekinesis;* 6th—*geas/quest, greater glyph of warding, true seeing;* 7th—*delayed blast fireball, disintegrate, giant size*[CAr]

Book of Geometry (Ex) Every spell Valbryn learns requires only a single page in her spellbook. It still takes 24 hours to write each spell into her book and requires materials costing 100 gp per page. In addition, the DC of Spellcraft checks for a nongeometer to decipher or prepare spells from Valbryn's spellbook is increased by 5.

NONASSOCIATED CLASS LEVELS

Valbryn has pursued an atypical profession for fire giants by becoming an arcane spellcaster. As such, her levels of wu jen and geometer are considered nonassociated class levels. Adding nonassociated class levels to a monster increases its Challenge Rating by 1/2 per level until its nonassociated class levels equal its original Hit Dice. For details, see *MM* 294.

Pass Sigil (Su) Valbryn can temporarily negate magical wards based on written symbols, sigils, runes, or glyphs. As a standard action, she can make a caster level check (DC 6 + the sigil creator's caster level). If successful, she can suppress the effects of the device for as long as she maintains concentration. Valbryn must be able to see the device.

Rapid Metamagic Valbryn uses this feat to spontaneously cast metamagic versions of *fireball* and still have a move action afterward.

Sigilsight (Ex) Valbryn can use a Search check to find magic traps based on runes, glyphs, sigils, symbols, and other writing, as a rogue can. She gains a +11 bonus on Search checks to find traps of this sort. If she comes within 10 feet of a magic rune, glyph, sigil, or symbol, or within the threshold of danger for such a device, she is entitled to make a Search check as if she were actively searching for a magic trap.

Spellglyph (Su) Valbryn can cast spells using spellglyphs. Such spells have a special material component (the spellglyph) that substitutes for the spell's verbal component and any other material components it might normally require. When Valbryn casts a spell using a spellglyph, the spell is treated as if it were affected by the Silent Spell feat.

Spell Secrets Whenever Valbryn casts *alter self*, *greater invisibility*, or *polymorph*, those spells are modified as if affected by the Extend Spell metamagic feat, but without using any higher-level spell slots.

Taboos Valbryn may not cast spells of the metal element (see Elemental Mastery, *Complete Arcane* page 16), must face west when sitting and south when preparing spells, and must always wear something red and never wear anything white.

Thaden Felstorm and his animal companion

Illus. by E. Deschamps

Watchful Spirit Once per day, Valbryn can reroll initiative before knowing her place in the initiative order. She takes the better of the two rolls.

THADEN FELSTORM

"I gave up trying to escape a long time ago—not because I stopped craving my freedom, but because I realized that Gilgirn had become my home."

—Thaden Felstorm,
trusted advisor of the fire giant queen

Nobody knows the fire giant queen and princess better than Thaden does. He has occupied a cell beneath the royal suite for three decades, during which he has been privy to the two females' most private thoughts. Thaden has become the sole confidant of the queen in matters personal and strategic, and watched Helthra grow up, parenting by proxy.

GOALS

Thaden fought alongside the other heroes who visited Gilgirn to sue for peace, but he was knocked senseless during the battle and awoke imprisoned. From that point forward, his only goal was to stay alive. Valbryn intended to torture the human to death because he had killed several prominent fire giants, but whenever she visited him, he deflected her anger with flattery and personal inquiries. For months, the giantslayer managed to earn a stay of execution by candidly conversing with the queen.

Thaden had a seductive effect on Valbryn, giving her an audience for thoughts and feelings that she could not share with other fire giants. Once the ranger realized that his life was no longer in imminent danger, his goal became to ingratiate himself to the queen, and he has done exactly that. There is nobody with whom Valbryn is more relaxed.

USING THADEN FELSTORM

Thaden was a giantslayer of no small repute, unrivaled in his ability to fell the great folk like trees. In the early years of his imprisonment, he escaped from Gilgirn on more than one occasion—more to familiarize himself with his surroundings than anything else, since he knew that the Urdred would catch him eventually. Each time, Valbryn had him thrown back in his cell but did not punish him beyond that, since she was becoming emotionally attached to the human and she saw his escape attempts as Thaden's way of asserting his individuality and keeping his skills sharp.

After a decade in captivity, he escaped for the final time. Not only did he manage to leave the fortress unseen, he made it as far as the border of his former homeland before he found himself unwilling to continue. He realized that he had left something important behind—he did not want to live in a world that did not include the fire giant queen and her daughter. Thaden turned around, infiltrated the fire giant kingdom, snuck back into the fortress, and returned to his cell.

When Valbryn learned what had happened, she released him from captivity. Today, Thaden still spends some time in his unlocked cell, but he is no longer treated like a prisoner. He roams the fortress, often accompanied by his fleshraker animal companion—a 7-foot-tall dinosaur similar to a velociraptor. Thaden will defend or avenge Valbryn or Helthra to the death, motivated by his dedication to them both.

Appearance and Behavior

Although he is in late middle age, Thaden Felstorm has not lost his vitality. He stays healthy by sparring with the Urdred and teaching young fire giants how to protect themselves from giantslayers like him. His hair has long since turned gray, but his build is still powerful—in fact, living among giants has made Thaden a prodigy of strength (see the sidebar). He outfits himself in a mithral chain shirt and wields two giant-sized bastard swords.

Thaden has developed a sense of humor about his place in the fire giant kingdom, and he is treated with attentive respect by his adopted compatriots. The fire giants that he trains live in fear of his ability to kill them outright, and he enjoys nothing more than embarrassing cocksure young giantlings in front of their peers.

THADEN FELSTORM — CR 15

hp 98 (128 with *bear's endurance*) (15 HD)

Male human ranger 12/rogue 3
N Medium humanoid
Init +5; **Senses** Listen +13, Spot +13
Languages Common, Draconic, Giant

AC 23, touch 11, flat-footed 22
(+1 Dex, +7 armor, +5 natural [with *potion of barkskin*])
Resist evasion
Fort +10 (+12 with *bear's endurance*), **Ref** +12, **Will** +6

Speed 40 ft. (6 squares) (50 ft. with *longstrider*); woodland stride
Melee *+2 Large adamantine bastard sword* +19/+14/+9 (2d8+8/17–20) and
+2 Large adamantine bastard sword +19/+14 (2d8+8/17–20)
Ranged *+1 composite longbow* +16/+11/+6 (1d8+6/19–20×3)
Base Atk +14; **Grp** +20
Atk Options favored enemy giants +6, favored enemy humans +4, favored enemy dragons +2, sneak attack +2d6
Combat Gear *2 potions of cure moderate wounds, potion of barkskin +5*†
† Already used
Ranger Spells Prepared (CL 6th):
3rd—*water walk*
2nd—*bear's endurance*†
1st—*endure elements*†, *longstrider*†
† Already cast

Abilities Str 22, Dex 13, Con 12 (16 with *bear's endurance*), Int 11, Wis 13, Cha 10
SQ animal companion, link with companion, prodigy of strength (see sidebar), share spells, swift tracker, trapfinding, trap sense +1, wild empathy +12 (+8 magical beasts)
Feats Endurance[B], Exotic Weapon Proficiency (bastard sword), Greater Two-Weapon Fighting[B], Improved Critical (bastard sword), Improved Initiative, Improved Toughness[CW], Improved Two-Weapon Fighting[B], Monkey Grip[CW] (see page 25), Oversized Two-Weapon Fighting[CAd] (see page 25), Track[B], Two-Weapon Fighting[B], Weapon Focus (bastard sword)
Skills Bluff +9, Climb +25, Diplomacy +4, Disguise +0 (+2 when acting), Hide +16, Intimidate +2, Jump +34 (+38 with *longstrider*), Listen +13, Move Silently +16, Open Lock +10, Sense Motive +10, Spot +13, Survival +16
Possessions combat gear plus *+3 mithral shirt*, two *+2 Large adamantine bastard swords*, *+1 composite longbow* (+6 Str bonus) with 40 arrows, *belt of giant strength +4*, *boots of striding and springing*, 63 pp, 8 gp

FLESHRAKER[MM3] ANIMAL COMPANION — CR —

hp 39 (51 with *bear's endurance*) (6 HD)

N Medium animal (dinosaur)
Init +1; **Senses** low-light vision, scent; Listen +2, Spot +2

AC 26, touch 14, flat-footed 22
(+4 Dex, +4 armor, +8 natural)
Resist evasion
Fort +7 (+9 with *bear's endurance*), **Ref** +9, **Will** +4

Speed 50 ft. (10 squares) (60 ft. with *longstrider*)
Melee 2 claws +8 each (1d6+4 plus poison) and
bite +6 (1d6+2) and
tail +6 melee (1d6+2 plus poison)
Base Atk +4; **Grp** +8
Atk Options leaping pounce, poison (Fort DC 14, 1d6 Dex/1d6 Dex), rake 1d6+2

Abilities Str 18, Dex 19, Con 15 (19 with *bear's endurance*), Int 2, Wis 14, Cha 12
SQ two bonus tricks
Feats Improved Natural Attack (claw), Multiattack, Track
Skills Hide +12 (+14 in forested areas), Jump +27 (+31 with *longstrider*), Listen +2, Spot +2
Possessions *collar of mage armor*

PRODIGY OF STRENGTH

Thaden has lived among fire giants for much of his adult life. To survive in a world meant for much larger creatures—or to simply move from room to room—he was forced to open giant sized-doors, scale giant-sized stairs, and use giant-sized utensils. As such, he eventually became a prodigy of strength (see DMG2 page 160), gaining a +2 bonus to his Strength score and a +4 bonus on Strength-based checks, including ability checks and skill checks.

HELTHRA MORLYDD

"My mother has devoted her life to studying the portal to Elemental Fire. If I had half as much physical determination as she has mental resolve, then I'd stop fighting only when I died. If I could match her in full, then beware my ghost."

—Helthra Morlydd,
heir apparent to the fire giant throne

After Valbryn had successfully brutalized the other nations into submission, the fire giants heralded her as a conquering hero, and all the highest-ranking males of the nation vied for her attention. The queen had no interest in being married again (after her unpleasant experience with Balthur), but needed to keep the warriors mollified, so the queen began holding monthly contests of combative skill for the honor of her company. When she eventually became pregnant, Valbryn declined to identify the father and announced to her followers that she intended to name and raise the child herself. As a result, Valbryn's daughter Helthra grew up profoundly influenced by her mother—and to a lesser but still significant degree by Thaden.

Helthra is aware that she lives in the shadow of her mother, but she cares too much about furthering her kingdom to let that bother her. The princess has embraced the traditional ways of her kin by becoming a pious fire giant warrior. Helthra revels in the harsh life of her kinfolk, accepting no special treatment for being royalty.

Illus. by T. Giorello

Helthra Morlydd, Princess of the Fire Giants, and an Urdred

GOALS

Since she stands to inherit the kingdom one day, Helthra has a personal stake in the quest to open the Elemental Plane of Fire. The princess is committed to assembling the *planar trestle* at any cost, and she leads the Urdred on missions to find its components. Her unwavering single-mindedness during these expeditions can make her oblivious to the collateral damage that she and the death maidens sometimes cause. When at home, Helthra is the voice of reason for her mother, advocating caution and discretion with respect to the portal.

USING HELTHRA MORLYDD

Whenever Valbryn sends the Urdred to recover a piece of the *planar trestle*, Helthra is in command. The queen is confident that her daughter will obtain what is needed—by sheer stubbornness if nothing else. Helthra does not accept failure lightly and rails against seemingly insurmountable odds, destroying any obstacle that stands in her way. She is known for digging in to fight when it would be smarter to change her tactics. Regardless of the situation, the Urdred that accompany Helthra never leave her side.

NONASSOCIATED CLASS LEVELS

Helthra has pursued an atypical profession for fire giants by becoming a divine spellcaster. As such, her levels of cleric are considered nonassociated class levels. Adding nonassociated class levels to a monster increases its Challenge Rating by 1/2 per level until its nonassociated class levels equal its original Hit Dice. For details, see the *Monster Manual*, page 294.

If Helthra is able to cast most or all of her self-buffing spells (such as *bull's strength* and *shield of faith*) before combat begins, or if she uses Divine Vigor more than once, consider increasing her Challenge Rating by 1 or 2.

Appearance and Behavior

Fire giants are a sturdy race, harsh in countenance and solidly built. A typical fire giant weighs around 7,000 pounds, with a chest circumference that measures three-quarters of her height. Helthra has a softer appearance than the other members of her clan. This perceived shortcoming drives the princess to work harder at fitting in among her peers.

Helthra wears black full plate armor whenever possible, and when not clad for battle, she makes an effort to look disheveled and dour. Despite her minor physical quirks, she is all fire giant, right down to her long orange hair.

HELTHRA MORLYDD **CR 15**

hp 246 (292 with Divine Vigor) (23 HD)

Female fire giant cleric 6/fighter 2
LE Large giant (fire)
Init +5; **Senses** darkvision 60 ft., low-light vision; Listen +5, Spot +17
Languages Common, Giant

AC 32, touch 13, flat-footed 31
(–1 size, +1 Dex, +11 armor, +3 deflection, +8 natural)
Immune fire, giant immunities
Fort +23, **Ref** +8, **Will** +15
Weakness vulnerability to cold, giant vulnerabilities

Speed 30 ft. (6 squares) (40 ft. with Divine Vigor)
Melee *+2 adamantine flaming greataxe* +33/+27/+23/+17 (3d6+23/19–20/×3 plus 1d6 fire) or
Melee 2 slams +30 each (1d4+14)
Ranged rock +31 (2d6+14 plus 2d6 fire)
Base Atk +17; **Grp** +35
Atk Options Awesome Blow, Improved Bull Rush, Improved Sunder, Power Attack
Special Actions command undead 4/day (+1, 2d6+7, 6th), Divine Vigor†, rock catching, rock throwing, spontaneous casting
† Already used
Combat Gear 2 *potions of lesser restoration, wand of cure moderate wounds* (30 charges)
Cleric Spells Prepared (CL 10th):
3rd—*inflict serious wounds*[D] (+33 melee touch), *dispel magic, protection from energy, ring of blades*[CAr]
2nd—*bull's strength*†, *inflict moderate wounds*[D] (+33 melee touch), *deific vengeance*[CD] (DC 17), *spiritual weapon* (2)
1st—*cause light wounds*[D] (+33 melee touch), *comprehend languages, divine favor* (2), *obscuring mist, shield of faith*†
0—*cure minor wounds* (2), *detect magic, purify food and drink, read magic*
D: Domain spell. Domains: Trickery, War
† Already cast

Abilities Str 34 (38 with *bull's strength*), Dex 12, Con 22, Int 10, Wis 20, Cha 12
SQ giant traits
Feats Awesome Blow, Brutal Throw[CAd], Combat Casting, Divine Vigor[CW] (see page 25), Improved Bull Rush, Improved Critical[B] (greataxe), Improved Initiative, Improved Sunder[B], Power Attack, Practiced Spellcaster[CAr], Weapon Focus (greataxe)[B]
Skills Climb +15, Concentration +13 (+17 when casting defensively), Hide +2, Intimidate +13, Jump +15 (+19 with Divine Vigor), Listen +5, Move Silently +2, Spot +17
Possessions combat gear plus *+3 shadow silent moves full plate, +2 adamantine flaming greataxe, amulet of health +4,* silver holy symbol, noble's outfit, 18 pp, 5 gp

Spontaneous Domain Casting This alternative class feature allows Helthra to sacrifice any prepared spell (other than a domain spell) to cast any spell of the same level or lower from the Trickery domain. In addition, when preparing spells, she can choose to fill any or all of her domain spell slots with *cure* or *inflict* spells of the same level. For details, see *PH2* 37.

GILGIRN

Since before fire giants can remember, Gilgirn (Fiery Mountainhold in the Fire Giant language) has existed. The mountain was an active volcano many millennia ago, but there have been no signs of geologic activity since, aside from the simmering pools of lava. For this reason, fire giants regard the mountain as their sacred home—they believe that their deity has used divine power to prevent eruptions so that Gilgirn could be carved out of the volcanic rock directly above the lava throat.

Mythology has led fire giants to believe that they were originally birthed out of the magma that now feeds Gilgirn's protective moat. This viewpoint still prevails, but Valbryn Morlydd wanted to test it. The fire giant queen descended into the molten rock to explore, and she found a dimensional barrier in the lava throat; this portal was adorned with a ring of ancient runes in a forgotten language, carved into the stone.

Valbryn became fascinated with the runes and memorized the lava-submerged symbols by touch until she could scribe them herself. She then concentrated on learning the script (through study of the runes coupled with research into other similar symbols) until she understood the writing perfectly. After thirty years of work on this project, Valbryn came to realize that the fire giants' ancestors had not only emerged from the lava pool, but had originated on the Elemental Plane of Fire. The lava throat contained a portal to that plane, which her forebears had sealed shut.

When Valbryn took control of the kingdom, its fire giants had lost their way in the world. She changed that by attacking the nations that had preyed on her people. These battles were successful, but they somewhat depleted the kingdom's military resources, leaving Valbryn hesitant to launch further attacks on its foes. She thinks that opening the portal is the solution, imagining that legions of fire giants await on the other side.

KEY FEATURES

Gilgirn has always been inhabited by the fire giants' ruling caste, who treat the hold as the kingdom's seat of power. Valbryn has devoted considerable resources to restoring the dilapidated portions of the volcanic fortress, and Gilgirn is now no less impressive than when it was first constructed. The queen has taken up residence there with her daughter Helthra, her confidant Thaden, a garrison of warriors, and her own private guard, the Urdred.

Structural Properties

The following general properties apply to all rooms unless otherwise noted in the area descriptions.

Walls: The curtain walls around Gilgirn are reinforced masonry. They are 20 feet thick and 50 feet high, and have hardness 8 and 3,600 hit points. The barracks, gatehouse, and tower walls are also reinforced masonry, but are only 5 feet thick, with hardness 8 and 900 hit points. Scaling reinforced masonry walls requires a successful DC 15 Climb check. The volcanic cavern walls are unworked stone and have hardness 8 and 900 hit points per 5 feet of thickness. Scaling unworked walls requires a successful DC 20 Climb check.

Floors: The floors throughout Gilgirn are flagstone. Each floor is at least 5 feet thick by necessity, since a typical fire giant weighs approximately 7,000 pounds.

Doors: The ground-level doors are carved from 8-inch-thick stone. Each door is 10 feet wide and 15 feet high and has hardness 8 and 120 hit points. The doors on the second and third levels are carved from 4-inch-thick stone. Each upper-level door is 5 feet wide and 13-1/2 feet high and has hardness 8 and 60 hit points.

Ceilings: In the rooms of the fortress, the ceilings are 20 feet high. Outside the walls, the ceiling of the volcanic cavern is 150 feet above the main lava throat.

Staircases: All staircases in Gilgirn are made for fire giants and are considered steep, affecting the movement of creatures climbing up or down (*DMG* 63). In addition, while on the stairs and attacking opponents below them, creatures gain a +1 bonus on melee attack rolls for fighting from higher ground.

Cover: Murder holes grant fire giants a +8 bonus to Armor Class and a +4 bonus on Reflex saves. Battlements atop each barracks, curtain wall, gatehouse, and tower grant fire giants a +4 bonus to Armor Class and a +2 bonus on Reflex saves.

Lava Canals: Canals of lava have been redirected off the central lava throat to feed the moat around Gilgirn. These canals are 5 feet deep and filled with rocks that fire giants can reach in and grab for throwing. Coming into contact with lava deals 2d6 points of fire damage per round of exposure, except in the case of total immersion, which deals 20d6 points of damage per round. Damage from lava continues for 1d3 rounds after exposure ceases, but this additional damage is only half the amount dealt during actual contact.

Steam Vents: In lieu of natural chimneys that release pressure from the magma reservoir beneath Gilgirn, artificial chimneys were installed in the fortress during its construction thousands of years ago. These vents randomly discharge superheated steam once every minute (roll 1d10 to determine the round in which a vent discharges). Anyone caught within 15 feet of a discharging vent must make a DC 16 Reflex save. Those who fail take 2d6 points of fire damage and are permanently blinded. Those who succeed take 1d6 points of fire damage and are not blinded.

Illumination: Any lava source emits shadowy illumination to a radius of 30 feet (60 feet for those with low-light vision). In places where lava is not present, nonremovable sconces built into the walls every 40 feet emit light to a radius of 20 feet.

Traps: Valbryn has cast a number of *greater glyphs of warding* around Gilgirn, most of which are keyed to remain inactive around creatures of the fire subtype. Some are *greater blast glyphs* that deal 10d8 points of sonic damage to the intruder and anyone else within 5 feet (Reflex DC 34 half), while others are *greater spell glyphs*, detailed individually. A sonic *greater blast glyph* also alerts fire giant guards. The entire surface of every foot bridge over a lava canal is covered with a sonic *greater blast glyph*. A rogue can find a *greater glyph of warding* with a successful DC 31 Search check and thwart it with a successful DC 31 Disable Device check.

Temperature: The volcanic cavern is bearably hot, but the temperature within Gilgirn is 90 degrees F, requiring visitors to make successful Fortitude saves to avoid nonlethal damage (*DMG* 303). Within 30 feet of lava, the temperature exceeds 110 degrees F, requiring more frequent saves.

DEFENSES

If the PCs set off a *greater glyph of warding* or are detected by fire giant guards or death maidens, the entire fortress goes on alert. Valbryn, Helthra, and Thaden cast or use their buffing abilities and spells, while brigades of fire giants and hell hounds arrive to attack the intruders. These warriors soften up the PCs for the Urdred, who enter melee using their ghost step ability to make sudden strikes. Helthra and Thaden appear next, focusing on the lead melee fighter and spellcaster, respectively. Meanwhile, Valbryn casts *dimension door* to position herself atop a tower or wall within 60 feet of the battle, and then begins casting offensive and defensive spells.

AREA DESCRIPTIONS

Gilgirn had fallen into disrepair, but Valbryn spared no expense to restore the fortress to its former glory. The following areas correspond with those on the map on page 120.

1. Archway: Myriad, mazelike tunnels leading in from outside the mountain eventually connect and widen to accommodate an archway cut out of the volcanic rock. The opening is 15 feet wide and 15 feet high, and sculptures of hell hounds carved into the sides seem to threaten anybody who walks through. Just beyond the archway, a flagstone bridge 15 feet above a lava moat leads to a gatehouse that guards the entrance to the inner ward of Gilgirn. (See tactical encounter 7–1, page 122.)

A sonic *greater blast glyph* (Search DC 31 to find; Disable Device DC 31 to thwart) is set to activate if any creature that is not of the fire subtype walks through the archway.

2. Barracks: Gilgirn has a total of twenty-eight fire giant guards. Each of the four enclosures that frame the inner towers serves as a combination lookout tower and barracks, with modest living quarters for seven of the guards.

Under normal circumstances (if the complex is not on alert), one fire giant is training on the first floor of each tower, two more are relaxing on the second level, and a fourth stands atop the tower next to a pile of unheated rocks. The

Gilgirn (Fiery Mountainhold)

other three fire giants who live in each tower are on duty elsewhere around Gilgirn.

The guards rotate their locations approximately every 8 hours. If an alarm sounds, the fire giants on duty around the complex are the first to respond, followed by the training fire giants 1 round later, followed by the resting fire giants 1 round after that. The fire giant that stands atop each tower holds his position and directs the others to any perceived disturbances.

On the first floor of each tower, the guards keep their armor, weapons, an extra bunk bed, and two strongboxes for personal storage. The second floor features three sets of bunk beds, a table and chairs, and six strongboxes.

Fire Giant Guards: hp 142 each (15 HD); see page 122

3. Southwest Tower: The southwest tower contains a basement, three levels, and a lookout. The basement is a dungeon for prisoners. The first floor is a hell hound kennel where the fire giant stablehand works. The second and third floors are split into four private bedrooms for the Urdred.

The fire giant stablehand defends himself if attacked, but otherwise avoids conflict.

Fire Giant Stablehand — CR 7

hp 82 (11 HD)

Male fire giant expert 1
LE Medium giant (fire)
Init –1; **Senses** darkvision 60 ft., low-light vision; Listen +2, Spot +12
Languages Giant

AC 17, touch 9, flat-footed 17
(–1 Dex, +8 natural)
Immune fire, giant immunities
Fort +10, **Ref** +2, **Will** +5
Weakness vulnerability to cold, giant vulnerabilities

Speed 40 ft. (8 squares)
Melee quarterstaff +16/+11 (1d6+8)
Base Atk +8; **Grp** +16
Atk Options Cleave, Great Cleave, Improved Overrun, Power Attack
Special Actions rock catching, rock throwing

Abilities Str 27, Dex 9, Con 17, Int 10, Wis 14, Cha 11
SQ giant traits
Feats Cleave, Great Cleave, Improved Overrun, Power Attack
Skills Climb +13, Jump +17, Listen +2, Profession (stablehand) +6, Spot +12

4. Southeast Tower: The southeast tower contains a basement, three levels, and a lookout. The basement is for livestock that produce food. The first floor is for meat-yielding livestock. The second floor is a kitchen where the fire giant butcher/cook works. The third floor is a gathering place for eating and meetings.

The fire giant defends himself if attacked, but otherwise avoids conflict. He has access to hot rocks, used in cooking, that deal extra fire damage when thrown.

Fire Giant Butcher/Cook CR 10

hp 137 (16 HD)

Male fire giant expert 1
LE Large giant (fire)
Init –1; **Senses** darkvision 60 ft., low-light vision; Listen +3, Spot +15
Languages Giant

AC 16, touch 8, flat-footed 16
(–1 size, –1 Dex, +8 natural)
Immune fire, giant immunities
Fort +13, **Ref** +4, **Will** +10
Weakness vulnerability to cold, giant vulnerabilities

Speed 40 ft. (8 squares)
Melee cleaver +21/+16/+11 (1d6+11/18–20) and slam +16 (1d4+5) or
Melee 2 slams +21 each (1d4+11)
Ranged rock +10 (2d6+11 plus 2d6 fire)
Base Atk +11; **Grp** +26
Atk Options Cleave, Great Cleave, Improved Overrun, Power Attack
Special Actions rock catching, rock throwing

Abilities Str 32, Dex 9, Con 19, Int 10, Wis 17, Cha 8
SQ giant traits
Feats Cleave, Great Cleave, Improved Overrun, Skill Focus (Profession [butcher]), Skill Focus (Profession [cook]), Power Attack
Skills Climb +16, Jump +20, Listen +3, Profession (butcher) +12, Profession (cook) +12, Spot +15

5. **Lava Throat:** This opening continually produces lava that runs through canals and feeds the moat around Gilgirn. The lava then drains into the natural magma reservoir deep

beneath the fortress. Valbryn discovered the sealed portal to the Elemental Plane of Fire after swimming down into the molten rock here.

This area is easily the hottest part of Gilgirn. Within 5 feet of the lava, the temperature exceeds 140 degrees F and deals lethal damage (*DMG* 303).

6. Northeast Tower: The northeast tower contains a basement, three levels, and a lookout. The basement is a storage area for the fortress's finest metal goods. The first floor is a masterwork blacksmithy where the fire giant artisan works. The second floor is a study and place of reflection, adorned with antiques that belonged to fire giant ancestors. The third floor is the personal quarters of Helthra Morlydd, though she is not currently present.

The fire giant artisan defends himself if attacked, but otherwise avoids conflict. He has access to hot rocks, used in the smithy, that deal extra fire damage when thrown.

Fire Giant Artisan — CR 11

hp 152 (18 HD)

Male fire giant expert 3
LE Large giant (fire)
Init –1; **Senses** darkvision 60 ft., low-light vision; Listen +2, Spot +14
Languages Common, Giant

AC 16, touch 8, flat-footed 16 (–1 size, –1 Dex, +8 natural)
Immune fire, giant immunities
Fort +14, **Ref** +5, **Will** +10
Weakness vulnerability to cold, giant vulnerabilities

Speed 40 ft. (8 squares)
Melee warhammer +22/+17/+14 (2d6+10/×3) and slam +17 (1d4+5) or
Melee 2 slams +22 each (1d4+10)
Ranged rock +12 (2d6+10 plus 2d6 fire)
Base Atk +13; **Grp** +27
Atk Options Cleave, Great Cleave, Improved Overrun, Power Attack
Special Actions rock catching, rock throwing

Abilities Str 31, Dex 8, Con 19, Int 14, Wis 14, Cha 9
SQ giant traits
Feats Cleave, Great Cleave, Improved Overrun, Skill Focus (Craft [armorsmithing]), Skill Focus (Craft [stonemasonry]), Skill Focus (Craft [weaponsmithing]), Power Attack
Skills Climb +16, Jump +20, Craft (armorsmithing) +14, Craft (stonemasonry) +14, Craft (weaponsmithing) +14, Knowledge (architecture and engineering) +11, Listen +2, Profession (blacksmith) +11, Spot +14

7. Northwest Tower: The northwest tower contains a basement, three levels, and a lookout. The basement is a storage area for valuable gifts and tomes. The first floor is a library where the fire giant elder works. The second floor is split between a study full of books and journals, and a cell for Thaden Felstorm, which is outfitted with all the comforts of a guest room. The third floor is the personal quarters of Valbryn Morlydd. Neither she nor Thaden is currently present.

The fire giant elder defends himself if attacked, but otherwise avoids conflict.

Fire Giant Elder — CR 12

hp 132 (18 HD)

Male fire giant aristocrat 5
LE Large giant (fire)
Init –3; **Senses** darkvision 60 ft., low-light vision; Listen +4, Spot +16
Languages Common, Giant

AC 14, touch 6, flat-footed 14 (–1 size, –3 Dex, +8 natural)
Immune fire, giant immunities
Fort +12, **Ref** +3, **Will** +13
Weakness vulnerability to cold, giant vulnerabilities

Speed 40 ft. (8 squares)
Melee dagger +21/+16/+11 (1d6+8/19–20) and slam +16 (1d4+4) or
Melee 2 slams +21 each (1d4+8)
Ranged rock +11 (2d6+8)
Base Atk +14; **Grp** +26
Atk Options Cleave, Great Cleave, Improved Overrun, Power Attack
Special Actions rock catching, rock throwing

Abilities Str 27, Dex 4, Con 15, Int 16, Wis 18, Cha 13
SQ giant traits
Feats Cleave, Great Cleave, Improved Overrun, Skill Focus (Knowledge [history]), Skill Focus (Knowledge [nature]), Skill Focus (Knowledge [the planes]), Power Attack
Skills Climb +14, Diplomacy +8, Jump +18, Knowledge (history) +13, Knowledge (nature) +13, Knowledge (the planes) +13, Listen +4, Sense Motive +9, Spot +16

8. Meditation Chamber: Valbryn comes to this room to prepare her spells. She keeps her spellbook here, along with a highly polished silver mirror for scrying and an extensive library of focus components, material components, and spellglyph ink. A *flame breath (cold) glyph* cast on each door (Search DC 31 to find; Disable Device DC 31 to thwart) is keyed to activate by touch.

THE GUARDS

Encounter Level 16

SETUP

Beyond the archway with its sculpted hell hounds (area 1), a flagstone bridge crosses a lava moat and leads to a gatehouse on the other side. The bridge, 15 feet above the lava, is the only way to approach the gatehouse on foot.

If the PCs pass through the archway without setting off the sonic *greater blast glyph* and make an effort to conceal their position, they might remain undetected. The two fire giants standing guard outside the gatehouse and the two fire giants standing atop the gatehouse make Listen checks and Spot checks with a penalty of –1 per 10 feet of distance.

If they succeed on either check, they notice the PCs. The two fire giants outside the gatehouse enter the structure, closing and bracing the stone doors from within, while the two guards atop the gatehouse hurl hot rocks at the party.

When the PCs pass through the archway, read:

As you step onto the flagstone bridge, a wave of heat envelops you from the lava moat that bubbles and churns below. The bridge spans over 100 feet, and leads up to a gatehouse 50 feet high. The curtain walls and structures are made of worked stone reinforced with iron braces. On both sides of the gatehouse, lava pours out of the lower curtain walls, feeding the moat. The entire stronghold is blackened from fire and heat, but no less sturdy for the exposure. The cavern roof above curves upward into a darkened dome.

TACTICS

The fire giants atop the gatehouse start hurling hot rocks at the PCs, targeting any airborne characters first. The flagstone bridge can take the punishment easily, having been designed to withstand such attacks. If the player characters eliminate at least two rock-throwing fire giants from a distance, or if they take cover behind the archway, the stone doors of the gatehouse open again and four fire giants emerge to attack the intruders. Four more fire giants (minus any that were defeated from a distance) charge the characters as a second wave of combatants.

6–8 FIRE GIANT GUARDS **CR 10**
hp 142 (15 HD)

Male or female fire giant
LE Large giant (fire)
Init –1; **Senses** darkvision 60 ft., low-light vision; Listen +2, Spot +14
Languages Giant

AC 23, touch 8, flat-footed 23
(–1 size, –1 Dex, +7 armor, +8 natural)
Immune fire, giant immunities
Fort +14, **Ref** +4, **Will** +7
Weakness vulnerability to cold, giant vulnerabilities

Speed 30 ft. (6 squares) in half-plate, base speed 40 ft.
Melee greatsword +20/+15/+10 (3d6+15/19–20) or
Melee 2 slams +20 each (1d4+10)
Ranged rock +21 (2d6+10 plus 2d6 fire)
Base Atk +11; **Grp** +25
Atk Options Cleave, Great Cleave, Improved Overrun, Improved Sunder, Power Attack
Special Actions rock catching, rock throwing

Abilities Str 31, Dex 9, Con 21, Int 10, Wis 14, Cha 11
SQ giant traits
Feats Brutal Throw[CAd], Cleave, Great Cleave, Improved Overrun, Improved Sunder, Power Attack
Skills Climb +9, Craft (weaponsmithing) +6, Intimidate +6, Jump +9, Listen +2, Spot +14
Possessions half-plate, greatsword

If the battle takes place before the archway (and not on the bridge), the fire giants charge and attempt to sunder the characters' weapons before cutting them down. Each charging sunder attempt uses a 5-point Power Attack (opposed attack +25 [+4 per difference in size category that fire giants are larger than their foes], damage 2d6+25). After making a sunder attempt, each fire giant uses a 5-point Power Attack (attack +15/+10/+5, damage 2d6+25/19–20), unless reducing their attacks proves ineffective.

If anybody attempts to block a charging fire giant from attacking a designated foe, the giant uses Improved Overrun against the obstacle, gaining a bonus of +20 on Strength checks to knock it down.

If the battle takes place on the bridge, the fire giants attempt to sunder the characters' weapons (as described above) and then grapple with their designated foes. If a grappled PC whose weapon has been destroyed makes an attack of opportunity against a fire giant, he might provoke an attack of opportunity from the giant if he is not proficient in unarmed combat.

Features of the Area

The gatehouse shares some of the structural properties of Gilgirn (page 118), but differs in the following features.

Doors: The double doors of the gatehouse are carved from 1-foot-thick stone. Each door is 10 feet wide and 15 feet high and has hardness 8 and 180 hit points.

Rooms: The gatehouse contains two levels and a lookout. Two fire giants stand outside the open stone doors, two more are stationed on the second floor to operate the portcullises, and two more stand atop the gatehouse. The ground level corridor is 130 feet long and 20 feet wide.

Portcullis: When the encounter begins, both the front gate portcullis and the back gate portcullis are raised. Each is made of iron and is 25 feet wide, 25 feet high, and 6 inches thick, with hardness 8 and 180 hit points. If either portcullis is dropped, the PCs can raise it by making a successful DC 30 Strength check.

Traps: An area *greater dispel magic glyph* has been cast on the area to the north that leads to the inner ward of Gilgirn. The *glyph* can be found with a successful DC 31 Search check and thwarted with a successful DC 31 Disable Device check.

Password: A daily password allows fire giants and invited guests to pass through the gatehouse without being contested by the guards.

A fire giant who successfully grapples with a PC tries to pin that character down and use an additional attack to toss him. To do this, the giant must succeed on an opposed grapple check to pick up the PC (each guard can lift 3,680 pounds) and then make a Strength check. If the result is at least 10, the fire giant tosses the character 5 feet over the nearest edge of the bridge into the waiting lava below (to resolve the effects, see Lava Canals, above). For every 5 points that the giant's check result exceeds 10, he tosses the character another 5 feet, to a maximum of 25 feet.

If the PCs enter the gatehouse, the two fire giants on the second floor drop portcullises to block the entrance and the exit, trying to trap the party inside. If successful, the giants drop hot rocks on the PCs through murder holes in the floor (attack +22, damage 2d6+10 plus 2d6 fire).

Conclusion

The fire giant guards fight to the death to protect Gilgirn and their queen.

INNER WARD

Encounter Level 18

SETUP

The gatehouse guards will sound the alarm before engaging the PCs in tactical encounter 7–1. Hearing the alarm, Helthra leaves her study in the northeast tower and summons four Urdred, keeping two at her side and sending two to accompany her mother. Helthra casts *bull's strength* and *shield of faith* on herself, both of which last for 10 minutes.

If the PCs enter the inner ward of Gilgirn, they are greeted by eight advanced hell hounds (X) in the first round. Eight fire giant guards (G), Helthra (H), and her two death maidens (U) arrive on the second round. If the PCs are using cold-based attacks, the princess casts *protection from energy (cold)* on herself, which lasts for 100 minutes or until it absorbs 120 points of cold damage. Helthra can cast all her spells on the defensive without failing.

The princess next casts *spiritual weapon*, sending a greatsword of force against the toughest-looking melee character (attack +22/+17/+12/+7, damage 1d8+3/19–20). Finally, if Helthra did not cast *protection from energy* earlier, she uses a rebuke undead attempt to empower herself with Divine Vigor, which grants her 46 temporary hit points and increases her base speed to 40 feet. The effects of *spiritual weapon* and Divine Vigor last for 1 minute.

When the PCs pass through the gatehouse, read:

The gatehouse opens to the inner ward of Gilgirn, revealing the central keep in its entirety; the ceiling here rises to a height of 75 feet. A lava-filled canal flows out at ground level from between the two closest towers, then splits into two canals that run off in different directions under the curtain walls—presumably feeding the moat outside. Three different foot bridges cross the lava canals at different points, and blackened hounds the size of wolves are running across the bridges toward you, slavering and snorting flames. More fire giants are not far behind.

TACTICS

The hell hounds attack first, using their breath weapon attacks against as many opponents as possible. The fire giant guards attack on the following round, charging into combat with 5-point Power Attacks (attack +17, damage 2d6+25/19–20); they make unmodified multiple attacks in subsequent rounds. Helthra and the two Urdred arrive at the same time as the fire giant guards, and the princess begins casting spells (as described in Setup, above).

NONASSOCIATED CLASS LEVELS

The Urdred have pursued an atypical profession for fire giants by becoming ninjas. As such, their levels of ninja are considered nonassociated class levels. Adding nonassociated class levels to a monster increases its Challenge Rating by 1/2 per level until its nonassociated class levels equal its original Hit Dice. For details, see *MM* 294.

HELTHRA MORLYDD — **CR 15**
hp 243 (289 with Divine Vigor) (23 HD); see page 117

2 URDRED — **CR 14**
hp 197 each (19 HD)

Female fire giant ninja 4
NE Large giant (fire)
Init +6; **Senses** darkvision 60 ft., low-light vision; Listen +5, Spot +15
Languages Common, Giant, Infernal

AC 28, touch 11, flat-footed 26
(–1 size, +2 Dex, +4 class, +3 armor, +10 natural)
Immune fire, giant immunities
Fort +16, **Ref** +11, **Will** +10 (+12 while at least one use of *ki* power remains)
Weakness vulnerability to cold, giant vulnerabilities

Speed 40 ft. (8 squares)
Melee *+1 longsword* +23/+18/+13 (2d6+10/17–20) and slam +17 (1d4+4) or
Melee *+1 dagger* +23/+18/+13 (1d6+10/19–20 plus poison) and slam +17 (1d4+4) or
Melee 2 slams +22 each (1d4+9)
Ranged *+1 composite longbow* +18/+13/+8 (2d6+9/×3) or
Ranged *+1 composite longbow* +16/+16/+11/+6 (2d6+9/×3) with Rapid Shot or
Ranged rock +16 (2d6+9 plus 2d6 fire)
Base Atk +14; **Grp** +27
Atk Options Improved Critical (longsword), Point Blank Shot, Precise Shot, Telling Blow, poison (deathblade, Fort DC 20, 1d6 Con/2d6 Con), poison (Large scorpion venom, Fort DC 14, 1d6 Con/1d6 Con), sudden strike +2d6
Special Actions *ki* power 6/day (ghost step), rock catching, rock throwing
Combat Gear dose of deathblade poison, dose of Large scorpion venom

Abilities Str 28, Dex 14, Con 22, Int 13, Wis 18, Cha 10
SQ giant traits, great leap, trapfinding
Feats Improved Initiative, Improved Critical (longsword), Point Blank Shot, Precise Shot, Rapid Shot, Telling Blow[PH2] (see page 25), Zen Archery[CW]
Skills Climb +20, Hide +17, Intimidate +10, Jump +20, Listen +5, Move Silently +17, Spot +15
Possessions combat gear plus *+1 longsword, +1 composite longbow* (+9 Str bonus) with 40 arrows, *+1 dagger, amulet of natural armor +2, bracers of armor +3,* 16 pp, 2 gp

8 FIRE GIANT GUARDS — **CR 16**
hp 142 each (15 HD); see page 122

8 Advanced Hell Hounds CR 12
hp 44 each (8 HD)

LE Medium outsider (evil, extraplanar, fire, lawful)
Init +5; **Senses** darkvision 60 ft., scent; Listen +11, Spot +11
Languages understands Infernal

AC 20, touch 11, flat-footed 19
(+1 Dex, +4 armor, +5 natural)
Immune fire, outsider immunities
Fort +7, **Ref** +7, **Will** +6
Weakness vulnerability to cold, outsider vulnerabilities

Speed 40 ft. (8 squares)
Melee bite +10 (2d6+2 plus 1d6 fire)
Base Atk +8; **Grp** +10
Atk Options fiery bite
Special Actions breath weapon

Abilities Str 14, Dex 13, Con 13, Int 6, Wis 10, Cha 6
SQ outsider traits
Feats Improved Initiative, Improved Natural Attack (bite), Run, Track[B]
Skills Hide +17, Jump +17, Listen +11, Move Silently +17, Spot +11, Survival +11 (+19 tracking by scent)
Possessions *collar of mage armor*

Fiery Bite (Su) A hell hound deals an extra 1d6 points of fire damage each time it bites an opponent, as if its bite were a flaming weapon.
Breath Weapon (Su) 10-ft. cone, once every 2d4 rounds, damage 3d6 fire, Reflex DC 15 half.

If the PCs were trapped in the gatehouse and managed to enter the inner ward by lifting the back gate portcullis, the fire giants inside the gatehouse close it again to prevent them from retreating from the battle.

Helthra tries to position herself so that a chosen foe stands between her and a lava canal, so that she can use her Awesome Blow feat (*MM* 303). If successful, she subtracts 4 from her melee attack roll with her +2 *adamantine flaming greataxe* (attack +29), hoping to knock her target 10 feet through the air into the lava.

If her chosen foe is not close enough to the lava or has immunity to fire, Helthra tries to make sunder attempts instead (opposed attack +41/+36/+31/+26 [+4 per difference in size category that Helthra is larger than foe], damage 3d6+23). If the princess sunders the character's weapon with her greataxe, she begins making normal melee attacks with a 5-point Power Attack (attack +27/+22/+17/+12, damage 3d6+33/19–20/×3 plus 1d6 fire).

On the same round in which Helthra casts *protection from energy* (or *spiritual weapon*, if the PCs are not using cold-based attacks), the Urdred attack. They close to within 30 feet of the PCs, activate ghost step as a swift action, and ready an action to shoot any spellcaster who does anything threatening (attack +21, damage 2d6+9/×3 plus 2d6 sudden strike). Their intent is to disrupt spells, but they attack even if none are cast. Ghost step attacks give the death maidens a bonus of +2 on attack rolls and ignore their targets' Dexterity bonus to Armor Class (if any).

On subsequent rounds, the Urdred fire Rapid Shot volleys into melee until the fire giant guards and hell hounds are reduced to between one-half and one-quarter of their number. At that point, the Urdred drop their longbows and begin making melee attacks with their +1 *longswords*. On the first round in which they can make a full attack, they activate ghost step as a swift action and make four attacks

Features of the Area
The inner ward shares the same structural properties of Gilgirn (page 118), with no new features.

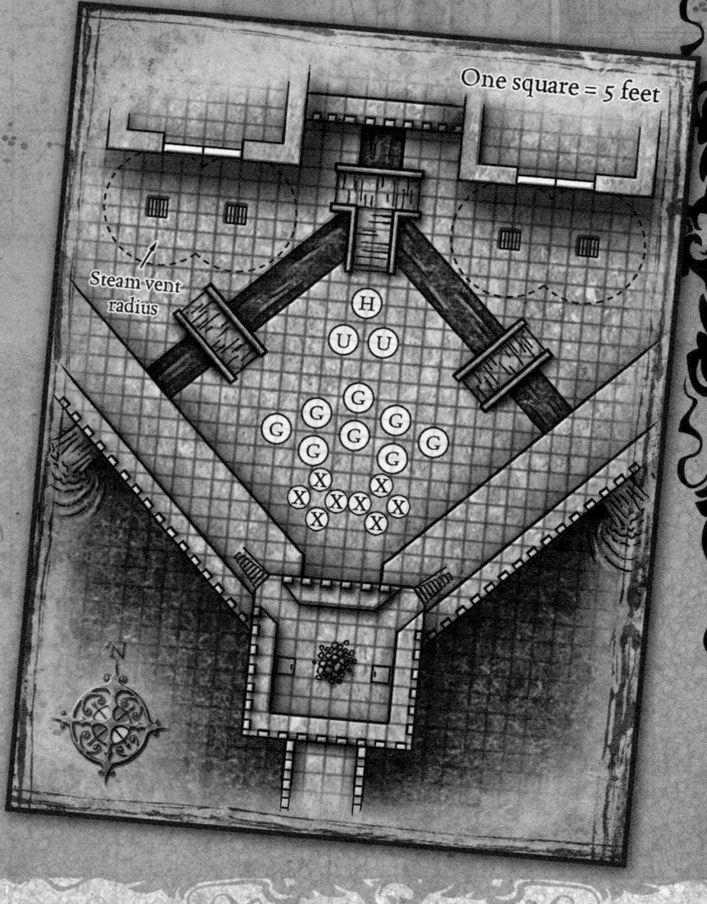

while remaining invisible for 1 round (attack +25/+20/+15, damage 2d6+9/17–20 plus 2d6 sudden strike and +19 slam, damage 1d4+4 plus 2d6 sudden strike).

If the Urdred are taking a beating and Helthra is not harried by the PCs, she spontaneously casts *invisibility* on herself so that she can walk around, healing the death maidens with her *wand of cure moderate wounds*.

Conclusion

The hell hounds and fire giant guards fight to the death to protect Gilgirn and their queen. If one of the two Urdred fall, the other attacks the PC most responsible with a deathblade-poisoned dagger.

If Helthra is reduced to 50 or fewer hit points, she spontaneously casts *invisibility* on herself and retreats to the rear gatehouse (see tactical encounter 7–3, page 126). Along the way, she heals herself with her *wand of cure moderate wounds*.

Any remaining Urdred use ghost step to retreat when Helthra does, but they cross the nearest footbridge first, hoping that one or more PCs will pursue and activate the bridge's sonic *greater blast glyph*.

If the PCs end up alone on the battlefield, any fire giant guards atop the barracks and gatehouses that have line of sight to the characters begin throwing rocks at them. If approached by multiple PCs, these fire giants retreat to tactical encounter 7–3, along the curtain wall.

GATEHOUSE

Encounter Level 19 (20 if Helthra and her Urdred from tactical encounter 7–2 are present)

SETUP

When Helthra sent two of the Urdred to join her mother, the ninjas also collected Thaden and his fleshraker animal companion and retreated to the rear gatehouse. There, the surviving occupants of Gilgirn make their final stand, with Valbyrn's firepower to aid them.

First, Valbryn casts *protection from energy* (*cold*) on herself, which lasts for 3-1/2 hours or until it absorbs 120 points of damage from cold-based attacks. Next, she casts extended *greater invisibility* on herself, which lasts for 38 rounds. Third, she casts *polymorph* on an Urdred to create a spitting image of herself. Finally, she casts *globe of invulnerability* where the Urdred stands atop the gatehouse. Valbryn can cast all her spells on the defensive without failing.

The *polymorph*-disguised Urdred remains atop the rear gatehouse and yells down at the PCs, matching her gestures with the spells that Valbryn casts while invisible. Thaden and his fleshraker remain beside the so-called queen for protection. This ruse is possible because Valbryn has created spellglyphs for nearly all her prepared spells, which allows her to cast them with no verbal or material components. However, there is one spell that she prefers to cast with its focus component for dramatic effect: *decapitating scarf* (see Tactics, below).

Thaden begins every day in Gilgirn by casting *endure elements* on himself. At the first sign of conflict, he casts *longstrider* on himself, which lasts for 6 hours, and he drinks his *potion of barkskin +5*, which lasts for 2 hours. He casts *bear's endurance* on himself at the last possible moment before combat begins, since the effect of that spell lasts for only 6 minutes. All of Thaden's spells also affect his animal companion.

When the PCs approach the rear gatehouse, read:

Valbryn, the fire giant queen, looks like a crimson force of nature standing atop the rear gatehouse, calling down spells with wild abandon. She appears to be in her element, neither forgiving nor merciful, much like every story about her unchecked wrath has led you to believe.

TACTICS

Though she prepares spells from a book, Valbryn is a surprisingly versatile spellcaster. Using elemental mastery, she can spontaneously exchange any prepared spell of 3rd level or higher for a *fireball* spell. Using the Energy Substitution feat, she can make the spell deal cold damage instead. Moreover, because of her Maximize Spell feat

VALBRYN MORLYDD **CR 17**
hp 248 (29 HD); see page 113

THADEN FELSTORM **CR 15**
hp 98 (128 with *bear's endurance*) (15 HD); see page 115

HELTHRA MORLYDD **CR 15**
hp 243 (289 with *bear's endurance*) (23 HD); see page 117

4 URDRED **CR 16**
hp 197 each (19 HD); see page 124

12 FIRE GIANT GUARDS **CR 17**
hp 142 each (15 HD); see page 122

and her Rapid Metamagic feat, Valbryn can exchange any spell of 6th level or higher for a maximized *fireball* that deals fire damage or cold damage, without increasing her casting time.

If Helthra or any member of the Urdred survives tactical encounter 7–2 and joins the battle at the rear gate, they tell Valbryn everything they know about the intruders—including whether the PCs have immunity to fire or not. If the PCs do not have immunity, the queen casts *wall of fire* on them when they arrive, and sends Helthra (if present) and any remaining Urdred and fire giant guards into battle.

If the PCs do have immunity to fire, Valbryn uses Energy Substitution to hit them with cold-based *fireballs* instead, warning Helthra, the Urdred, and the fire giants to stand clear until they can enter melee combat safely. If a PC uses magical means to fly, Valbryn waits until the character flies over lava and then targets him with a *greater dispel magic* spell.

After raining *fireballs* down on the PCs, Valbryn targets the most bothersome character with a *sword of darkness* spell (attack +19/+14/+9/+4, damage 1d4/19–20 plus one negative level [two negative levels on a critical hit], no save). The spell lasts for 19 rounds and could devastate the PCs if they cannot dispel the effect. If the *sword of darkness* kills a member of the party, Valbryn redirects it to a new target.

While still invisible, Valbryn casts *dimension door*, transporting herself, Thaden, and the dinosaur into melee combat and leaving the disguised Urdred atop the gatehouse. In doing so, Valbryn leaves the safety of the immobile *globe of invulnerability*. The queen follows Thaden into battle and casts *stoneskin* on him, which lasts for 190 minutes.

Valbryn is a vain individual, and takes great pride in revealing herself after a particularly devastating series of spells, wanting credit where it is due. Thus, if the adventuring party has been largely defeated, she turns visible, approaching to within 70 feet of the PC who has shown the most resilience and casting *decapitating scarf* (CAd 102) in an attempt to cut off his head. She uses her red sash as the focus component; indeed, she wears it specifically for this purpose. *Decapitating scarf* is a metal spell, and as such is forbidden by Valbryn's wu jen taboos. Accordingly, the queen commits to this action only after most of the spells in her repertoire have already been cast.

During the battle, Helthra (if present) does her best to harry the PCs, relying on spells such as *divine favor, ring of blades* (CAd 121), and *spiritual weapon*. If it looks as if her side is not faring well, Helthra spontaneously casts *invisibility* on herself and walks around healing the Urdred and the fire giants with her *wand of cure moderate wounds*.

The Urdred use their ghost step ability liberally to gain sudden strike attacks against the PCs.

DEVELOPMENT

If Helthra falls in battle, Thaden becomes unhinged and attacks the party without concern for his own welfare. If Valbryn does not protect Thaden during such a frenzy, he fights to the death to avenge the princess. His animal companion joins Thaden in battle at all times, creating flanking sneak attacks when possible.

If Thaden falls in battle, Valbryn loses her confidence in the fire giants' ability to defeat the intruders. She travels to the lava throat (area 5) by the fastest means possible and pulls the *planar trestle* (which had been completed before the encounter) out of her *bag of holding*. The queen throws the artifact into the lava. It takes 3 rounds for the *planar trestle* to sink down far enough to reach the closed portal, at which point the seal violently ruptures and Gilgirn becomes directly connected to the Elemental Plane of Fire.

All the lava in the pool is sucked downward for one second before spewing back up in a powerful geyser of molten rock that blankets all of Gilgirn, dealing 6d6 points of fire damage to anybody standing out in the open (DC 23 Reflex save for half). Damage from the lava continues for 1d3 rounds after exposure ceases, but this additional damage is only half the amount dealt during contact.

If the PCs previously came upon Thaden in his cell, the human begins this encounter by pretending to be a prisoner of the fire giants. Thaden claims that he was captured while

8 Noble Salamanders **CR 16**
hp 112 each (15 HD); *MM* 218

trying to escape from Gilgirn, which is true and therefore grants him a +2 bonus on his Bluff check. He attacks the PCs on his first opportunity, relying on his animal companion to help him gain a flanking bonus on his sneak attack.

CONCLUSION

The Urdred and the fire giant guards fight to the death protecting Gilgirn and their queen. Valbryn loves Helthra and Thaden, but if they are killed in battle, she can still see a future for herself. She casts *teleport* to escape or *transfix* (CAd 127) to paralyze the PCs, assuming that she has not exchanged either spell for *fireball*. If all the characters are paralyzed, the queen delivers a coup de grace on each one. She casts *transfix* only if Thaden has already fallen, since the spell might paralyze him as well.

Alternatively, if Valbryn reaches the lava throat and succeeds in opening the portal, the magma geyser sucks eight noble salamanders into Gilgirn from the Elemental Plane of Fire. These chaotic evil creatures take no sides in the conflict between the PCs and the fire giants, creating a battle on three fronts. The self-serving noble salamanders try to claim Gilgirn as their own stronghold.

With the portal now stuck open, salamander reinforcements soon begin arriving from Elemental Fire, presenting a grave new threat to the region. The PCs can abandon the fire giants, or they can try to find a way to drive the salamanders back and seal the portal again.

Features of the Area

The rear gatehouse area is nearly identical to the front gatehouse (tactical encounter 7–1), with the following exceptions.

Doors: The stone double doors of the rear gatehouse face the inner ward to the south. Each door is 10 feet wide, 15 feet high, and 1 foot thick, with hardness 8 and 180 hit points.

Traps: An area *greater dispel magic glyph* has been cast on the corridor just north of the gatehouse. The *glyph* can be found with a successful DC 31 Search check and thwarted with a successful DC 31 Disable Device check.

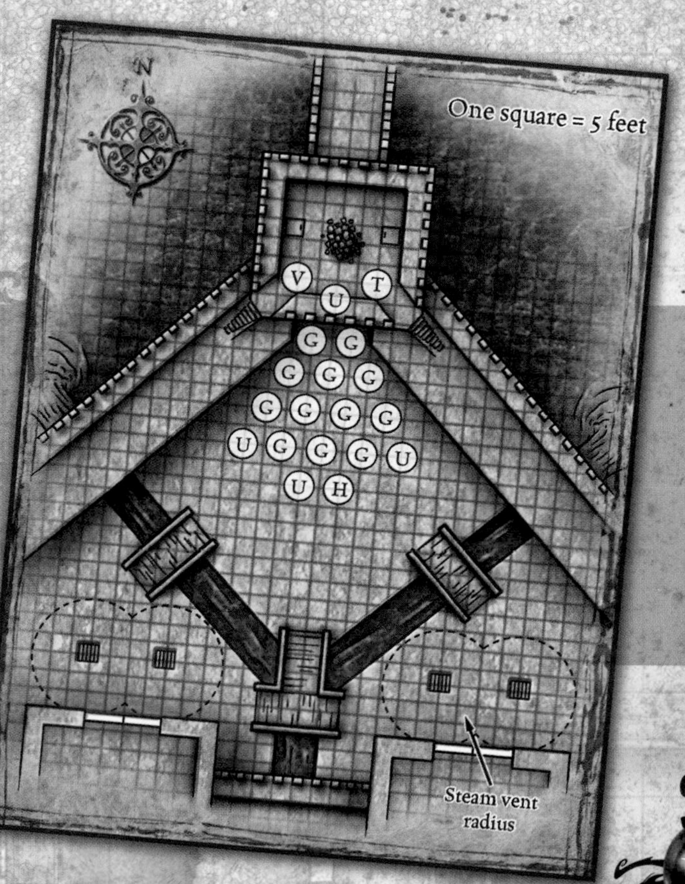

Illus. by E. Widermann

The lich-queen tolerates no rivals, no one that might threaten her stranglehold on our society. It is not out of a desire to rule that I commit myself to the study of necromancy, but rather out of a desire to survive—to defy a tyrant that is no better than the illithids that oppressed our people so long ago."

—Kastya Zurith-Movya

Formerly an advisor of Vlaakith, the lich-queen of the githyanki, Kastya Zurith-Movya renounced his allegiance and fled to the Negative Energy Plane. There, he desperately searches for a way to restore the great lich Acererak and gain his assistance to help him usurp the githyanki tyrant.

BACKGROUND

For over one thousand years, Vlaakith the lich-queen (*Planar Handbook* page 150) has ruled the githyanki race with an iron grip. Through her guidance and wisdom, the githyanki secured a truce with the red dragons, spread their influence across the Astral Plane, and became a considerable force for evil throughout the multiverse. Within Vlaakith's militaristic society, each githyanki strives for excellence, hoping to achieve perfection and the admiration or envy of its peers. Although ambition is encouraged, it is tempered by the obedience demanded from the race's dreaded undead mistress.

Kastya Zurith-Movya held a place of prominence in this tyrant's court. A gifted necromancer, he advised the lich-queen in matters of war, governance, and espionage. The fact that Vlaakith tolerated his arrogance astounded the other members of the court, leading many to wonder what magic Kastya had wrought to remain in her good graces. In truth, Kastya had seduced the lich-queen, appealing to her vanity and pride, and used his status to delve into forbidden treatises on magic, pursuing a treacherous aim. The necromancer knew that he would eventually grow mighty enough for Vlaakith to see him as a threat, and that she would not hesitate to devour his essence once that day came. He hoped to protect himself against his mistress by becoming a lich, and it was not long before he had stolen enough supplies and information to complete his transformation.

The lich-queen saw that act as a supreme betrayal and ordered Kastya's death. The palace swarmed with githyanki knights as Kastya fled through its cavernous corridors, heading for his vampiric red dragon steed and ally, Albrathax. Amid a spectacular exchange of spells and dragon breath, the new lich escaped the great githyanki city of Tu'narath (*Planar Handbook* page 147) and fled through the vast emptiness of the Astral Plane. The wing of dragons and knights that pursued might have captured them, but the precipitous appearance of a shimmering black portal enabled Kastya and his mount to escape into the leaching void of the Negative

Energy Plane, where even the boldest githyanki knights dared not follow.

The undead pair explored the endless night until they came upon a ruined and crumbling city—a metropolis issuing streams of decaying stones, putrid water, and the rotting flesh of primeval corpses. Kastya knew this place: accursed Moil, the ancient city cast down by Orcus and later exploited by the lich lord Acererak in his campaign to become a deity. Believing his destiny was at hand, Kastya set out to unlock Acererak's secrets, and to gain enough power to return to Tu'narath and slay his former mistress.

GOALS

Kastya knew that Vlaakith would take her revenge if he ever left the Negative Energy Plane. He refused to spend eternity trapped by his fears, so he sought a way to destroy the lich-queen and take her throne. However, Vlaakith is one of the mightiest beings in the multiverse, and it would take the power of a god to shatter her control. Kastya was an outcast, freed from laws of his people, but still he could not bring himself to appeal to a deity—the ways of the githyanki were too ingrained within him. Luckily, an alternate solution lay within the rotting city of Moil.

Kastya Zurith-Movya

As the necromancer explored the various towers, avoiding the few remaining traps and denizens, he learned much about the fate of Acererak. Evidently, the elder lich's bid for divinity failed and he was consigned to a tortured existence, trapped between realities as a vestige (see *Tome of Magic*). Kastya believed that if he freed Acererak and restored him to a living vessel, he would gain a powerful ally in his war against the lich-queen.

What Kastya intends is no small task. Overthrowing the legendary githyanki tyrant is daunting enough, but restoring one of the most formidable liches ever known borders on madness. Kastya is resolved to succeed, however, because he knows that otherwise Vlaakith will find and destroy him eventually.

Fortunately for him, Kastya is not alone. Some githyanki are willing to flee Tu'narath rather than sacrifice their lives to the lich-queen's endless hunger, and it is these rebels that Kastya lures to his cause. The few insurgent githyanki that can withstand the drain of the void, whether because they are shielded from it or because they are undead, join the necromancer in Bleak Hold, his floating tower on the Negative Energy Plane. Many others are scattered across the planes, serving Kastya in exile—though those that later have second thoughts are brought to the Hold, where they are slain and raised as zombies to fight in the necromancer's growing legions.

Kastya is content to let some of his minions sow unrest and disrupt life in and around Tu'narath, but he commits many of them to his larger goal: the restoration of Acererak. He believes that he must complete four tasks to accomplish this objective. First, he must locate the mysterious Fortress of Conclusion, where Acererak worked to ascend to godhood. Second, he must recruit a binder who has sufficient power to summon and bargain with the lich's vestige. Third, he needs a suitable vessel to contain the restored Acererak. And fourth, he must find and destroy the *tooth of Acererak,* one of the *teeth of Dahlver-Nar* (*Tome of Magic* page 77). Only when all four components of his plan are accomplished can he restore the lost lich successfully.

Illus. by K. Tanner

USING THIS VILLAIN

As a lich necromancer, Kastya is a major villain who has great power and resources. He controls hundreds of agents across the planes who watch, search, and fight for his cause, and his well-protected lair is far beyond the reach of most adventurers, floating in the fatal nothingness of the Negative Energy Plane. Thus, he works particularly well as a faceless villain, a mastermind who moves his servants like pieces in a terminally dangerous game.

There are a number of ways to inject Kastya into your campaign. The necromancer employs a vast network of followers, and his objectives are clear (locate a fortress, recruit a binder, and so on), so they can easily intersect with the PCs' adventures. Keep in mind, however, that most low- to mid-level player characters lack the means to travel the planes and are not likely to stumble across the main threads of the lich's overall scheme. Furthermore, the necromancer's minions are powerful in their own right, so the PCs should not deal with these foes directly until they have attained enough levels to have a chance of victory.

Thus, rather than plunging the player characters into the thick of the plot, reveal the story gradually over the life of the campaign. Early on, the adventures need not relate to the villain's goals, but as the PCs plunder dungeons, defeat minor villains, and contend with the dark forces of the world, you can start to introduce elements of Kastya's plan. As the characters reach higher levels, they can begin to deal with his lackeys and perhaps his minions as well, while undertaking missions that relate directly to his objectives.

These guidelines assume that Kastya is a recurring villain within the campaign. If you would rather use him as a one-shot villain, just accelerate the plot and decide that he is close to completing his plans by the time the PCs confront him in his lair. To this end, consider adding a binder (see *Tome of Magic*) of at least 14th level to the encounters described in Bleak Hold, and designate a vessel that Kastya has chosen to host the summoned vestige; the latter might be an ally of the party or an NPC who has not previously been introduced.

KASTYA ZURITH-MOVYA IN EBERRON

From the githyanki city of Tu'narath, Kastya fled to the plane of Mabar, the Endless Night. There, he brokered an arrangement with the yugoloths—they would help him locate the elusive *tooth of Acererak*, and he would provide them with undead servants for their own inscrutable schemes. But the yugoloths are far from trustworthy, and they spend as much time hampering Kastya and his allies as they do helping them. The necromancer's hands are tied, since the yugoloths have threatened to reveal his hidden lair to the lich-queen if he fails to make good on his promises.

KASTYA ZURITH-MOVYA IN FAERÛN

In his search for the *tooth of Acererak*, Kastya has inadvertently drawn the attention of Orcus, who rightly believes that the destruction of the *tooth* will create a conduit through which other vestiges might escape their torments. In no hurry to see Tenebrous restored, Orcus has forged a pact with Vlaakith and sends his demonic hordes to deal with Kastya's renegades.

APPEARANCE AND BEHAVIOR

The Negative Energy Plane has not been kind to Kastya. Its energy has spiritually bolstered his undead body but rendered him physically emaciated, his parchment skin pulled taut over sharp bones. Also, the necromancer has become infested with a strange parasite, and his body crackles with the movement of undead mites crawling through the wreckage of his flesh.

To conceal his hideous form, Kastya wears long, moldering white robes trimmed in crimson, with a cloak of a matching color. Around his slight waist is a wide belt made of interlocking brass plates; from these, he hangs pouches containing the components, dusts, stones, and runebones used in the performance of his dark arts.

Although Kastya commits most of his time and attention to his plot against Vlaakith, he is easily distracted by magical study. The lich spends a portion of each day exploring Moil's floating ruins, examining inscriptions and runes on the walls, delicately leafing through degenerating manuscripts, and performing vivisections on undead beings of his own creation to gain a deeper understanding of how negative energy animates the dead.

For the most part, Kastya's minions and lackeys are loyal, but some are growing concerned about his sanity (or lack thereof). On many occasions, Albrathax and others have found him explaining necromantic theory to the mute zombies and skeletons that shuffle mindlessly about Bleak Hold. Kastya never seems to think that his behavior is strange, and claims that he speaks aloud to work through the difficult aspects of spellcraft.

In truth, Kastya merely craves company. He is desperate for the camaraderie he enjoyed back in Tu'narath, and he often orders his minions to kidnap intelligent beings from the Material Plane for conversation. Such visitors to the floating tower are rarely talkative for long—the plane inexorably sucks away their life and turns them into twitching, lifeless husks. When they finally die, Kastya raises them as zombies to add to the countless walking corpses already in his service.

KASTYA ZURITH-MOVYA **CR 19**

hp 118 (15 HD); fast healing 3; **DR** 15/bludgeoning and magic

Male evolved lich githyanki necromancer 5/master specialist[LM] 10
CE Medium undead (augmented humanoid, extraplanar)
Init +8; **Senses** darkvision 60 ft.; Listen +27, Spot +19
Aura fear (60 ft., DC 25)
Languages Celestial, Common, Draconic, Gith, Infernal, Undercommon

AC 30, touch 17, flat-footed 26
(+4 Dex, +6 armor, +3 deflection, +1 insight, +6 natural)
Miss Chance 20% *blur*
Immune cold, electricity, *polymorph* (except spells with a range of personal), mind-affecting spells and abilities, undead immunities
Resist +4 turn resistance; **SR** 20
Fort +4, **Ref** +8, **Will** +14; +8 against spells and spell-like effects
Weakness undead vulnerabilities

Speed 30 ft. (6 squares)
Melee damaging touch +11 (1d8+5 negative energy plus paralysis)
Base Atk +7; **Grp** +8
Atk Options cursed glance 9/day, damaging touch, magic strike, paralyzing touch
Special Actions major school esoterica, minor school esoterica
Combat Gear 3 *oils of inflict serious wounds*, *staff of necromancy* (11 charges), *wand of dispel magic* (CL 10th, 10 charges)
Wizard Spells Prepared (CL 16th, prohibited schools evocation and illusion):
8th—*blackfire*[SC] (CL 18th, +11 ranged touch, DC 29), *horrid wilting* (CL 18th, DC 29), Moilian *blackfire*[SC] (CL 18th, +11 ranged touch, +9d6 damage, DC 29), *protection from spells*†
7th—*avasculate*[SC] (CL 18th, +11 ranged touch, DC 28), Moilian *finger of death* (CL 18th, +8d6, DC 28), *greater teleport*, *limited wish*, *waves of exhaustion* (CL 18th)
6th—*circle of death* (CL 18th, DC 27), *disintegrate* (+11 ranged touch), *globe of invulnerability*, *greater dispel magic*, *mass suggestion* (DC 25)
5th—*cloudkill* (DC 24), *dominate person* (DC 24), *feeblemind* (DC 24), *magic jar* (CL 18th, DC 26), *overland flight*, *wall of force*, *waves of fatigue* (CL 18th)

4th—Moilian *burning blood*[SC] (CL 18th, +5d6 damage, DC 25), *crushing despair* (DC 23), *enervation* (CL 18th, +11 ranged touch), *Evard's black tentacles* (grapple +23), *Rary's mnemonic enhancer*†, *solid fog, stoneskin*
3rd—*acid breath*[SC] (DC 22), *blink, clairaudience/clairvoyance, ray of exhaustion* (CL 18th, +11 ranged touch, DC 24), *slow* (DC 22), *suggestion* (DC 22), *vampiric touch* (CL 18th, +11 melee touch)
2nd—*blindness/deafness* (CL 18th, DC 23), *cat's grace*†, *command undead* (CL 18th, DC 23), *death armor*[SC] (CL 18th), *false life* (CL 18th), *ghoul touch* (CL 18th, +11 melee touch, DC 23), *spectral hand* (CL 18th), *touch of idiocy* (CL 18th, +11 melee touch)
1st—*chill touch* (CL 18th, +11 melee touch, DC 22), *expeditious retreat, feather fall, ray of enfeeblement* (CL 18th, +11 ranged touch), *shield* (2), *spirit worm*[SC] (CL 18th, +11 melee touch, DC 22), *true strike* (2)
0—*detect magic, read magic, resistance, touch of fatigue* (2) (melee touch +11, DC 21)
† Already cast
Psionics (CL 15th):
3/day—*blur*†, *daze* (DC 18), *dimension door, mage hand, telekinesis* (DC 23)
1/day—*plane shift* (DC 25)
† Already used once
Spell-Like Abilities (CL 15th):
1/day—*greater invisibility*

Abilities Str 12, Dex 16 (18 with *cat's grace*), Con —, Int 29, Wis 17, Cha 26
SQ undead traits
Feats Black Lore of Moil[CAr] (see page 25), Craft Wondrous Item[B], Greater Spell Focus (necromancy)[B], Improved Initiative, Improved Toughness[CW], Lifebond[LM] (see page 25), Scribe Scroll[B], Skill Focus (Spellcraft)[B], Spell Focus (necromancy), Weapon Finesse
Skills Concentration +18, Craft (alchemy) +13, Decipher Script +27, Hide +12, Intimidate +17, Knowledge (arcana) +27, Knowledge (the planes) +27, Listen +27, Move Silently +12, Search +17, Sense Motive +11, Spellcraft +32, Spot +19, Survival +3 (+5 on other planes)
Possessions combat gear plus *deadwalker's ring*[CM] (see below), *ring of protection +3, bracers of armor +6, cloak of Charisma +6*, crystal ball with *see invisibility, dusty rose ioun stone, orange ioun stone, gloves of Dexterity +2, headband of intellect +6*, crystal focus for *magic jar* (1,000 gp), 2 diamonds for *protection from spells* (500 gp each), powder of crushed black pearl for *circle of death* (500 gp), 2 pinches of diamond dust for *stoneskin* (250 gp each), 4 onyxes for *death armor* (50 gp each), runebone for Moilian *blackfire* (225 gp), 2 runebones for Moilian *finger of death* (200 gp), runebone for Moilian *burning blood* (125 gp), spell component pouch, phylactery
Spellbook spells prepared plus 0—all except evocation and illusion; 1st—*alarm, comprehend languages, identify, mage armor*; 7th—*control undead*; 8th—*create greater undead*

Fear Aura (Su) At the end of each of Kastya's turns, creatures of less than 5 HD within 60 feet of him must attempt DC 25 Will saves. Those that fail are panicked for 10 rounds. Those that succeed are shaken for 1 round and cannot be affected again by Kastya's aura for 24 hours.
Cursed Glance (Sp) Nine times per day, when a visible enemy within 60 feet targets Kastya with an attack or a spell, he can as an immediate action force the enemy to make a DC 21 Will save. On a failed save, the enemy takes a –2 penalty to Armor Class and on saves until the start of Kastya's next turn. On a successful save, the enemy is not affected. This ability is the equivalent of a 2nd-level spell.
Damaging Touch (Su) Any living creature that is touched by Kastya takes 1d8+5 points of negative energy damage (Will DC 25 half).
Magic Strike (Su) Kastya's touch attack is treated as a magic weapon for the purpose of overcoming damage reduction.
Paralyzing Touch (Su) Any living creature that Kastya hits with his damaging touch attack must succeed on a DC 25 Fortitude save or become paralyzed. A *remove paralysis* spell or any spell that can remove a curse frees the victim. This effect cannot be dispelled. Anyone paralyzed by Kastya appears to be dead, though a successful DC 20 Spot check or DC 15 Heal check reveals that the victim is alive.
Major School Esoterica (Ex) Whenever Kastya casts a necromancy spell, all undead allies within 60 feet gain fast healing 10 for 5 rounds.
Minor School Esoterica (Ex) Whenever Kastya casts a necromancy spell, all undead allies within 60 feet gain +10 turn resistance for 10 rounds.
Deadwalker's Ring When Kastya wears this ring and creates undead by using spells, the undead gain 2 Hit Dice. Bonus hit points do not stack with those gained from the *desecrate* spell.

If you use *Expanded Psionics Handbook*, Kastya gains the psionic subtype and uses the following statistics in place of spell resistance and psionics.
PR 20
Power Points/Day: 3
Psi-Like Abilities (ML 7th):
3/day—*concealing amorpha, far hand, psionic daze* (DC 19), *psionic dimension door, telekinetic thrust* (350 lbs., DC 21)
1/day—*psionic plane shift*

ALBRATHAX

"The ancient pact binding my kind to the githyanki prevents me from severing my ties to the exiled one, and for my dedication to the old agreements, I have endured unspeakable suffering. If ever the terms of the pact can be severed, I shall loose myself from this wretched master and take the revenge to which I am entitled."

—Albrathax the Dread

Albrathax aided Kastya in his flight from Tu'narath and the Astral Plane, carrying him through a color pool onto the Negative Energy Plane. For now, he continues to work for the necromancer, but the bonds between them have weakened, and the dragon plots revenge.

GOALS

In many ways, Albrathax is not like other vampiric dragons (see *Draconomicon* page 195). He has no recollection of his living existence, and—to put it mildly—he does not particularly appreciate being an undead creature. He believes that his current state is a curse imposed on him by the evil dragon deity Tiamat for having betrayed the lich-queen. Also, this vampiric dragon is not forever bound to his treasure hoard—nonetheless, being a dragon by nature, he did bring his treasure along when he and Kastya fled to the Negative Energy Plane.

Desperate to be free of his ravenous thirst for life and blood, Albrathax secretly searches for a way to lift his vampiric malady. At the same time, his fear of absolute death is strong enough to prevent him from committing suicide.

The dragon accepts some responsibility for his undead existence, but lays most of the blame at Kastya's feet. Although not openly hostile to his master, Albrathax is not particularly loyal and serves the lich as it suits his purpose.

USING ALBRATHAX

Kastya employs the dragon as his steed, prowling the expanse of the void in search of ways to expand their influence. The lich sometimes dispatches Albrathax to serve as a messenger, deal with troublesome allies, and spy on his rivals.

The vampiric dragon uses Kastya's lackeys to spread word throughout the planes of his fabulous treasures, hoping to lure bold heroes or greedy mercenaries to Bleak Hold. Albrathax wants to feed on such foolish adventurers, of course, but he also seeks to expose Kastya to danger. Given his tenuous ties to the necromancer, Albrathax could be a useful, if untrustworthy, ally.

Albrathax

Illus. by J. Zhang

Appearance and Behavior

Appearing much as he did in life, Albrathax is a massive dragon covered in a thick hide of crimson scales. Unlike other dragons of his hue, his scales have faded to white at the edges, giving him a mottled appearance. Thorny spurs of bone pierce his hide at his joints. His eyes are feral and gleam with malevolence, and his sinister appearance is enhanced by the long fangs that fill his maw.

Albrathax is cunning, cruel, and treacherous. He remains loyal to Kastya only as long as it benefits him to do so, and he has plots in motion that he believes will ultimately ruin the necromancer.

ALBRATHAX **CR 17**

hp 231 (22 HD); fast healing 5; **DR** 5/magic

Male adult vampiric[Dra] red dragon
CE Huge undead
Init +7; **Senses** blindsense 60 ft., darkvision 120 ft., keen senses; Listen +40, Spot +40
Aura frightful presence (range 180 ft., 22 HD, Will DC 26 negates)
Languages Abyssal, Celestial, Common, Draconic, Gith

AC 36, touch 13, flat-footed 33; Dodge (–2 size, +3 Dex, +2 deflection, +23 natural)
Immune fire, paralysis, sleep, undead immunities (*MM* 317)
Resist cold 20, electricity 20; +4 turn resistance; **SR** 21
Fort +15, **Ref** +20, **Will** +20
Weakness vampire vulnerabilities

Speed 40 ft. (8 squares), fly 150 ft. (poor); Flyby Attack, Hover, Wingover
Melee bite +35 (2d8+15) and 2 claws +33 each (2d6+7 plus energy drain) and 2 wings +33 each (1d8+7) and tail slap +33 (2d6+22)
Space 15 ft.; **Reach** 10 ft. (15 ft. with bite)
Base Atk +22; **Grp** +45
Atk Options Combat Reflexes, Power Attack, blood drain, energy drain, frightful presence, magic strike
Special Actions Clinging Breath, Maximize Breath, Quicken Breath, breath weapon, *charm*, create spawn, crush, domination
Combat Gear *wand of greater invisibility* (10 charges), *wand of inflict critical wounds* (7 charges), *wand of magic missiles* (CL 5th, 7 charges)
Sorcerer Spells Known (CL 7th):
3rd (4/day)—*displacement, fireball* (DC 18)
2nd (6/day)—*scorching ray* (+23 ranged touch), *see invisibility, web*
1st (6/day)—*expeditious retreat, mage armor, shield, silent image* (DC 16), *true strike*
0 (6/day)—*arcane mark, detect magic, ghost sound* (DC 15), *mage hand, prestidigitation, read magic, touch of fatigue* (+35 melee touch, DC 15)
Spell-Like Abilities (CL 7th):
6/day—*locate object*

Abilities Str 41, Dex 16, Con —, Int 18, Wis 21, Cha 20
SQ undead traits
Feats Alertness[B], Clinging Breath[Dra] (see page 25), Combat Reflexes[B], Dodge[B], Flyby Attack, Hover, Improved Initiative[B], Lightning Reflexes[B], Maximize Breath[Dra] (see page 25), Power Attack, Quicken Breath[Dra] (see page 25), Wingover
Skills Bluff +13, Concentration +25, Diplomacy +9, Escape Artist +28, Hide +3, Intimidate +30, Jump +19, Knowledge (arcana) +29, Knowledge (the planes) +29, Listen +40, Move Silently +11, Search +37, Sense Motive +38, Spot +40, Survival +3 (+5 on other planes or following tracks), Use Magic Device +30, Use Rope +3 (+5 bindings)
Possessions combat gear plus *ring of protection +2, belt of giant Strength +4, vest of resistance +2*, treasure hoard (see page 143)

Keen Senses (Ex) Albrathax sees four times as far as a human does in shadowy illumination.

Frightful Presence (Ex) Albrathax can inspire terror by flying overhead, charging, or attacking. Creatures within 180 feet are subject to the effect if they have fewer than 22 Hit Dice. Affected creatures must attempt a DC 26 Will save. Those that fail the save and that have 4 or fewer Hit Dice become panicked for 4d6 rounds. Those that fail the save and that have 5 or more Hit Dice become shaken for 4d6 rounds. Those that save successfully cannot be affected by Albrathax's frightful presence for 24 hours. Dragons are immune to this effect.

Blood Drain (Ex) Albrathax can suck blood from a living victim by making a successful grapple check. If he pins the foe, he drains 1d4 points of Constitution from the victim each round that he maintains the pin. This ability does not affect elementals, plants, or creatures that lack a Constitution score.

Energy Drain (Su) Living creatures hit by Albrathax's claw attack gain one negative level (DC 26 Fortitude save to remove).

Magic Strike (Su) Albathrax's natural weapons are treated as magic weapons for the purpose of overcoming damage reduction.

Breath Weapon (Su) 50-ft. cone, once every 1d4 rounds, 12d10 fire, Reflex DC 26 half.

Charm (Su) At will, as a full-round action, Albrathax can try to *charm* creatures with his voice. When the dragon speaks, any creature within 180 feet that hears his voice must succeed on a DC 26 Will save or be *charmed* as the *charm monster* spell. This effect ends if Albrathax attacks or uses his frightful presence on the affected creature.

Create Spawn (Su) A humanoid or monstrous humanoid of any size that Albrathax slays with his energy drain attack rises as a vampire spawn 1d4 days after death. If Albrathax instead drains the victim's Constitution to 0, the victim returns as a spawn if it had 4 or fewer Hit Dice and as a vampire if it had 5 or more Hit Dice. In either case, the new vampire or spawn is under Albrathax's command and remains enslaved until its death.

An adult or older dragon slain by Albrathax's blood drain returns as a vampiric dragon under the command of Albrathax, as noted above. Young adult or younger dragons slain by Albrathax's blood drain attack, or any dragon slain by his energy drain attack, rise instead as mindless zombie dragons[Dra].

Crush (Ex) When flying or jumping, Albrathax can as a standard action land on Small or smaller opponents. Victims must succeed on a DC 26 Reflex save or be pinned, taking 2d8+22 points of bludgeoning damage on the next round and on each subsequent round the pin is maintained.

Domination (Su) Albrathax can *dominate* foes as the *dominate monster* spell (range 90 ft., Will DC 26 negates, CL 18th).

ILISS GITHOM-VAAS

"Can you blame me? Why should I submit to Vlaakith's hunger, when there is so much left to experience, to savor, to enjoy? What right has she to lay claim to my life?"

—Iliss Githom-vaas, renegade githyanki lich

Like Kastya, Iliss Githom-Vaas is an exile who fled from Tu'narath after she attained enough power that the lich-queen found her threatening. Iliss escaped certain death and took up with Kastya, who promised to extend his protection to her in exchange for her perpetual service. Now, Iliss commands the githyanki that are loyal to the necromancer, and she organizes expeditions to gain the tools Kastya needs to destroy the lich-queen.

GOALS

Iliss has little interest in Kastya's goals, and if she could destroy Vlaakith on her own, she would. In fact, she does not hate the cruel githyanki ruler, but she realizes that she can never return to her people as long as the lich-queen demands her soul.

She has reluctantly joined the necromancer in undeath. Although becoming a lich has provided her some benefits (including the ability to avoid damage on the Negative Energy Plane), it has also given Kastya more power over her. Her fear of the necromancer is enough to ensure that she remains a useful servant. If she failed Kastya, she could face a fate worse than the oblivion promised by Vlaakith.

USING ILISS

Having ridden on the backs of the eldest dragons, destroyed countless illithid strongholds, and orchestrated the invasion of the githzerai monastery Sheth-maal, Iliss was widely regarded as one of the most skilled warriors in Tu'narath. Although her flight and exile has disgraced her to most githyanki, some consider her a martyr, and they occasionally seek her out to join her cause.

Iliss is an agitator. She often sows unrest and confusion in githyanki cities, working to loosen Vlaakith's hold on them.

Iliss Githom-Vaas

Illus. by J. Hodgson

Many gith reject Iliss out of hand, but her long and exemplary career lends weight to her revolutionary words, leading some to set aside their prior allegiances and join her (and, by extension, Kastya). She knows that her recruits are more loyal to her than to Kastya, and she hopes to gain enough support one day to turn the tables on the necromancer and force him to back her own bid for the githyanki throne.

Appearance and Behavior

By githyanki standards (notwithstanding the fact that she is now a lich), Iliss is an attractive female whose ocher skin is laced with scars. She wears her rust-red hair in an elaborate topknot woven with black stones. Her unusual suit of full plate armor is decorated in draconic flanges and spurs, with a stylized roaring dragon skull worked into the breastplate.

Iliss has a fiery personality and an instinctual understanding of githyanki psychology that allows her to inspire and intimidate her fellow warriors. She uses rhetoric and threats to inflame emotions and entice others to serve her.

Iliss Githom-Vaas — CR 17

hp 166 (15 HD); **DR** 15/bludgeoning and magic

Female githyanki lich fighter 6/death's chosen[LM] 3/blackguard 5
CE Medium undead (augmented humanoid, extraplanar)
Init +7; **Senses** darkvision 60 ft.; Listen +2, Spot +4
Aura fear (60 ft., DC 25), despair (10 ft., –2 on saves), evil (strong), unnatural (30 ft.)
Languages Common, Gith

AC 29, touch 17, flat-footed 26 (+3 Dex, +12 armor, +4 deflection)
Miss Chance 20% *blur*
Immune cold, electricity, *polymorph* (except spells with a range of personal), mind-affecting spells and abilities, undead immunities
Resist +4 turn resistance; **SR** 21
Fort +23 (+27 against disease), **Ref** +13, **Will** +12 (+14 when within 60 feet of Kastya)

Speed 20 ft. (4 squares) in full plate, base speed 30 ft.
Melee *+1 flaming silver sword* +22/+17/+12 (2d6+12/17–20 plus 1d6 fire) or
Melee damaging touch +20 (1d8+5 negative energy plus paralysis)
Base Atk +14; **Grp** +20
Atk Options Cleave, Improved Sunder, Power Attack, Quicken Spell-Like Ability (*blur*), bravery of the chosen, magic strike, paralyzing touch, smite good 2/day (+4 attack, +7 damage), sneak attack +2d6
Special Actions rebuke undead 7/day (+4, 2d6+9, 5th)
Combat Gear *oil of curse weapon, potion of cure moderate wounds, potion of hide from undead, potion of invisibility*
Blackguard Spells Prepared (CL 5th):
2nd—*cure moderate wounds, shatter* (DC 16)
1st—*corrupt weapon, doom* (DC 15)
Psionics (CL 7th):
3/day—*blur*†, *daze* (DC 14), *dimension door, mage hand, telekinesis* (DC 19)
1/day—*plane shift* (DC 20)
† Already used once

Abilities Str 22, Dex 17, Con —, Int 10, Wis 14, Cha 18
SQ dark blessing, poison use, shield of the master, vigor of the chosen, will of the chosen
Feats Cleave[B], Endurance[B], Gruesome Finish (see page 24), Improved Critical (greatsword), Improved Initiative[B], Improved Sunder[B], Power Attack[B], Quicken Spell-Like Ability (*blur*), Weapon Focus (greatsword), Weapon Specialization (greatsword)
Skills Hide +3, Intimidate +18, Knowledge (religion) +2, Listen +2, Ride +15, Spot +4
Possessions combat gear plus *+4 full plate, +1 flaming silver sword, ring of feather falling, ring of protection +4, amulet of health +2, belt of giant strength +4, cloak of Charisma +2, vest of resistance +2,* 1,100 gp

Fear Aura (Su) At the end of each of Iliss's turns, creatures of less than 5 HD within 60 feet of her must attempt DC 22 Will saves. Those that fail are panicked for 7 rounds. Those that succeed are shaken for 1 round and cannot be affected again by Iliss's aura for 24 hours.

Aura of Despair (Su) All enemies within 10 feet of Iliss take a penalty of –2 on saves.

Unnatural Aura (Su) Animals will not approach within 30 feet of Iliss willingly, and they panic if forced to do so.

Damaging Touch (Su) Any living creature that is touched by Iliss takes 1d8+5 points of negative energy damage (Will DC 22 half).

Bravery of the Chosen (Ex) Whenever Iliss is within 30 feet of Kastya, she gains a +1 morale bonus on melee attack rolls and melee damage rolls. If Iliss is reduced to half her hit points or fewer, these bonuses increase to +2. Iliss loses these bonuses if Kastya is destroyed.

Magic Strike (Su) Iliss's touch attack is treated as a magic weapon for the purpose of overcoming damage reduction.

Paralyzing Touch (Su) Any living creature that Iliss hits with his damaging touch attack must succeed on a DC 22 Fortitude save or become paralyzed. A *remove paralysis* spell or any spell that can remove a curse frees the victim. This effect cannot be dispelled.

Shield of the Master (Ex) Whenever Kastya casts a spell or uses an extraordinary ability, a spell-like ability, or a supernatural ability, he can choose (as a free action) to exempt Iliss from its effects.

Vigor of the Chosen (Ex) Iliss needs to consume only one-tenth the normal amount of food and water each day and can subsist on only 2 hours of sleep each night.

If you use *Expanded Psionics Handbook*, Iliss gains the psionic subtype and uses the following statistics in place of spell resistance and psionics.
PR 20
Power Points/Day: 3
Psi-Like Abilities (ML 7th):
3/day—*concealing amorpha, far hand, psionic daze* (DC 15), *psionic dimension door, telekinetic thrust* (350 lbs., DC 17)
1/day—*psionic plane shift*

BLEAK HOLD

Ages ago, the accursed city of Moil sank into the Negative Energy Plane. The debilitating nature of the environment made short work of the city: Mortar crumbled, stones slipped free, structures collapsed, and chunks of Moil simply drifted away. The undead horrors that remained clung to the rocks, silently shrieking in hate against the living—bolstered by the vile energy that empowered them.

Little now remains of old Moil, except for a few impressive spires that managed to hold together despite the drain of the void. Like islands in a sea of death, these lost towers are havens for the few inhabitants of the plane, and dramatic battles of apocalyptic proportions are waged here for precious little territory. Those who lose are cast off wailing into the dark, while the victors enjoy a brief respite before their prize crumbles into frozen bits of gravel.

When Kastya crossed through the Astral Plane color pool onto the Negative Energy Plane, he discovered, though luck or design, a massive tower that had escaped destruction. He and Albathrax purged the complex of squatters and claimed it for themselves, naming it Bleak Hold. Many portions of the tower have since broken off, and other parts house terrifying, indescribable things, making the slowly spinning structure no more hospitable than any other location on this deathly plane.

KEY FEATURES

Centuries of decay have all but dissolved the top and bottom sections of Bleak Hold, leaving nothing but hollow areas shrouded in darkness. Only one level of the tower now remains more or less intact, and that level is where Kastya makes his home.

Planar Traits

Bleak Hold drifts through the Negative Energy Plane, which has the following traits. (For more details, see Chapter 5 of the *Dungeon Master's Guide.*)

Subjective Directional Gravity: Within Bleak Hold, there is a clear up and down.

Minor Negative-Dominant: Bleak Hold exists in an area of doldrums, which minimizes the deadlier traits of the plane. Most areas within the tower are minor negative-dominant, meaning that living creatures within take 1d6 points of damage each round, unless protected by *death ward* or similar magic. If they fall to 0 or fewer hit points, they crumble into ash.

Major Negative-Dominant: Outside Bleak Hold, and in certain locations within the tower, living creatures must succeed on a DC 25 Fortitude save each round or gain one negative level. If a living creature's negative levels equal its Hit Dice, the creature dies and instantly rises as a wraith.

Enhanced Magic: Spells and spell-like abilities that use negative energy, such as *inflict* spells, are maximized (as if affected by the Maximize Spell metamagic feat, but without changing the effective spell slot). Spells and spell-like abilities that are maximized already are not affected by this benefit. Class abilities that use negative energy, such as rebuking and controlling undead, gain a +10 bonus on the roll to determine how many Hit Dice of creatures are affected.

Impeded Magic: Spells and spell-like abilities that use positive energy, such as *cure* spells, are impeded. To cast such a spell, the caster must succeed on a Spellcraft check (DC 20 + the level of the spell). On a failed check, the spell does not work and is lost. Characters on the Negative Energy Plane take a penalty of –10 on Fortitude saves to remove negative energy levels bestowed by an energy drain attack.

Illus. by M. Phillippi

Bleak Hold

Structural Properties

The following properties apply to all areas in Bleak Hold unless otherwise noted in the area descriptions.

Walls: The walls are superior masonry covered in a rime of bone-chilling ice. Living creatures that touch a wall take 1d6 points of cold damage. A wall can be scaled with a successful DC 30 Climb check.

Floors: The floors are clear of debris but are covered in ebony ice (*Frostburn* 15). It costs 2 squares of movement to enter a square containing ebony ice, and the DC of Balance and Tumble checks increases by 5 in such a square. A successful DC 10 Balance check is required to run or charge across the ice. Undead creatures in an area of ebony ice gain a +2 profane bonus on attack rolls and saves and a +4 profane bonus to turn resistance.

Ceiling Height: Throughout the tower, the ceilings rise 20 feet high.

Doors: The stone doors are 10 feet wide and 4 inches thick, with hardness 8 and 60 hit points. They bear horned demonic faces with mouths stretched wide open.

Illumination: The Negative Energy Plane devours light greedily. Within Bleak Hold, all clear vision (including darkvision) is halved. Outside the tower, all clear vision is reduced to 5 feet.

Encounter Levels: All listed Encounter Levels in the following tactical encounters are 1 higher than normal due to the deadly nature of the environment.

DEFENSES

If Kastya becomes aware of intruders in Bleak Hold, he immediately commands Albrathax to fly to the landing (area 1) and be ready to prevent the trespassers from leaving the tower. The lich then uses *dimension door* to travel to one of the holding chambers (area 2). From there, he unleashes his zombie hordes, sending them forth in waves to congregate at the site of tactical encounter 8–1 (page 138). One mob of zombies arrives every 2 rounds until all seven mobs are present. Finally, Kastya and Iliss prepare to make their stand in a chamber loaded with defensive advantages (see tactical encounter 8–2).

AREA DESCRIPTIONS

Although Bleak Hold's exterior is almost completely in ruins, its rooms are more or less intact. The following areas correspond with those on the map on page 137.

1. Landing: From the outside of the slowly spinning tower, a half-destroyed bridge extends. Its surface is broken and pitted, and streams of debris float away from it into the void, vanishing in the darkness. An enormous archway leads into the tower, framed by the snarling face of a demon with twin horns curling down from each side of its green head.

If Kastya ordered Albrathax to guard the landing, the vampiric dragon waits just outside the archway, ready to prevent anyone from leaving Bleak Hold.

Albrathax: hp 231 (22 HD); see page 132

2. Holding Chambers: Scattered throughout the complex are a number of holding chambers; Kastya sets these rooms aside for the zombies he creates. The undead creatures await his eventual order to wage war on Vlaakith's githyanki subjects. Until that day comes, they shuffle about their chambers and attack anyone other than Kastya who enters.

Mob of Zombies — CR 8

hp 198 (30 HD); **DR** 5/slashing
NE Gargantuan undead (extraplanar) (mob[DMG2] of 48 Medium undead)
Init +0; **Senses** darkvision 60 ft.; Listen –2, Spot +2

AC 13, touch 6, flat-footed 13
(–4 size, +5 armor, +2 natural)
Immune undead immunities
Resist +4 turn resistance
Fort +11, **Ref** +11, **Will** +19
Weakness undead vulnerabilities

Speed 10 ft. (2 squares) in breastplate, base speed 20 ft.; cannot run
Melee mob (5d6)
Space 20 ft.; **Reach** 0 ft.
Base Atk +15; **Grp** +31
Atk Options expert grappler, trample 2d6+3

Abilities Str 15, Dex 11, Con —, Int —, Wis 10, Cha 8
SQ mob anatomy, single actions only, undead traits
Feats Improved Bull Rush[B], Improved Overrun[B], Toughness[B]
Skills Listen –2, Spot +2
Possessions breastplate, various weapons (individuals only)

Mob A mob attacks like a swarm, dealing damage to any creature whose space it occupies at the end of its move. A mob's attacks ignore concealment and cover.
Expert Grappler (Ex) A mob can maintain a grapple without penalty and still make attacks against other targets. A mob is never considered flat-footed while grappling.
Trample (Ex) A mob that moves over a creature and does not end its movement while that creature is in one of its occupied squares can trample the creature, dealing 2d6+3 points of damage. A trampled victim can make an attack of opportunity against the mob or attempt a DC 27 Reflex save for half damage.
Mob Anatomy (Ex) The mob consists of 48 Medium undead. For each individual creature that is slain, disabled, or otherwise incapacitated by spells or effects that target specific creatures, the mob gains two negative levels (an exception to the rule that undead do not gain negative levels). If the mob's negative levels equal its Hit Dice, it is destroyed. A mob takes half again as much damage (+50%) from spells or effects that affect an area, such as splash weapons or evocation spells.
Single Actions Only (Ex) A zombie can perform only a single action each round, a standard action or a move action.

3. Haunted Chamber: The floor of this room is similar to that of the other barren chambers—it is laced with ebony ice and laden with grime. The walls, however, are different. On each wall is a bas-relief of bald men wearing long robes with voluminous sleeves, bowing before a fat, ram-headed demon seated on a throne of skulls. In the background of each image, spirits dance above another knot of men who are trying to hold a struggling sacrifice down on an altar.

Four dread wraiths lurk in this room. They hide in the walls, their shadowy features blending in with the carvings of the spirits flying over the men. Two rounds after the PCs enter the chamber, the dread wraiths attack. Each one uses Spring Attack to dart from the wall, attack the characters, and slide into the floor. The undead target obvious divine spellcasters first, while using Dodge to avoid attacks from the other PCs.

Dread Wraiths (4): hp 104 each (16 HD) each; *MM* 258

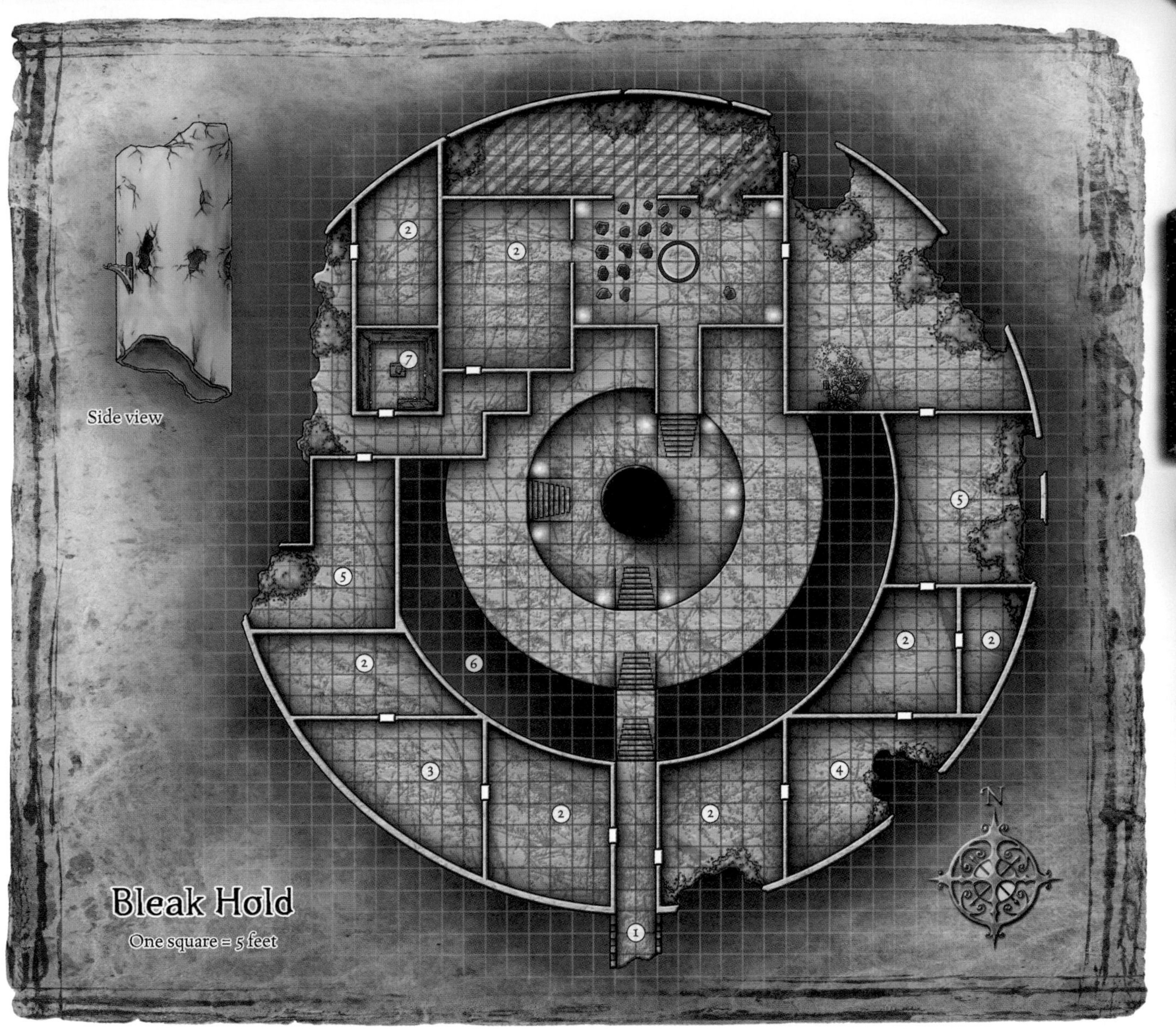

4. Corroded Room: This empty room is similar to other barren chambers in the tower. However, a serious breach in the outer wall exposes the room to the Negative Energy Plane, making it a major negative-dominant area (see Planar Traits, above).

5. Necromantic Seepage: A foul liquid known as necromantic seepage oozes from rents in the walls of these chambers. It collects in areas as indicated on the map. If left alone, the seepage bubbles harmlessly. If removed from this room, it dries to a foul powder in 1d6 rounds.

If the seepage comes into contact with a living creature or other organic material, it deals 1d6 points of damage (ignoring hardness) and swiftly grows, enveloping whatever touched it. If a PC is caught in the seepage, he must attempt a DC 20 Fortitude save. A successful save indicates that the seepage dries up and flakes away. On a failed save, the victim takes 1d6 points of damage plus 1d6 extra points of damage for each previous failed save. If the victim takes a total of 10d6 points of damage, he is completely encased and in danger of suffocation.

A Small or Medium creature is cleansed of necromantic seepage on a successful turning check against a 10 HD creature that also affects 10 or more total Hit Dice of creatures.

6. Pit: The floor of this area rotted away long ago. Creatures that fall into the pit slip out of the protective zone of Bleak Hold and tumble into the major negative-dominant area that surrounds the tower (see Planar Traits, above).

7. Library: This chamber serves as Kastya's personal quarters. Shelves line the walls, holding decomposed, now-useless manuscripts. The lich's spellbook sits on a reading stand in the center of the room. A magnificent lamp equipped with a *continual flame* spell hangs above the stand, illuminating the book's pages in soft blue light. Hidden in the lamp (Search DC 30) is Kastya's phylactery—a fake dragon egg studded with diamonds. The phylactery has hardness 20, 40 hit points, and a break DC of 40.

VOIDSTONE PILLAR

Encounter Level 17

SETUP

A pillar of utterly black voidstone (*DMG* 157) rises through the floor in the center of the room. A hullathoin lurks at the base of the pillar, and eight xeg-yi float near the top.

As soon as the PCs enter the room, the hullathoin makes a Listen check with a penalty of –1 per 10 feet of distance. If it hears the intruders, the creature exudes a bloodfiend locust swarm every other round until it has produced four swarms. The characters can hear the swarms if they succeed on DC 10 Listen checks.

When the PCs cross the bridge, read:

Across the bridge, you see a massive gallery in the shape of a bowl. Three staircases descend to the bottom—a relatively flat area from which a pillar of absolute darkness rises. At the base of a thick column is a grotesque abomination. Its oversized head is little more than exposed bone, and its vaguely reptilian body has a mottled, gray-and-black hide that is spotted with bloody sores. Bloated locusts wriggle out of the sores and swarm about the creature.

With a deep chuckle, the horrifying beast rises from its supine position and lumbers toward you. As it moves, disembodied, pulsing red spheres descend from the top of the spire, touching the creature with long, strange tendrils.

TACTICS

When the hullathoin comes within reach of a lightly armored foe, it attacks with its bite, using a 5-point Power Attack (attack +14, damage 2d8+20). When it can make a full attack, it stops using Power Attack. If the hullathoin hits with a tentacle attack, it and the target make opposed grapple checks. If the hullathoin wins the opposed check, it deals an extra 1d6+5 points of damage, and the target must succeed on a DC 19 Fortitude save or take 1d10 points of Strength damage from the creature's poison.

If the hullathoin gets a hold on a target, it moves 6 squares back toward the voidstone pillar on the next round by making another opposed grapple check. On its next turn, the creature releases its prey as a free action and makes a bull rush attempt to push the target against the pillar. The target can make an attack of opportunity, after which the hullathoin and the target make opposed Strength checks. The hullathoin gains a +8 bonus on the check, for a total modifier of +18. If the beast pushes the target against the pillar, the target must succeed on a DC 25 Fortitude save or be destroyed.

Meanwhile, the xeg-yi use the Flyby Attack feat to deliver negative energy lashes that heal the undead creature. If prevented from doing so, they fly 30 feet overhead and fire negative energy rays at the hullathoin instead.

The bloodfiend locusts are mindless and attack the closest living creature.

HULLATHOIN[FF] **CR 15**

hp 104 (16 HD); fast healing 8; **DR** 15/magic and silver

NE Huge undead (extraplanar)
Init –1; **Senses** blindsight 60 ft., scent; Listen +22, Spot +22
Languages Common, Draconic

AC 27, touch 7, flat-footed 27
(–2 size, –1 Dex, +20 natural)
Immune cold, electricity, undead immunities
Resist fire 10, sonic 10; +8 turn resistance; **SR** 26
Fort +9, **Ref** +6, **Will** +15
Weakness undead vulnerabilities

Speed 60 ft. (12 squares)
Melee bite +19 (2d8+10/19–20 plus poison)
Melee 2 stamps +16 each (1d8+5) and
2 tentacles +16 each (1d6+5 plus poison)
Space 15 ft.; **Reach** 10 ft. (20 ft. with tentacle)
Base Atk +8; **Grp** +28
Atk Options Cleave, Power Attack, deform, improved grab, improved grapple, poison (DC 19, 1d10 Str/1d10 Str)
Special Actions exude bloodfiend locusts, rebuke undead 4/day (+1, 2d6+21, 20th), ring of pus

Abilities Str 30, Dex 8, Con —, Int 12, Wis 16, Cha 12
SQ undead traits
Feats Cleave, Great Fortitude, Improved Critical (bite), Multiattack, Power Attack, Weapon Focus (bite)
Skills Balance +18, Climb +29, Listen +22, Spot +22, Swim +29

Deform (Su) Whenever a hullathoin deals damage with a grapple attack, the target must succeed on a DC 19 Fortitude save or take an extra 1d6 points of Charisma damage.
Improved Grab (Ex) To use this ability, a hullathoin must hit an opponent of up to Large size with a tentacle attack. It can then attempt to start a grapple as a free action without provoking attacks of opportunity.
Improved Grapple (Ex) A hullathoin does not take a penalty of –20 to grappling checks when using a tentacle to hold its opponent.
Exude Bloodfiend Locusts (Su) As a standard action, a hullathoin can produce from its body a swarm of bloodfiend locusts that attacks its foes.
Ring of Pus (Ex) Once per day, a hullathoin can spray pus in a 30-foot radius. All creatures in the area become nauseated for 1d10 rounds, take 5d6 points of acid damage, and take 1d6 points of Strength damage. A successful DC 19 Reflex save negates the nauseated condition, halves the acid damage, and negates the Strength damage.

4 BLOODFIEND LOCUST SWARMS[FF] **CR 8**
hp 91 each (14 HD)

CE Fine vermin (extraplanar, swarm)
Init +4; **Senses** darkvision 60 ft.; Listen +1, Spot +1

AC 19, touch 14, flat-footed 15
(+4 Dex, +5 natural)
Immune swarm immunities, vermin immunities
Fort +11, **Ref** +8, **Will** +5
Weakness swarm vulnerabilities, vermin vulnerabilities

Speed 20 ft. (4 squares), fly 20 ft. (perfect)
Melee swarm (3d6 plus energy drain)
Space 5 ft.; **Reach** 0 ft.
Base Atk +10; **Grp** —
Atk Options distraction, energy drain
Special Actions reanimate

Abilities Str 1, Dex 18, Con 14, Int —, Wis 13, Cha 11
SQ swarm traits, vermin traits
Skills Listen +1, Spot +1

Distraction (Ex) Any creature that begins its turn with a swarm in its square must make a successful DC 19 Fortitude save or be nauseated for 1 round. Spellcasting or concentrating on spells requires a successful Concentration check (DC 20 + spell level). Using skills involving patience and concentration requires a DC 20 Concentration check.
Energy Drain (Su) Living creatures hit by a bloodfiend locust swarm gain one negative level (Fortitude DC 17 to remove).
Reanimate (Su) A humanoid or monstrous humanoid killed by the energy drain attack of a bloodfiend locust swarm rises 2d6 hours later as a fiendish vampire spawn. For details, see the vampire spawn (*MM* 253) and the fiendish template (*MM* 108).

8 ADVANCED XEG-YI[MoP] **CR 5**
hp 49 (9 HD)

N Medium elemental (extraplanar, incorporeal)
Init +4; **Senses** darkvision 60 ft.; Listen +0, Spot +6

AC 18, touch 17, flat-footed 14; Dodge
(+4 Dex, +4 deflection)
Immune elemental immunities
Fort +4, **Ref** +10, **Will** +3
Weakness elemental vulnerabilities

Speed fly 20 ft. (good); Flyby Attack
Melee 4 incorporeal touches +10 each (1d6)
Ranged negative energy ray +10 (1d8)
Base Atk +6; **Grp** —
Atk Options Combat Reflexes, negative energy lash
Special Actions explosion, rebuke undead 10/day (+4, 2d6+13, 9th)

Abilities Str —, Dex 18, Con 12, Int 7, Wis 10, Cha 18
SQ elemental traits
Feats Combat Reflexes, Dodge, Extra Turning, Flyby Attack
Skills Hide +10, Listen +0, Spot +6

Negative Energy Ray (Ex) A xeg-yi's negative energy ray has a range of 30 feet.
Negative Energy Lash (Su) Five times per day, a xeg-yi can make a ranged touch attack or hit with an incorporeal touch attack to infuse a target with negative energy. The lash either deals 2d8+9 points of damage to a living creature or heals an undead creature of that amount of damage.
Explosion (Su) When reduced to 0 hit points, a xeg-yi explodes in a 20-foot-radius burst that deals 1d8+9 points of negative energy damage to everything in the area (Reflex DC 15 half).

FEATURES OF THE AREA

The chamber has the following features.

Illumination: Because of the debilitating nature of the plane, *everburning torches* spaced around the rim of the bottom level give off only 10 feet of bright light and 20 feet of shadowy illumination.

Ceiling: The ceiling in this room is 40 feet high.

Floors and Walls: The floors and walls are covered in ebony ice. It costs 2 squares of movement to enter a square containing ebony ice, and the DC of Balance and Tumble checks increases by 5 in such a square. A successful DC 10 Balance check is required to run or charge across the ice. Undead creatures in an area of ebony ice gain a +2 profane bonus on attack rolls and saves and a +4 profane bonus to turn resistance.

Staircase: Staircases lead from the bottom of the bowl-shaped gallery up to the promenade. Characters who stand on a staircase while fighting creatures below can gain a +1 melee attack bonus for fighting from higher ground.

Promenade: The promenade stands 20 feet above the bottom level of this room.

Pit: Any creature that falls into the pit drops for 80 feet and leaves the protection of the tower, drifting into the void. If the creature is living, it must succeed on a DC 25 Fortitude save each round or gain one negative level. If the creature's negative levels equal its Hit Dice, the creature dies and instantly rises as a wraith.

Voidstone Pillar: Rising through the floor in the center of this room is a pillar of black voidstone (*DMG* 157). A creature that comes into contact with the pillar must succeed on a DC 25 Fortitude save or be destroyed as if it had come into contact with a *sphere of annihilation*.

Lich Lair

Encounter Level 21

SETUP

Once Kastya hears the sounds of combat from tactical encounter 8–1, he uses *dimension door* to round up his zombie mobs and send them to converge on the PCs. Afterward, he casts *death armor*, which lasts for 19 rounds; during this time, any creature that strikes Kastya with its body or a handheld weapon takes 1d4+10 points of damage. He follows up by casting *stoneskin* and *protection from spells*, each of which lasts for 160 minutes.

The lich then sends Albrathax to the landing (area 1) to cut off the intruders' escape route. After the dragon departs, Kastya prepares to make his stand in a chamber that contains numerous defensive aids, including blood rocks, negative energy, absolute darkness, and a corrupt circle that boosts his Armor Class and caster level. For details, see Features of the Area, below.

Iliss joins him in the chamber, and Kastya casts *stoneskin* on her. The necromancer then uses *greater invisibility* and casts *globe of invulnerability* on himself. If he still has time, he readies an action to cast Moilian *blackfire* at the first player character he sees.

Iliss uses a rebuke undead attempt to bolster her master. She then drinks her *potion of invisibility* and moves to one of the blood rock squares, making sure to stay within 60 feet of the lich so that he gains a +4 bonus to turn resistance and a +2 bonus on saves through his Lifebond feat.

When the PCs reach the top of the steps leading to this encounter, read:

About 30 feet down the corridor, a rotating crimson sphere rises up from the floor. From the center of the sphere, a ray of crackling black energy streaks directly toward you.

When the PCs enter the room, read:

This large chamber has a strange, coppery scent. Torches cast a dim blue light throughout the area, revealing dark stone sheathed in black ice. Here and there, ruddy outcroppings appear through the rime. A glowing red circle is set into the floor in the center of the room, and two 10-foot-wide alcoves in the far wall seem to lead to utter blackness.

KASTYA ZURITH-MOVYA CR 19

Refer to his full statistics on page 130. The changed statistics below represent the results of protective measures taken prior to the start of the encounter.

Resist +8 turn resistance

Fort +6, **Ref** +10, **Will** +16; +8 against spells and spell-like effects

Melee damaging touch +13 (1d8+5 negative energy plus paralysis)

ILISS GITHOM-VAAS CR 17

Refer to her full statistics on page 134. The changed statistics below represent the results of protective measures taken prior to the start of the encounter.

hp 166 (15 HD); **DR** 10/adamantine (*stoneskin*)

TACTICS

Kastya casts spells from the center of the corrupt circle, which grants him a +2 bonus to Armor Class and an effective caster level of 17th (or 19th for necromancy spells). If the lich has readied his Moilian *blackfire* spell but has not yet used it, he casts it now against a spellcasting PC.

While still invisible, Kastya casts *magic jar*, sending his essence into the crystal he carries for this purpose. Each round thereafter, the lich attempts to possess one of the player characters. He prefers lightly armored rogues and similar hosts so that he can cast spells without fear of arcane spell failure. He continues his attempts to possess one of the PCs until he succeeds. Characters who make a successful Will save or who are under the effect of *protection from evil* or *magic circle* are immune to his attempts at possession.

If the lich takes over a PC, he retains his Intelligence, Wisdom, Charisma, classes, levels, base attack bonus, base save bonuses, alignment, and mental abilities, but he gains the physical attributes of the character. He casts *avasculate* on the closest PC and then uses *telekinesis* to move a light character into a square containing negative energy. He continues this tactic until his host is destroyed or until he is forced out of the body, at which point he jumps back to the crystal as a free action and tries to possess another character.

If Kastya's own lifeless body is threatened by a PC, he focuses on stopping the attacker. If he cannot, he shifts back to his body, ending the *magic jar* spell, and unleashes a barrage of attack spells, switching between rays and area spells depending on the threat.

Features of the Area

The room has the following features.

Illumination: Because of the debilitating nature of the plane, *everburning torches* in the corners of the chamber containing the corrupt circle give off only 10 feet of bright light and 20 feet of shadowy light.

Floors and Walls: The floors and walls are covered in ebony ice. It costs 2 squares of movement to enter a square containing ebony ice, and the DC of Balance and Tumble checks increases by 5 in such a square. A successful DC 10 Balance check is required to run or charge across the ice. Undead creatures in an area of ebony ice gain a +2 profane bonus on attack rolls and saves and a +4 profane bonus to turn resistance.

Blood Rock: If a creature is standing in a blood rock square and makes an attack that threatens a critical hit, the critical hit is automatically confirmed—no roll is necessary.

Negative Energy: Each round that a living creature remains in a square containing negative energy, it must succeed on a DC 25 Fortitude save or gain one negative level. If the creature's negative levels equal its Hit Dice, the creature is slain and instantly rises as a wraith.

Corrupt Circle: Evil creatures that stand even partly within the area of the corrupt circle receive a +2 profane bonus to Armor Class, and their effective caster level is increased by 1.

Absolute Darkness: Squares containing absolute darkness greedily devour light, reducing the range of bright light to 5 feet, the range of shadowy illumination to 0 feet, and the range of darkvision to 5 feet.

Iliss also tries to protect Kastya's body. At the start of the encounter, she is invisible, and when her master casts *magic jar*, she moves near his body to keep it safe. If a PC threatens the lich's body or comes with reach of Iliss, she lashes out with her *+1 flaming silver sword*, dealing an extra 2d6 points of sneak attack damage. If possible, she fights while standing in blood rock squares so that she is more likely to make critical hits. If that proves difficult, Iliss uses *dimension door* to cut across the battlefield and engage weaker foes.

Against a warrior or a similar character, Iliss starts by making a 5-point Power Attack in conjunction with smite good. If that does not work, she becomes a bit more conservative, making a 3-point or a 1-point Power Attack depending on the opponent. She works with Kastya (or whichever PC he possesses) to get a flanking bonus, which she uses to increase her Power Attack.

If the necromancer takes a significant amount of damage from a single opponent's melee attack, Iliss uses Improved Sunder in an attempt to destroy the offending weapon. She and the PC make opposed attack rolls; Iliss has a +22 bonus against Medium PCs and a +26 bonus against Small PCs. If her result beats the PC's result, her attack deals 2d6+12 points of damage to the targeted weapon. For the hardness and hit points of common weapons, see PH 158; remember that each +1 enhancement bonus adds 2 to a weapon's hardness and 10 to its hit points. If Iliss fails to destroy the weapon, she does not try again.

Conclusion

If the PCs reduce Kastya to 10 or fewer hit points, he casts *greater teleport* and appears in the landing (area 1), where Albrathax waits to block the intruders from leaving. The lich flies off into the Negative Energy Plane to repair his wounds and plot revenge.

If Iliss is reduced to 50 or fewer hit points, she uses *plane shift* to flee to the Astral Plane.

LAIR OF THE WYRM

Encounter Level 18

SETUP

If Kastya is aware of intruders in Bleak Hold, he orders Albrathax to move to the landing (area 1) and block the exit. Otherwise, the vampiric dragon does not take the initiative to help his master; instead, he remains in this chamber to defend his treasure hoard, which fills a whole corner.

The room is completely dark; huge breaches in the walls allow the plane's negative energy to suck up light. Ebony ice and heavy debris on the floor make it hard to move through the room on foot. A trilloch flits near the largest breach, waiting for the battle to begin so that it can steal the ebbing life force of the dying. The creature is invisible, but if the PCs are able to see it, the trilloch resembles a roiling cloud of darkness mixed with sparkling light.

To prepare for the intruders, Albrathax uses his *wand of greater invisibility* on himself, and then uses Hover to hang near the ceiling.

When the PCs enter this room, read:

The wall opposite the door curves gently toward the south. Huge fissures in the ancient stone provide a disturbing view of the inky void beyond. Debris litters the floor near the rents. In the far corner, where the two walls form an angle, you see a massive, frost-covered heap of coins, gemstones, and other miscellaneous items.

ALBRATHAX **CR 17**
hp 231 (22 HD); see page 132

If the trilloch uses its *control rage* ability on Albrathax, substitute the following statistics for the duration of the effect.
AC 32, touch 9, flat-footed 29; Dodge
(–2 size, +3 Dex, +2 deflection, +23 natural, –4 rage)
Fort +17, **Ref** +22, **Will** +24
Melee bite +37 (2d8+17) and
2 claws +35 each (2d6+8 plus energy drain) and
2 wings +35 each (1d8+8) and
tail slap +35 (2d6+25)
Grp +47
Abilities Str 45
Skills Jump +21

TACTICS

Once at least two player characters have entered the room, Albrathax uses *charm* in an attempt to seduce the PCs. Any character within 180 feet who can hear the dragon's voice must succeed on a DC 26 Will save or become friendly. The dragon commands *charmed* characters to head back

ADVANCED TRILLOCH[MM3] **CR 12**
hp 120 (16 HD); **DR** 15/lawful

CN Small outsider (chaotic, extraplanar, incorporeal)
Init +8; **Senses** blindsight 60 ft., darkvision 60 ft.; Listen +23, Spot +23
Languages understand all spoken languages

AC 19, touch 19, flat-footed 15; Dodge, Mobility
(+1 size, +4 Dex, +4 deflection)
Miss Chance 50% natural invisibility
Immune magic, incorporeal immunities
Fort +13, **Ref** +14, **Will** +14
Weakness incorporeal vulnerabilities

Speed fly 40 ft. (perfect); Hover
Base Atk +16; **Grp** —
Special Actions *control rage*, *death knell*

Abilities Str —, Dex 19, Con 17, Int 11, Wis 18, Cha 20
SQ incorporeal traits, natural invisibility
Feats Ability Focus (*control rage*), Dodge, Hover, Improved Initiative, Mobility, Quicken Spell-Like Ability (*death knell*)
Skills Concentration +22, Diplomacy +7, Hide +27, Intimidate +24, Listen +23, Search +19, Sense Motive +23, Spot +23, Survival +23 (+25 following tracks)

Immunity to Magic (Ex) A trilloch is immune to any spell or spell-like ability that allows spell resistance. In addition, certain spells and effects function differently against the creature. *Detect magic* and *deathwatch* reveal the trilloch's location. *Death ward* protects a creature from the trilloch's *control rage* and *death knell* abilities. If a trilloch is encountered somewhere other than the Negative Energy Plane, *holy word* or *banishment* forces it back to its native plane. Finally, a trilloch is considered an undead creature for the purposes of being affected by *cure* spells and positive and negative levels.
Control Rage (Sp) As the *rage* spell; at will; DC 25; caster level 8th. This ability affects all living creatures within 180 feet. Each creature gains a +4 morale bonus to Strength and Constitution, a +2 morale bonus on Will saves, and a penalty of –4 to Armor Class. When the *rage* effect ends, the creatures are not fatigued. The effect lasts as long as the trilloch concentrates and for 8 rounds thereafter.
An affected creature can end its rage prematurely by making a successful DC 25 Will save. The trilloch can end the effect for any number of creatures prematurely without affecting other raging creatures. It can also end a rage caused by any other effect.
Death Knell (Sp) As the *death knell* spell; at will; DC 17; caster level 8th. This ability affects all creatures within 180 feet. The trilloch steals the fading life force of the dying to sustain itself, but the creature gains no hit points or other benefits.
Natural Invisibility (Su) As the *greater invisibility* spell; always active; caster level 8th. This ability is not subject to the *invisibility purge* spell.

the way they came, and then uses a clinging maximized breath weapon to fill the room with fire.

If any PCs survive the flaming assault, Albrathax descends from his hiding place to start a grapple with the closest one, provoking an attack of opportunity. If the dragon succeeds on a melee touch attack with any of his attack forms, he and his foe make opposed grapple checks. If the dragon wins, he pulls the PC into his space. On the next round, Albrathax makes another grapple check to pin his opponent. If he succeeds, he starts sucking the victim's blood, draining 1d4 points of Constitution each round that he maintains the pin.

Once Albrathax has engaged a foe, the trilloch flies in from outside and uses *control rage* on the dragon, hoping to hasten the deaths of the PCs. The creature also tries to enrage any spellcasters in the room to prevent them from casting spells. Thereafter, it flies around the chamber, using *death knell* on any creatures that fall below 0 hit points.

DEVELOPMENT

The trilloch is far more interested in the PCs than in the dragon. If the characters manage to destroy Albrathax or drive him off, the trilloch stops using *death knell* and begins hounding the PCs' steps as they proceed through Bleak Hold. The trilloch uses *control rage* to disrupt the party's spellcasters and aid the party's enemies.

CONCLUSION

Albrathax does not intend to let the player characters slaughter him. He fights until reduced to 30 or fewer hit points and then tries to escape through one of the breaches in the walls. Since he is bound to his treasure hoard just as a vampire is bound to his coffin, Albrathax remains just outside the tower, letting the negative energy repair his injuries. Once restored to at least 150 hit points, the dragon flies back into Bleak Hold to seek revenge.

Treasure: The dragon's hoard contains the following gems: 2 alexandrites (400 gp each), 1 amber (80 gp), 1 amethyst (110 gp), 1 banded agate (10 gp), 2 bloodstones (50 gp each), 2 blue diamonds (5,000 gp each), 2 citrines (80 gp and 70 gp), 1 freshwater pearl (6 gp), 2 golden yellow topazes (600 gp), 1 jacinth (4,400 gp), 1 jasper (60 gp), 2 obsidian (11 gp each), 1 tiger eye turquoise (9 gp), 1 tourmaline (90 gp), and 1 zircon (20 gp).

The hoard also contains a pair of blink dog fur boots (1,300 gp), a bronze amulet (90 gp), bronze inlaid earrings (200 gp), an engraved fir brooch with agate setting (900 gp), an engraved mahogany amulet (200 gp), an etched onyx scepter (5,000 gp), a glass crown inlaid with amber stones (500 gp), a granite pendant (500 gp), a mahogany plate (50 gp), a pillar of solid yew (700 gp), a steel-plated circlet (3,000 gp), a tapestry depicting githyanki soldiers marching to war (900 gp), an ornate zither (200 gp), 17,472 gp, and 2,190 pp.

FEATURES OF THE AREA

The dragon's lair has the following features.

Illumination: None. The lair is completely dark and exposed to the light-devouring plane. The negative energy reduces the range of bright light to 5 feet, the range of shadowy light to 0 feet, and the range of darkvision to 5 feet.

Floors and Walls: The floors and walls are covered in ebony ice. It costs 2 squares of movement to enter a square containing ebony ice, and the DC of Balance and Tumble checks increases by 5 in such a square. A successful DC 10 Balance check is required to run or charge across the ice. Undead creatures in an area of ebony ice gain a +2 profane bonus on attack rolls and saves and a +4 profane bonus to turn resistance.

Heavy Debris: It costs 4 squares of movement to enter a square that contains heavy debris, which is also covered in ebony ice. Heavy debris increases the DC of Balance and Tumble checks by 4, and it imposes a penalty of –2 on Move Silently checks. Running or charging through heavy debris is impossible.

Negative Energy: Any living creature that is exposed to negative energy (either by standing in a square adjacent to a breach or by stepping out into the plane) must make a DC 25 Fortitude save on each round of exposure. On a failed save, the creature gains one negative level. If the creature's negative levels equal its Hit Dice, the creature is slain and instantly rises as a wraith.

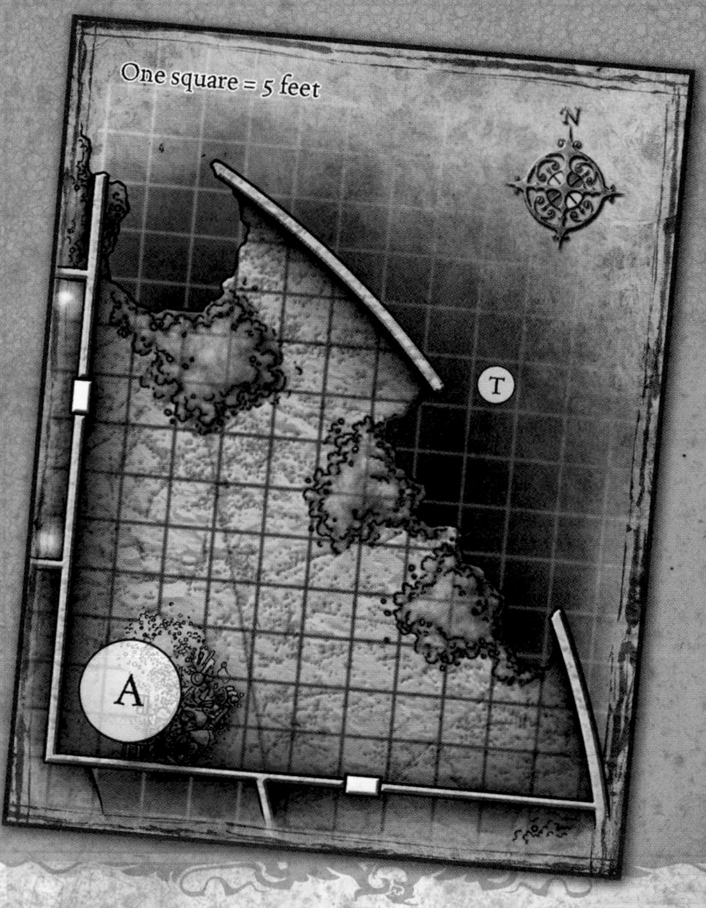

Illus. by E. Widermann

"Others have defied me over the years. They are no more than ashes and bleached bones amid these ruins, as you shall soon be."

—Borak the Thunder Tyrant

Legends say that surrounding an oasis deep in the desert is the ruined city of Imer, which long ago fell to the ravages of a mighty dragon. The beast made her lair in the wreckage and claimed dominion over the scattered former inhabitants, who had fled across the burning sands to escape the destruction of their city. Today, the descendants of those exiles pay a yearly tithe to the monster they call the "Thunder Tyrant," suffer the cruelties of the dragon's half-human spawn, and live in the shadow of their ancient conqueror. Yet they still cling to the hope that one day, someone will overthrow the tyrant and free them.

BACKGROUND

The Thunder Tyrant of the Desert is Boraksaghegirak, more commonly known as Borak—an ancient blue dragon that dwells in the ruins of a city she destroyed.

Centuries ago, Borak encountered an ambitious human wizard in Imer and became enamored of his power and confidence. Together they worked sophisticated magic and accumulated vast treasures from every part of the world, including a magic ring that granted the wearer command of a mighty djinni.

Borak's paramour eventually allowed his greed to get the better of him and sought to bind the dragon to his service forever. The affront caused Borak to slay the human and lay waste to the city of Imer, driving its people into the desert and claiming the ruins as her lair.

Thereafter, Borak demanded reparations, insisting that the new desert tribes tithe their gold and gems in regular tribute. Worse, the people of the sands also had to supply her with young males and females to serve in her ruined palace—or to be eaten as sacrifices, at her whim. Fearing the power of the dragon and that of her noble djinni servant, the desert folk could do nothing but accede to her demands.

Some of those sent to the palace served Borak capably, and those that became her meals were always replaced by new tribe members. As the years went by, the dragon grew restless and bade her male servants to form a harem for her amusement. She had developed a taste for human flesh in more ways than one, and often visited the harem in humanoid form.

Occasionally Borak chose to spawn, laying clutches of eggs that hatched into half-dragons. Female offspring were slain so that they could present no challenge to her rule, but the males were allowed to live and mature, becoming their mother's servants and protectors. This elite group became known as the Al-Iborak, or the "Sons of the Dragon." They took over the duties of safeguarding Borak's lair and enforcing her will among the desert people, acting as her hands and eyes. The most favored

Sons were allowed to claim mates from among the dragon's human servants, thus securing Borak's bloodline.

Generations of would-be champions of the desert folk have sought to slay the dragon—but their bleached bones now decorate her palace in Imer, and their goods have been added to her hoard. Indeed, most members of the desert tribes have come to believe that the Thunder Tyrant cannot be slain, that she sees and knows all, and that they can do nothing but continue to meet her demands in the hope of avoiding her wrath.

GOALS

Borak dwells comfortably in the ruins of Imer. From the desert tribes, she receives annual tribute to fatten her hoard and satisfy her various appetites for human flesh. The dragon is safeguarded by Rajief—her djinni servant—and her half-dragon guardians, and she is feared and practically worshiped by the scattered descendants of the Imerians.

Maintaining her power is her primary concern, of course, but she takes an exceptionally long view. Generations have passed since she laid waste to Imer, and she expects that decades or even centuries more will pass before she is roused sufficiently to destroy another city.

The dragon passes the time by taking an interest in obscure arcana. Now and then, a particular item or bit of arcane lore catches her attention, and she decides that she must have it. She usually has the Al-Iborak track such articles down, but if her object is particularly far away or difficult to acquire, she might send Rajief instead. Borak's servants have practically picked her domain clean of such things, so a character who brings a unique magic item or knowledge of an unusual spell within Borak's grasp might have the misfortune of attracting her attention.

Borak still has two *wishes* remaining from Rajief. Rather than squandering them on trivial matters, she holds the *wishes* in reserve as her ultimate "aces in the hole"—particularly the third *wish*, since granting it will release Rajief from servitude.

USING THIS VILLAIN

The legendary Thunder Tyrant is best utilized as a campaign's climactic villain. Even the people dwelling in her domain rarely, if ever, see the dragon. Her isolation allows you to spread intriguing story seeds early on, with hushed tales about Borak's merciless reign over the desert people and the cruel deeds of her minions.

Rajief and the Al-Iborak can provide challenges and opportunities for lower-level adventurers. For example, the PCs might run afoul of the Sons of the Dragon early in their careers, finding the remains of a caravan or village that refused to tithe. Although the PCs do not find the culprits, they start to learn about the Al-Iborak—preparing them for a later encounter with the Sons of the Dragon themselves. During this face-to-face confrontation, you can adjust the quantity, levels and abilities of the half-dragons to suit your needs, giving the PCs a reasonable challenge and piquing their interest in the master dragon behind the Al-Iborak.

Once word of the characters reaches Borak's ears, she might send Rajief to learn more about them, while she uses divinations and other methods for additional research. In this case, the noble djinni sees the party as a means to be rid of Borak once and for all. Perhaps he makes contact with the PCs, or he could simply observe them from a distance at first, quietly helping them from behind the scenes.

For her part, Borak determines whether or not the PCs could threaten her reign. If she thinks that they might, she dispatches the Al-Iborak to eliminate them, giving the characters even more reason to oppose her.

If assassination attempts and the promise of a dragon's hoard are not enough to tempt the PCs into action, Rajief might offer them a *wish*, or an NPC friend of the party might be chosen as a potential sacrifice and taken to the ruined palace. If necessary, you can have the Thunder Tyrant take the offensive and launch direct attacks on the characters, as well as on anyone who aids or shelters them, until they have no choice but to strike back.

BORAK IN EBERRON

The depths of the Blade Desert in Khorvaire conceal the crumbling city that Borak claims as her own. Parts of the ruins feature cryptic passages from the draconic Prophecy, which the Thunder Tyrant has been studying.

The halflings of the Talenta Plains and the elves of Valenar know of the blue dragon and her spawn, but they consider it wise to let sleeping dragons lie as long as Borak preys only on the nomadic desert folk. However, halflings and elves on both sides warn that it is only a matter of time before the Thunder Tyrant becomes more ambitious.

BORAK IN FAERÛN

Borak's lair lies in the depths of Calimshan's Calim Desert, half-buried beneath sands that blow and shift in frequent storms. The powerful blue is a remnant of the dragons that menaced Calimshan centuries ago, now driven into desolation far from ports and cities.

Borak and her spawn deal primarily with the nomadic desert tribes, but she is beginning to draw the attention of the pashas and the caliphs, who worry that the dragon will not remain content in her isolation for long. They might recruit explorers to journey into the desert to learn more.

BORAK THE CONQUEROR

This chapter treats the Thunder Tyrant as a distant but growing menace for a valiant group of adventurers to seek out and destroy. If you prefer a more immediate and epic threat, you can make the Thunder Tyrant's plans more sweeping and ambitious. In this case, having dwelt in the desert for untold generations, the great dragon has built an army led by her half-dragon offspring, and uses it to conquer the surrounding lands.

This plot can make Borak the mastermind villain that defines an entire campaign. For example, an arrogant Al-Iborak commander could lead the army to destroy the homes of the player characters, forcing them into the rootless lives of adventurers. Swearing to learn all they can about the ancient blue dragon, they vow that one day they will seek her lair and slay her.

At one point in such a campaign, the djinni Rajief could secretly find a way to spare the player characters from certain death. In return, he gains their friendship, though his ultimate desire is to turn the PCs into cat's-paws to use against his master.

APPEARANCE AND BEHAVIOR

The Thunder Tyrant is a gargantuan blue dragon in the prime of her life. Her scales vary in hue from deep cobalt along her back to almost turquoise near her belly and flanks, fading to pale on her underbelly. They also vary in size: Along her back and shoulders, they are bigger than a human's hand, while along her flanks and tail they are as fine and shimmering as iridescent mail.

Borak has dark, curving horns like those of a ram, and a blunt snout filled with teeth as big and as sharp as daggers. Her powerful wings stay furled close to her body when she lies at ease, but when extended to their full span, they nearly brush the walls of the former sultan's great hall, where she resides. The immense chamber within the palace is large enough to contain the dragon comfortably, and she likes to curl up on the dais, around her hoard.

The dragon spends much of her time resting her head on her forelimbs in repose, barely raising it to acknowledge an audience. Only when her curiosity or ire is roused does she lift her great head toward the domed ceiling, and if she stands, it never bodes well for her visitors.

On occasion, Borak magically assumes humanoid form. Her typical shape is that of a beautiful female human with long, lustrous black hair, deep blue eyes, and the dark skin of a desert dweller. When in this form, she wears whatever the circumstance requires, from simple clothing when she travels in disguise to the richest finery when she appears in all her glory.

BORAKSAGHEGIRAK **CR 21**

hp 445 (33 HD); **DR** 15/magic

Female ancient blue dragon
LE Gargantuan dragon (earth)
Init +0; **Senses** blindsense 60 ft., darkvision 120 ft., keen senses; Listen +35, Spot +35
Aura frightful presence (range 300 ft., fewer than 32 HD, Will DC 31 negates)
Languages Draconic, Common

AC 38, touch 6, flat-footed 38
(–4 size, +32 natural)
Immune electricity, *sleep*, paralysis
SR 27
Fort +25, **Ref** +18, **Will** +23

Speed 40 ft. (8 squares), burrow 20 ft., fly 200 ft. (clumsy)
Melee bite +33 (4d6+12) and
2 claws +27 each (2d8+6) and
2 wings +27 each (2d6+6) and
tail slap +27 (2d8+18)
Space 20 ft.; **Reach** 15 ft. (20 ft. with bite)
Base Atk +33; **Grp** +57
Atk Options Combat Expertise, Great Cleave, Multiattack, Power Attack
Special Actions breath weapon, crush, sound imitation, tail sweep
Sorcerer Spells Known (CL 13th; 1d20+15 to overcome SR):
6th (4/day)—*chain lightning* (DC 24), *guards and wards* (DC 24)

Illus. by M. Phillippi

Boraksaghegirak

5th (7/day)—*dominate person* (DC 23), *Mordenkainen's faithful hound, prying eyes*
4th (7/day)—*bestow curse* (DC 22), *lesser globe of invulnerability, polymorph, scrying*
3rd (7/day)—*dispel magic, gaseous form, lightning bolt* (DC 21), *nondetection*
2nd (7/day)—*arcane lock, blindness/deafness* (DC 20), *detect thoughts* (DC 20), *misdirection* (DC 20), *whispering wind*
1st (8/day)—*charm person* (DC 19), *protection from good, silent image, true strike, ventriloquism*
0 (6/day)—*arcane mark, detect magic, detect poison, flare* (DC 18), *light, mage hand, message, open/close, touch of fatigue* (DC 18)
Spell-Like Abilities (CL 13th):
3/day—*create/destroy water, ventriloquism* (DC 19)
1/day—*hallucinatory terrain, veil* (DC 22)

Abilities Str 35, Dex 10, Con 25, Int 20, Wis 21, Cha 20
Feats Ability Focus (frightful presence), Alertness, Cleave, Combat Expertise, Eschew Materials, Flyby Attack, Great Cleave, Hover, Improved Initiative, Multiattack, Power Attack, Spell Penetration, Wingover
Skills Bluff +37, Concentration +39, Diplomacy +33, Hide +28, Intimidate +35, Knowledge (arcana) +33, Knowledge (history) +29, Knowledge (nature) +29, Knowledge (the planes) +29, Listen +35, Search +31, Sense Motive +33, Spellcraft +37, Spot +35
Possessions *ring of djinn calling*

Keen Senses (Ex) Borak sees four times as well as a human does in shadowy illumination.
Frightful Presence (Ex) Borak can inspire terror by flying overhead, charging, or attacking. Creatures within 300 feet are subject to the effect if they have fewer than 32 Hit Dice. Affected creatures must attempt a DC 31 Will save. Those that fail the save and that have 4 or fewer Hit Dice become panicked for 4d6 rounds. Those that fail the save and that have 5 or more Hit Dice become shaken for 4d6 rounds. Those that save successfully cannot be affected by Borak's frightful presence for 24 hours.
Breath Weapon (Su) 120-ft. line of lightning, once every 1d4 rounds, 20d8 electricity, Reflex DC 33 half.
Crush (Ex) When flying or jumping, Borak can as a standard action land on Medium or smaller opponents. Victims must succeed on a DC 31 Reflex save or be pinned, taking 4d6+18 points of bludgeoning damage on the next round and on each subsequent round the pin is maintained.
Sound Imitation (Ex) Borak can mimic any voice or sound she has heard, anytime she likes. Listeners must succeed on DC 31 Will saves to detect the ruse.
Tail Sweep (Ex) As a standard action, Borak can sweep her tail (attack +33, damage 2d6+18) in a half circle with a radius of 30 feet, affecting Small and smaller creatures (Reflex DC 33 half).

AL-IBORAK, SONS OF THE DRAGON

"You have entered the domain of the all-powerful Boraksaghegirak, terrible mother of the desert, from whom all power flows. Obey her or die!"

—A friendly greeting from one of the Sons of the Dragon

From time to time, Borak has chosen to spawn following a tryst with a promising human, producing half-dragon offspring. The females are killed, but the males are raised by the dragon's servants. Born of her all-powerful blood, these children are known as the Al-Iborak, or the Sons of the Dragon. Generations of the Sons have served their tyrant mother, and those who are too weak or too ambitious to do so meet a swift end—often beneath the blades or claws of their brethren, who prize loyalty to Borak above all.

GOALS

The only goals of the Al-Iborak are to serve their dragon mother in every way, and to honor and revere her as the source of all life, power, and meaning. They are raised from birth with a fanatical devotion to the Thunder Tyrant, worshiping her as if she were a deity.

Although the Al-Iborak are humble before Borak, they are tremendously arrogant to everyone else. They consider themselves superior to all other creatures—a blessed elite whose divine blood makes them worthy to serve. They enjoy lording their power over the desert tribes: Anyone who fails to bow and scrape sufficiently before them feels their wrath.

USING THE AL-IBORAK

The Sons of the Dragon offer a range of adversaries for adventuring parties of all levels. The statistics block below describes a typical member of the Al-Iborak, but the organization runs the gamut from novices with lower class levels to elite soldiers that can challenge a high-powered party.

The Al-Iborak should be an ongoing challenge for the player characters. At first, the PCs can encounter the Sons on the fringes of Borak's domain, as the half-dragons are collecting tribute from the desert folk or delivering punishment for some slight. Alternatively, the PCs might find evidence of the Al-Iborak's handiwork before meeting any of the Sons in person. As events progress and the adventurers prove to be a thorn

Al-Iborak

Illus. by E. Widermann

in the dragon's side, encounters with Al-Iborak become more frequent and more difficult.

The Al-Iborak are accustomed to victims that cower in fear, so they might underestimate the PCs at first. However, the Sons of the Dragon are hardened warriors and will not make the same mistake twice.

Appearance and Behavior

All Sons of the Dragon are powerfully muscled humanoids that wear loose-fitting robes and head covers bound with scarves. From a distance, they might be mistaken for any group of desert warriors. Up close, however, their draconic heritage is apparent. They are covered in deep blue scales and have reptilian faces, golden eyes with slit pupils, and mouths full of sharp teeth. They have no wings, but their fingers are tipped with sharp claws.

Beneath their outer garb, the Al-Iborak wear armor and bear weapons in the service of their mother and queen. They favor curved desert scimitars for close combat.

Al-Iborak Warrior **CR 11**
hp 68 (9 HD)
See full statistics block on page 154

Rajief, Prince of the Djinn

"As my mistress commands, so must it be done. I only hope my regrets will be of some small comfort to you, o doomed ones."

—Rajief, about to deliver a message from Borak

That the noble Rajief, Prince of the Djinn, Caliph of Clouds, should be reduced to a mere servant—surely there is no justice in all the planes. At least, that is how the noble djinni sees it. Rajief was magically bound long ago to an enchanted ring—for an hour each day, the owner of the ring can summon and command him, and Rajief must obey. He is tied to the ring until he grants the wearer three wishes, at which point he will be free and need deal no longer with the creatures of the Material Plane.

Unfortunately for Rajief, he has been the bound servant of Borak for centuries, ever since she slew the wizard who originally found the ring and claimed it (and the djinni) as her own. The dragon puts the Caliph of Clouds' speed to good use, using him as her long-range spy and agent. He also whips up sandstorms to hinder desert caravans and spirits the dragon's enemies away.

Illus. by W. Maby

Rajief

The subjugation is almost intolerable, but Borak refuses to use her remaining two wishes. Why should she, when she benefits so much from Rajief's continued service?

Goals

Rajief has one overriding goal: freedom. More than anything, he wants to quit the base creatures of the Material Plane, especially his blue dragon mistress. However, as long as she has the ring to which he is bound, the djinni is all but helpless. He cannot harm Borak in any way or take the ring away from her; his only hope is for someone else to take the ring and either destroy it or grant Rajief his freedom.

Of course, such a task is easier said than done, and Rajief is understandably wary of potential liberators. Even if some mighty creature managed to take the ring from Borak, could the new owner be trusted to release the noble djinni, or would Rajief merely have a different master?

Using Rajief

Rajief is a potential ally in Borak's camp, provided that the PCs are willing to help him achieve his freedom. The noble djinni has been privy to the dragon's affairs for centuries and knows more about the Thunder Tyrant than anyone else alive. He hates his servitude to Borak and will do almost anything to end it.

Still, Rajief is no fool. He has little reason to trust the natives of the Material Plane, who have proven treacherous and greedy, and he has every reason to fear the Thunder Tyrant, who literally holds his life in her talons. If Rajief chooses to aid a group of adventurers in their quest to overcome the ancient blue, he will try to remain behind the scenes. Of course, if the PCs treated the noble djinni poorly in their early encounters, he will be even less inclined to trust them later on, though he might still use them as pawns to achieve his objective.

Appearance and Behavior

Nearly three times the height of a typical human, Rajief towers over most mortals, looking down on them with a haughty glare. He resembles an overly muscular man with deeply tanned skin. His head is bald except for a single long lock wrapped in a golden band, and his spade-shaped black beard is always neatly trimmed.

Rajief dresses in loose blue pantaloons and fine slippers, but no shirt; he wraps a golden sash across his broad chest instead. On his wrists, he wears iron bracelets–enduring reminders of his servitude.

Rajief **CR 12**

hp 154 (19 HD)

Male advanced noble djinni
CG Huge outsider (air, extraplanar)
Init +8; **Senses** darkvision 60 ft.; Listen +24, Spot +24
Languages Auran, Celestial, Common, Ignan; telepathy 100 ft.

AC 18, touch 12, flat-footed 14; Mobility
(–2 size, +4 Dex, +6 natural),
Immune acid, outsider immunities
Fort +15, **Ref** +14, **Will** +13
Weakness outsider vulnerabilities

Speed 20 ft. (4 squares), fly 60 ft. (perfect)
Melee 2 slams +29 each (2d6+10)
Space 10 ft.; **Reach** 10 ft.
Base Atk +19; **Grp** +33
Atk Options Stunning Fist
Special Actions air mastery, spell-like abilities, whirlwind
Spell-Like Abilities (CL 20th):
At will—*invisibility* (self only)
1/day—*create food and water, create wine, gaseous form* (as the spell, up to 1 hour), *major creation, persistent image* (DC 17), *wind walk*

Abilities Str 31, Dex 17, Con 18, Int 14, Wis 15, Cha 15
SQ grant wishes, outsider traits, plane shift
Feats Combat Casting, Combat Reflexes, Dodge, Improved Grapple, Improved Initiative[B], Improved Unarmed Strike, Mobility, Stunning Fist
Skills Appraise +20, Concentration +24, Craft (masonry) +24, Diplomacy +16, Escape Artist +17, Knowledge (arcana) +24, Listen +24, Move Silently +25, Sense Motive +24, Spellcraft +24, Spot +24, Use Rope +3 (+5 with bindings)
Air Mastery (Ex) Airborne creatures take a penalty of –1 on attack rolls and damage rolls against a djinni.
Whirlwind (Su) Rajief can transform into a whirlwind once every 10 minutes and remain in that form for up to 7 rounds.
Grant Wishes (Su) Rajief can grant three *wishes* to the owner of the magic ring to which he is bound.

IMER THE LOST

In the desert depths lies the fabled city of Imer: once a sizable walled city and a jewel of civilization, now little more than a crumbling ruin that serves as the lair of Borak and her spawn. The hot wind piles sand against the remnants of the outer walls, and many of the buildings—long ago crushed or burned by the dragon—are buried under the shifting dunes.

Only the heart of Imer remains relatively intact. The great palace of the Sultan still stands, although it has been cracked and blasted by the stinging sands, and its paved plazas and beautiful fountains have been buried.

KEY FEATURES

The ground floor of the palace remains intact, though its once-soaring towers have collapsed and its fabled gardens turned to dust. The area provides sufficient space for Borak and her minions, and that is all that concerns the dragon.

Sinkholes

The foundations of the palace and the surrounding buildings are buried beneath the surface of the desert, and the shifting sands create dangerous sinkholes. At any moment, an area of sand can give way without warning, enveloping a victim. Borak adds to the danger by using *hallucinatory terrain* to cover any evidence of the sinkholes, making intruders or escaping prisoners more likely to stumble into them. Only she and the Al-Iborak know the safe routes to and from the palace.

For every 30 feet a character moves within 100 feet of the palace, he has a 50% chance of encountering a sinkhole. When a sinkhole opens, anyone within 10 feet must make a successful DC 18 Reflex save to jump aside in time. A failed save means that the victim is sucked beneath the sand and takes 2d6 points of damage. The victim is buried under the collapsing sand and must make a DC 20 Strength check to climb back out. While buried, a victim takes 1d6 points of nonlethal damage per minute. Those reduced to 0 hit points fall unconscious and must make a DC 15 Constitution check to avoid taking 1d6 points of lethal damage per minute.

The Palace

The palace was originally a much larger structure, but Borak's destruction of Imer and the subsequent march of years have left only parts of the building intact. The great hall remains, under the palace's towering dome—as do parts of the wings off the entryway, which hold the dragon's harem and barracks for Al-Iborak warriors. The courtyard behind the great hall also escaped devastation; Borak sometimes goes there to sun herself in relative shelter and safety.

Structural Properties

The following structural properties apply to the ruins of the sultan's palace.

Walls: Most of the palace walls are made of stout stone, and have hardness 8 and 90 hit points.

Ceilings: In most areas of the palace, the ceilings are 10 feet high. The ceiling of the harem chamber rises to 20 feet, and the ceiling of the great hall is a vaulted dome that is 45 feet high at its center.

Doors: The palace's original doors succumbed long ago to dry rot and age. Most doorways have no doors, but some—such as the doorways of the harem or the quarters of the Al-Iborak—have simple curtains of fabric or beads that provide a small measure of privacy.

Illumination: During the day, sunlight streams in through tall windows, creating bright illumination. The windows have iron shutters that can be closed if desired; the shutters have hardness 10 and 30 hit points. At night, the great hall and the human-inhabited areas are lit with torches and braziers that provide shadowy illumination.

DEFENSES

If the player characters make it past the concealed sinkholes outside the palace, they face additional challenges within from the dragon and her followers.

If alerted to the presence of intruders, Borak immediately casts *guards and wards* to protect the palace. She then casts *polymorph* and assumes the form of an innocent desert girl trapped in the harem.

Meanwhile, fully armed Al-Iborak begin searching for the intruders, with orders to capture them if possible and kill them if necessary. If it becomes clear that the PCs are too formidable for the Sons of the Dragon, Borak either intervenes directly, assuming her natural form and attacking the characters with surprise, or she summons Rajief and commands the djinni to destroy her enemies.

AREA DESCRIPTIONS

The remains of the sultan's palace are home to Borak, her Al-Iborak spawn, and her human servants—the sacrifices sent to her over the years that have managed to survive in the ancient dragon's shadow. The following areas correspond with those on the map on page 151.

1. **Entry Hall:** The entry hall has been stripped of its former grandeur. Wide sets of stairs spiral up to the broken floor above (area 6), and the once-fine tile floor is cracked and in poor repair. The hall is now used as a guard post and common area by the Al-Iborak, and servants pass through it as quickly as they can when carrying out their duties.

2. **The Great Hall:** This part of the palace is the only chamber large enough to accommodate the Thunder Tyrant, and thus has become her lair. When supplicants come to Imer to offer tribute, they present themselves to Borak in this room.

Though the hall is in bad shape, it retains much of its original majesty. Rising up from the 20-foot-high walls, a vaulted dome arcs high overhead; it is inlaid with lapis and resembles the night sky. Heavy pillars support the dome along two sides, and an archway on the north wall opens onto what was once a verdant courtyard, providing Borak with easy access to the great hall from the outside.

The Thunder Tyrant reclines on the raised dais, which is piled high with her treasure hoard. The sultan's throne still stands on the dais as well, half-buried by the contents of the hoard. Borak rarely sits on the throne in human form, preferring to take her natural shape while in this chamber.

3. **Harem Quarters:** This suite of rooms centers around a long, rectangular chamber that contains a richly tiled bath filled with magically heated and replenished water, as well as sun-heated stones for resting and reclining. In the old days, these rooms belonged to the sultan's harem, and Borak uses the suite for a similar purpose, housing her most "interesting" human servants here. The harem slaves dwell in relative comfort, awaiting the desires of the dragon—or that of her most senior and favored Al-Iborak sons.

Few of the members of Borak's harem entertain notions of escape. Even if they could evade Al-Iborak hunters and the all-seeing eyes of the Thunder Tyrant, they consider it folly to cross the burning desert alone.

4. **Al-Iborak Barracks:** The rooms of this wing serve as the barracks for the Sons of the Dragon—this is where they live, train, and await the bidding of their mother and ruler. These spare, militant quarters are adorned with weapons and grisly trophies claimed by the half-dragon warriors, including the skulls of slain enemies.

The northeast chamber houses the human servants who were not favored to join the dragon's harem. They live in constant fear of their Al-Iborak overseers, to say nothing of their draconic mistress's cruel whims.

5. **Courtyard:** Once a magnificent garden of flowering hedges, fruit trees, and statuary, the courtyard behind the palace is now little more than a sand-choked area of cracked stone, surrounded by a 10-foot-high stone wall. Borak likes to sun herself here on occasion, and also uses the courtyard to come and go from the palace.

6. **Stairs to the Broken Floor:** The upper floors of the palace were sheared away in Borak's assault on Imer. All that remains is the floor of what used to be the second level, piled with accumulated sand and rubble from the destroyed walls. Here and there, various fixtures and low remnants of the old walls stick up from the floor. Through the debris, the ancient tile and carpet are still visible, though ruined by age and weathering.

The Al-Iborak sometimes use the broken floor to gain a higher vantage point for watching over the approaches to the palace, and they guard the wide stairs that connect it with the entry hall (area 1). Otherwise, this section of the palace is of little use to anyone.

Illus. by W. Mahy

Imer the Lost

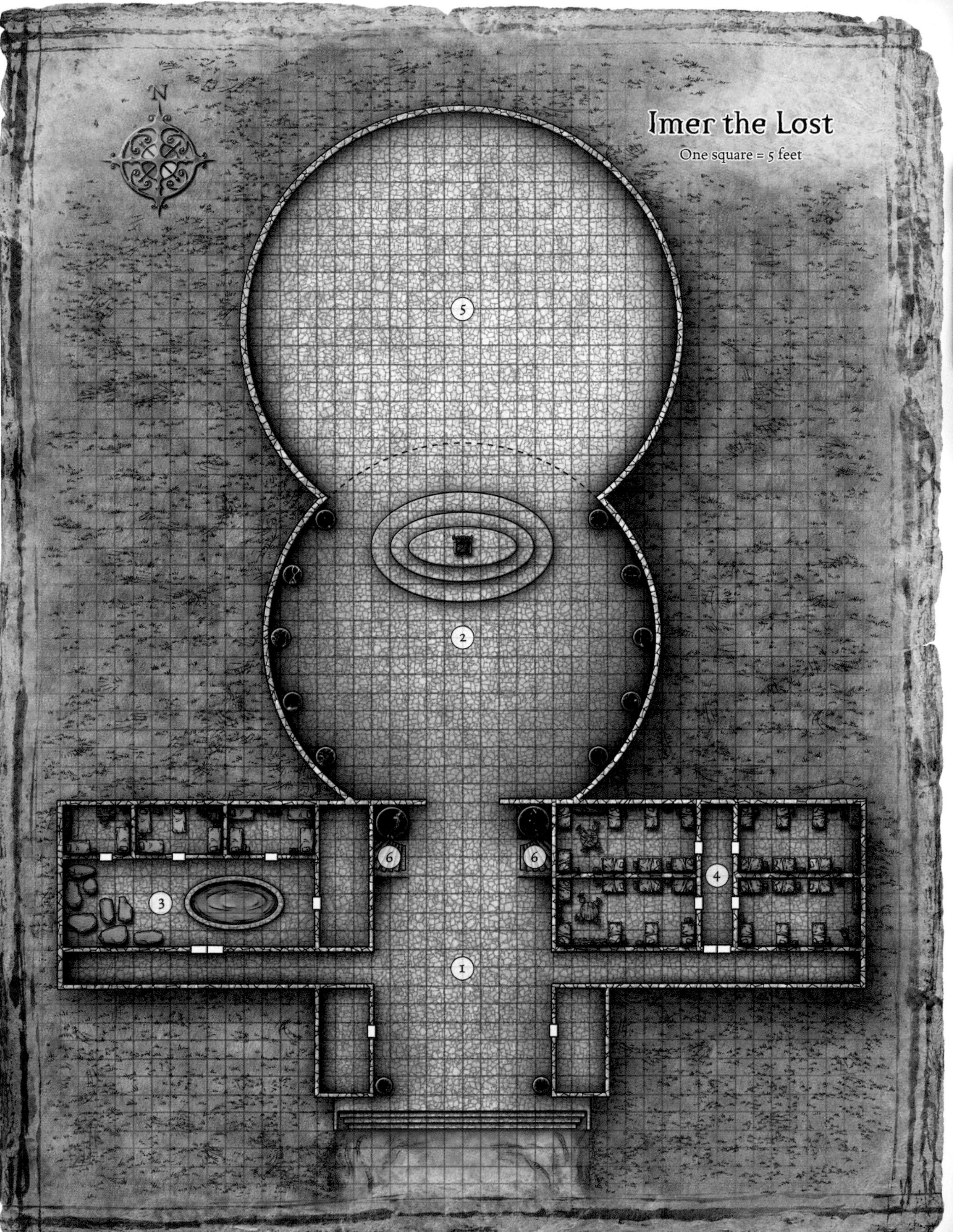
N
Imer the Lost
One square = 5 feet
5
2
6
6
3
4
1

Al-Iborak Camp

Encounter Level 19

SETUP

The PCs can come upon the Al-Iborak camp in a variety of ways. It might be an established outpost or guard point on way to Imer, or it could be temporarily set up near a desert oasis or settlement where the Sons of the Dragon are collecting tribute. The half-dragon warriors could even be a random encounter for a band of PCs trekking through the desert, hoping to find or a friendly encampment.

When the PCs approach the camp, read:

Three white linen tents stands in the desert before you, their fabric snapping and fluttering in the hot wind. Supported by central poles, the tents are tall enough for a human to stand upright inside them. A small campfire burns amid the tents, and a dozen swift desert horses are hobbled nearby.

When the PCs first see one of the Al-Iborak, read:

The desert warrior is clad in long, flowing layers of linen wrappings, including a headwrap and a scarf, to block the heat of the day. A sudden breeze pulls the scarf loose, revealing the warrior's face—an inhuman visage covered in deep blue scales, with a blunt snout and golden, reptilian eyes.

Twelve Al-Iborak occupy the camp. One tent belongs to the commander and his second, while the remaining warriors crowd into the other two tents. Use the statistics block below for all the Al-Iborak.

Whether the PCs attack, approach the camp openly, try to sneak in unseen, or are caught spying from a distance, the result is more or less the same. The half-dragons attempt to take them prisoner, seize their belongings, and bring them all—or the survivors of the battle, at least—to Borak as gifts.

12 Al-Iborak Warriors CR 11
hp 68 each (9 HD)

Male blue half-dragon fighter 5/sorcerer 4
LE Medium dragon (augmented humanoid)
Init +5; **Senses** darkvision 60 ft., low-light vision; Listen +7, Spot +7
Languages Common, Draconic

AC 21, touch 11, flat-footed 20 (+1 Dex, +6 armor, +4 natural)
Immune electricity, *sleep*, paralysis
Fort +9, **Ref** +3, **Will** +6

Speed 30 ft. (6 squares)
Melee *+1 shock scimitar* +14 (1d6+7 plus 1d6 electricity/18–20) and bite +8 (1d6+6) or
Melee whip +13 (1d3+6 or trip) or
Melee 2 claws +13 each (1d4+6) and bite +8 (1d6+6)
Ranged *javelin of lightning* +8 (5d6 electricity, Reflex DC 14 half) or
Ranged javelin +8 (1d6)
Space 5 ft.; **Reach** 5 ft.
Base Atk +7; **Grp** +13
Atk Options Combat Expertise, Power Attack, whip (trip attack)
Special Actions breath weapon
Sorcerer Spells Known (CL 4th):
2nd (3/day)—*bull's strength*
1st (7/day)—*disguise self, shocking grasp, true strike*
0 (6/day)—*daze, detect magic, detect poison, flare, mage hand, message, resistance*

Abilities Str 22, Dex 13, Con 18, Int 10, Wis 13, Cha 13
Feats Combat Expertise, Combat Reflexes, Exotic Weapon Proficiency (whip), Improved Initiative, Iron Will, Power Attack, Weapon Focus (scimitar)
Skills Intimidate +5, Listen +7, Ride +5, Search +4, Spot +7
Possessions *+1 shock scimitar, +1 chainmail, 2 javelins of lightning*, 2 javelins, whip, spell components, 6d6 gp

Breath Weapon (Su) 60-ft. line of lightning, once per day, 6d8 electricity, Reflex DC 14 half.

TACTICS

The half-dragons' tactics depend on whether or not they are forewarned of the assault on their camp.

If they have the opportunity to prepare, the Al-Iborak cast *bull's strength* and *resistance* to enhance their combat prowess. They use their *javelins of lightning* and breath weapons before closing with the PCs, and they use their *scimitars of shock* in melee. They use their natural weapons only as secondary attacks or if they are disarmed.

The half-dragons take advantage of their great numbers. At range, some of them cast *daze* or *flare* in an attempt to hinder the party, while others hurl *javelins of lightning* or mundane weapons. In close combat, the Al-Iborak pair up, fighting back to back to prevent flanking and sneak attacks as much as possible. If they have the chance, some of the half-dragons use their whips to trip opponents so that their brethren can attack the downed characters. If the PCs prove too difficult to strike one on one, the Sons of the Dragon use aid another actions and flanking maneuvers

The tactics of surprised Al-Iborak are similar, except that they do not have the opportunity to cast enhancing spells such as *bull's strength*, and they might not be able to use their *javelins of lightning*. They still use their breath weapons, however, since the half-dragons have immunity to electricity damage and need not worry about catching their brethren in the area of effect.

If the party retreats, the Al-Iborak pursue on horseback unless they have lost more than a third of their number.

Features of the Area

The Al-Iborak make camp either in the desert wilderness between Imer and an oasis, or a short distance from a settlement where they collect tribute from the desert folk. Regardless, the camp has the following features:

Illumination: The encounter takes place at night, where the desert illumination is limited to the moon and stars. The central fire creates an area of bright illumination in a 20-foot radius and an area of shadowy illumination in a 40-foot radius. If forewarned of the party's approach, the half-dragons douse the flames to take advantage of their darkvision.

Tents: The Al-Iborak tents are made of ordinary cloth and have hardness 0 and 1 hit point. Each tent is supported by a wooden pole that has hardness 5 and 10 hit points. The tents offer concealment but do not provide cover.

Horses: A dozen desert-bred light war horses (*MM* 274) are hobbled near the camp. These well-trained animals do not panic when combat breaks out, but they attempt to escape if directly attacked when not under the control of their riders. The Al-Iborak mount their horses only if they need to chase fleeing enemies or if they seek to escape themselves.

In that scenario, the Sons of the Dragon simply count themselves fortunate and take any prisoners to Imer for interrogation.

CONCLUSION

The half-dragon warriors fight fiercely and surrender only if they have no means of escape. Their devotion to Borak is absolute; consider them fanatical in attitude (see *Epic Level Handbook*). They are not likely to betray the Thunder Tyrant or provide the party with any meaningful aid.

If the Al-Iborak defeat the characters, they finish off any foes who are disabled or dying and loot the corpses. Then they strip survivors of any equipment before taking them back to Imer as prisoners. Borak might choose to slay the adventurers or consign them to her harem for her future amusement (see tactical encounter 9–2, page 154).

Treasure: The tents hold a collection of tribute bound for Imer, where it will become part of Borak's hoard. If the PCs overcome the half-dragons and search the tents, they find the following: 25,000 sp; 18,000 gp; 1,200 pp; fine rugs and tapestries worth 2,400 gp total; assorted semiprecious stones worth 4,000 gp total; a sapphire worth 1,000 gp; a gold pitcher, serving platter, and gem-encrusted goblets worth 3,600 gp total; fine incense in a golden and sandalwood cask worth 600 gp total; and four *potions of cure moderate wounds* (used to treat battle injuries and such). In addition, the tents contain the mundane equipment and magic items of the Al-Iborak.

The Rescue

If you wish, the camp might contain prisoners from the desert tribes who were captured in raids or offered willingly to stay the Thunder Tyrant's wrath. If the PCs intend in advance to free the captives, the encounter can be set up as a rescue mission; alternatively, the adventurers could be unaware of the human cargo until they defeat the half-dragons and discover the prisoners chained up in one of the tents.

In either case, the Al-Iborak commander is more than willing to use the prisoners as hostages if he has any reason to believe that the party cares about their lives. If he does, the encounter can change tone and become a tense standoff. A sudden escape by the prisoners can also alter the balance if the PCs are losing the battle, or the breakout might simply add confusion to the melee.

Any rescued prisoners ask the party's aid in returning to their homes. Some promise rich rewards for the PCs' assistance (truthfully or not, as you see fit).

Harem Room

Encounter Level 13

SETUP

The player characters can arrive at this encounter in several different ways. They might come across the harem while exploring the ruined palace, while posing as human tribute to the dragon, or as prisoners captured by the Al-Iborak.

If the PCs stumble upon the harem on their own, the Al-Iborak guards attack if it is clear that the adventurers do not belong there. If the PCs evade the guards, they still must deal with the human prisoners in the harem, any of whom might sell out the party to curry favor with the Thunder Tyrant. The PCs can attempt Diplomacy checks to win the trust of the slaves, whose initial attitude is indifferent. If the party clearly intends to help the prisoners escape, the PCs receive a +5 bonus on the check.

Alternatively, cunning or foolhardy characters might infiltrate a desert tribe and volunteer to become tribute for the dragon—or the party could have been captured by the Al-Iborak and brought to the palace as prisoners. In either case, the PCs are searched, stripped of any valuables or equipment, and taken to the great hall to explain themselves to Borak. The mighty dragon is initially indifferent to the characters, but a sincere effort and successful Bluff, Diplomacy, or Perform checks can improve her attitude to friendly—and earn the PCs spots in the harem rather than the servants' quarters. However, if the characters cause Borak's attitude to shift to hostile, she simply eats them.

If the player characters enter the harem during daylight hours, read:

Half-dragon guards swathed in desert robes keep watch over this room, which is dominated by a large bath tiled in blue and white. A dozen or so humans bathe, lounge on warm rocks at the far end of the room, or help each other wash, dress, and primp.

Hegira

Hegira, a desert woman who has black hair and eyes and deeply tanned skin, is actually a disguise that Borak adopts using polymorph. The other harem slaves believe that Hegira is a particularly favored servant of the dragon, though one who has no love for the Thunder Tyrant. She claims to be the daughter of a tribal sheik and has a proud and noble bearing.

Borak often entertains herself by assuming Hegira's form and spending time in the harem. She finds it a pleasant game and a handy way to learn about her servants. The dragon is a consummate actress, and her Bluff skill modifier is more than sufficient to fool the harem slaves, though she might have a harder time with seasoned adventurers who are more likely to be dubious.

6 Al-Iborak Guards — CR 11

hp 68 each (9 HD)

Male blue half-dragon fighter 5/sorcerer 4
LE Medium dragon (augmented humanoid)
Init +5; **Senses** darkvision 60 ft., low-light vision; Listen +7, Spot +7
Languages Common, Draconic

AC 21, touch 11, flat-footed 20
(+1 Dex, +6 armor, +4 natural)
Immune electricity, *sleep*, paralysis
Fort +9, **Ref** +3, **Will** +6

Speed 30 ft. (6 squares)
Melee *+1 shock scimitar* +14 (1d6+7 plus 1d6 electricity/18–20) and bite +8 (1d6+6) or
Melee whip +13 (1d3+6 or trip) or
Melee 2 claws +13 each (1d4+6) and bite +8 (1d6+6)
Ranged *javelin of lightning* +8 (5d6 electricity, Reflex DC 14 half) or
Ranged javelin +8 (1d6)
Space 5 ft.; **Reach** 5 ft.
Base Atk +7; **Grp** +13
Atk Options Combat Expertise, Power Attack, whip (trip attack)
Special Actions breath weapon
Sorcerer Spells Known (CL 4th):
2nd (3/day)—*bull's strength*
1st (7/day)—*disguise self, shocking grasp, true strike*
0 (6/day)—*daze, detect magic, detect poison, flare, mage hand, message, resistance*

Abilities Str 22, Dex 13, Con 18, Int 10, Wis 13, Cha 13
Feats Combat Expertise, Combat Reflexes, Exotic Weapon Proficiency (whip), Improved Initiative, Iron Will, Power Attack, Weapon Focus (scimitar)
Skills Intimidate +5, Listen +7, Ride +5, Search +4, Spot +7
Possessions *+1 shock scimitar*, *+1 chainmail*, 2 *javelins of lightning*, 2 javelins, whip, spell components, 6d6 gp

Breath Weapon (Su) 60-ft. line of lightning, once per day, 6d8 electricity, Reflex DC 14 half.

If the PCs use stealth to enter the harem at night, read:

The only sound in the dimly lit chamber is that of water gurgling in a pool, which is tiled in shades of blue and white. The shimmering pool takes up much of the room, and the smooth slate floor rises to a pile of rocks at the far end. Several curtained doorways lead off to other chambers.

Features of the Area

The main chamber and the connected rooms have the following features.

Illumination: Windows provide bright illumination during the day, and torches and braziers provide shadowy illumination at night. When the harem slaves sleep, the guards extinguish all sources of light; the Al-Iborak prefer to use their darkvision. Characters who enter or leave the harem late at night find it almost completely dark.

Ceilings: The ceilings in the chambers are 12 feet high.

Doors: The main door into the harem chamber is made of bronze-bound wood and has hardness 5, 12 hit points, and a break DC of 25. The doorways into the other chambers lack doors but have beaded curtains, which provide concealment but no cover.

Pool: The bathing pool in the main chamber is 3 feet deep at the edges and 4 feet deep in the middle. Magically warmed and cleansed water fills the pool, and a tiled step runs around the inside of the basin at half its depth.

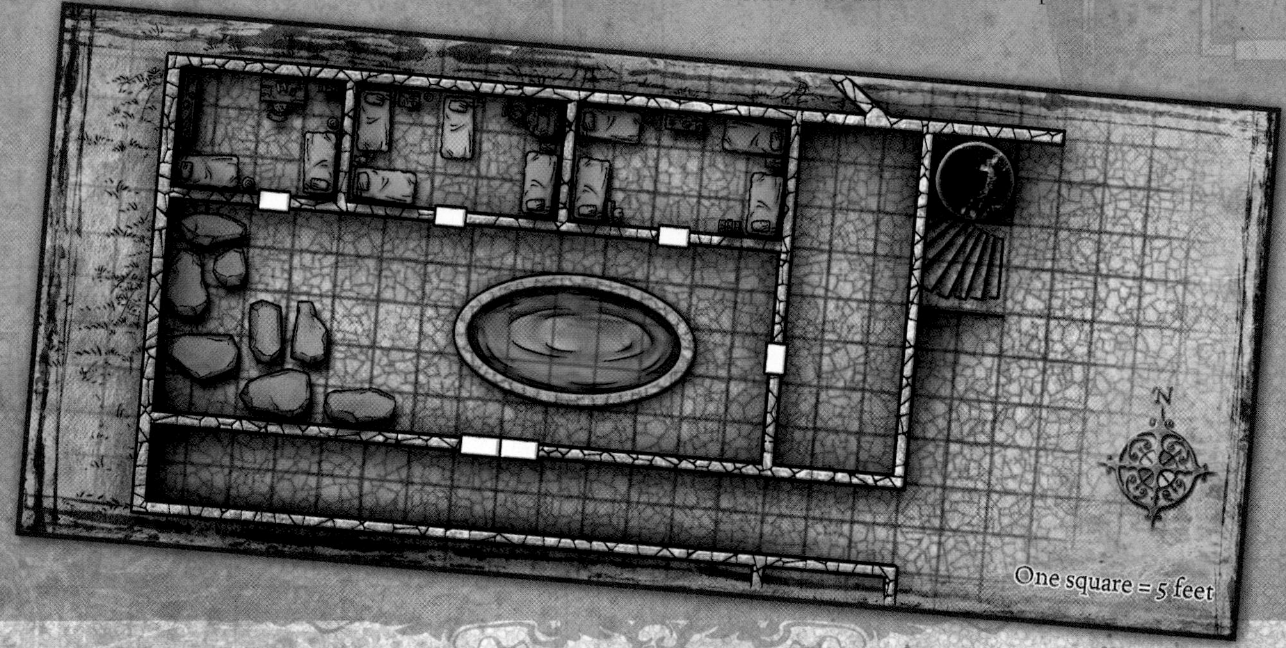

Six Sons of the Dragon guard the harem, including two standing watch outside the entrance from the corridor. They remain alert for signs of rebellion, plotting, or general trouble among the slaves. Since such disruptions rarely occur, the Al-Iborak consider guarding the harem to be soft duty and just take 10 on Listen checks, Spot checks, and the like.

Borak's harem consists of human males and females, mostly low-level commoners or experts with an occasional aristocrat. They have no weapons, and they fight only if absolutely necessary. Currently, fourteen slaves make up the harem, including a purported ex-noblewoman named Hegira (see the sidebar).

Tactics

Unless the characters storm the harem to clear out the Al-Iborak guards and free the prisoners by force, this encounter is a test of their stealth and cunning. They can learn useful information from the slaves, including the layout of the palace, how often Borak sleeps, the truth about her *ring of djinn calling*, and so on. Of course, if they take "Hegira" into their confidence, they might inadvertently give away their plans to the Thunder Tyrant.

Conclusion

If the PCs have been consigned to the harem, they must acquire weapons before trying to escape. They might be able to take the guards by surprise and steal their whips or scimitars. Failing that, they could try to smuggle weapons into the palace somehow, or rely on extreme stealth to escape while unarmed.

Treasure: In addition to the equipment carried by the guards, the harem contains a few luxuries that are permitted to the slaves. These items include a gold and opal necklace (1,500 gp), a dozen gold rings (150 gp each), a gold ring set with a ruby (2,000 gp), five pairs of earrings set with precious stones (200 gp each), a dozen gold bangles and bracelets (200 gp each), a silver chain headdress set with precious stones (1,000 gp), a belt of gold-chased silver disks (300 gp), assorted perfumes and incenses (2,000 gp total), and rugs and tapestries worth 1,000 gp total to the right buyer.

Throne Room

Encounter Level 21

SETUP

One way or another, the PCs have an encounter with Borak in the great hall. The nature and development of the encounter depends on the manner in which they arrive.

When the PCs enter the great hall, read:

In the past, this circular chamber was probably the centerpiece of the palace. The floor is paved in fine marble, now cracked and buckled with age, and fluted columns support a balcony and a dome. The dome is truly majestic, inlaid with lapis lazuli to look like the night sky. The far side of the room is open to e a walled courtyard, now choked with sand. Piled on a raised dais in the middle of the chamber are years of invaluable tribute, including silver, gold, jewels, fine carpets, a golden decanter, and an ebony staff set with a fist-sized emerald. A carved throne is nearly buried under the mounds of riches.

If the PCs manage to reach the great hall without being detected or raising an alarm, they have a shot at catching Borak off her guard. The dragon often dozes coiled around her hoard, so there is a 50% chance that she is sleeping. Keep in mind that she has a bonus of +35 on her Listen check, so despite the penalty for being asleep, there is a good chance that she hears the PCs moving and awakens. Even if her Listen check fails, her *Mordenkainen's faithful hound* is likely to alert her before the characters get too close to do melee damage.

If the party assaults the palace and storms the great hall, they find only a desert slave-girl, chained to the throne on the dais. The black-haired beauty is actually Borak, disguised as Hegira (see the sidebar on page 154). She attempts to lure the party closer to her before assuming her true form and attacking.

Likewise, if Borak has led the PCs to the great hall while disguised as Hegira, she tries to take them by surprise by assumeing her true form and attacking.

TACTICS

Given the opportunity to prepare for the encounter, Borak casts *protection from good* and *lesser globe of invulnerability.*

BORAKSAGHEGIRAK **CR 21**

hp 445 (33 HD); **DR** 15/magic

Female ancient blue dragon
LE Gargantuan dragon (earth)
Init +0; **Senses** blindsense 60 ft., darkvision 120 ft., keen senses; Listen +35, Spot +35
Aura frightful presence (range 300 ft., fewer than 32 HD, Will DC 31 negates)
Languages Draconic, Common

AC 38, touch 6, flat-footed 38
(–4 size, +32 natural)
Immune electricity, *sleep*, paralysis
SR 27
Fort +25, **Ref** +18, **Will** +23

Speed 40 ft. (8 squares), burrow 20 ft., fly 200 ft. (clumsy)
Melee bite +33 (4d6+12) and
2 claws +27 each (2d8+6) and
2 wings +27 each (2d6+6) and
tail slap +27 (2d8+18)
Space 20 ft.; **Reach** 15 ft. (20 ft. with bite)
Base Atk +33; **Grp** +57
Atk Options Combat Expertise, Great Cleave, Multiattack, Power Attack
Special Actions breath weapon, crush, sound imitation, tail sweep
Sorcerer Spells Known (CL 13th; 1d20+15 to overcome SR):
6th (4/day)—*chain lightning* (DC 24), *guards and wards* (DC 24)
5th (7/day)—*dominate person* (DC 23), *Mordenkainen's faithful hound, prying eyes*
4th (7/day)—*bestow curse* (DC 22), *lesser globe of invulnerability, polymorph, scrying*
3rd (7/day)—*dispel magic, gaseous form, lightning bolt* (DC 21), *nondetection*
2nd (7/day)—*arcane lock, blindness/deafness* (DC 20), *detect thoughts* (DC 20), *misdirection* (DC 20), *whispering wind*
1st (8/day)—*charm person* (DC 19), *protection from good, silent image, true strike, ventriloquism*
0 (6/day)—*arcane mark, detect magic, detect poison, flare* (DC 18), *light, mage hand, message, open/close, touch of fatigue* (DC 18)
Spell-Like Abilities (CL 13th):
3/day—*create/destroy water, ventriloquism* (DC 19)
1/day—*hallucinatory terrain, veil* (DC 22)

Abilities Str 35, Dex 10, Con 25, Int 20, Wis 21, Cha 20
Feats Ability Focus (frightful presence), Alertness, Cleave, Combat Expertise, Eschew Materials, Flyby Attack, Great Cleave, Hover, Improved Initiative, Multiattack, Power Attack, Spell Penetration, Wingover
Skills Bluff +37, Concentration +39, Diplomacy +33, Hide +28, Intimidate +35, Knowledge (arcana) +33, Knowledge (history) +29, Knowledge (nature) +29, Knowledge (the planes) +29, Listen +35, Search +31, Sense Motive +33, Spellcraft +37, Spot +35
Possessions *ring of djinn calling*

Frightful Presence (Ex) See page 147
Breath Weapon (Su) 120-ft. line of lightning, once every 1d4 rounds, 20d8 electricity, Reflex DC 33 half.
Crush (Ex) See page 147
Sound Imitation (Ex) See page 147
Tail Sweep (Ex) See page 147

Features of the Area

The great hall of the palace has the following features:

Safeguard: Before falling asleep, Borak casts *Mordenkainen's faithful hound*; the spell lasts long enough for the dragon to awaken before it expires. The phantom watchdog alerts her if anyone approaches within 30 feet, and it can react to invisible and ethereal creatures.

Illumination: During the day, sunlight streams in through the courtyard archway, creating bright illumination in the chamber. At night, braziers flanking the entrance to the great hall provide bright illumination in a 20-foot radius and shadowy illumination in a 40-foot radius. That fails to make much difference in the gloom, but the braziers are meant to provide only token illumination for any servants who might need to enter the chamber at night. Borak and the Al-Iborak have darkvision and do not need the lights.

Ceiling: The domed ceiling rises 45 feet overhead, allowing Borak to rear up to her full height and to get far enough off the ground to make use of her crush attack if she desires.

Pillars: The dome is supported by heavy stone pillars that have hardness 8 and 180 hit points. The pillars are wide enough to provide cover for characters hiding behind them, whether for Hide checks or as possible protection from Borak's breath weapon.

Dais: The stone dais in the middle of the room rises by three steps to a height of about 4 feet. The dais is piled high with Borak's hoard, and the dragon typically coils around it—and the former sultan's throne—when she is relaxing or sleeping.

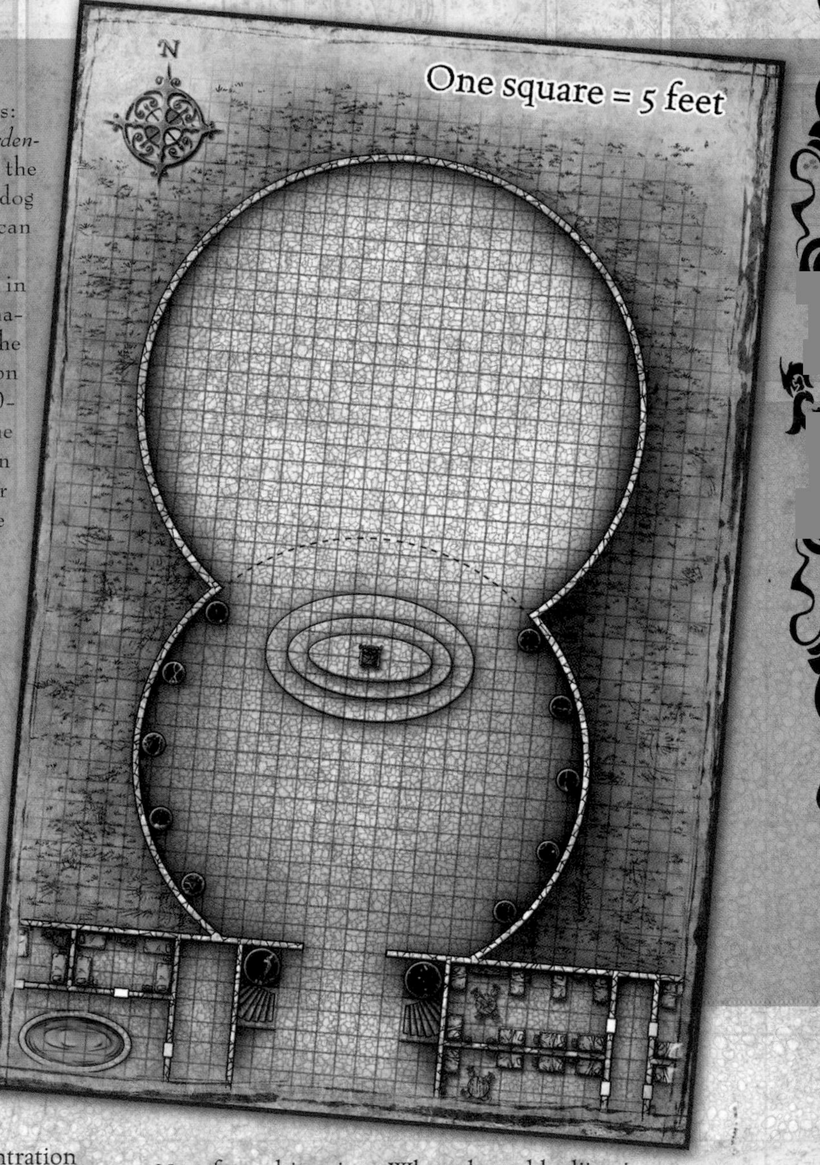

She might have already cast *guards and wards* over the palace and *Mordenkainen's faithful hound* to safeguard the great hall.

The dragon has a bonus of +39 on her Concentration check, which allows her to cast spells and use supernatural abilities defensively without fail. She makes liberal use of *chain lightning* (13d6 electricity damage, Reflex DC 24 half) and her lightning breath weapon during combat, even if the Al-Iborak are present—they have immunity to electricity damage. In addition, Borak might cast *blindness* on a PC whom she knows to be a spellcaster, or *dominate person* on a threatening party member (if she has not done so already prior to the encounter).

Otherwise, the Thunder Tyrant makes full use of her devastating attacks, exploiting any knowledge she has about the party to take out the most dangerous characters first. She makes crush attacks on groups of PCs that remain close enough together.

The dragon does not use her *ring of djinn calling* during the battle unless she is in serious danger of defeat, or is otherwise in dire need.

Conclusion

The dragon negotiates with the PCs only if she must, and even then she tries to deceive them. In particular, she does not reveal her *ring of djinn calling*, though she might summon Raijef—either at her first opportunity or if she is reduced to 20 or fewer hit points. When the noble djinni appears, she uses a *wish* to have him either heal all her damage or transport the characters far away where they can no longer trouble her (Will DC 31 negates).

Depending on how difficult you want to make the final encounter, Borak's death or defeat might break the will of the Al-Iborak, sending them fleeing into the desert, or it could drive them mad with grief and rage, causing them to attack the party heedless of their own safety.

Treasure: If the PCs defeat Borak or drive her off, they can claim her entire hoard, which includes the following: 67,000 sp, 44,000 gp, and 30,000 pp in sacks, barrels, and chests; assorted gems worth a total of 9,000 gp; and a collection of art objects (including fine tapestries; cloth-of-gold; and dishes, goblets, and serving trays made of silver and gold) worth a total of 8,000 gp. The hoard also contains a *Boccob's blessed book*, a *carpet of flying*, a *pearl of power* (5th level), a *staff of earth and stone*, and a *decanter of endless water*.

Depending on the outcome of the battle and their prior dealings with Rajief, the PCs might also acquire the *ring of djinn calling* to which he is bound. The noble djinni willingly grants the characters three *wishes* in exchange for his freedom. If they comply, he thanks them profusely before returning to the Elemental Plane of Air.

APPENDIX: PLACES OF EVIL

The locations described in *Exemplars of Evil* are designed to be generic enough so that they can be dropped into an existing campaign at any appropriate site. For games that use the EBERRON or FORGOTTEN REALMS setting, the following suggestions are provided as an aid to the Dungeon Master who wants to merge one or more of these sites into the campaign's existing geography and also tie them to story elements in those worlds.

ZAR'FELL IN EBERRON

Zar'Fell can be found in the low hills near the coast to the west of the Glum River. Although the place was undoubtedly built by dwarves, certain elements of the manor's original architecture suggest the touch of the daelkyr. No other trace of the daelkyr has been found in the region, however, and the reconstruction is erasing their influence from the house. Zargath has sent teams of prospectors to look for dragonshards in the rich fields nearby, but they have not yet found enough to make any significant money.

ZAR'FELL IN FAERÛN

Zar'Fell was once part of a Savage Frontier fortress guarding a large dwarf hold dug in one of the foothills of the Spine of the World. Most of the hold is gone now, having collapsed from excessive mining, monster attacks, and age. All that remains is the house and a large cavern where the majority of the orc tribe lives. Despite the brutal climate in the region, the deep valley is protected from the worst of the wind and thus is comparatively warm—at least, enough for construction to continue throughout most of the year.

TOLSTOFF KEEP IN EBERRON

Tolstoff Keep stands about 30 miles southeast of Korth, the capital of Karrnath, in the depths of the Nightwood. Not many people recall the keep or its surrounding village, and those who do presume that the place was swallowed by the darkness of the bleak forest. Instead of giving the guards the corrupted template, consider giving them the madborn template (*Five Nations* 123).

TOLSTOFF KEEP IN FAERÛN

The Tolstoffs' lands lie in the far north, at the edges of the Evermoors. Their crumbling castle is in poor condition, and the people in the village and the keep are thoroughly mad. Few others dare approach the place, and when barbarians tumble out of the wilds to raid and pillage the soft lands, the Tolstoffs can expect little in the way of help.

THE MUCH KILL IN EBERRON

The *Much Kill* is a stormship, but unlike other vessels powered by air elementals, this one derives its increased speed from a tempest (*MM2* 193). The *Much Kill* gains all the normal benefits of a stormship (*Explorer's Handbook* 38). However, a character with the Lesser Mark of Storm who grips the wheel can spend a use of the spell-like abilities associated with the mark to cast *ice storm* as a spell-like ability. Furthermore, all of this character's spells and spell-like abilities that have the cold, electricity, fire, or water descriptor are cast at +1 caster level. Given the ship's improved abilities, it is highly sought by half-elf corsairs all over the Sea of Lost Souls.

THE MUCH KILL IN FAERÛN

Captain Gnash gained the *Much Kill* through mutiny, but none of the crew is quite sure where the former captain acquired the vessel. In truth, the ogre stole it from a human captain, who had previously snatched it from a ghostly island ruled by an ancient lich lord. In the years since the *Much Kill* fell into goblinoid hands, the crew has discovered many oddities about the ship. For example, at certain times of the year, the planks ignite with pale green flames, and writhing runes and sigils appear on the hull. Pog suspects that the ship was once a spelljammer, a magic vessel that could sail the void between worlds, but he has not shared this theory with the captain. The goblin fears that the news would drive Gnash to awaken the ship's other powers, so that he could sail directly to the Eater of Worlds rather than trying to lure the Elder Evil to Toril.

THE CHELICERATA COMPLEX IN EBERRON

Tamesik's illicit trade complex is just a block from the worst part of the docks in Stormreach, making it easy for the drow to smuggle slaves. The group's current dealings include numerous transactions with the Lhazaar slaverunners and other disreputable residents.

THE CHELICERATA COMPLEX IN FAERÛN

Kesra Tanor'Thal, the de facto matron mother of Skullport, does not realize that a growing drow presence threatens to overwhelm her sovereignty. Under the control of Tamesik, the Chelicerata is rapidly becoming one of the most powerful drow organizations in Skullport. With its large contingent of agents, its resourceful and talented minions, and its potent divine magic, the trade ring is a significant (yet hidden) threat. Its members make use of secret tunnels and portals (both magical and mundane) between Waterdeep and Undermountain.

THE SOTH TARNEL IN EBERRON

Elliast's Spire stands within sight of the Grey Rakes, several hundred miles to the west of Sharn. The Soth Tarnel is dedicated to a hero who fought against the goblinoid remnants of the once-powerful Dhakaani Empire.

The hero—Minyu Colworn—and a small band of followers sought to stem an incursion by goblins from the north who searched for ancient places of Dhakaani power in the Grey Rakes. Minyu was slain, but a few of his devoted followers survived, and they built the Soth Tarnel to honor their friend and master. The last of the followers fell defending the tomb from hobgoblin raiders, who believed Minyu had been buried with several powerful Dhakaani antiquities.

THE SOTH TARNEL IN FAERÛN

The Soth Tarnel was built centuries ago, after the great battle that gave the Mere of Dead Men its name. Standing just off the coast of that desolate salt marsh, the tomb honors Marinnar, a great warrior who fell during the desperate fighting. Survivors of that terrible slaughter recovered his body and built the Soth Tarnel to mark his sacrifice.

Since the last survivors died out, harpies and pirates have tried to claim the Soth Tarnel. However, the turbulent waters that surround the spire—not to mention numerous aquatic predators—make any such occupation temporary at best.

GILGIRN IN EBERRON

The fiery mountainhold can be one of many volcanic locations in Xen' Drik. Alternatively, a Gilgirn located closer to civilization could be in Khorvaire, looking down upon the Eldeen Reaches from the demon wastes.

GILGIRN IN FAERÛN

Nestled in the Smoking Mountains, a region known for extensive mining, Gilgirn is mistakenly regarded as an active volcano by nearby communities. As a result, the miners avoid the fiery mountainhold completely.

BLEAK HOLD IN EBERRON

Bleak Hold is the remains of a shattered tower, protruding from an enormous floating rock in a sea of necromantic sludge. Flitting through the perpetual shadows are the xeg-yi (*Manual of the Planes* 168), who torment slaves stolen from the Material Plane and force them to mine the rock for precious ore. Meanwhile, the slaves wait their turn to perish, and become reanimated as mindless soldiers in the war machine.

BLEAK HOLD IN FAERÛN

Bleak Hold was once an impressive temple of Shar; planar travelers claim that it was thrust from the Material Plane during an ancient battle with Selûne. Legend holds that the tower once contained a potent artifact that was instrumental in the tearing of the weave. Luckily, the site no longer holds such power and now simply rots in the void.

IMER IN EBERRON

Imer the Lost dates back to the Age of Monsters, and legends say that it might be older still, built on foundations laid by efreet during the Age of Demons. Centuries ago, Borak came to Imer in pursuit of the draconic Prophecy and laid waste to the city when she was betrayed. Her fascination with humans stems partially from the dragonmarks and their relation to the Prophecy, and her hoard includes many sources of knowledge that hold clues to this mystery.

IMER IN FAERÛN

Imer the Beautiful was one of the jewels of Calimshan, built by djinn at the direction of powerful sorcerers. When its greatest wizard provoked the anger of Boraksaghegirak, the furious dragon razed the city, sending its dazzling spires crashing into the sands. Now Imer is a haunted ruin, half-buried in the desert and avoided by anyone with good sense.

ABOUT THE DESIGNERS

ROBERT J. SCHWALB is a staff designer and developer for Green Ronin Publishing, and he also works as a freelance designer for Wizards of the Coast. He has contributed to *Tome of Magic, Player's Handbook II, Fiendish Codex II, Complete Scoundrel, Drow of the Underdark,* and *Monster Manual V.* Robert lives in Tennessee with his wife Stacee and a pride of cats.

EYTAN BERNSTEIN is a freelancer designer and editor based in Long Island, New York. He has written and edited numerous articles, web enhancements and supplements for a variety of companies. Eytan is the PR and Marketing Manager and part owner of Silven Publishing, a Massachusetts-based company that publishes print and PDF roleplaying game supplements, music, fiction, and the Silven Trumpeter, the largest free roleplaying game magazine on the Internet.

CREIGHTON BROADHURST lives in a seaside town in merry old England, in a house he wants to rename the "Obsidian Citadel." Strangely, his wife won't let him. He is a member of Living Greyhawk's Circle of Six, a founding member of the Anoraks of the Coast (his local gaming group), and an occasional contributor to the *Oerth Journal.*

STEVE KENSON began writing for roleplaying games in 1995 with work on FASA's *Shadowrun.* Since then, he has written professionally for dozens of games and authored nine novels. Steve is a line developer for Green Ronin Publishing and the designer of the *Mutants & Masterminds* superhero roleplaying game. Steve lives in New Hampshire with his partner, metaphysical author and teacher Christopher Penczak. He maintains a web site at www.stevekenson.com.

KOLJA RAVEN LIQUETTE is perhaps best known for creating *The Waking Lands* web site. He has also written for *Races of the Dragon* and *Weapons of Legacy,* in addition to providing material for *Five Nations, Complete Mage,* and various articles and enhancements for the Wizards of the Coast web site.

ALLEN RAUSCH has been writing about games and gaming since 1996. His past projects include several *Orpheus* roleplaying game supplements for White Wolf, as well the novella *Dia de Los Muertos* for the *Haunting the Dead* collection. He's also worked on several computer games, including *Magic: the Gathering – Battlemage* and *Empire Earth.* His articles, interviews and game reviews can be seen regularly on GameSpy.com. Allen lives in Los Angeles with his wife Elizabeth and two stunningly amazing children, Lily and David.

Dungeons & Dragons

Dungeons & Dragons

Wizards of the Coast